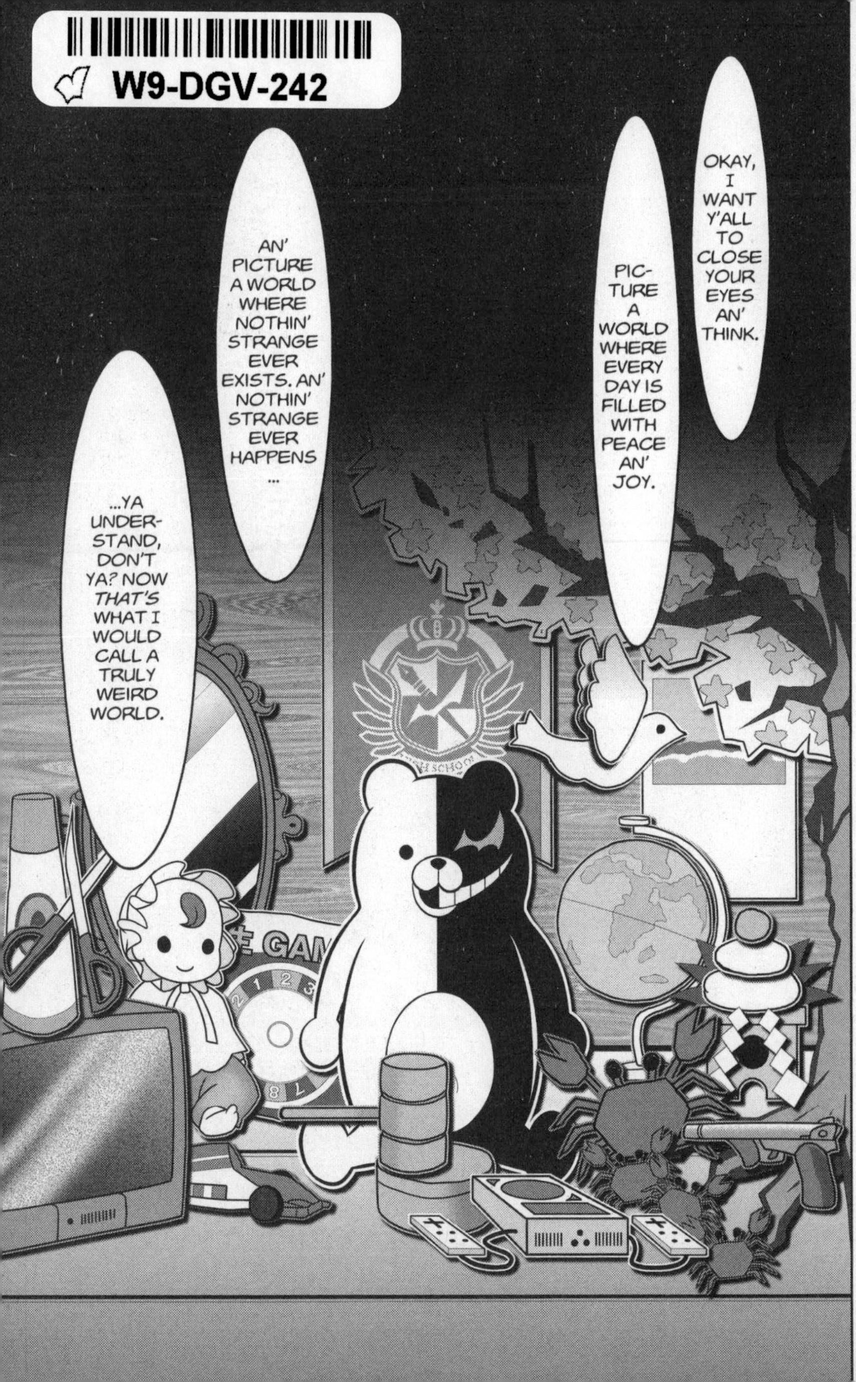
OKAY, I WANT Y'ALL TO CLOSE YOUR EYES AN' THINK.
PIC-TURE A WORLD WHERE EVERY DAY IS FILLED WITH PEACE AN' JOY.
AN' PICTURE A WORLD WHERE NOTHIN' STRANGE EVER EXISTS. AN' NOTHIN' STRANGE EVER HAPPENS ...
...YA UNDER-STAND, DON'T YA? NOW *THAT'S* WHAT I WOULD CALL A TRULY WEIRD WORLD.

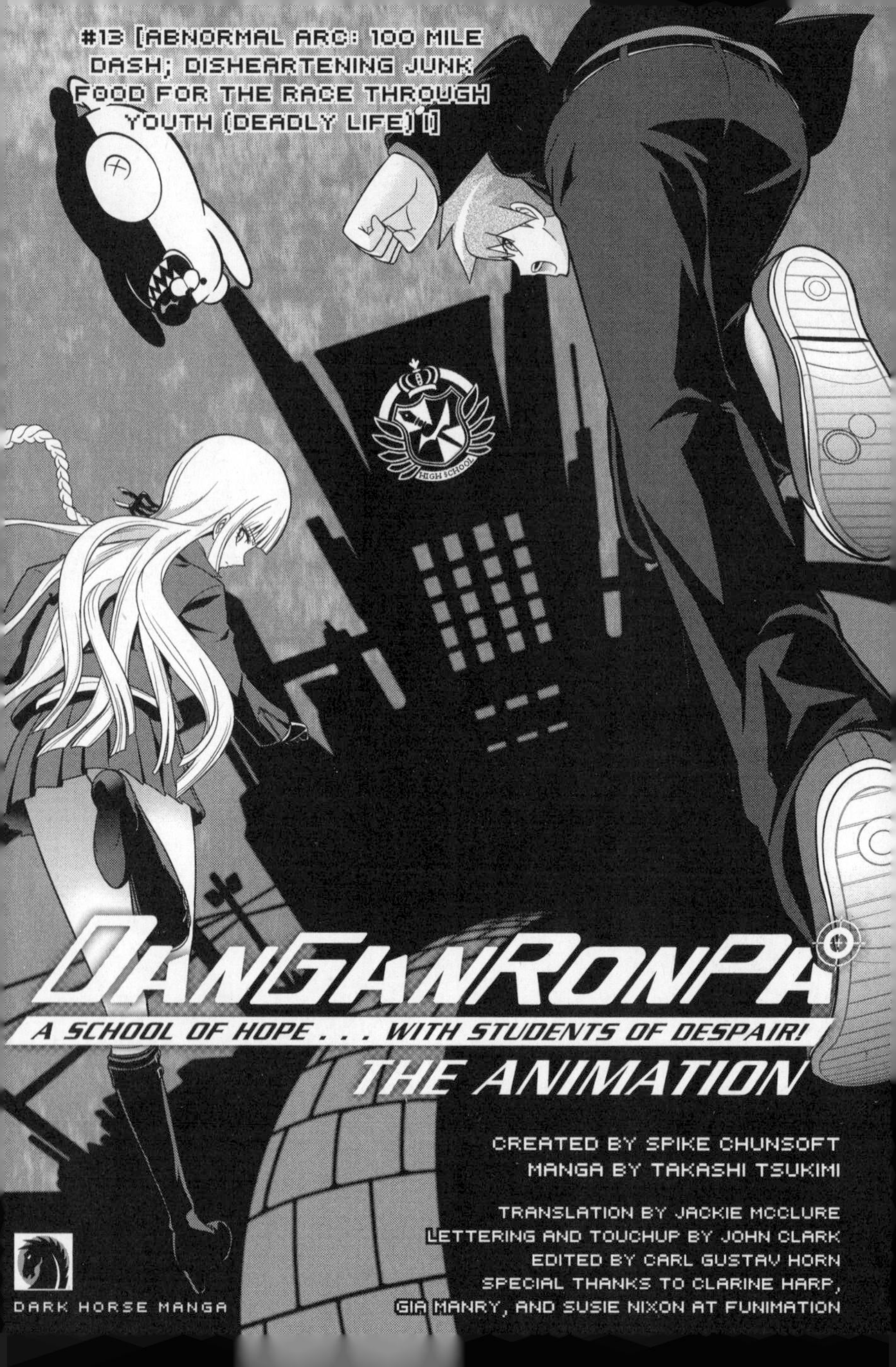

#13 [ABNORMAL ARC: 100 MILE DASH; DISHEARTENING JUNK FOOD FOR THE RACE THROUGH YOUTH (DEADLY LIFE) I]

DANGANRONPA

A SCHOOL OF HOPE . . . WITH STUDENTS OF DESPAIR!

THE ANIMATION

CREATED BY SPIKE CHUNSOFT
MANGA BY TAKASHI TSUKIMI

TRANSLATION BY JACKIE MCCLURE
LETTERING AND TOUCHUP BY JOHN CLARK
EDITED BY CARL GUSTAV HORN
SPECIAL THANKS TO CLARINE HARP, GIA MANRY, AND SUSIE NIXON AT FUNIMATION

DARK HORSE MANGA

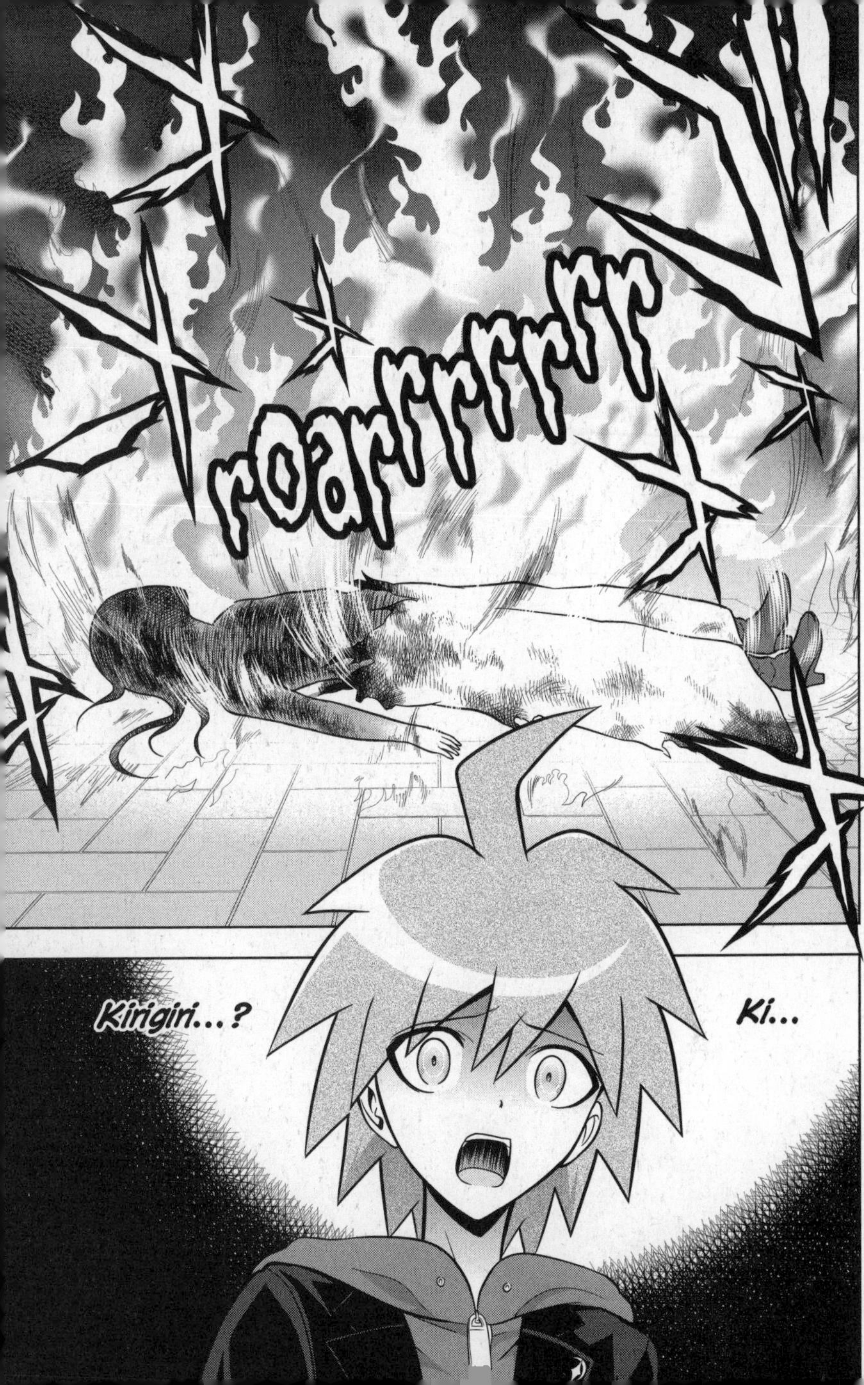
roarrrrrrr
Ki...
Kirigiri...?

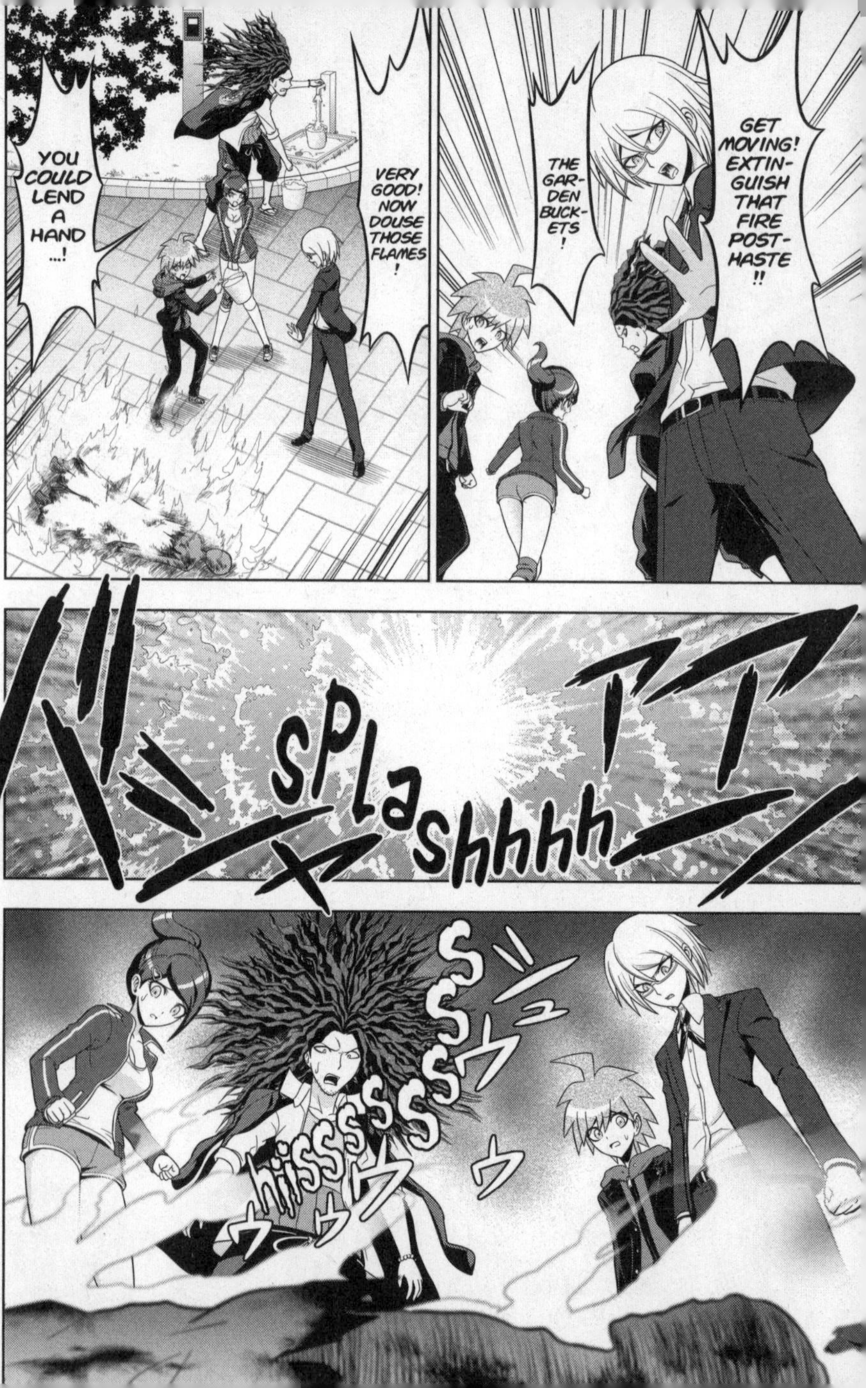
GET MOVING! EXTINGUISH THAT FIRE POSTHASTE!!
THE GARDEN BUCKETS!
VERY GOOD! NOW DOUSE THOSE FLAMES!
YOU COULD LEND A HAND...!
sPLashhhhh
SSSSS
hiSSSS

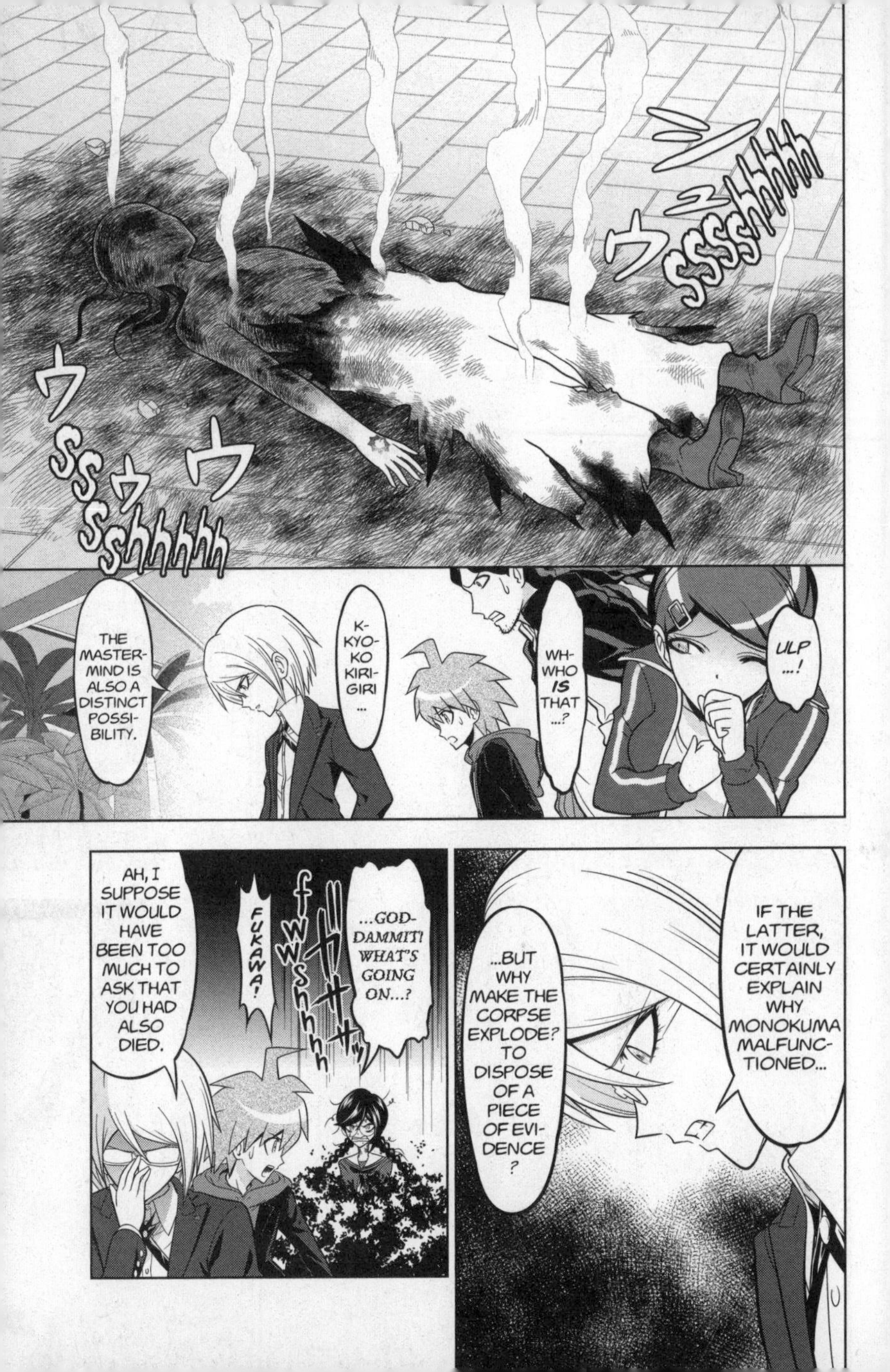
ウ SSSSSHHHHHH
ウ SS ウ ウ SSHHHHHH
ULP ...!
WH-WHO IS THAT ...?
K-KYOKO KIRIGIRI ...
THE MASTERMIND IS ALSO A DISTINCT POSSIBILITY.
IF THE LATTER, IT WOULD CERTAINLY EXPLAIN WHY MONOKUMA MALFUNCTIONED...
...BUT WHY MAKE THE CORPSE EXPLODE? TO DISPOSE OF A PIECE OF EVIDENCE?
...GODDAMMIT! WHAT'S GOING ON...?
FWWSHHHH
FUKAWA!
AH, I SUPPOSE IT WOULD HAVE BEEN TOO MUCH TO ASK THAT YOU HAD ALSO DIED.

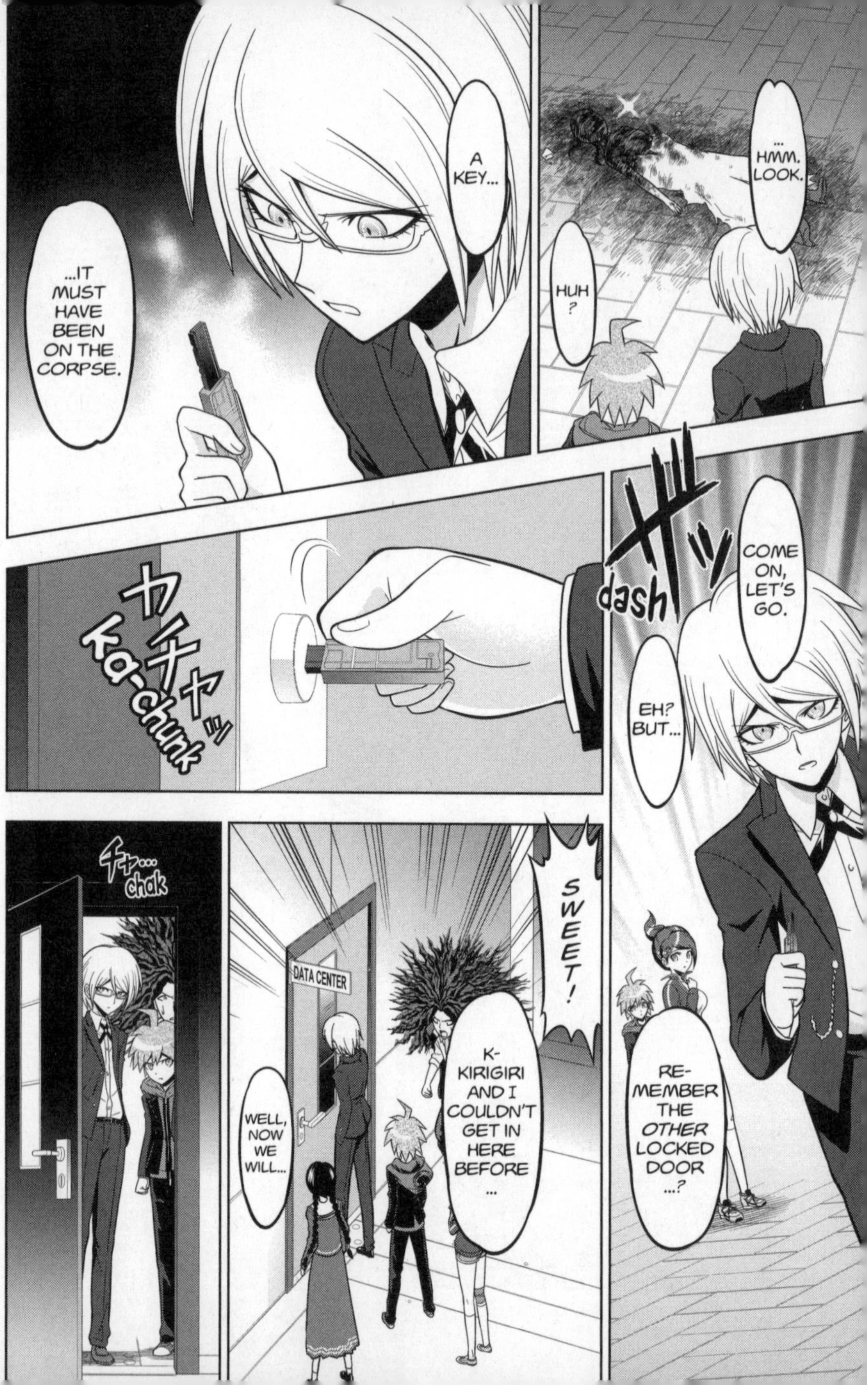

... HMM. LOOK.
HUH?
A KEY...
...IT MUST HAVE BEEN ON THE CORPSE.
dash
COME ON, LET'S GO.
EH? BUT...
RE-MEMBER THE OTHER LOCKED DOOR ...?
Ka-chunk
SWEET!
K-KIRIGIRI AND I COULDN'T GET IN HERE BEFORE ...
WELL, NOW WE WILL...
DATA CENTER
chak

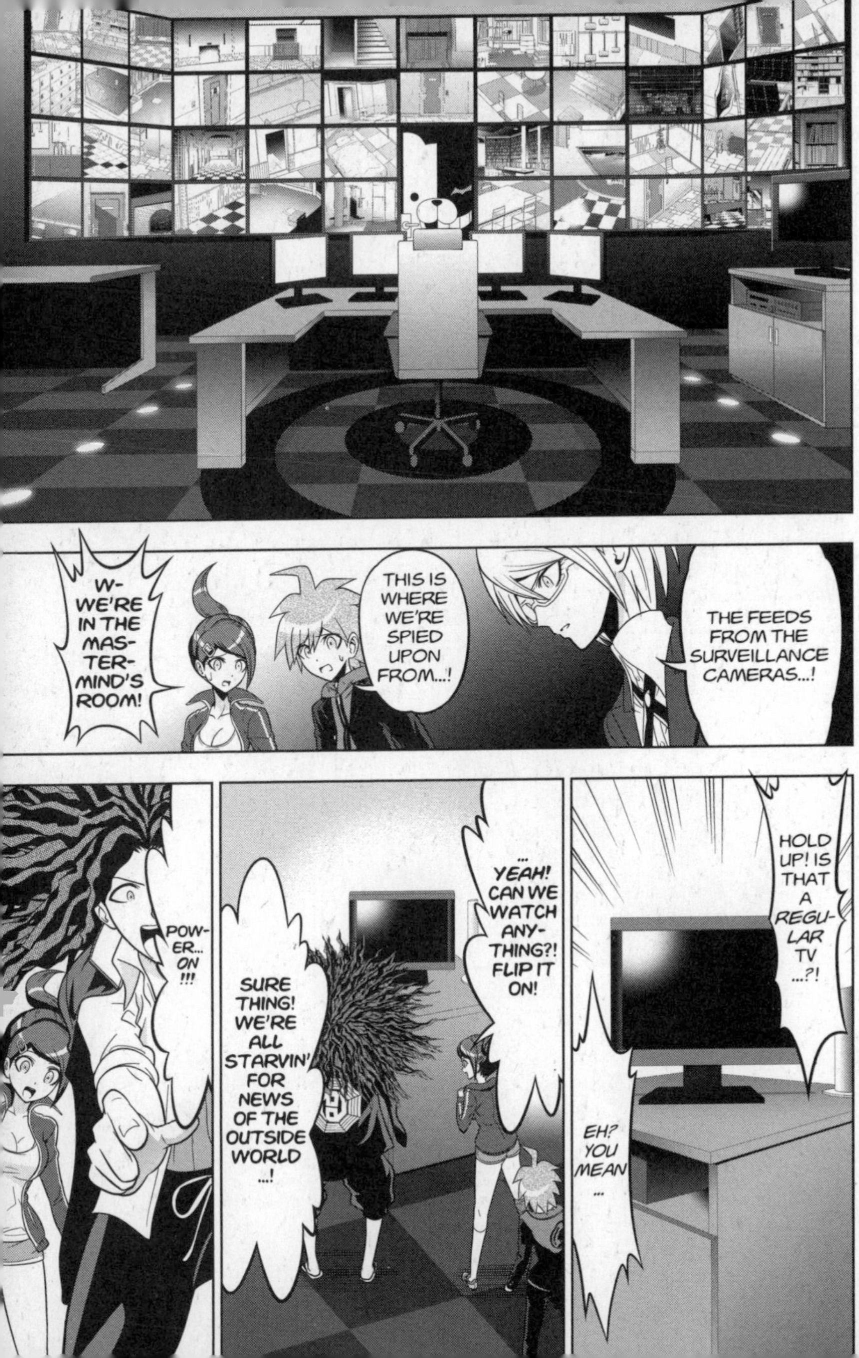
THE FEEDS FROM THE SURVEILLANCE CAMERAS...!
THIS IS WHERE WE'RE SPIED UPON FROM...!
W-WE'RE IN THE MASTER-MIND'S ROOM!
HOLD UP! IS THAT A REGULAR TV ...?!
EH? YOU MEAN ...
... YEAH! CAN WE WATCH ANYTHING?! FLIP IT ON!
SURE THING! WE'RE ALL STARVIN' FOR NEWS OF THE OUTSIDE WORLD ...!
POWER... ON !!!

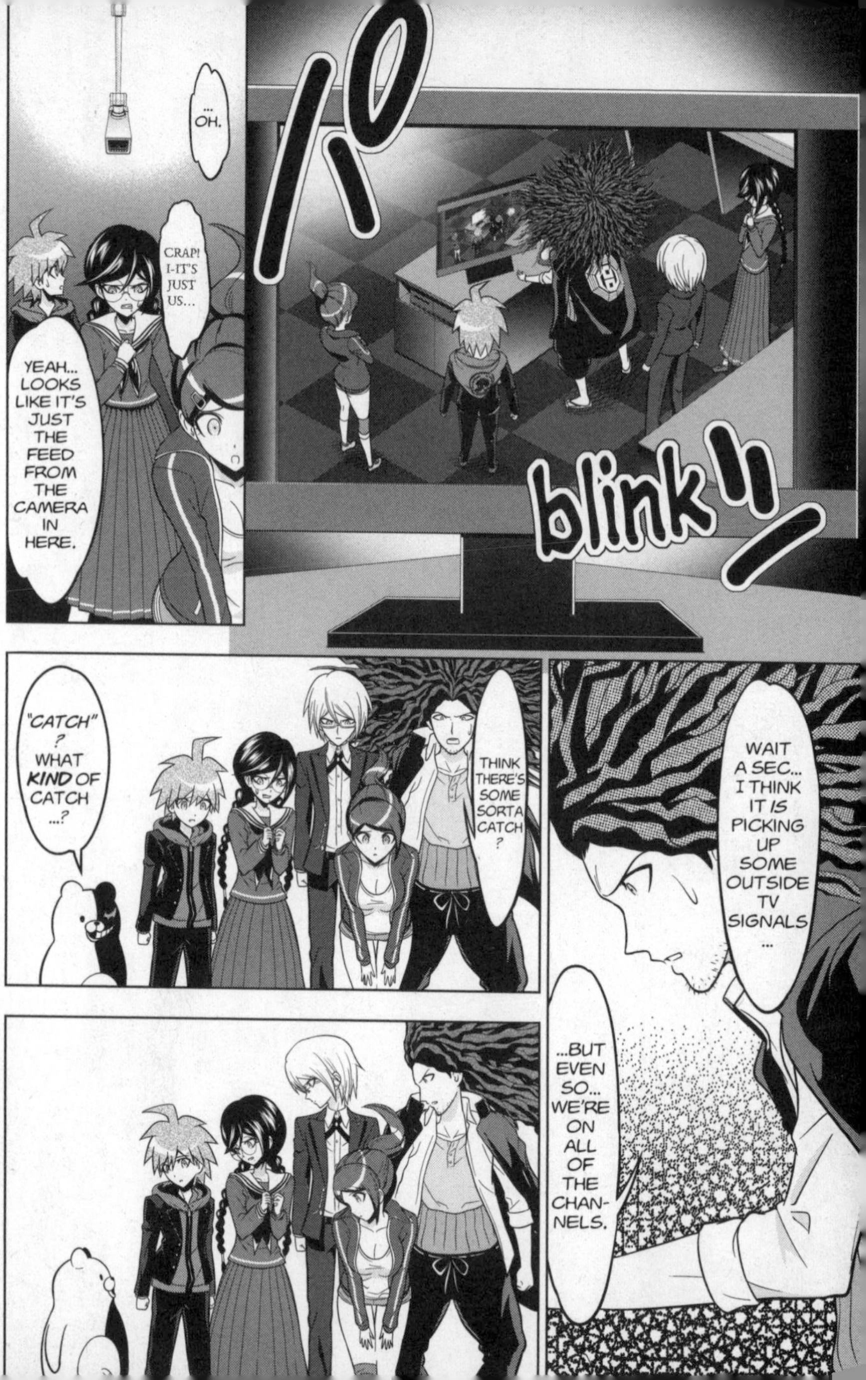
blink
... OH.
CRAP! I-IT'S JUST US...
YEAH... LOOKS LIKE IT'S JUST THE FEED FROM THE CAMERA IN HERE.
WAIT A SEC... I THINK IT IS PICKING UP SOME OUTSIDE TV SIGNALS ...
...BUT EVEN SO... WE'RE ON ALL OF THE CHANNELS.
THINK THERE'S SOME SORTA CATCH ?
"CATCH"? WHAT KIND OF CATCH ...?

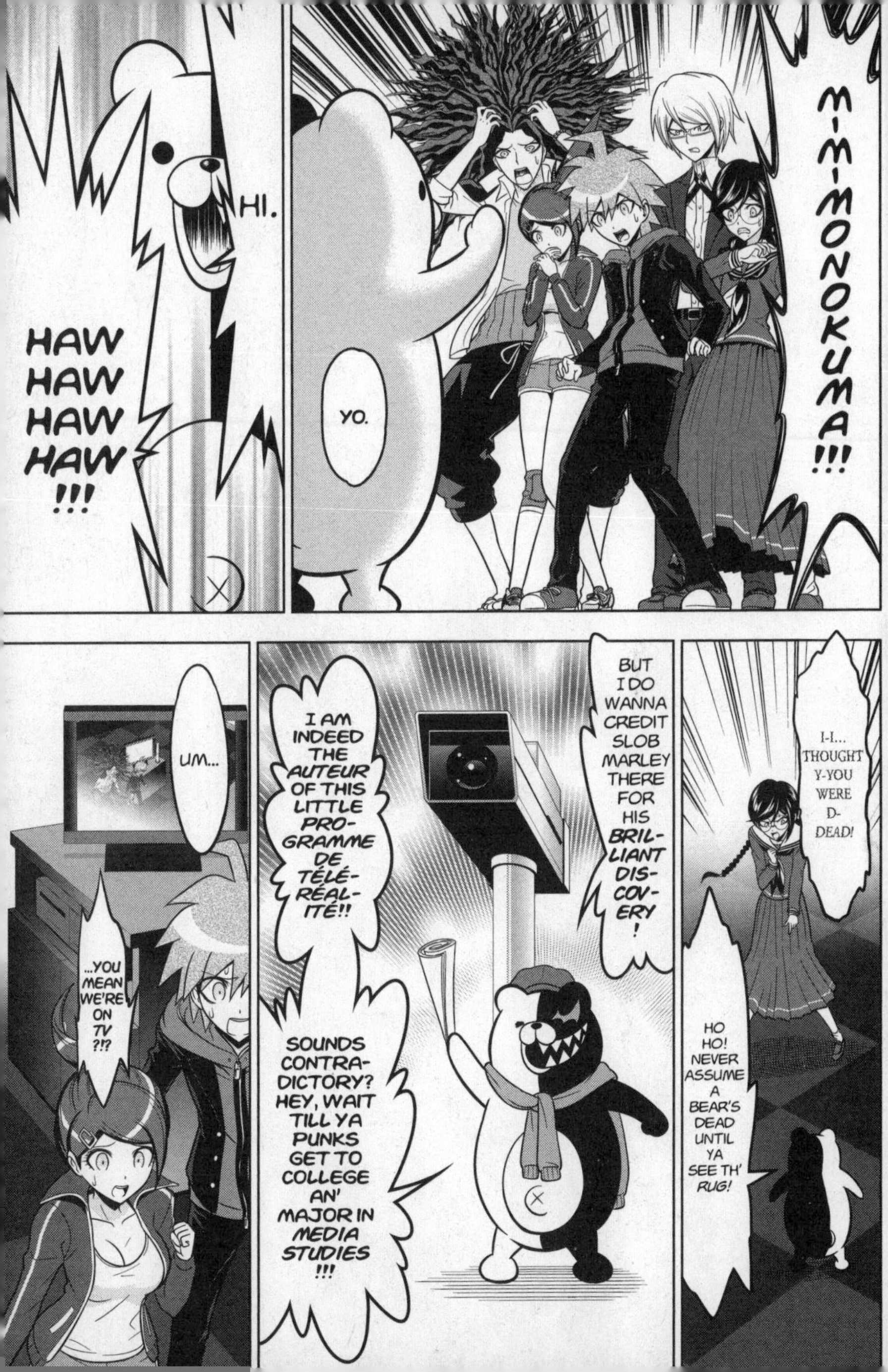

M-M-MONOKUMA!!!
YO.
HI.
HAW HAW HAW HAW!!!
I-I... THOUGHT Y-YOU WERE D-DEAD!
HO HO! NEVER ASSUME A BEAR'S DEAD UNTIL YA SEE TH' RUG!
BUT I DO WANNA CREDIT SLOB MARLEY THERE FOR HIS BRILLIANT DISCOVERY!
I AM INDEED THE AUTEUR OF THIS LITTLE PROGRAMME DE TÉLÉ-RÉALITÉ!!
SOUNDS CONTRADICTORY? HEY, WAIT TILL YA PUNKS GET TO COLLEGE AN' MAJOR IN MEDIA STUDIES!!!
UM...
...YOU MEAN WE'RE ON TV?!?

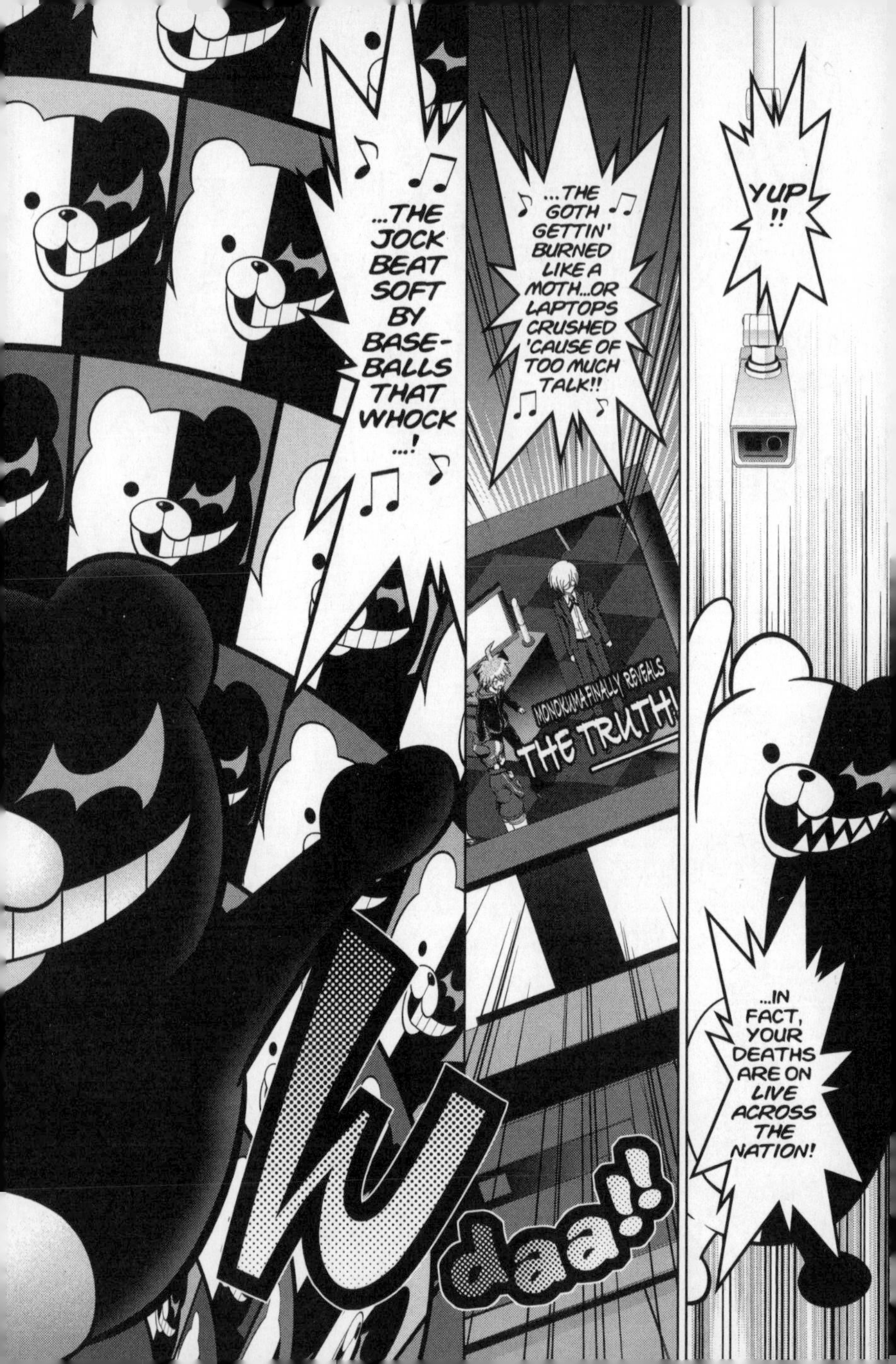
YUP!!
...IN FACT, YOUR DEATHS ARE ON LIVE ACROSS THE NATION!
...THE GOTH GETTIN' BURNED LIKE A MOTH...OR LAPTOPS CRUSHED 'CAUSE OF TOO MUCH TALK!!
MONOKUMA FINALLY REVEALS THE TRUTH!
...THE JOCK BEAT SOFT BY BASE-BALLS THAT WHOCK...!
Wdaa!!

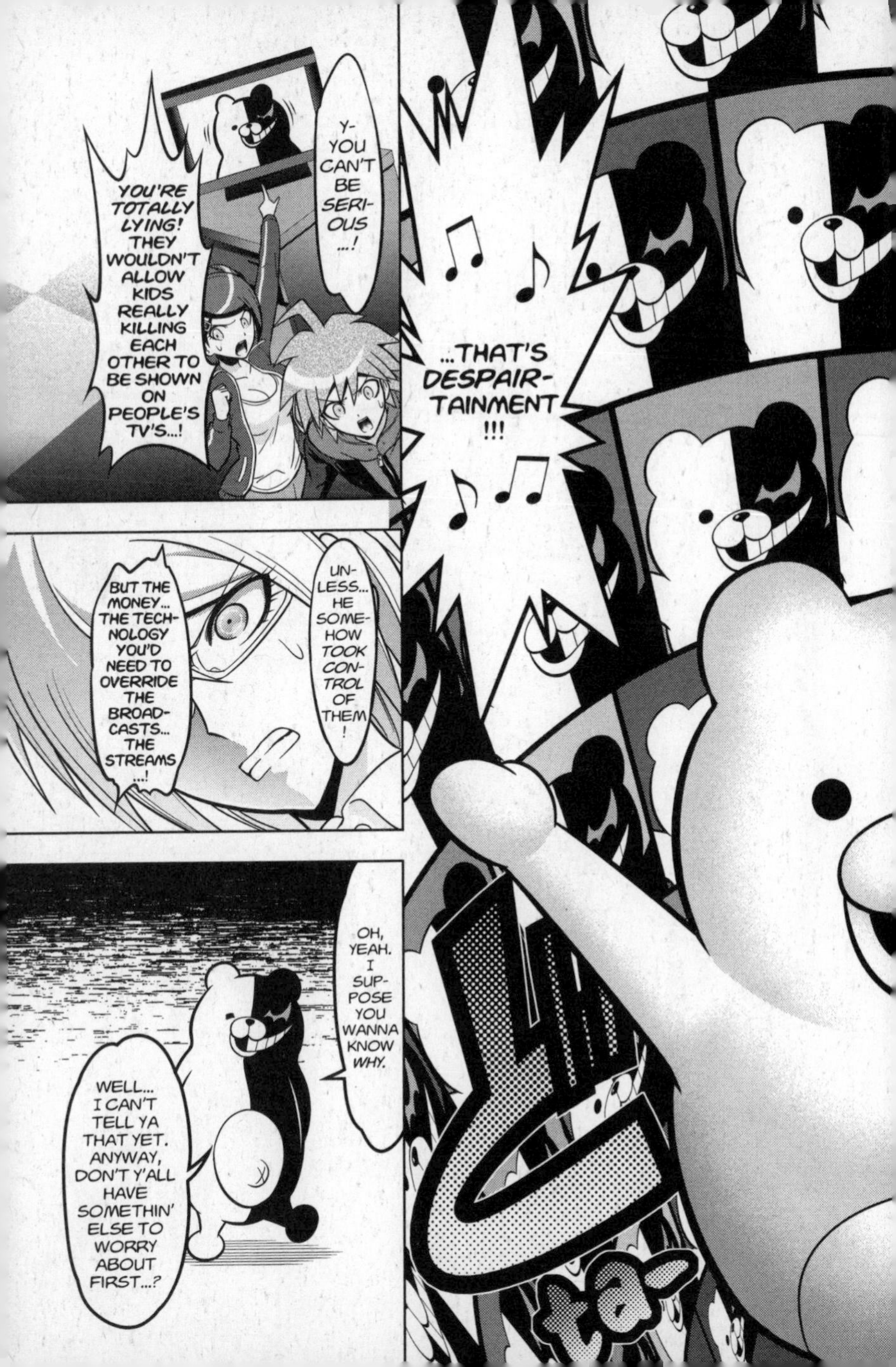
...THAT'S DESPAIR-TAINMENT!!!
Y-YOU CAN'T BE SERIOUS...!
YOU'RE TOTALLY LYING! THEY WOULDN'T ALLOW KIDS REALLY KILLING EACH OTHER TO BE SHOWN ON PEOPLE'S TV'S...!
UNLESS... HE SOMEHOW TOOK CONTROL OF THEM!
BUT THE MONEY... THE TECHNOLOGY YOU'D NEED TO OVERRIDE THE BROADCASTS... THE STREAMS...!
OH, YEAH. I SUPPOSE YOU WANNA KNOW WHY.
WELL... I CAN'T TELL YA THAT YET. ANYWAY, DON'T Y'ALL HAVE SOMETHIN' ELSE TO WORRY ABOUT FIRST...?

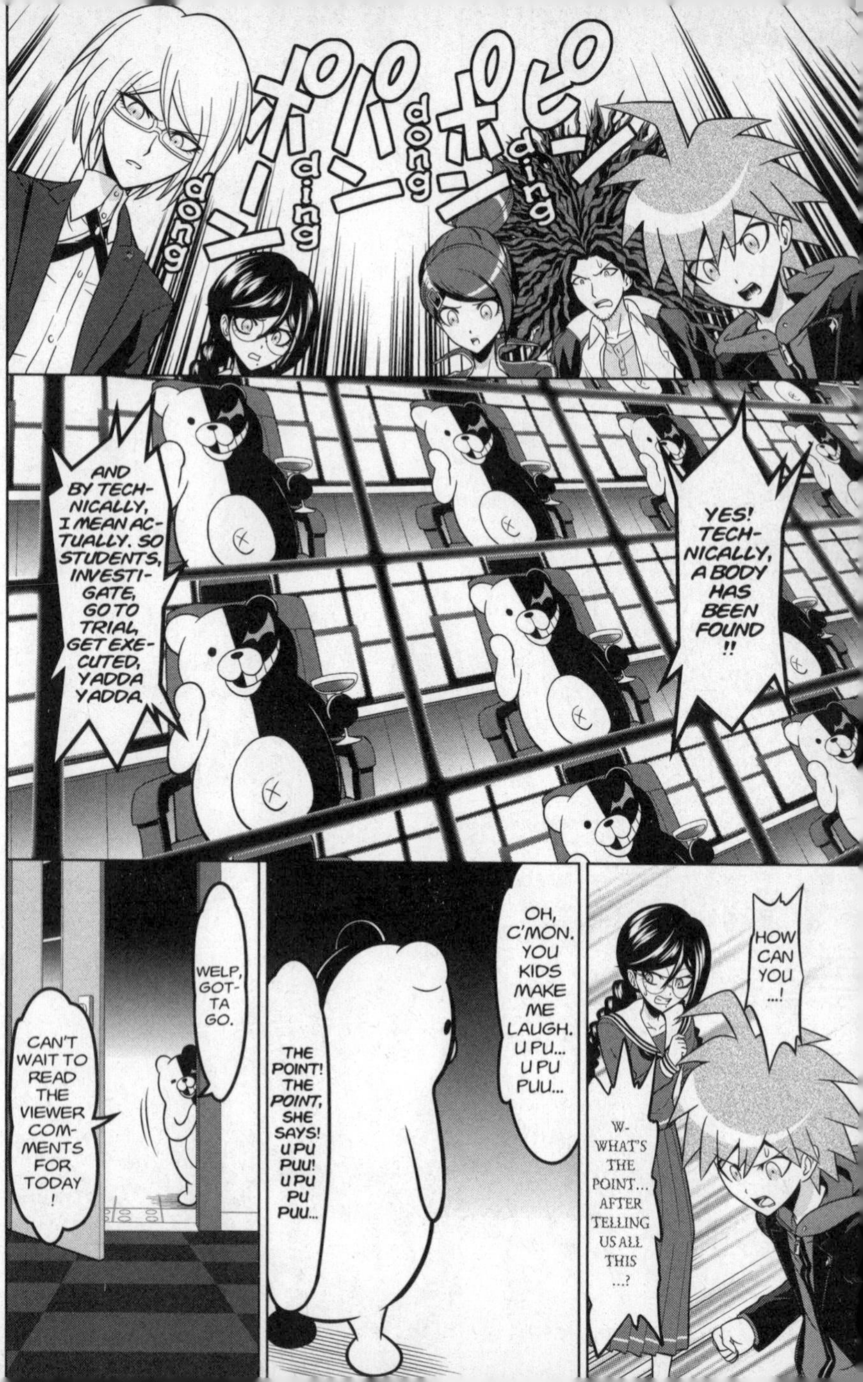
ding
dong
ding
dong
YES! TECHNICALLY, A BODY HAS BEEN FOUND!!
AND BY TECHNICALLY, I MEAN ACTUALLY. SO STUDENTS, INVESTIGATE, GO TO TRIAL, GET EXECUTED, YADDA YADDA.
HOW CAN YOU ...!
W-WHAT'S THE POINT... AFTER TELLING US ALL THIS ...?
OH, C'MON. YOU KIDS MAKE ME LAUGH. UPU... UPU PUU...
THE POINT! THE POINT, SHE SAYS! UPU PUU! UPU PU PUU...
WELP, GOTTA GO.
CAN'T WAIT TO READ THE VIEWER COMMENTS FOR TODAY!

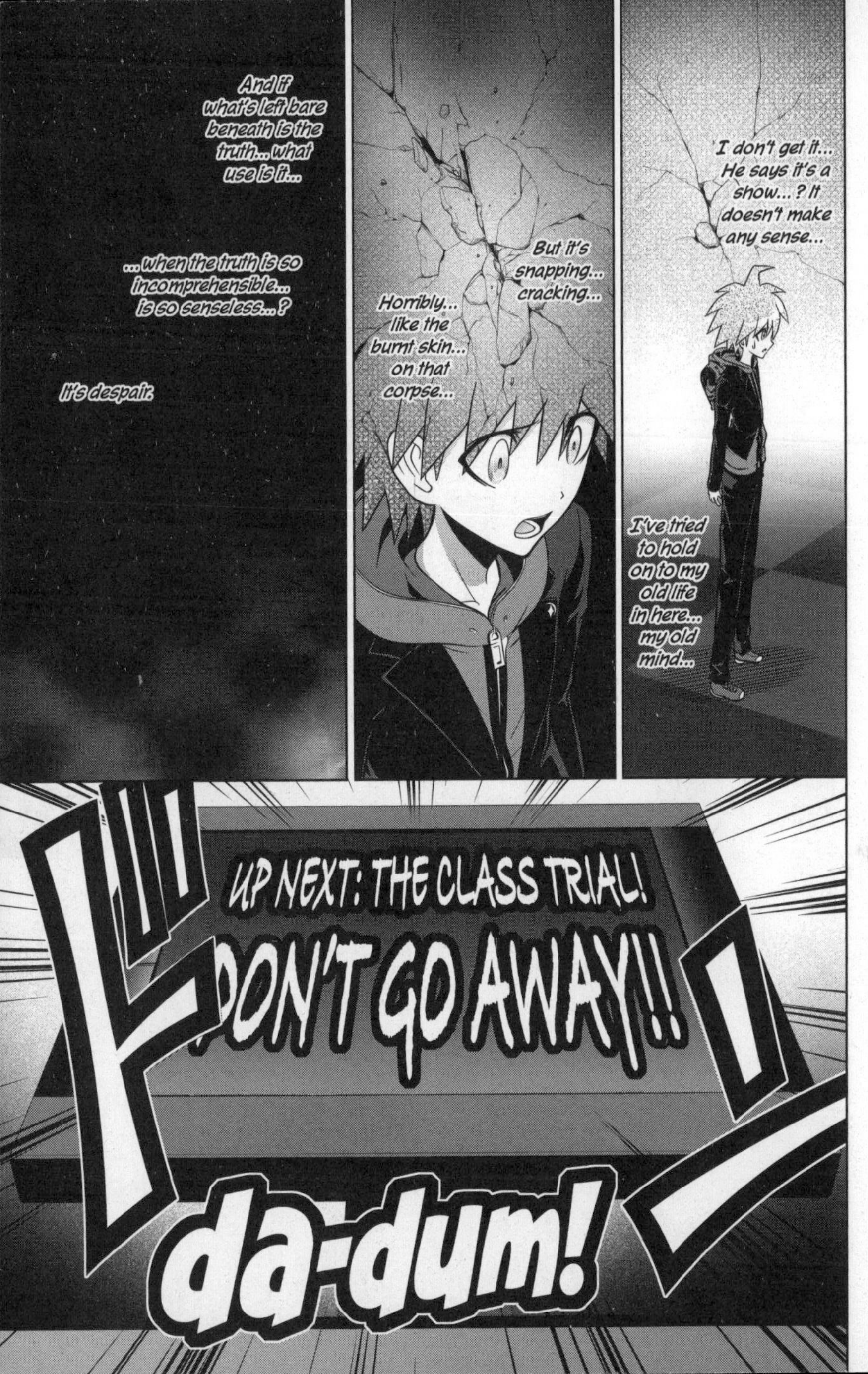
I don't get it... He says it's a show...? It doesn't make any sense...
I've tried to hold on to my old life in here... my old mind...
But it's snapping... cracking...
Horribly... like the burnt skin... on that corpse...
And if what's left bare beneath is the truth... what use is it...
...when the truth is so incomprehensible... is so senseless...?
It's despair.
UP NEXT: THE CLASS TRIAL!
DON'T GO AWAY!!
da-dum!

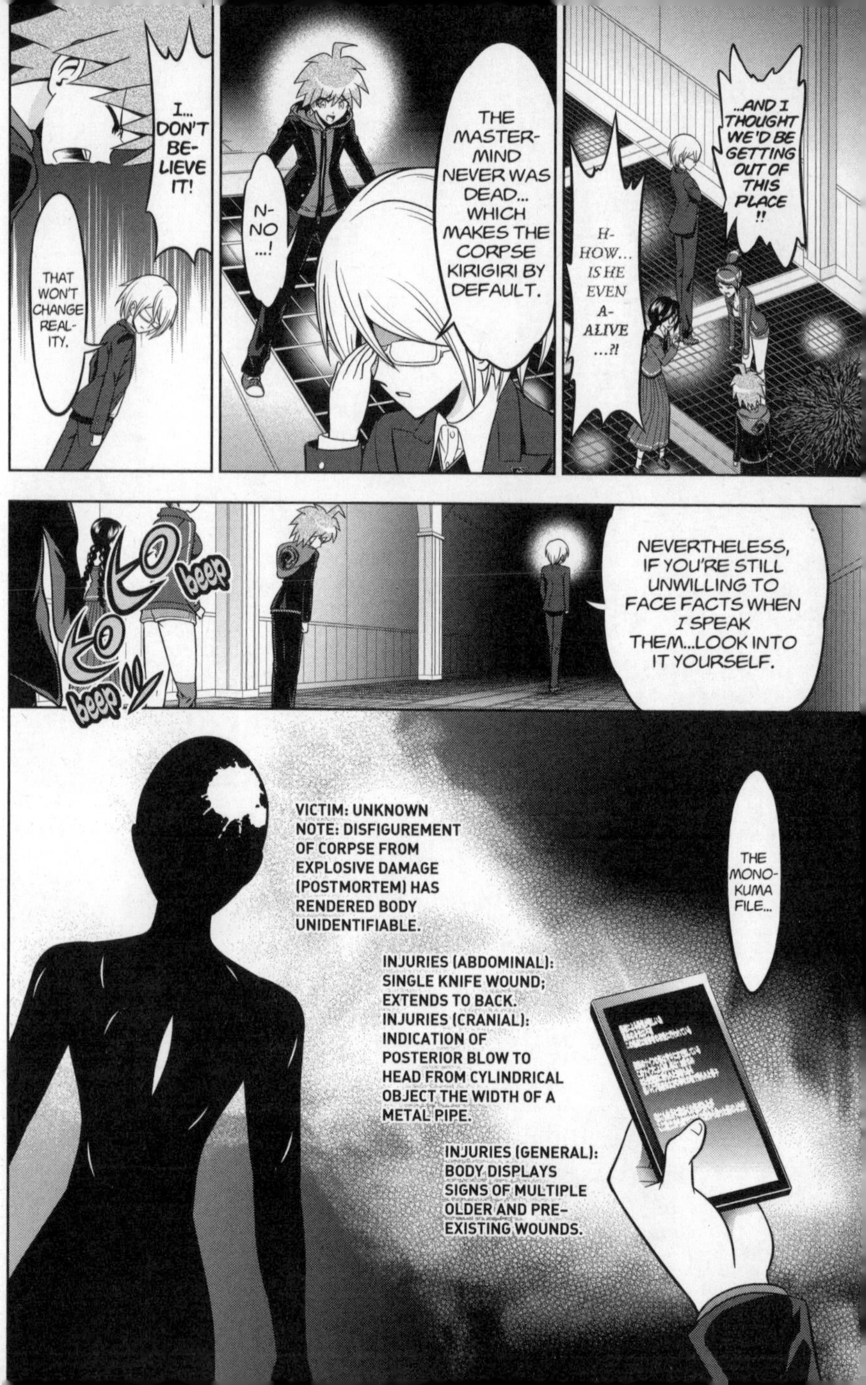
...AND I THOUGHT WE'D BE GETTING OUT OF THIS PLACE!!
H-HOW... IS HE EVEN A-ALIVE...?!
THE MASTERMIND NEVER WAS DEAD... WHICH MAKES THE CORPSE KIRIGIRI BY DEFAULT.
N-NO...!
I... DON'T BELIEVE IT!
THAT WON'T CHANGE REALITY.
NEVERTHELESS, IF YOU'RE STILL UNWILLING TO FACE FACTS WHEN I SPEAK THEM...LOOK INTO IT YOURSELF.
beep
beep!!
THE MONOKUMA FILE...
VICTIM: UNKNOWN
NOTE: DISFIGUREMENT OF CORPSE FROM EXPLOSIVE DAMAGE (POSTMORTEM) HAS RENDERED BODY UNIDENTIFIABLE.
INJURIES (ABDOMINAL): SINGLE KNIFE WOUND; EXTENDS TO BACK.
INJURIES (CRANIAL): INDICATION OF POSTERIOR BLOW TO HEAD FROM CYLINDRICAL OBJECT THE WIDTH OF A METAL PIPE.
INJURIES (GENERAL): BODY DISPLAYS SIGNS OF MULTIPLE OLDER AND PRE-EXISTING WOUNDS.

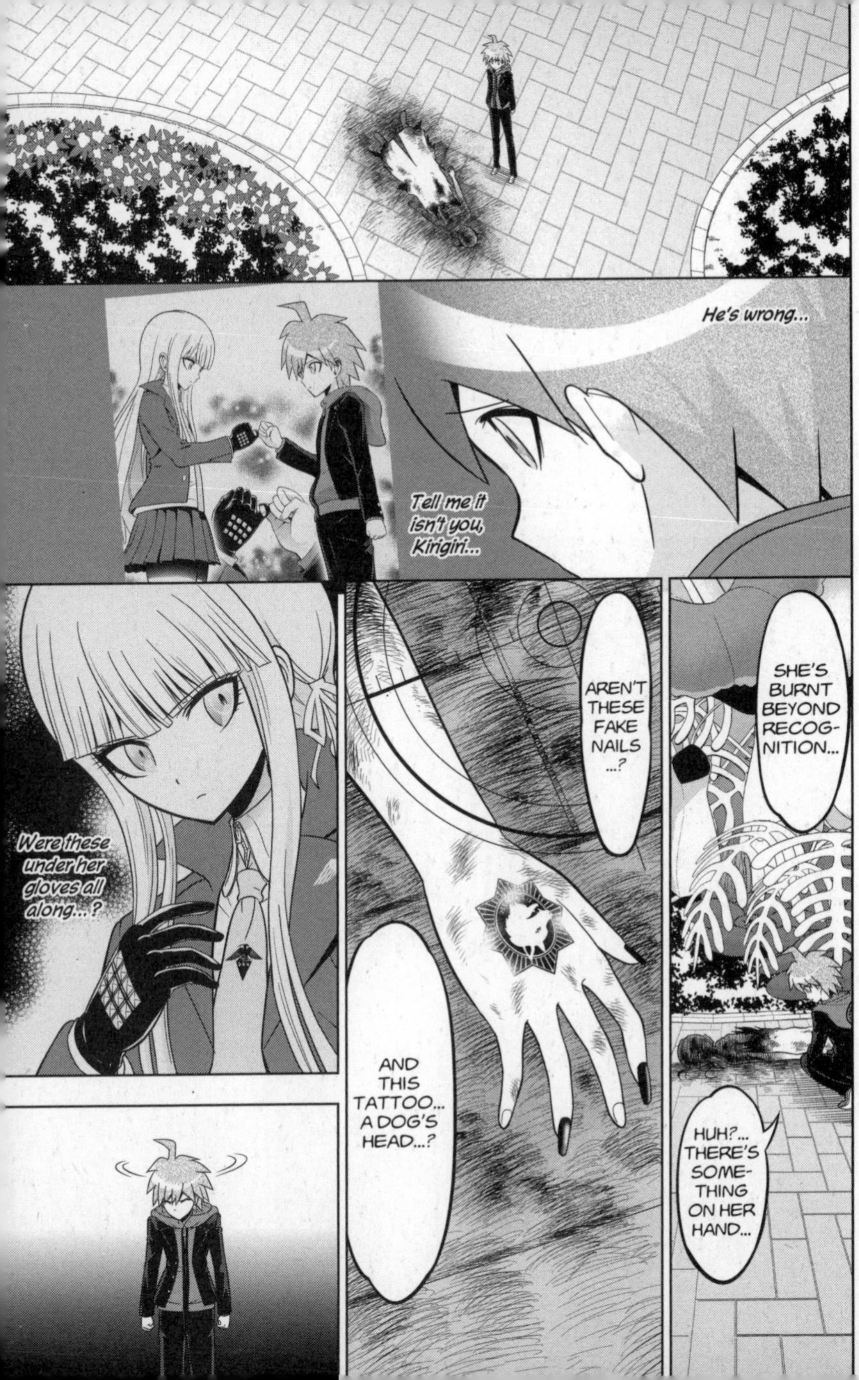
He's wrong...
Tell me it isn't you, Kirigiri...
SHE'S BURNT BEYOND RECOG-NITION...
HUH?... THERE'S SOME-THING ON HER HAND...
AREN'T THESE FAKE NAILS ...?
AND THIS TATTOO... A DOG'S HEAD...?
Were these under her gloves all along...?

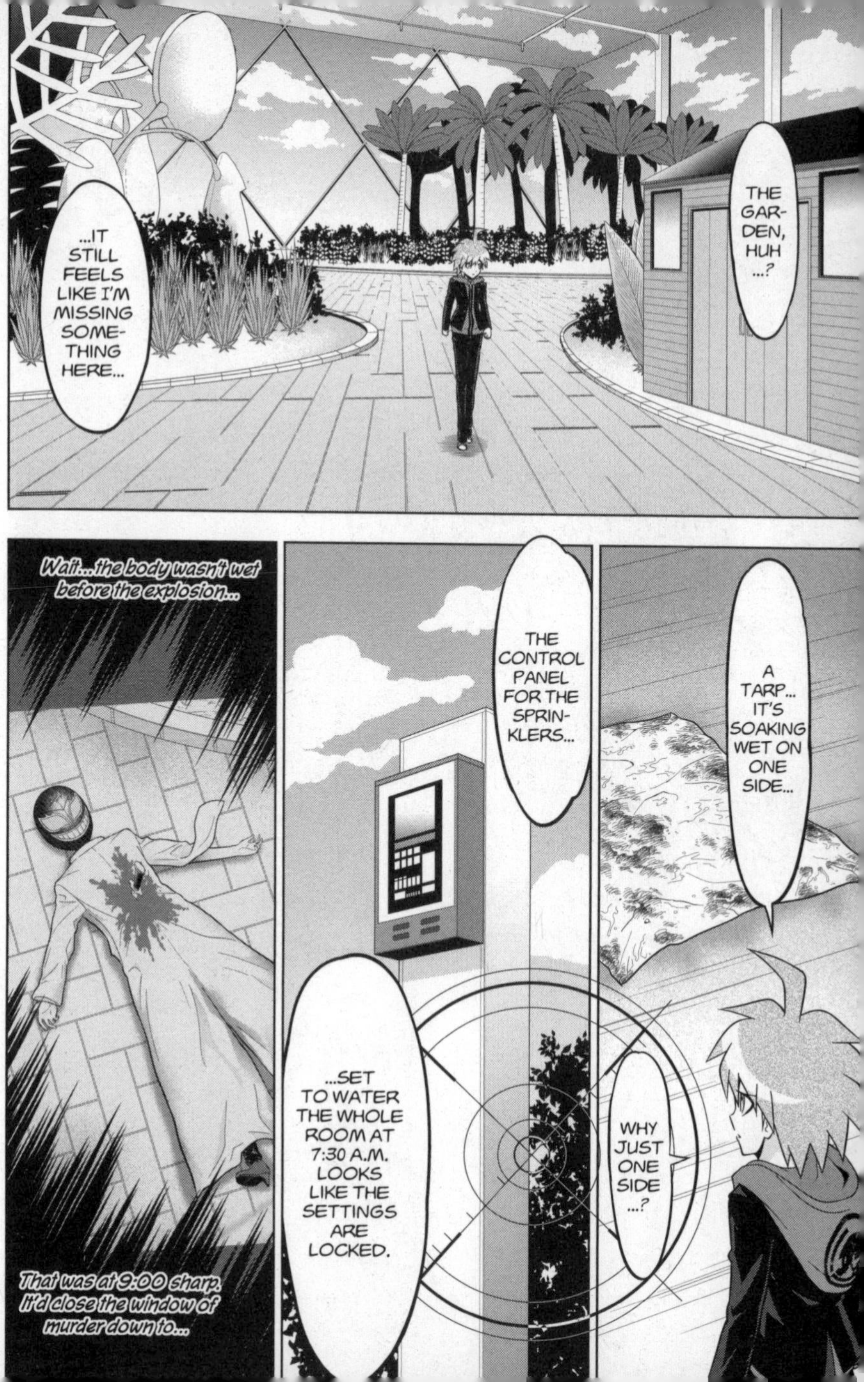
THE GARDEN, HUH...?
...IT STILL FEELS LIKE I'M MISSING SOMETHING HERE...
A TARP... IT'S SOAKING WET ON ONE SIDE...
WHY JUST ONE SIDE...?
THE CONTROL PANEL FOR THE SPRINKLERS...
...SET TO WATER THE WHOLE ROOM AT 7:30 A.M. LOOKS LIKE THE SETTINGS ARE LOCKED.
Wait...the body wasn't wet before the explosion...
That was at 9:00 sharp. It'd close the window of murder down to...

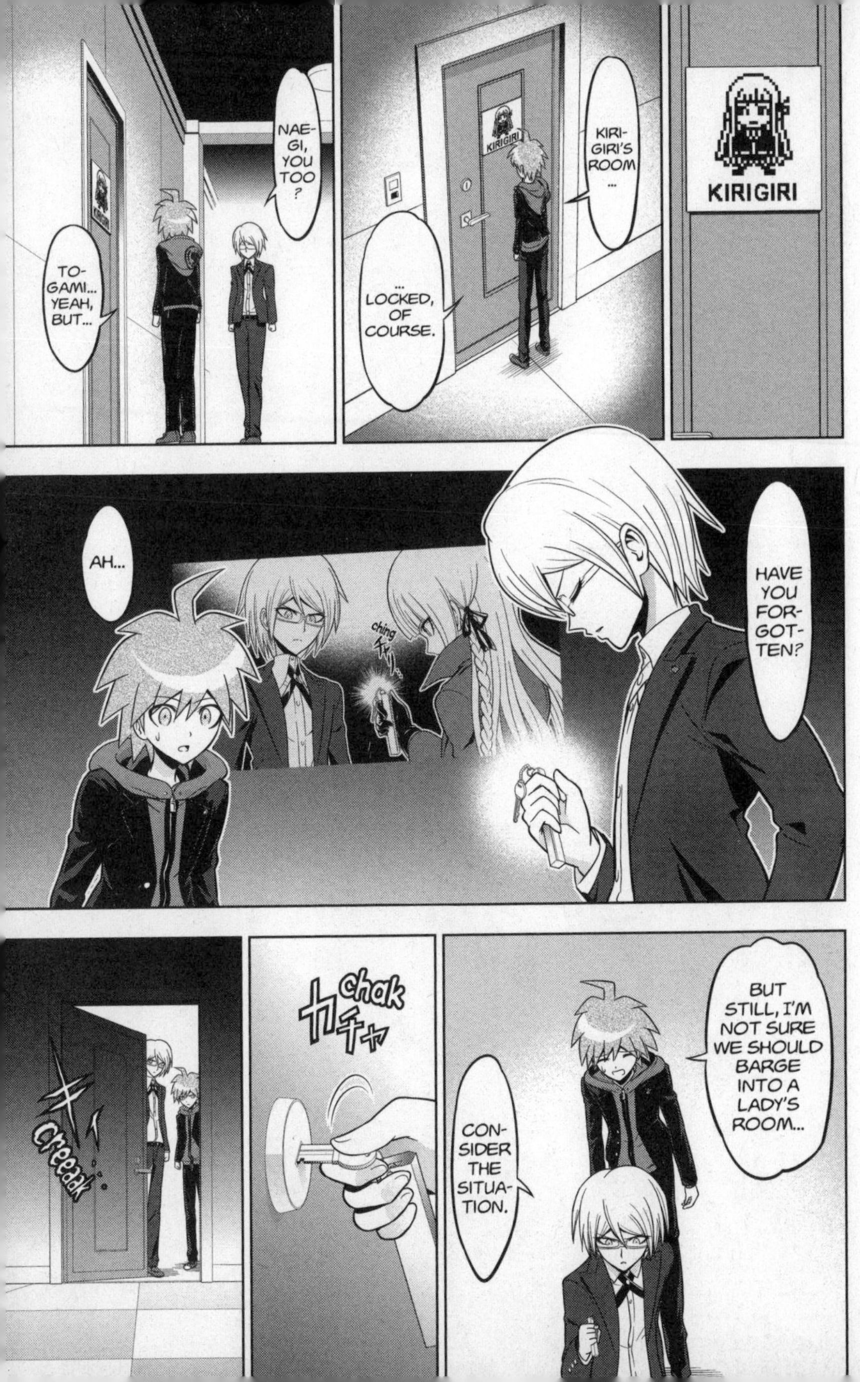
KIRIGIRI
KIRIGIRI'S ROOM ...
KIRIGIRI
... LOCKED, OF COURSE.
NAEGI, YOU TOO?
TOGAMI... YEAH, BUT...
HAVE YOU FORGOTTEN?
ching
AH...
BUT STILL, I'M NOT SURE WE SHOULD BARGE INTO A LADY'S ROOM...
CONSIDER THE SITUATION.
chak
creeaak

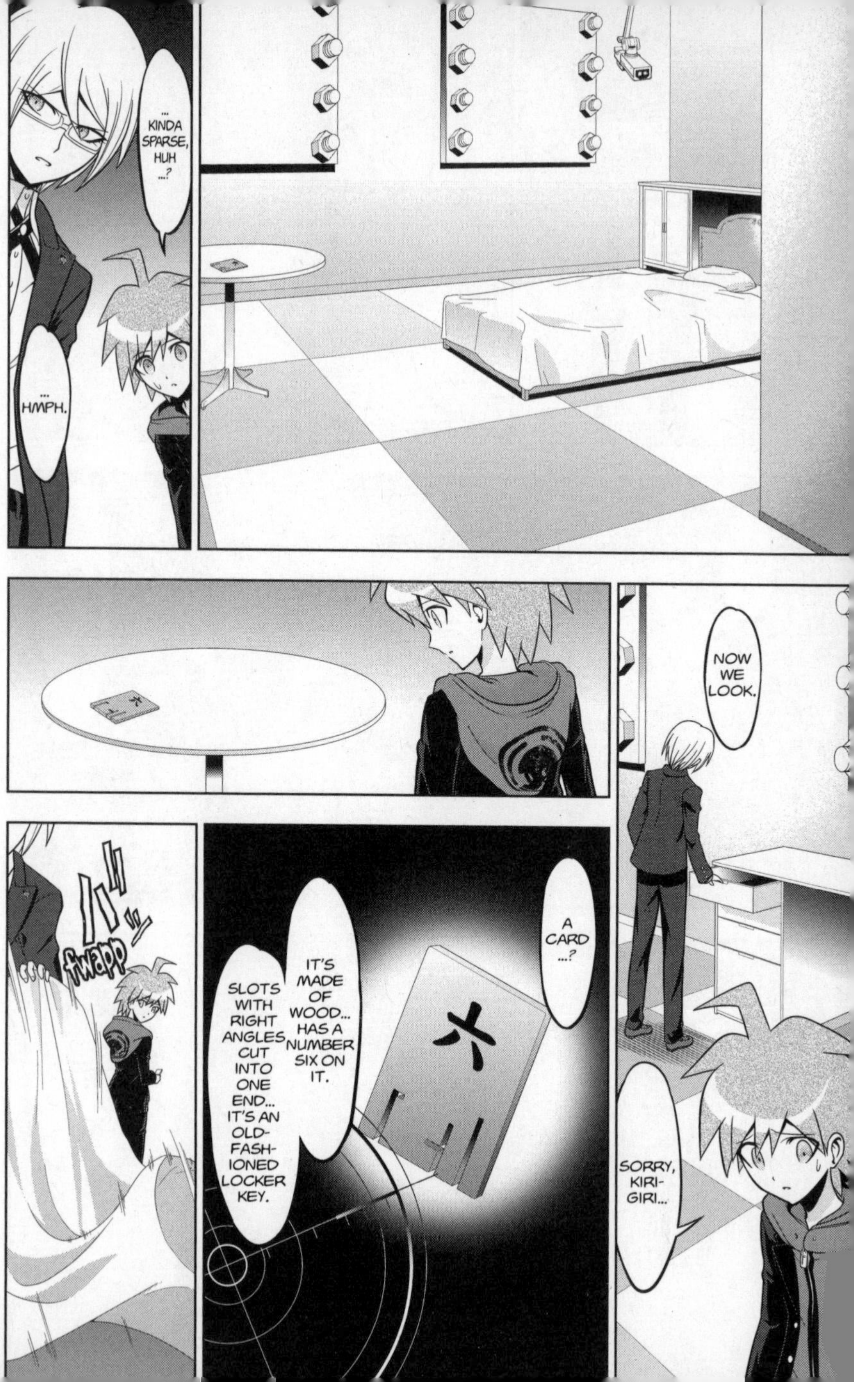

... KINDA SPARSE, HUH ...?
... HMPH.
NOW WE LOOK.
SORRY, KIRI-GIRI...
A CARD ...?
IT'S MADE OF WOOD... HAS A NUMBER SIX ON IT.
SLOTS WITH RIGHT ANGLES CUT INTO ONE END... IT'S AN OLD-FASH-IONED LOCKER KEY.
六
fwapp

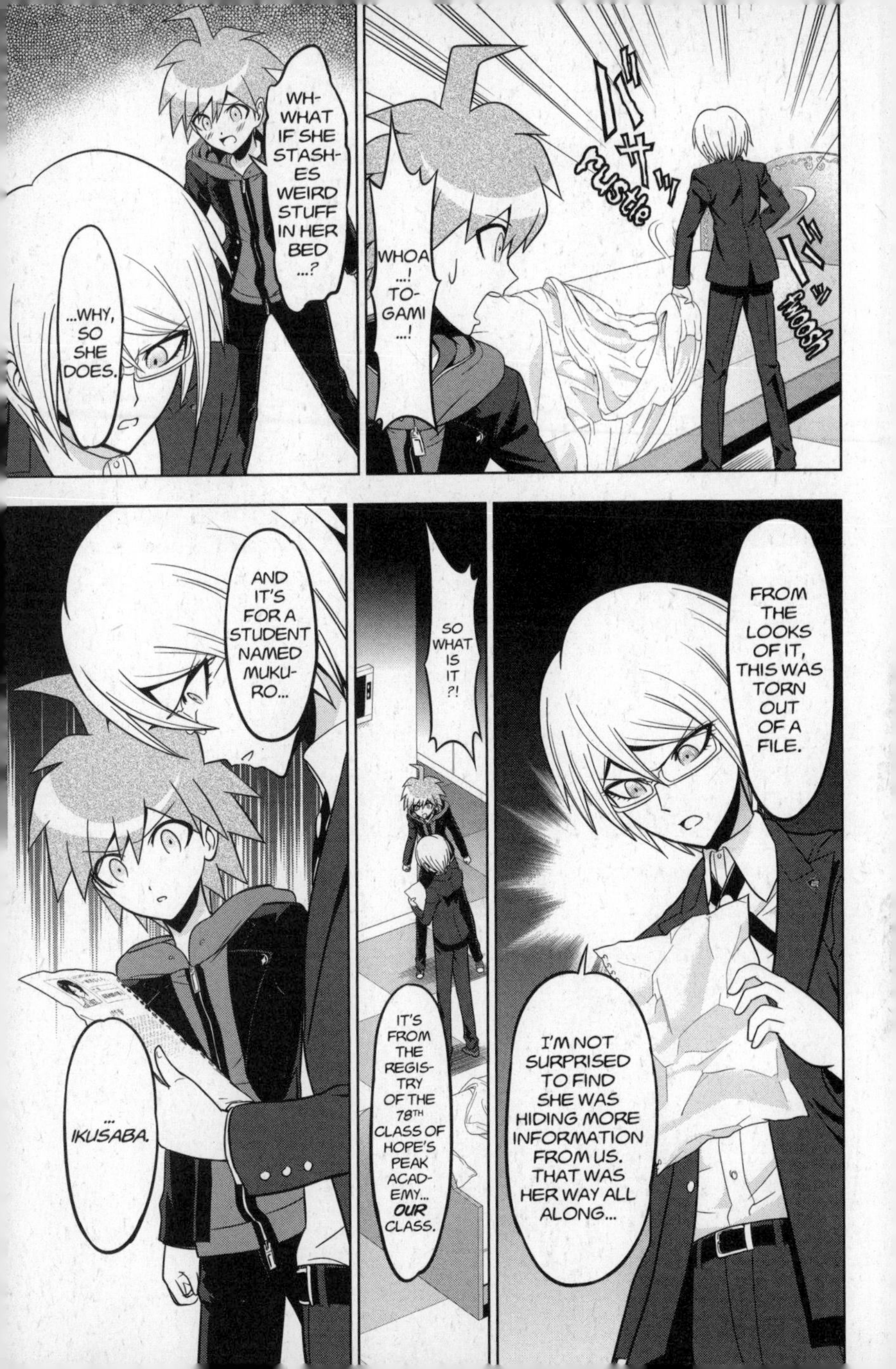

バサッ
rustle
fwoosh
WHOA...! TO-GAMI...!
WH-WHAT IF SHE STASHES WEIRD STUFF IN HER BED...?
...WHY, SO SHE DOES.
FROM THE LOOKS OF IT, THIS WAS TORN OUT OF A FILE.
I'M NOT SURPRISED TO FIND SHE WAS HIDING MORE INFORMATION FROM US. THAT WAS HER WAY ALL ALONG...
SO WHAT IS IT?!
IT'S FROM THE REGISTRY OF THE 78TH CLASS OF HOPE'S PEAK ACADEMY... *OUR* CLASS.
AND IT'S FOR A STUDENT NAMED MUKURO...
...IKUSABA.

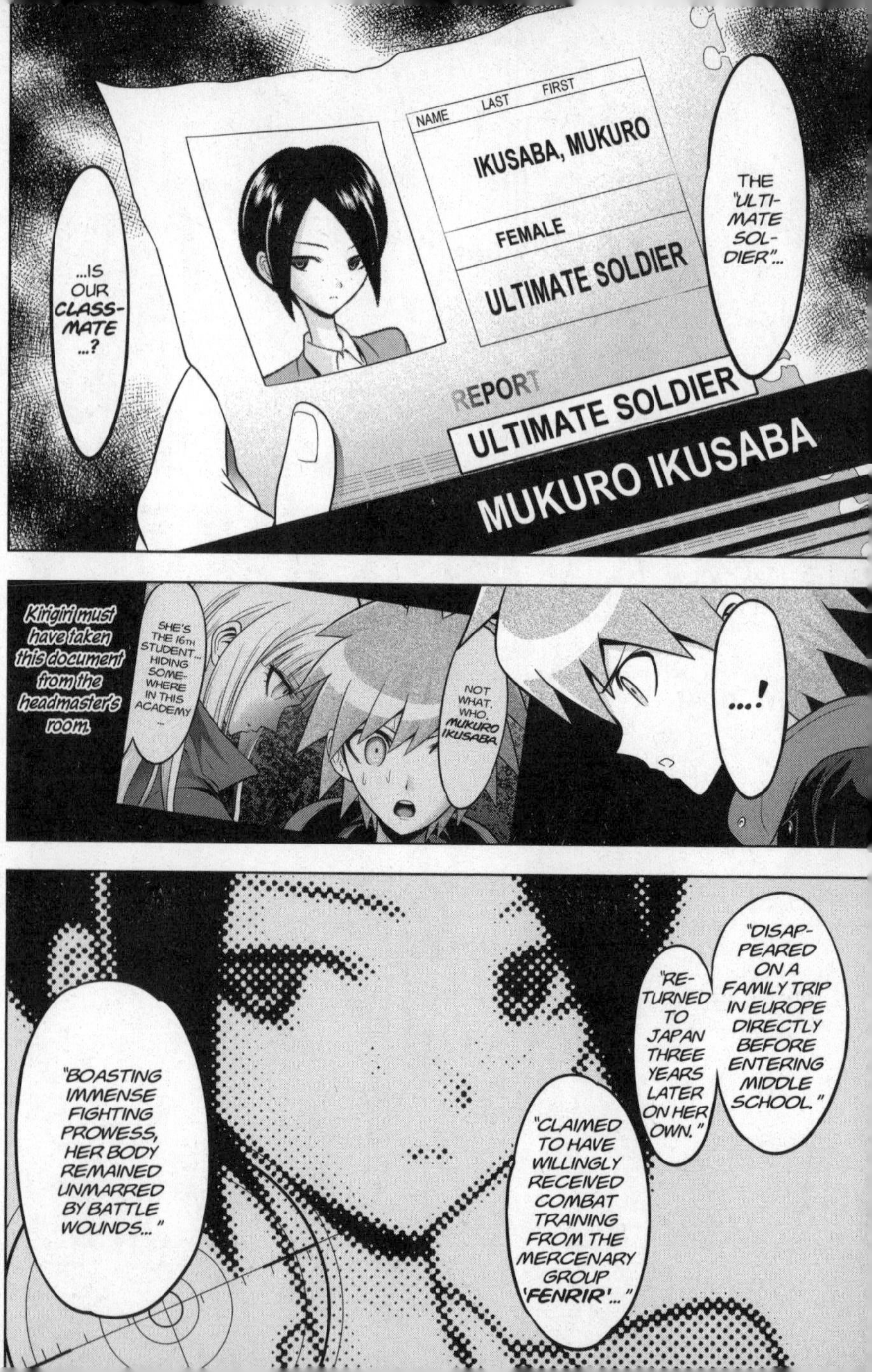
THE "ULTIMATE SOLDIER"...
NAME LAST FIRST
IKUSABA, MUKURO
FEMALE
ULTIMATE SOLDIER
...IS OUR CLASSMATE ...?
REPORT
ULTIMATE SOLDIER
MUKURO IKUSABA
...!
NOT WHAT. WHO. MUKURO IKUSABA
SHE'S THE 16TH STUDENT... HIDING SOMEWHERE IN THIS ACADEMY...
Kirigiri must have taken this document from the headmaster's room.
"DISAPPEARED ON A FAMILY TRIP IN EUROPE DIRECTLY BEFORE ENTERING MIDDLE SCHOOL."
"RETURNED TO JAPAN THREE YEARS LATER ON HER OWN."
"CLAIMED TO HAVE WILLINGLY RECEIVED COMBAT TRAINING FROM THE MERCENARY GROUP 'FENRIR'..."
"BOASTING IMMENSE FIGHTING PROWESS, HER BODY REMAINED UNMARRED BY BATTLE WOUNDS..."

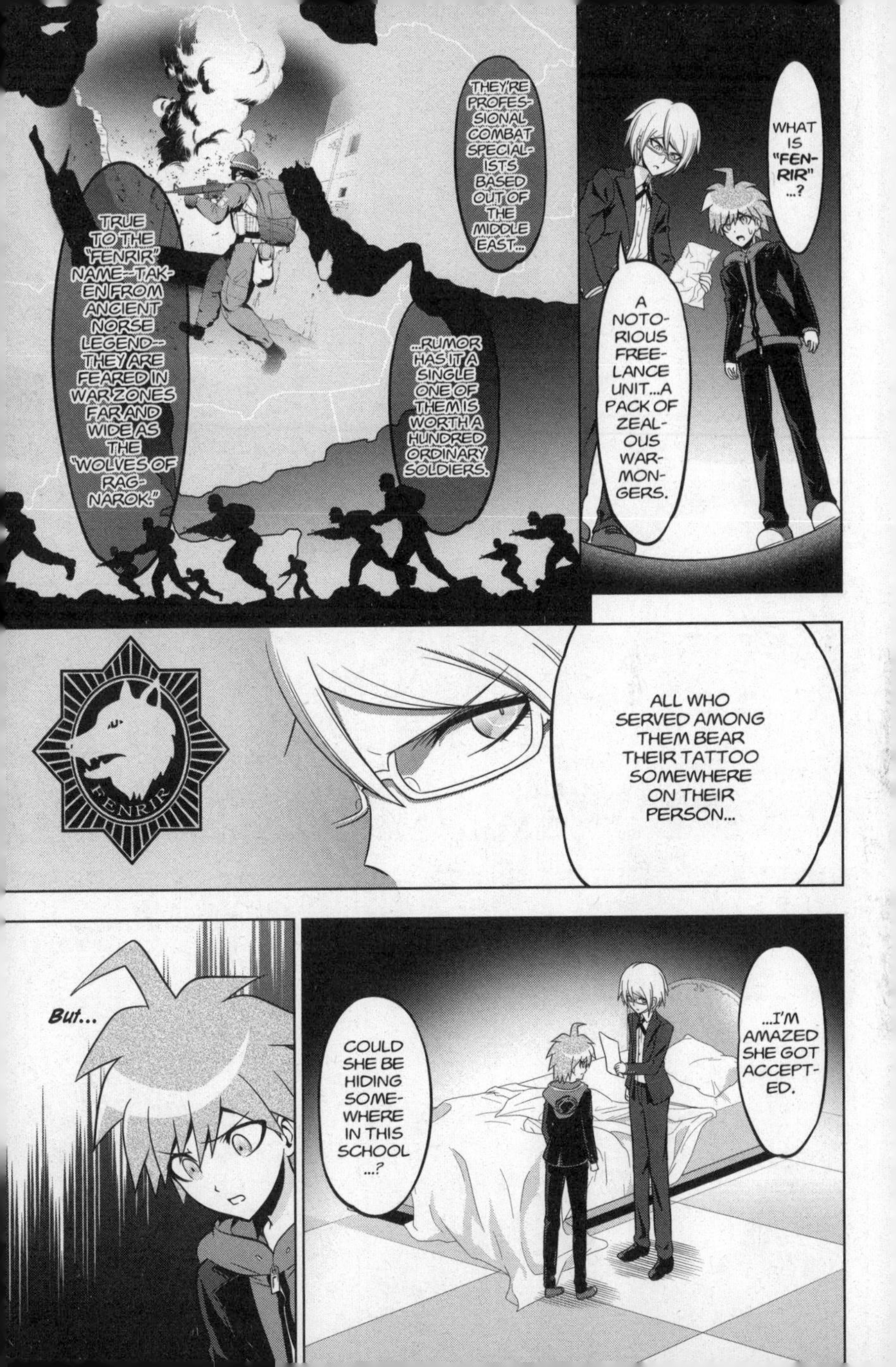
WHAT IS "FENRIR"...?
A NOTORIOUS FREELANCE UNIT...A PACK OF ZEALOUS WARMONGERS.
THEY'RE PROFESSIONAL COMBAT SPECIALISTS BASED OUT OF THE MIDDLE EAST...
...RUMOR HAS IT A SINGLE ONE OF THEM IS WORTH A HUNDRED ORDINARY SOLDIERS.
TRUE TO THE "FENRIR" NAME--TAKEN FROM ANCIENT NORSE LEGEND--THEY ARE FEARED IN WAR ZONES FAR AND WIDE AS THE "WOLVES OF RAGNAROK."
ALL WHO SERVED AMONG THEM BEAR THEIR TATTOO SOMEWHERE ON THEIR PERSON...
FENRIR
...I'M AMAZED SHE GOT ACCEPTED.
COULD SHE BE HIDING SOMEWHERE IN THIS SCHOOL...?
But...

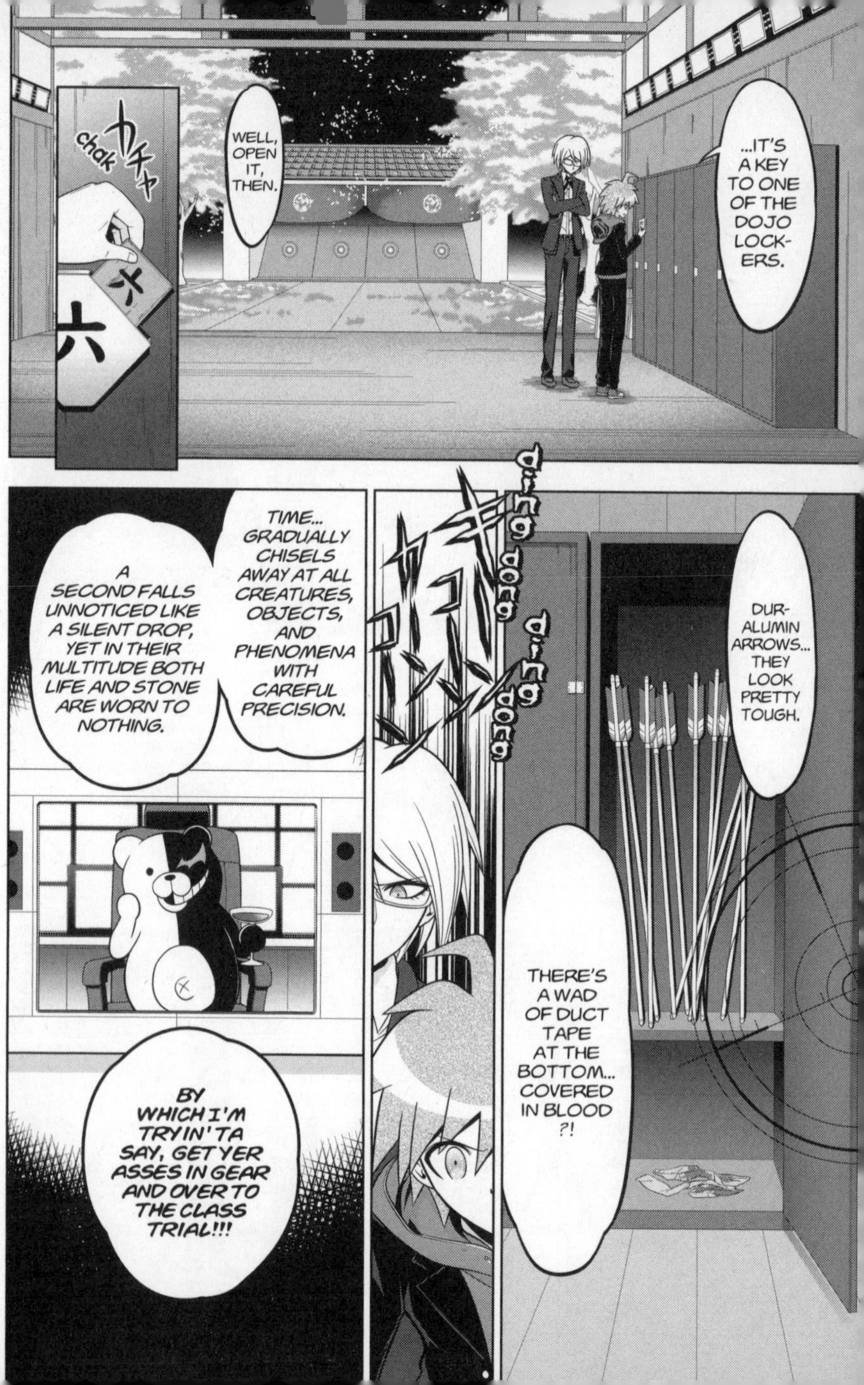
...IT'S A KEY TO ONE OF THE DOJO LOCKERS.
WELL, OPEN IT, THEN.
chak
六
六
DUR-ALUMIN ARROWS... THEY LOOK PRETTY TOUGH.
THERE'S A WAD OF DUCT TAPE AT THE BOTTOM... COVERED IN BLOOD?!
ding dong ding dong
TIME... GRADUALLY CHISELS AWAY AT ALL CREATURES, OBJECTS, AND PHENOMENA WITH CAREFUL PRECISION.
A SECOND FALLS UNNOTICED LIKE A SILENT DROP, YET IN THEIR MULTITUDE BOTH LIFE AND STONE ARE WORN TO NOTHING.
BY WHICH I'M TRYIN' TA SAY, GET YER ASSES IN GEAR AND OVER TO THE CLASS TRIAL!!!

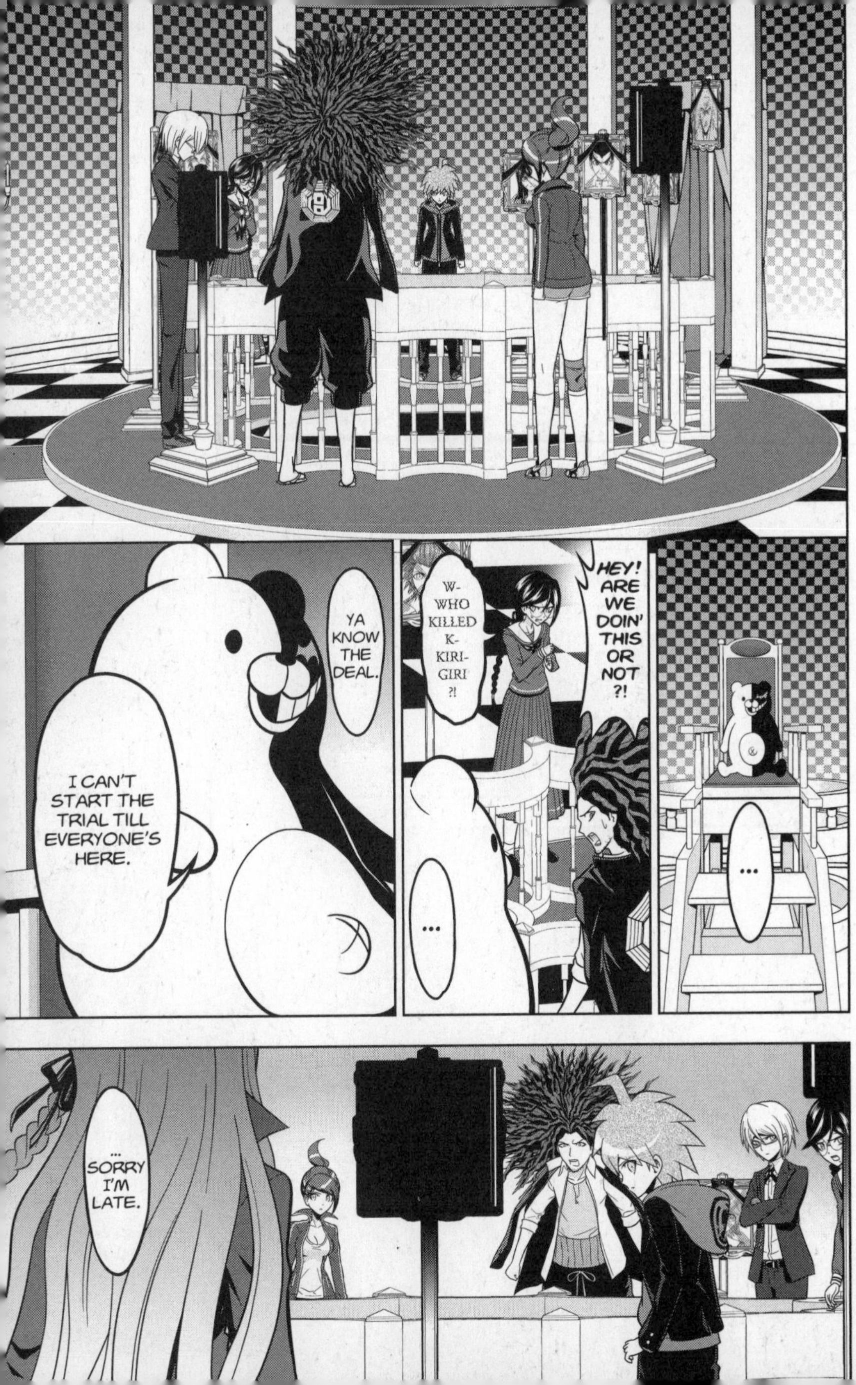
...
HEY! ARE WE DOIN' THIS OR NOT?!
W-WHO KILLED K-KIRI-GIRI?!
...
YA KNOW THE DEAL.
I CAN'T START THE TRIAL TILL EVERYONE'S HERE.
...SORRY I'M LATE.

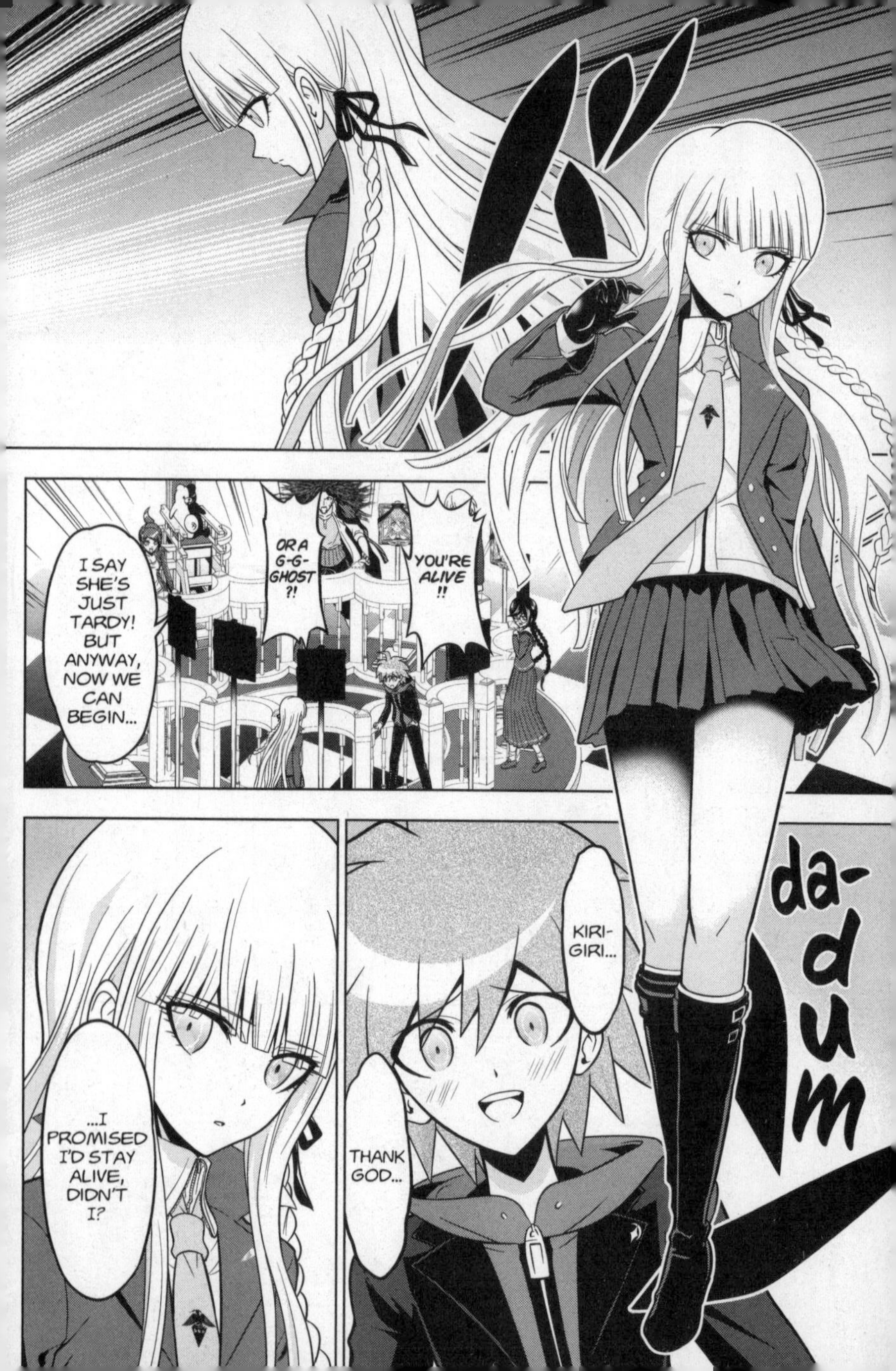
YOU'RE ALIVE!!
OR A G-G-GHOST?!
I SAY SHE'S JUST TARDY! BUT ANYWAY, NOW WE CAN BEGIN...
da-dum
KIRI-GIRI...
THANK GOD...
...I PROMISED I'D STAY ALIVE, DIDN'T I?

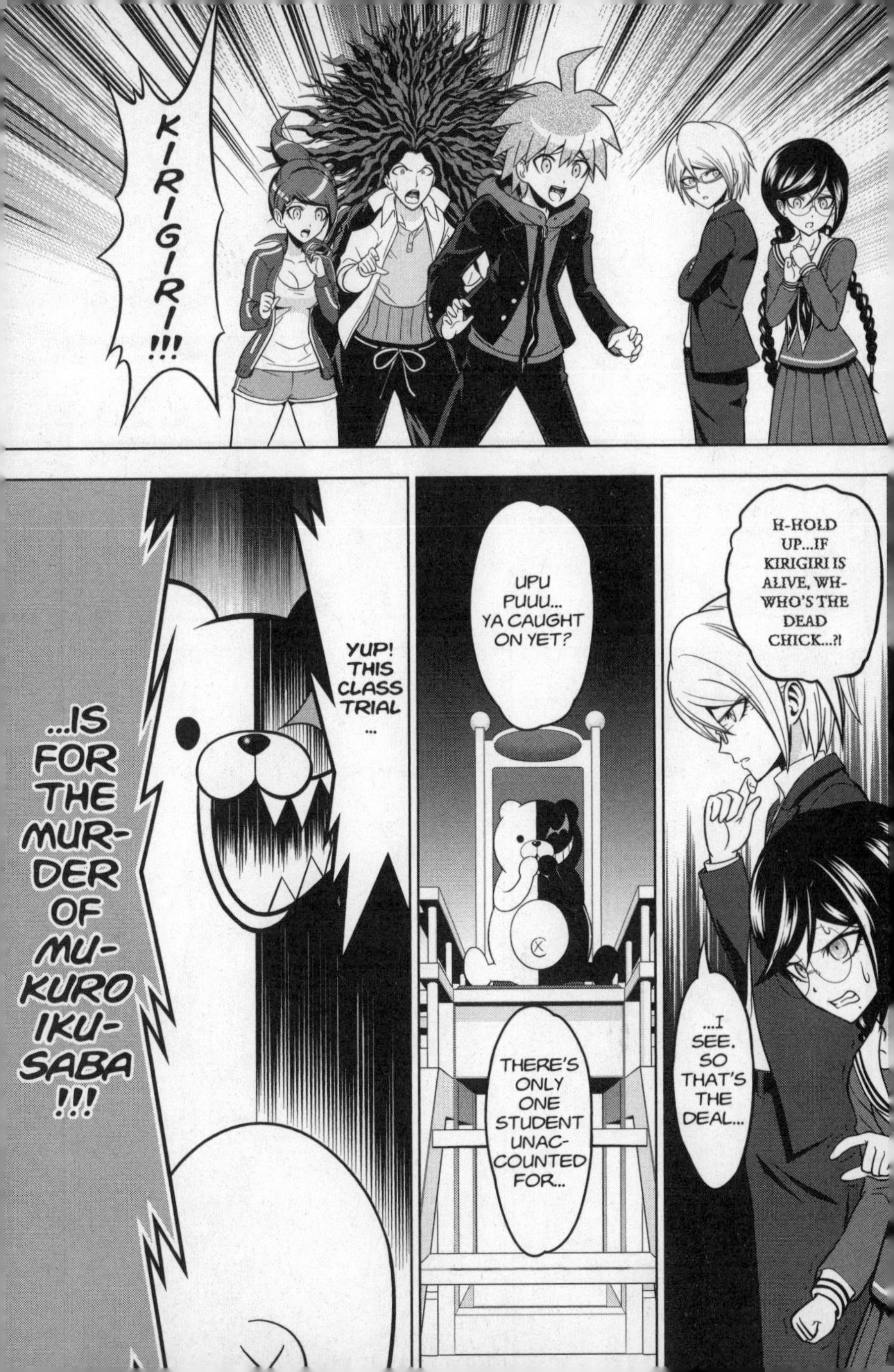
KIRIGIRI!!!
H-HOLD UP...IF KIRIGIRI IS ALIVE, WH-WHO'S THE DEAD CHICK...?!
...I SEE. SO THAT'S THE DEAL...
UPU PUUU... YA CAUGHT ON YET?
THERE'S ONLY ONE STUDENT UNACCOUNTED FOR...
YUP! THIS CLASS TRIAL...
...IS FOR THE MURDER OF MUKURO IKUSABA!!!

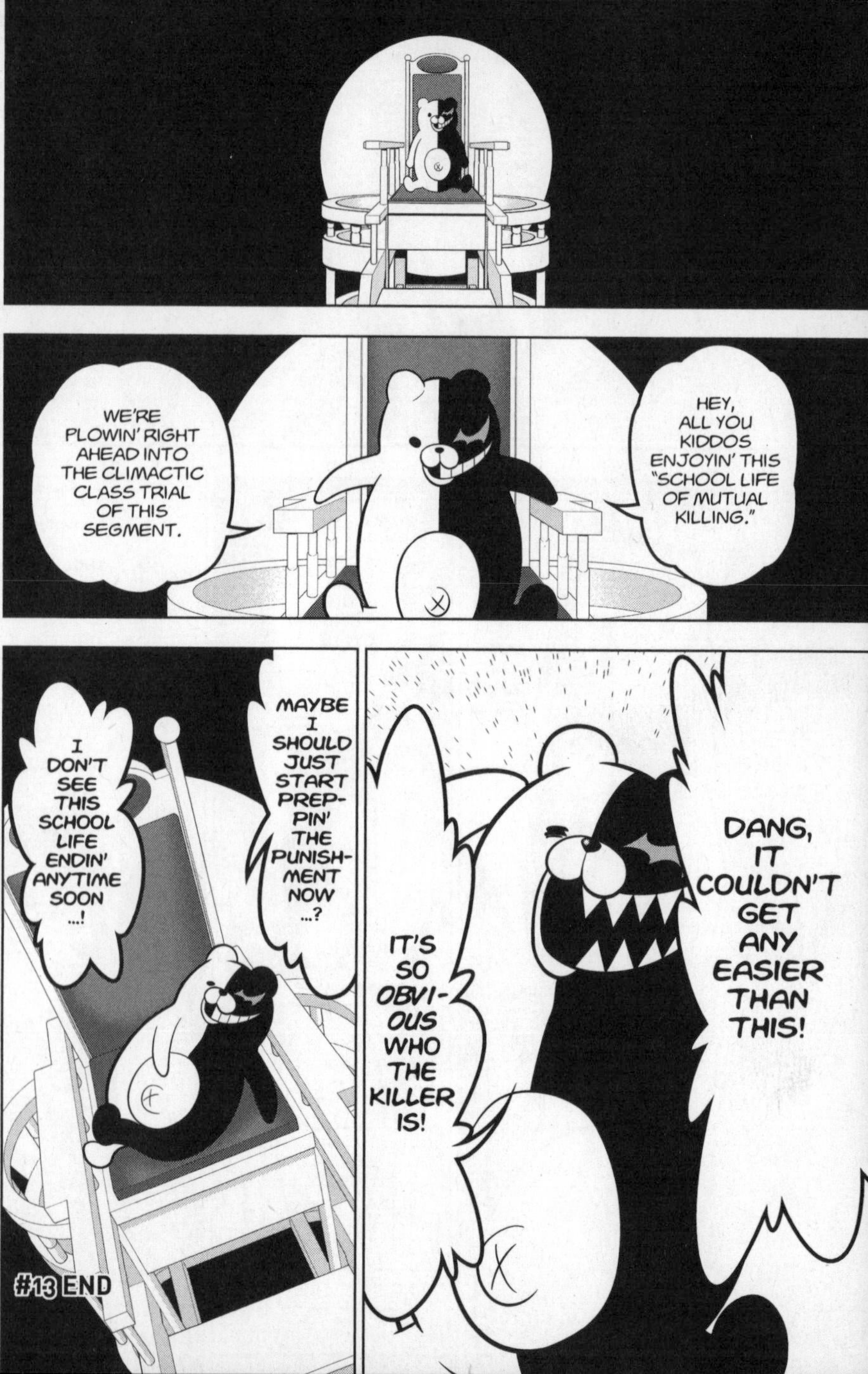
HEY, ALL YOU KIDDOS ENJOYIN' THIS "SCHOOL LIFE OF MUTUAL KILLING."
WE'RE PLOWIN' RIGHT AHEAD INTO THE CLIMACTIC CLASS TRIAL OF THIS SEGMENT.
DANG, IT COULDN'T GET ANY EASIER THAN THIS!
IT'S SO *OBVIOUS* WHO THE KILLER IS!
MAYBE I SHOULD JUST START PREPPIN' THE PUNISHMENT NOW ...?
I DON'T SEE THIS SCHOOL LIFE ENDIN' ANYTIME SOON ...!
#13 END

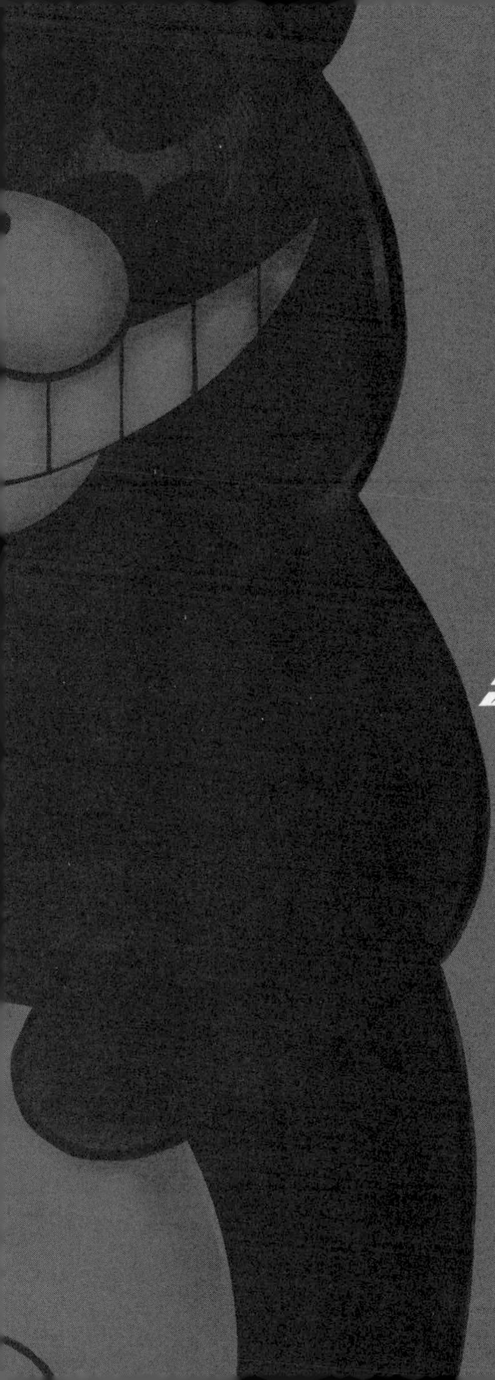

DANGANRONPA
A SCHOOL OF HOPE . . . WITH STUDENTS OF DESPAIR!
THE ANIMATION

DANGANRONPA

A SCHOOL OF HOPE . . . WITH STUDENTS OF DESPAIR!

THE ANIMATION

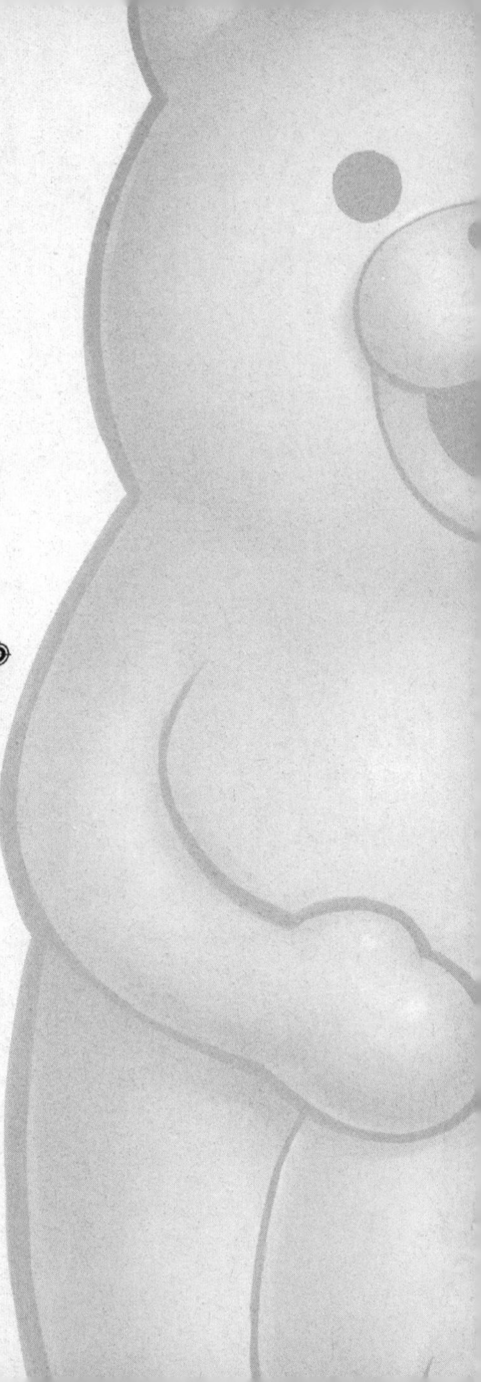

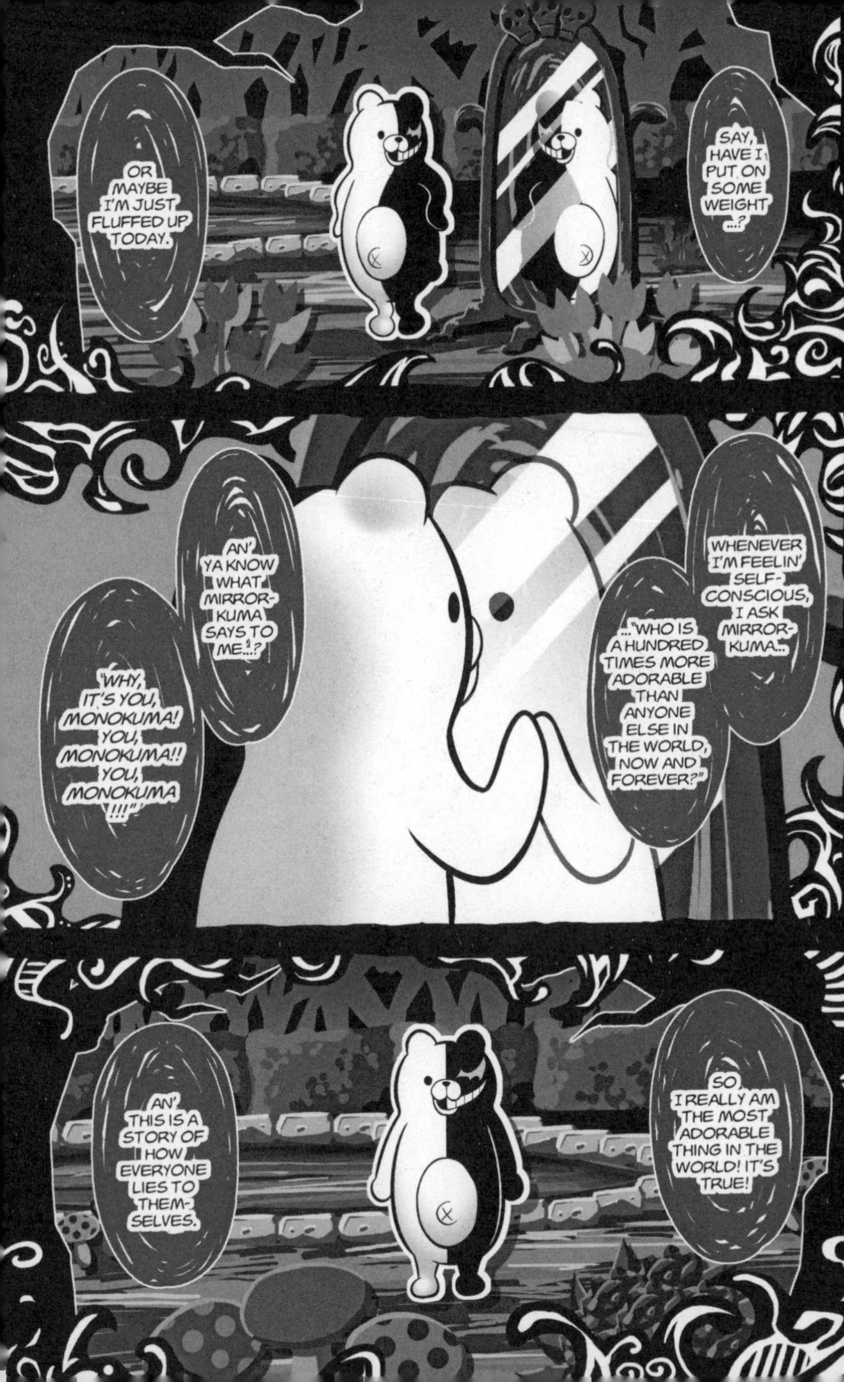
SAY, HAVE I PUT ON SOME WEIGHT ...?
OR MAYBE I'M JUST FLUFFED UP TODAY.
WHENEVER I'M FEELIN' SELF-CONSCIOUS, I ASK MIRROR-KUMA...
..."WHO IS A HUNDRED TIMES MORE ADORABLE THAN ANYONE ELSE IN THE WORLD, NOW AND FOREVER?"
AN' YA KNOW WHAT MIRROR-KUMA SAYS TO ME...?
"WHY, IT'S YOU, MONOKUMA! YOU, MONOKUMA!! YOU, MONOKUMA!!!"
SO, I REALLY AM THE MOST ADORABLE THING IN THE WORLD! IT'S TRUE!
AN' THIS IS A STORY OF HOW EVERYONE LIES TO THEMSELVES.

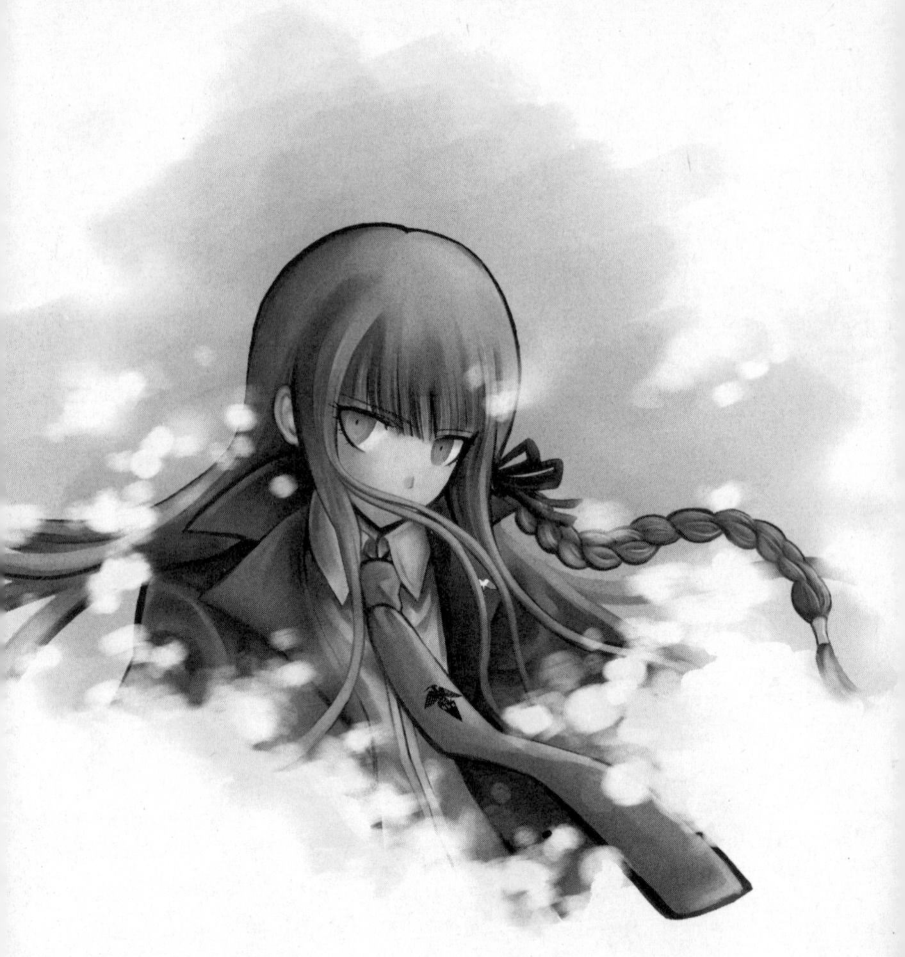

#14 [ABNORMAL ARC: 100 MILE DASH;
DISHEARTENING JUNK FOOD FOR THE RACE
THROUGH YOUTH (DEADLY LIFE) II]

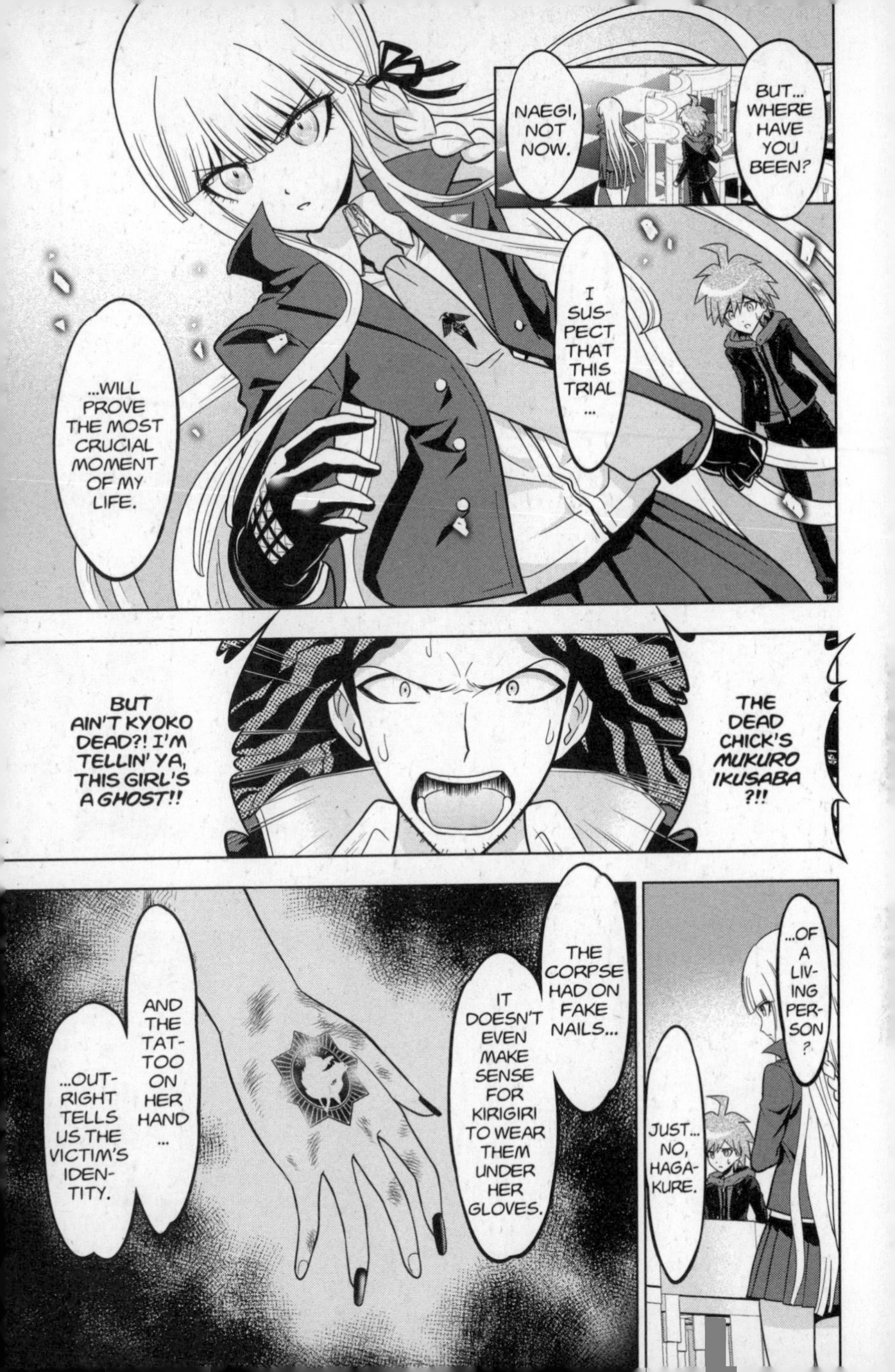
BUT... WHERE HAVE YOU BEEN?
NAEGI, NOT NOW.
I SUSPECT THAT THIS TRIAL...
...WILL PROVE THE MOST CRUCIAL MOMENT OF MY LIFE.
THE DEAD CHICK'S MUKURO IKUSABA?!!
BUT AIN'T KYOKO DEAD?! I'M TELLIN' YA, THIS GIRL'S A GHOST!!
...OF A LIVING PERSON?
JUST... NO, HAGAKURE.
THE CORPSE HAD ON FAKE NAILS...
IT DOESN'T EVEN MAKE SENSE FOR KIRIGIRI TO WEAR THEM UNDER HER GLOVES.
AND THE TATTOO ON HER HAND...
...OUTRIGHT TELLS US THE VICTIM'S IDENTITY.

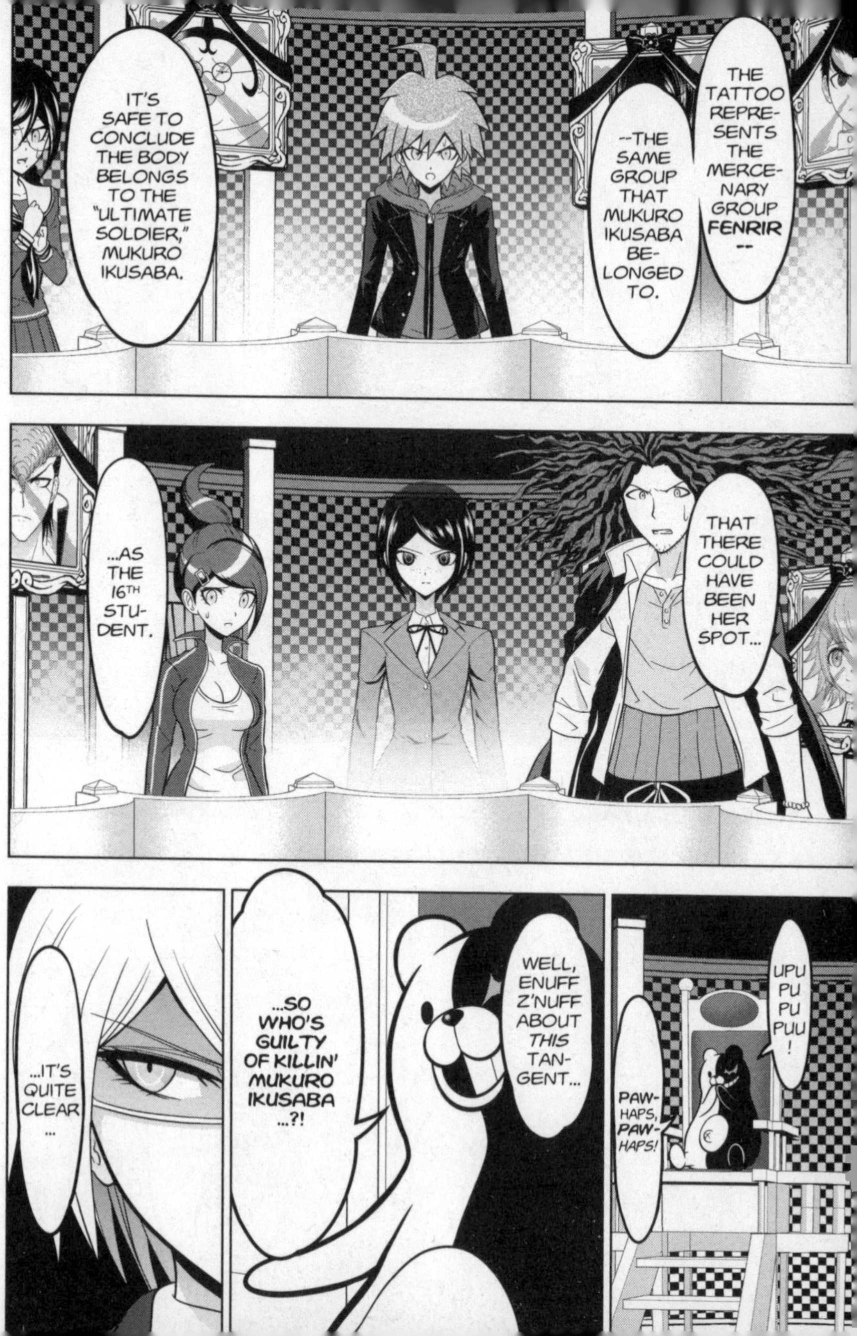
THE TATTOO REPRESENTS THE MERCENARY GROUP FENRIR --
--THE SAME GROUP THAT MUKURO IKUSABA BELONGED TO.
IT'S SAFE TO CONCLUDE THE BODY BELONGS TO THE "ULTIMATE SOLDIER," MUKURO IKUSABA.
THAT THERE COULD HAVE BEEN HER SPOT...
...AS THE 16TH STUDENT.
UPU PU PU PUU!
PAW-HAPS, PAW-HAPS!
WELL, ENUFF Z'NUFF ABOUT THIS TANGENT...
...SO WHO'S GUILTY OF KILLIN' MUKURO IKUSABA...?!
...IT'S QUITE CLEAR...

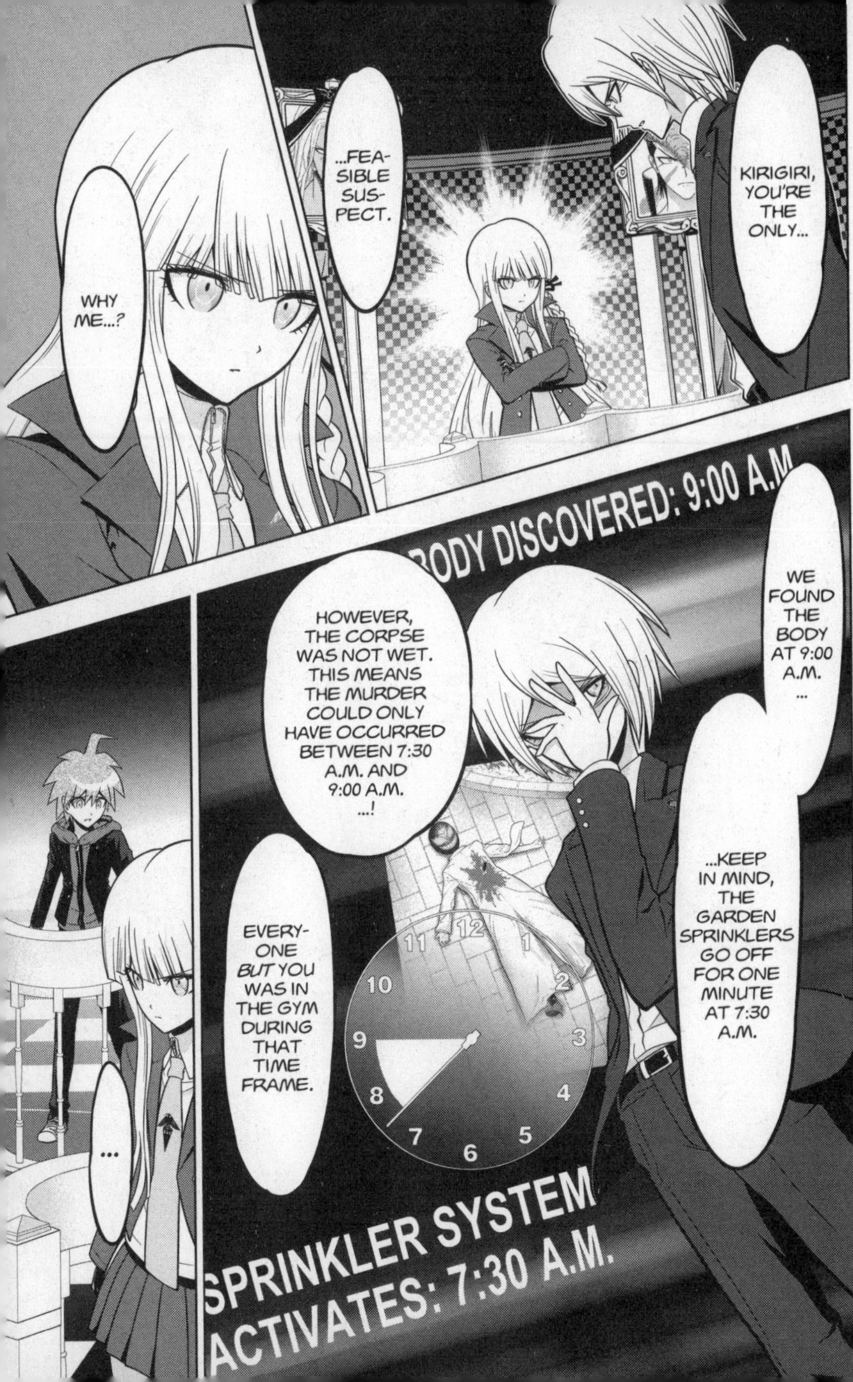
KIRIGIRI, YOU'RE THE ONLY...
...FEA-SIBLE SUS-PECT.
WHY ME...?
BODY DISCOVERED: 9:00 A.M
WE FOUND THE BODY AT 9:00 A.M. ...
...KEEP IN MIND, THE GARDEN SPRINKLERS GO OFF FOR ONE MINUTE AT 7:30 A.M.
HOWEVER, THE CORPSE WAS NOT WET. THIS MEANS THE MURDER COULD ONLY HAVE OCCURRED BETWEEN 7:30 A.M. AND 9:00 A.M. ...!
EVERY-ONE *BUT* YOU WAS IN THE GYM DURING THAT TIME FRAME.
SPRINKLER SYSTEM ACTIVATES: 7:30 A.M.
...

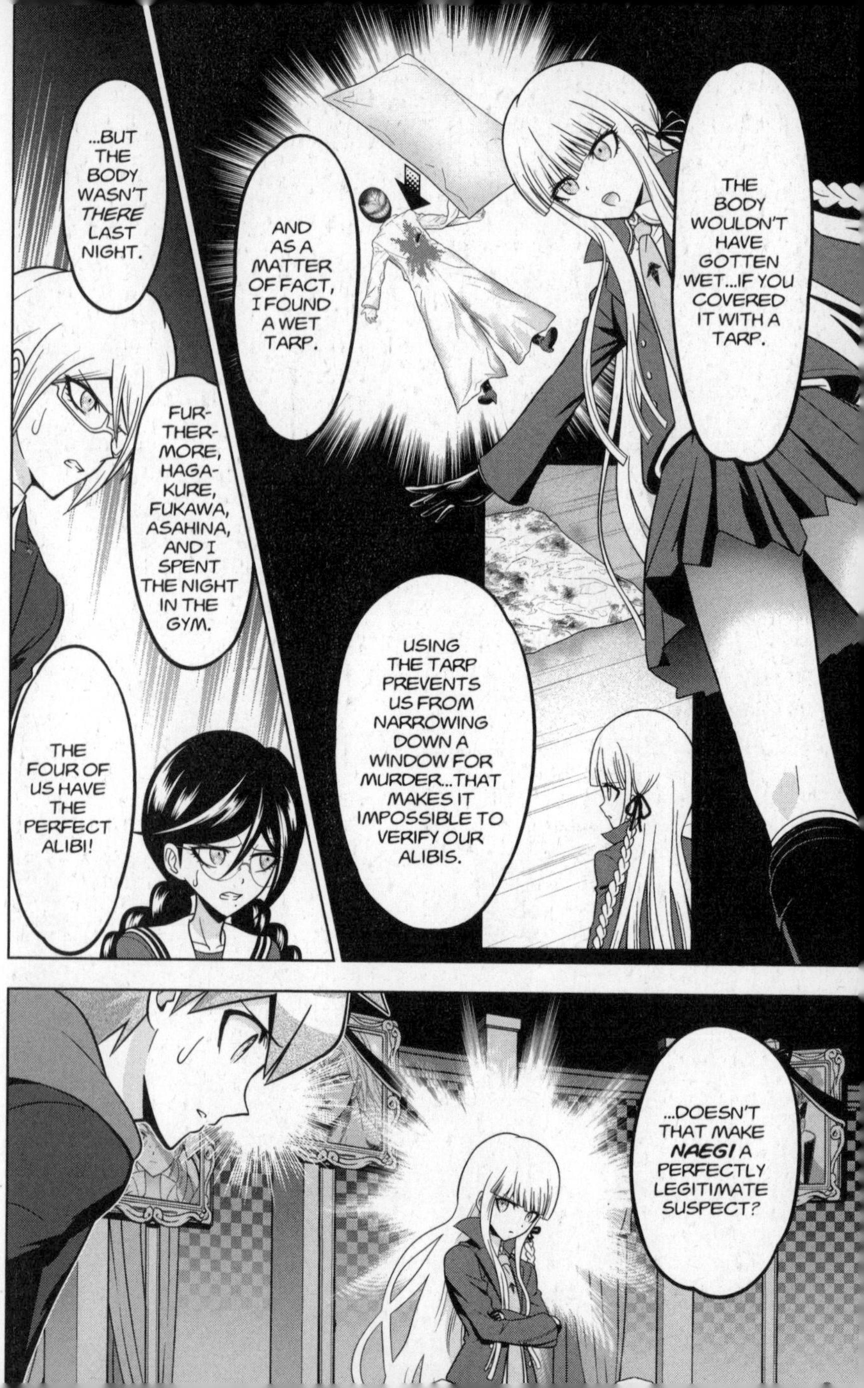
THE BODY WOULDN'T HAVE GOTTEN WET...IF YOU COVERED IT WITH A TARP.
AND AS A MATTER OF FACT, I FOUND A WET TARP.
USING THE TARP PREVENTS US FROM NARROWING DOWN A WINDOW FOR MURDER...THAT MAKES IT IMPOSSIBLE TO VERIFY OUR ALIBIS.
...BUT THE BODY WASN'T *THERE* LAST NIGHT.
FUR-THER-MORE, HAGA-KURE, FUKAWA, ASAHINA, AND I SPENT THE NIGHT IN THE GYM.
THE FOUR OF US HAVE THE PERFECT ALIBI!
...DOESN'T THAT MAKE ***NAEGI*** A PERFECTLY LEGITIMATE SUSPECT?

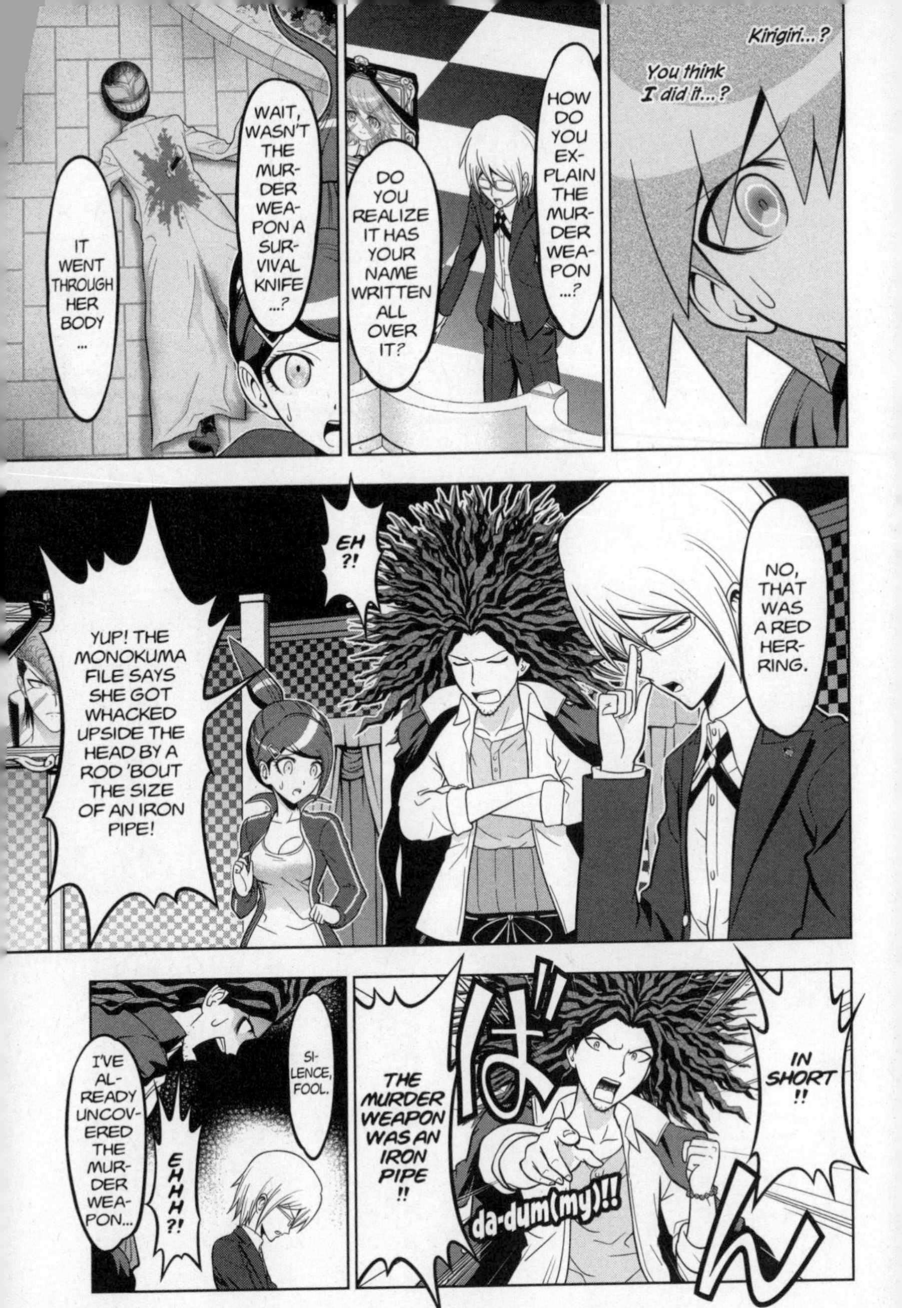
Kirigiri...?
You think I did it...?
HOW DO YOU EXPLAIN THE MURDER WEAPON...?
DO YOU REALIZE IT HAS YOUR NAME WRITTEN ALL OVER IT?
WAIT, WASN'T THE MURDER WEAPON A SURVIVAL KNIFE...?
IT WENT THROUGH HER BODY...
NO, THAT WAS A RED HERRING.
EH?!
YUP! THE MONOKUMA FILE SAYS SHE GOT WHACKED UPSIDE THE HEAD BY A ROD 'BOUT THE SIZE OF AN IRON PIPE!
IN SHORT!!
ばん
THE MURDER WEAPON WAS AN IRON PIPE!!
da-dum(my)!!
SILENCE, FOOL.
I'VE ALREADY UNCOVERED THE MURDER WEAPON...
EHHHH?!

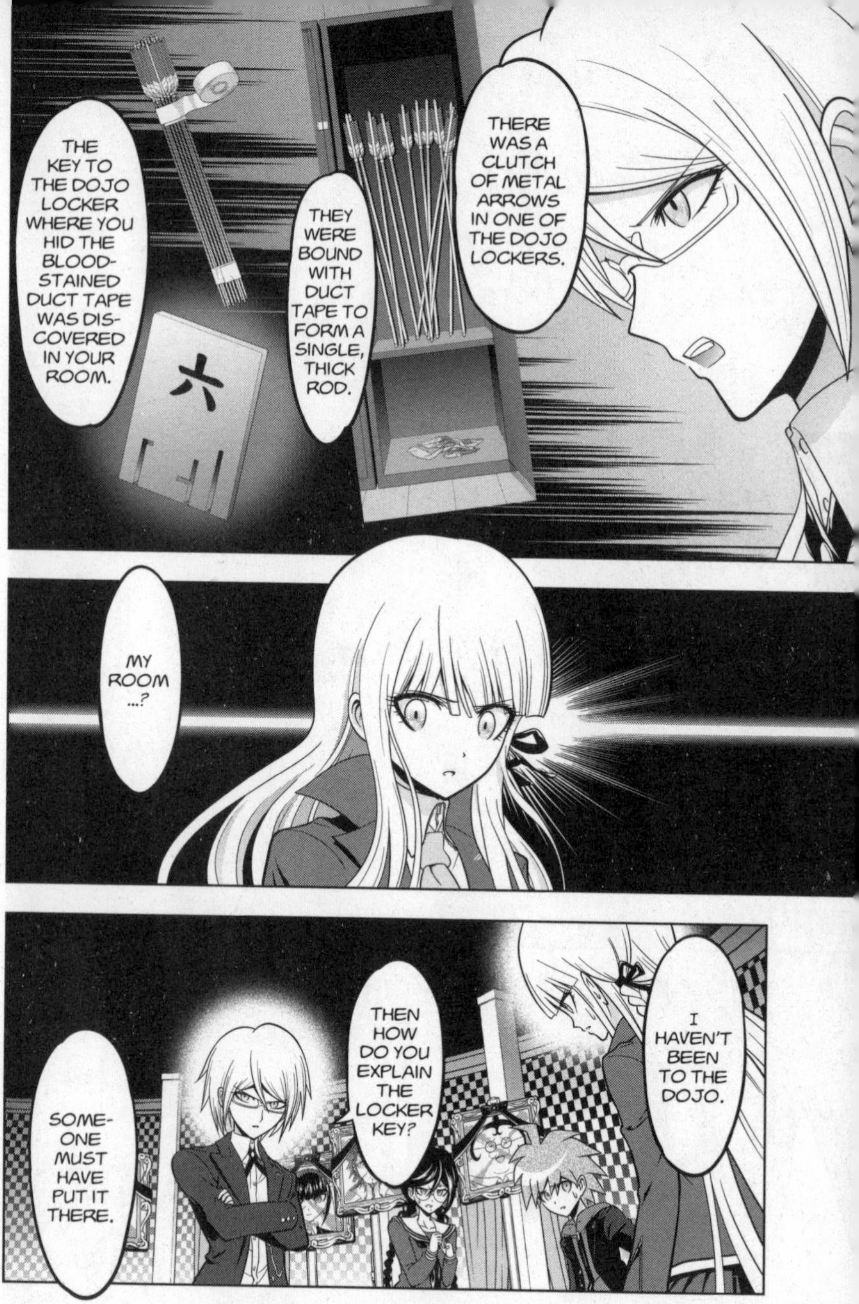
THERE WAS A CLUTCH OF METAL ARROWS IN ONE OF THE DOJO LOCKERS.
THEY WERE BOUND WITH DUCT TAPE TO FORM A SINGLE, THICK ROD.
THE KEY TO THE DOJO LOCKER WHERE YOU HID THE BLOOD-STAINED DUCT TAPE WAS DIS-COVERED IN YOUR ROOM.
MY ROOM ...?
I HAVEN'T BEEN TO THE DOJO.
THEN HOW DO YOU EXPLAIN THE LOCKER KEY?
SOME-ONE MUST HAVE PUT IT THERE.

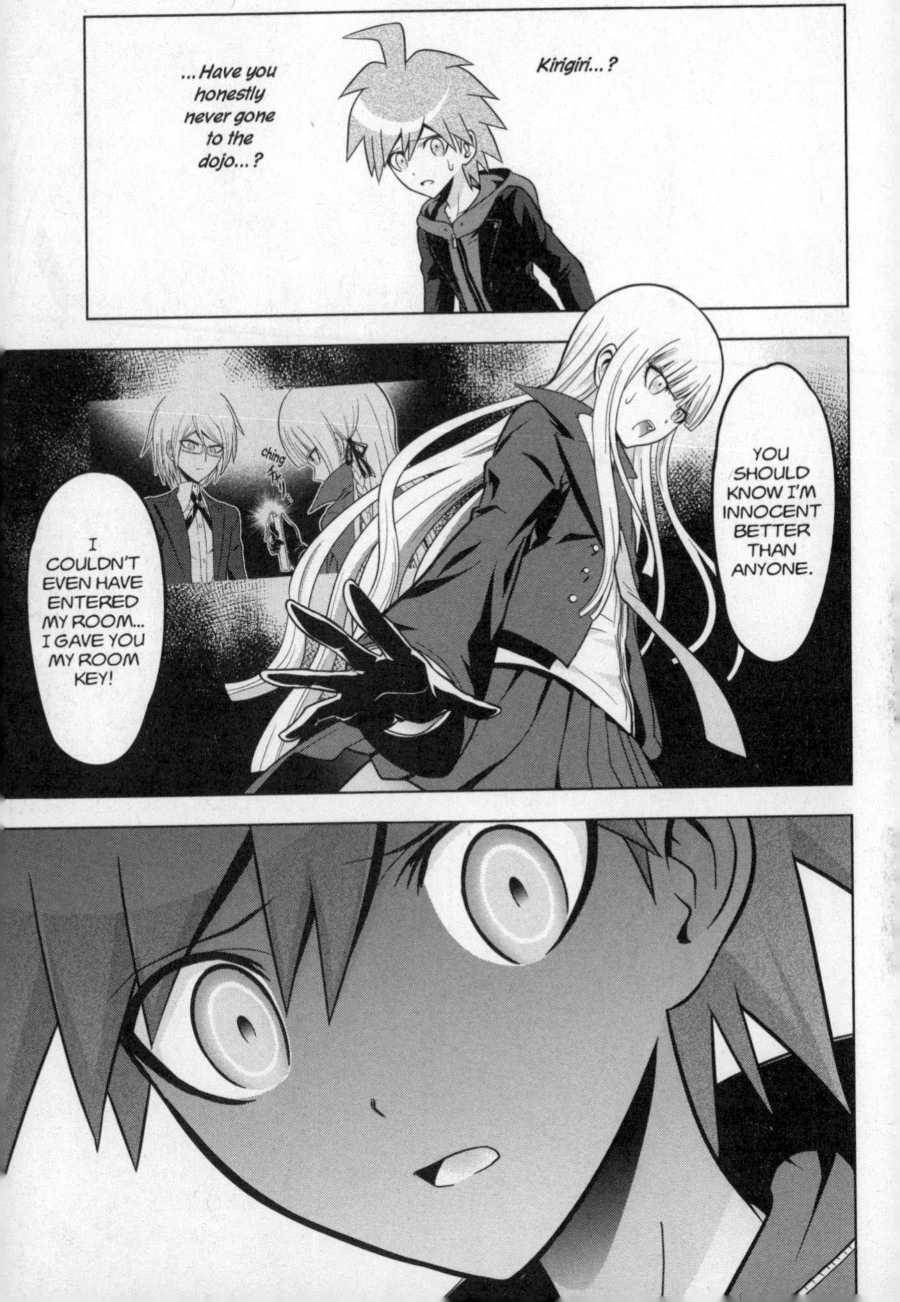
Kirigiri...?
...Have you honestly never gone to the dojo...?
YOU SHOULD KNOW I'M INNOCENT BETTER THAN ANYONE.
ching
I COULDN'T EVEN HAVE ENTERED MY ROOM... I GAVE YOU MY ROOM KEY!

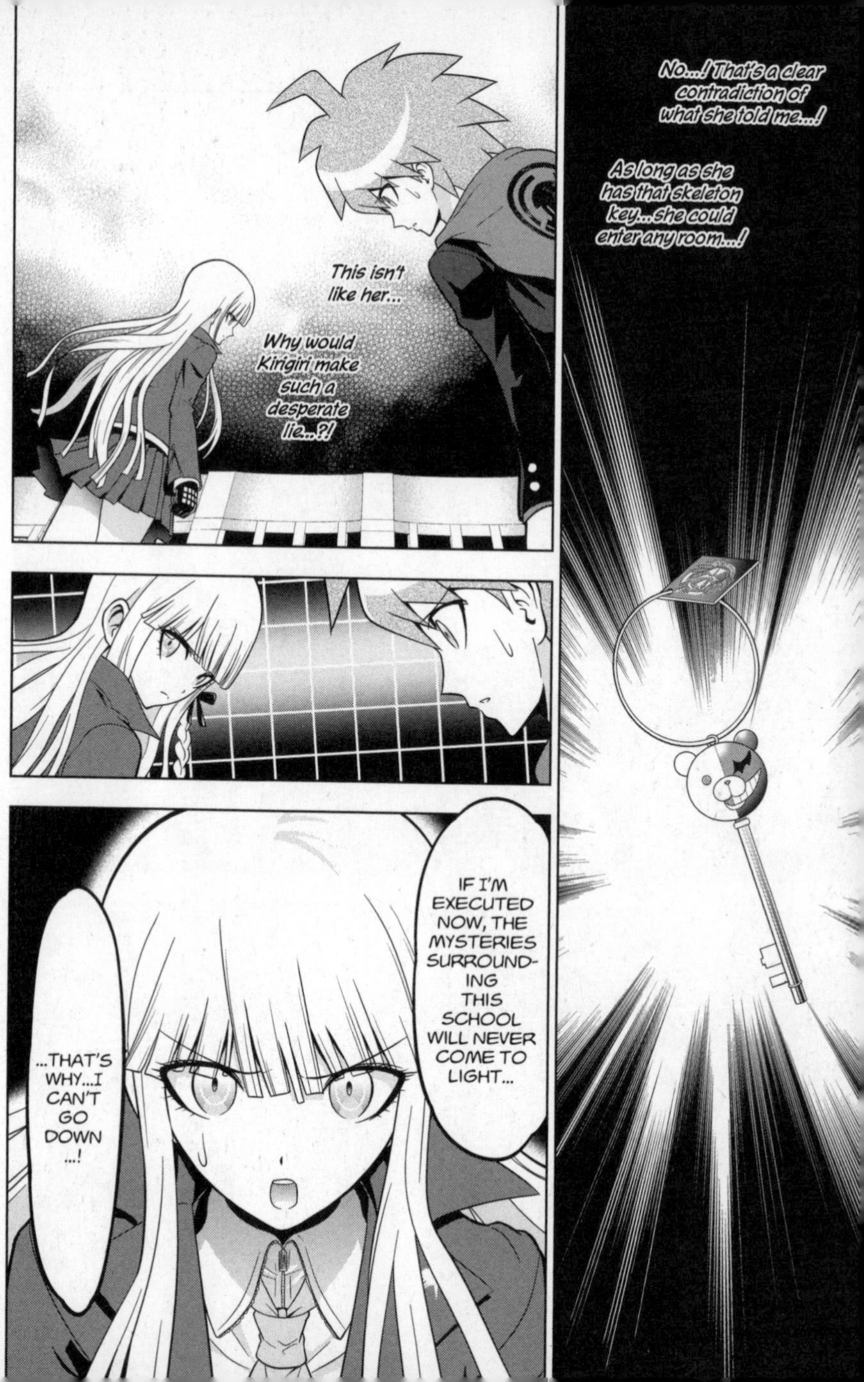
No...! That's a clear contradiction of what she told me...!
As long as she has that skeleton key...she could enter any room...!
This isn't like her...
Why would Kirigiri make such a desperate lie...?!
IF I'M EXECUTED NOW, THE MYSTERIES SURROUNDING THIS SCHOOL WILL NEVER COME TO LIGHT...
...THAT'S WHY...I CAN'T GO DOWN...!

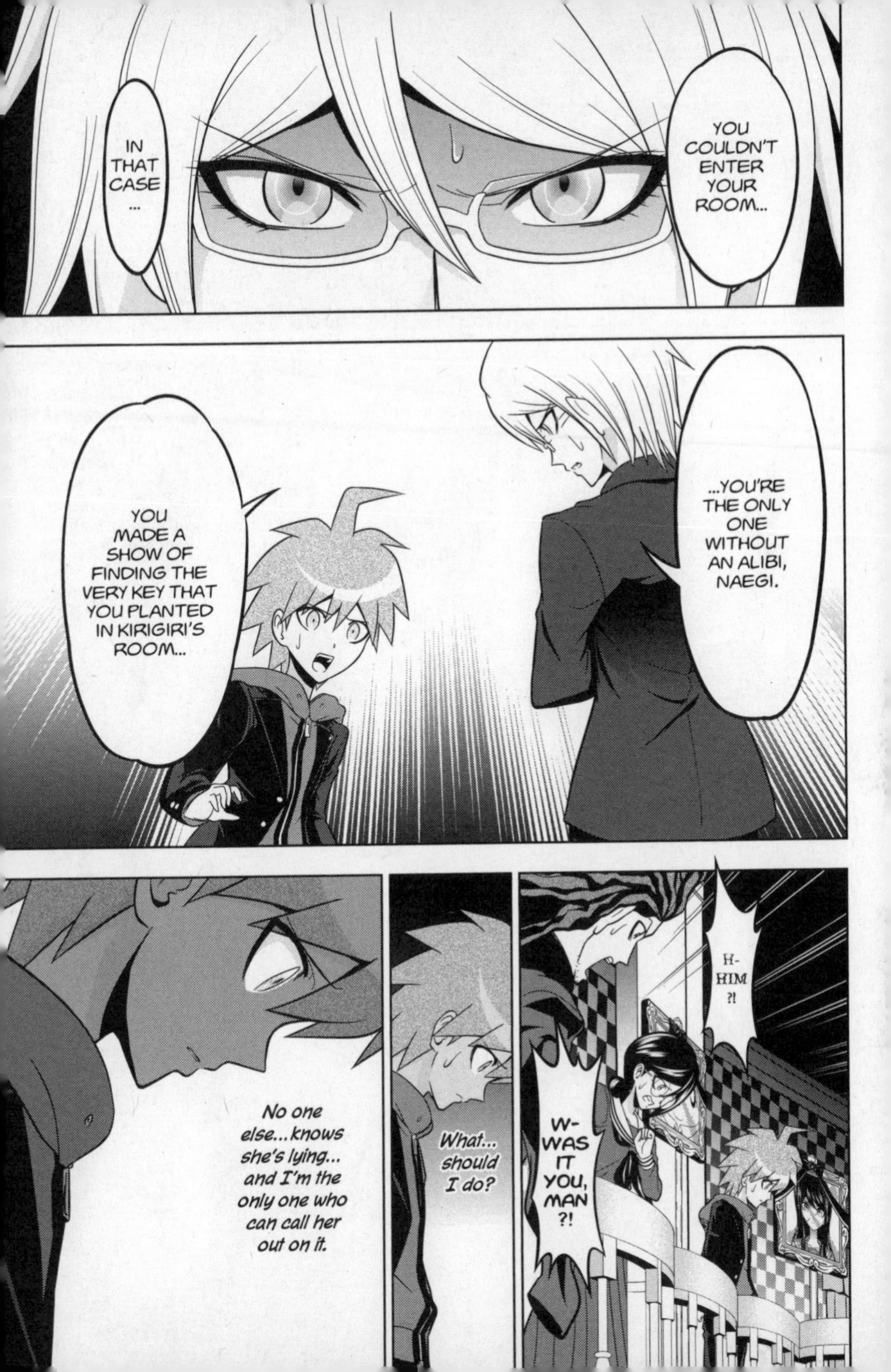
YOU COULDN'T ENTER YOUR ROOM...
IN THAT CASE ...
...YOU'RE THE ONLY ONE WITHOUT AN ALIBI, NAEGI.
YOU MADE A SHOW OF FINDING THE VERY KEY THAT YOU PLANTED IN KIRIGIRI'S ROOM...
H-HIM ?!
W-WAS IT YOU, MAN ?!
What... should I do?
No one else... knows she's lying... and I'm the only one who can call her out on it.

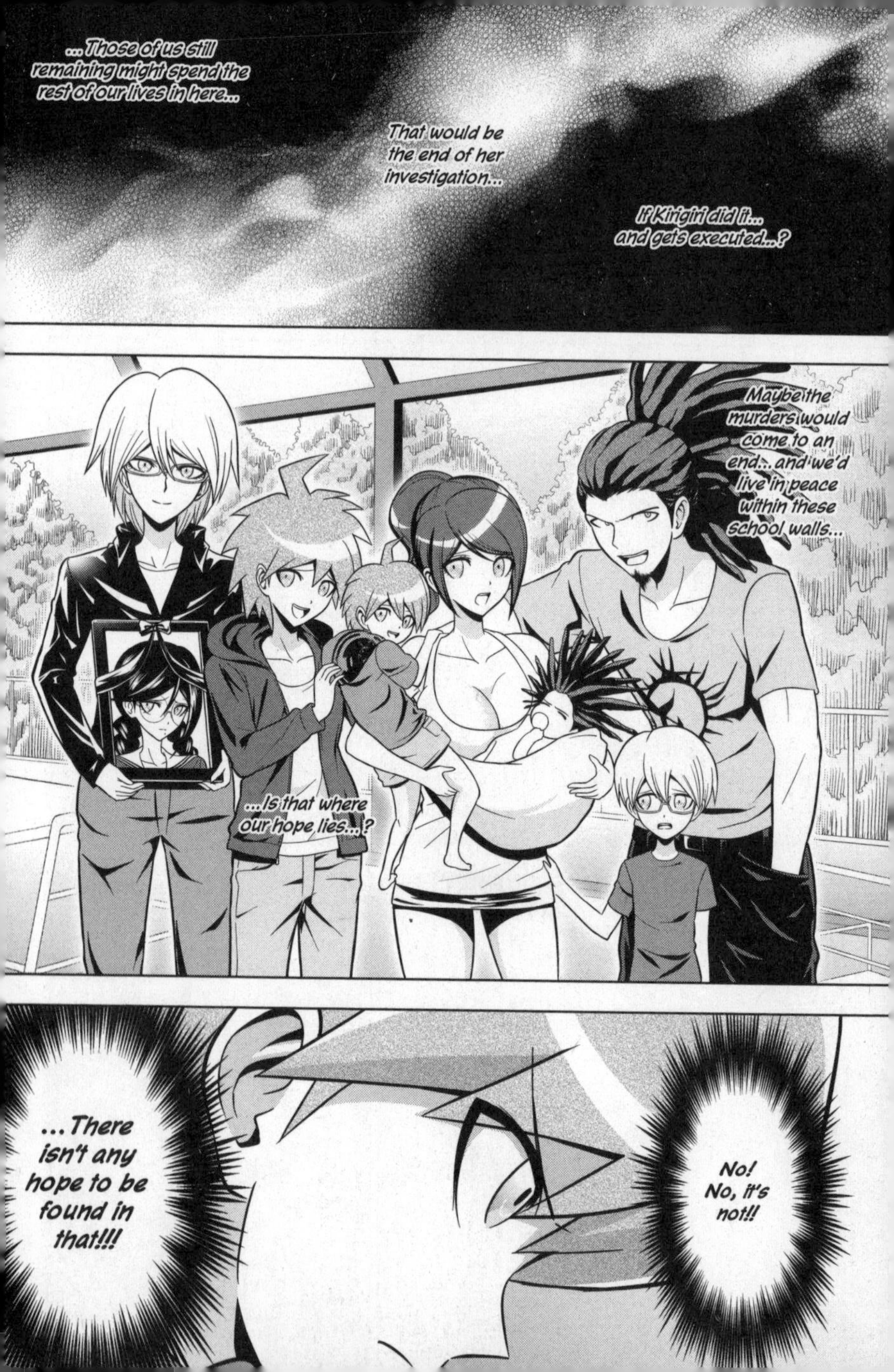
If Kirigiri did it... and gets executed...?
That would be the end of her investigation...
...Those of us still remaining might spend the rest of our lives in here...
Maybe the murders would come to an end... and we'd live in peace within these school walls...
...Is that where our hope lies...?
No! No, it's not!!
...There isn't any hope to be found in that!!!

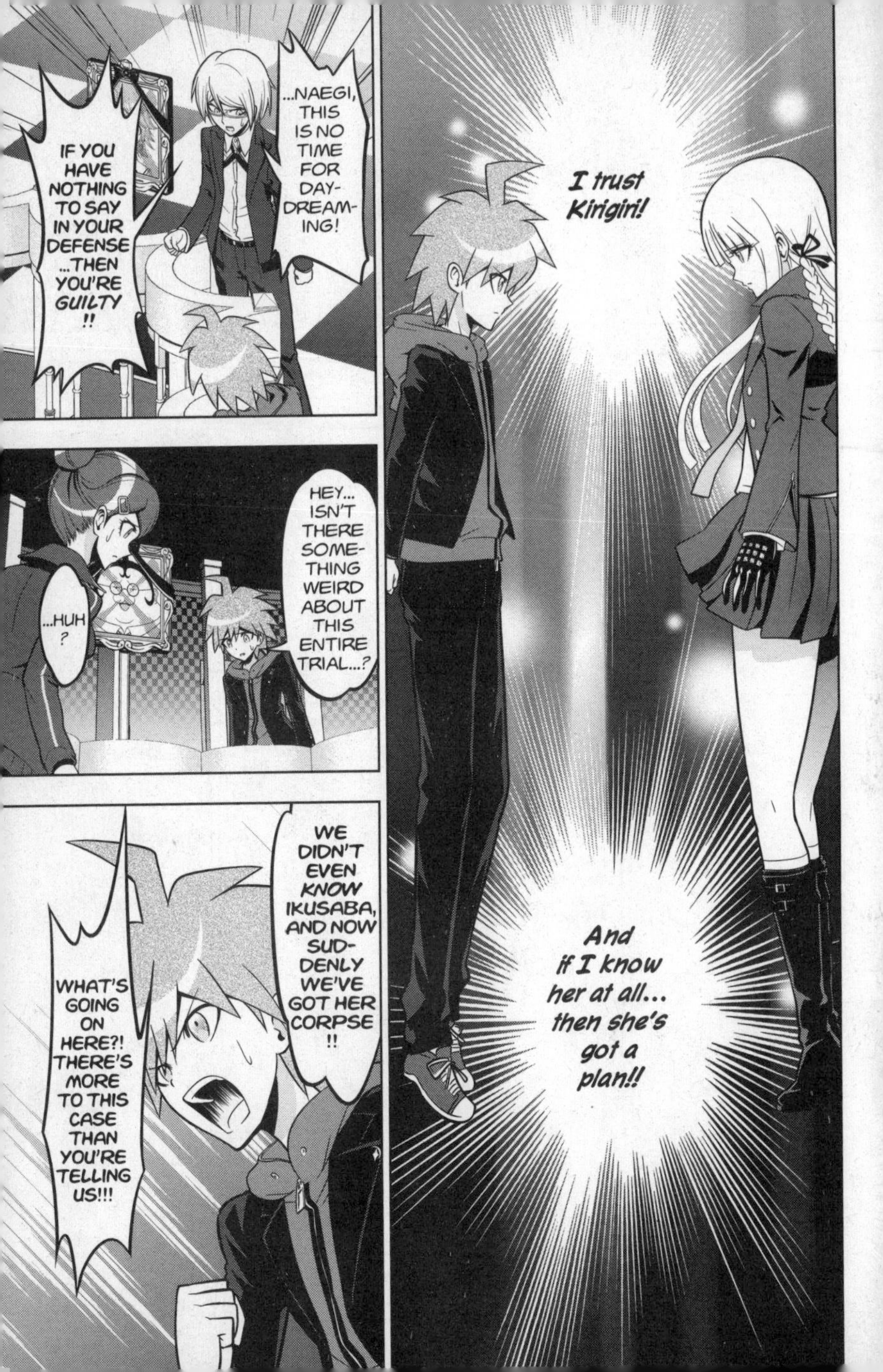

I trust Kirigiri!
And if I know her at all... then she's got a plan!!
...NAEGI, THIS IS NO TIME FOR DAY-DREAMING!
IF YOU HAVE NOTHING TO SAY IN YOUR DEFENSE ...THEN YOU'RE GUILTY !!
HEY... ISN'T THERE SOMETHING WEIRD ABOUT THIS ENTIRE TRIAL...?
...HUH?
WE DIDN'T EVEN KNOW IKUSABA, AND NOW SUDDENLY WE'VE GOT HER CORPSE!!
WHAT'S GOING ON HERE?! THERE'S MORE TO THIS CASE THAN YOU'RE TELLING US!!!

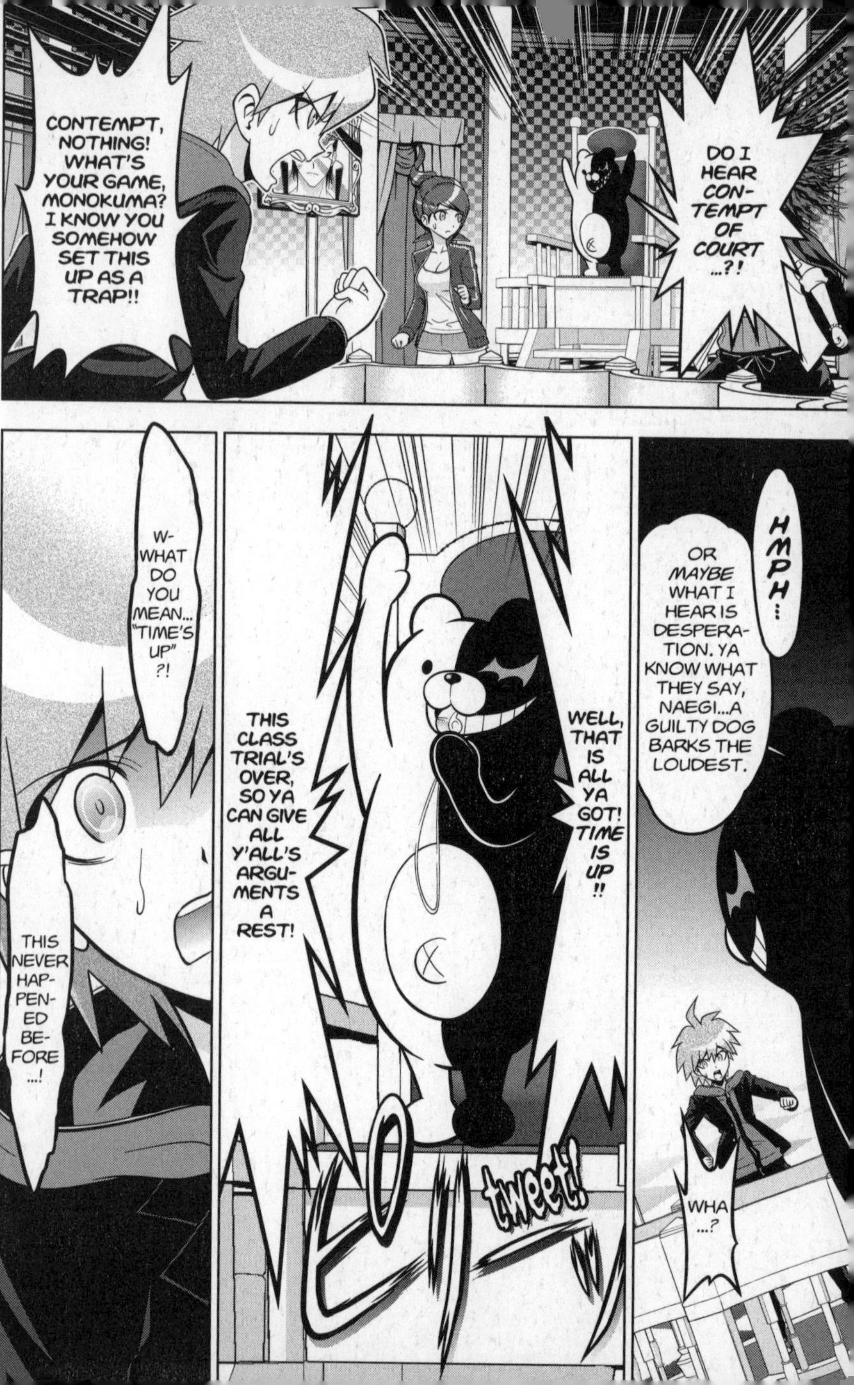
DO I HEAR CONTEMPT OF COURT ...?!
CONTEMPT, NOTHING! WHAT'S YOUR GAME, MONOKUMA? I KNOW YOU SOMEHOW SET THIS UP AS A TRAP!!
HMPH...
OR MAYBE WHAT I HEAR IS DESPERATION. YA KNOW WHAT THEY SAY, NAEGI...A GUILTY DOG BARKS THE LOUDEST.
WHA ...?
WELL, THAT IS ALL YA GOT! TIME IS UP!!
THIS CLASS TRIAL'S OVER, SO YA CAN GIVE ALL Y'ALL'S ARGUMENTS A REST!
tweet!
W-WHAT DO YOU MEAN... "TIME'S UP"?!
THIS NEVER HAPPENED BEFORE ...!

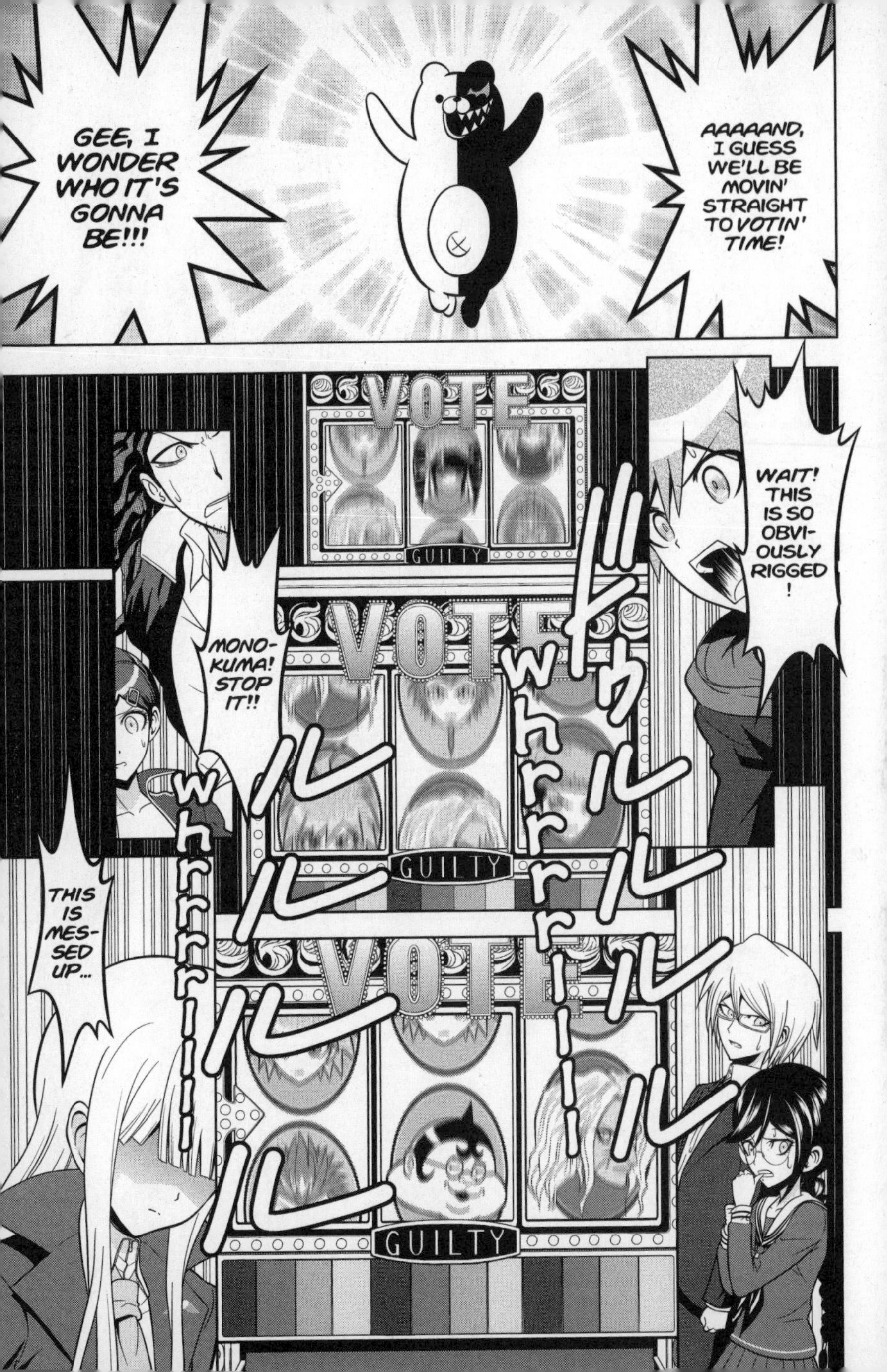
AAAAAND, I GUESS WE'LL BE MOVIN' STRAIGHT TO VOTIN' TIME!
GEE, I WONDER WHO IT'S GONNA BE!!!
VOTE
GUILTY
WAIT! THIS IS SO OBVIOUSLY RIGGED!
MONO-KUMA! STOP IT!!
whrrrrl
whrrrrl
THIS IS MESSED UP...

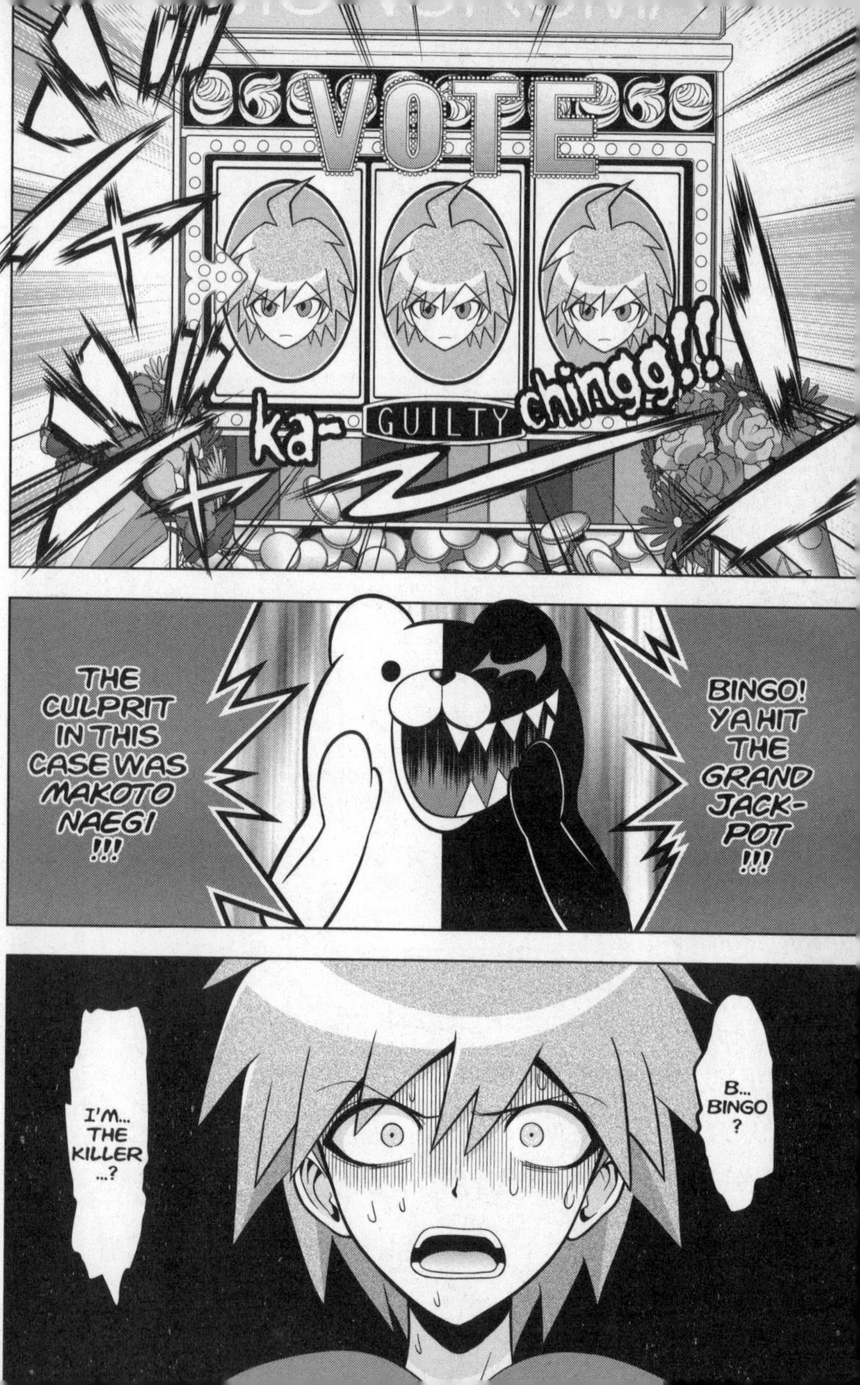
VOTE
GUILTY
ka-chingg!!
BINGO! YA HIT THE GRAND JACK-POT!!!
THE CULPRIT IN THIS CASE WAS MAKOTO NAEGI!!!
B... BINGO?
I'M... THE KILLER...?

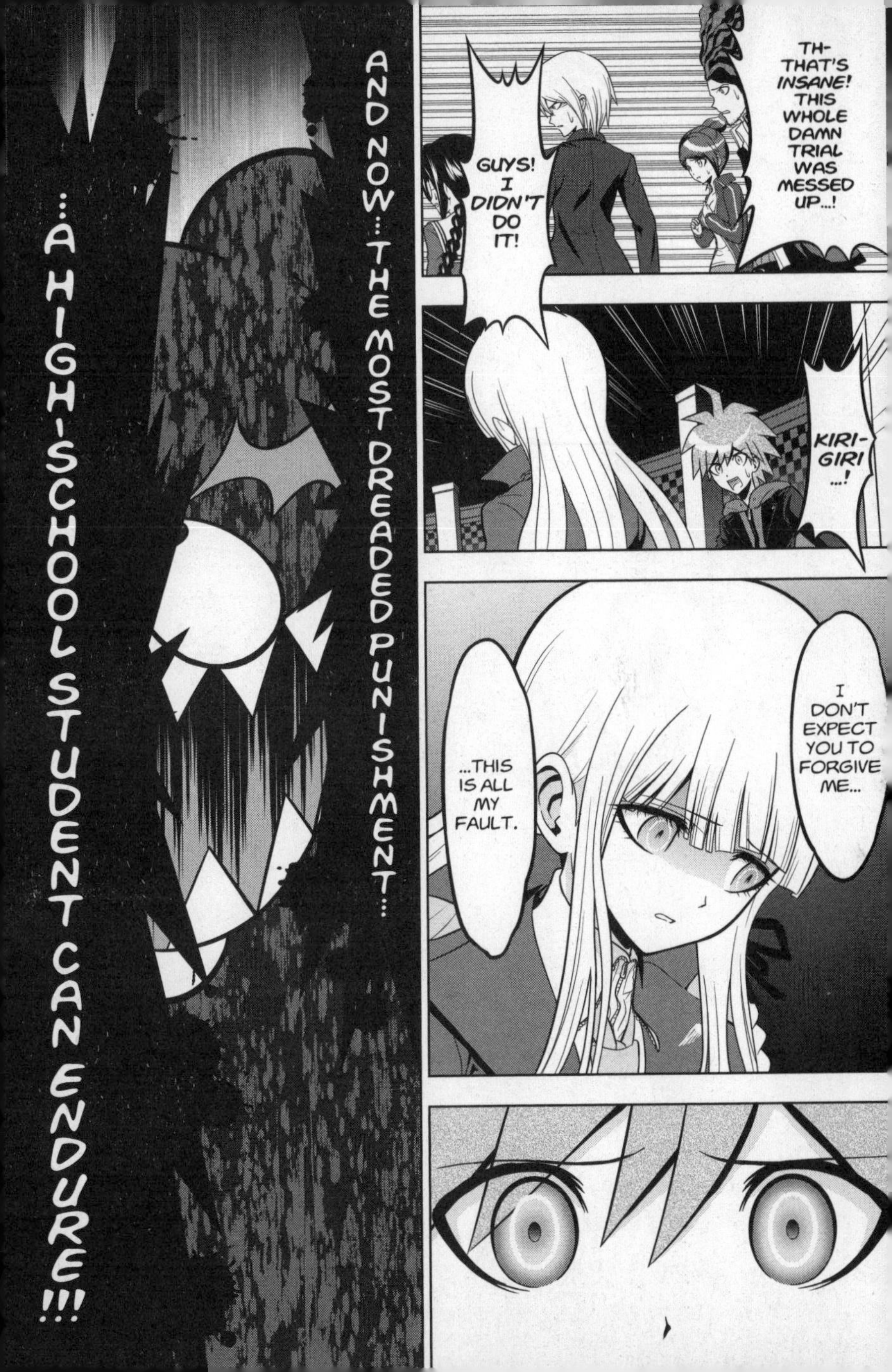
TH-THAT'S INSANE! THIS WHOLE DAMN TRIAL WAS MESSED UP...!
GUYS! I DIDN'T DO IT!
KIRI-GIRI ...!
I DON'T EXPECT YOU TO FORGIVE ME...
...THIS IS ALL MY FAULT.
AND NOW... THE MOST DREADED PUNISHMENT...
...A HIGH-SCHOOL STUDENT CAN ENDURE!!!

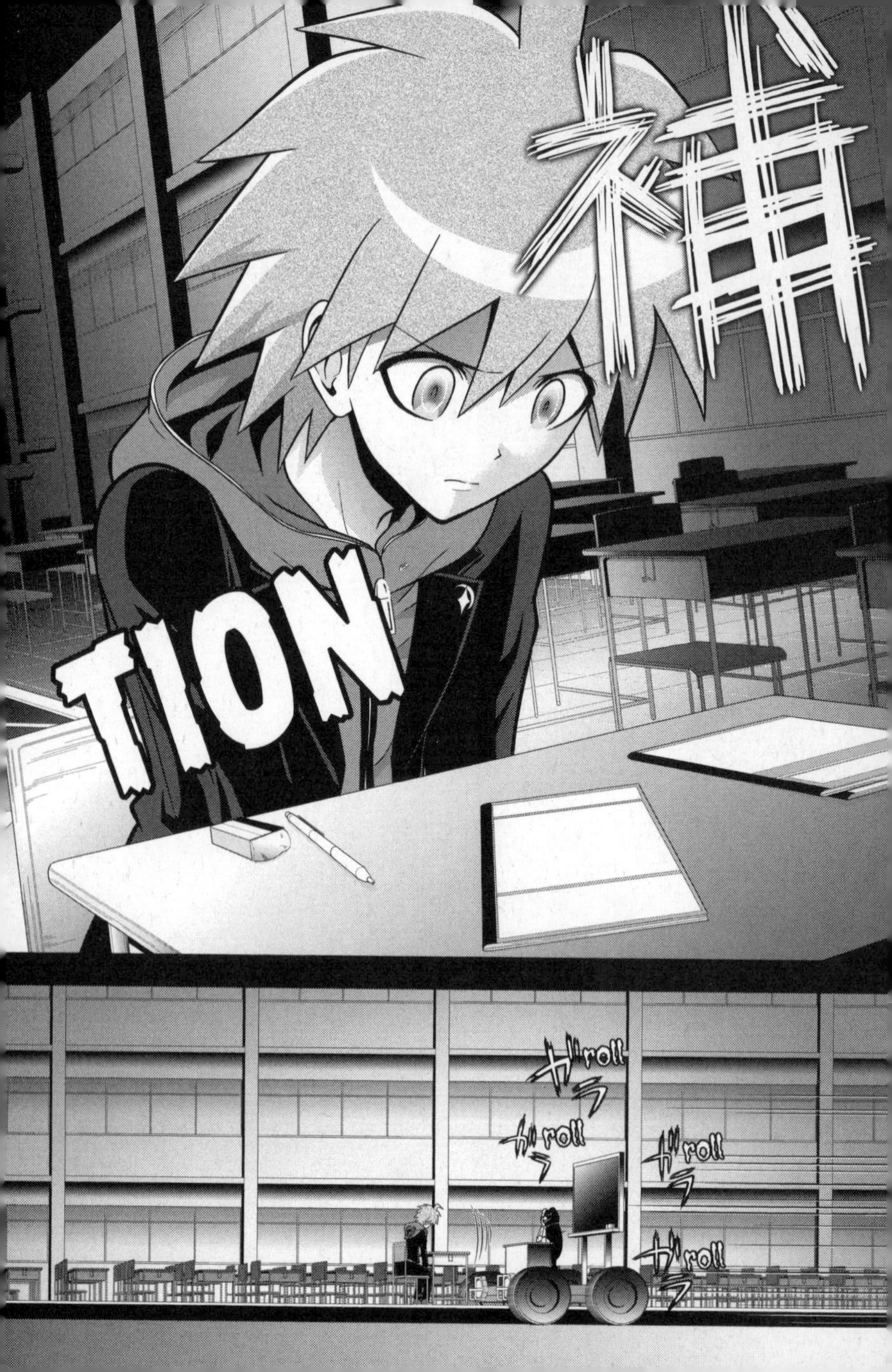
TION
ガラ roll
ガラ roll
ガラ roll
ガラ roll

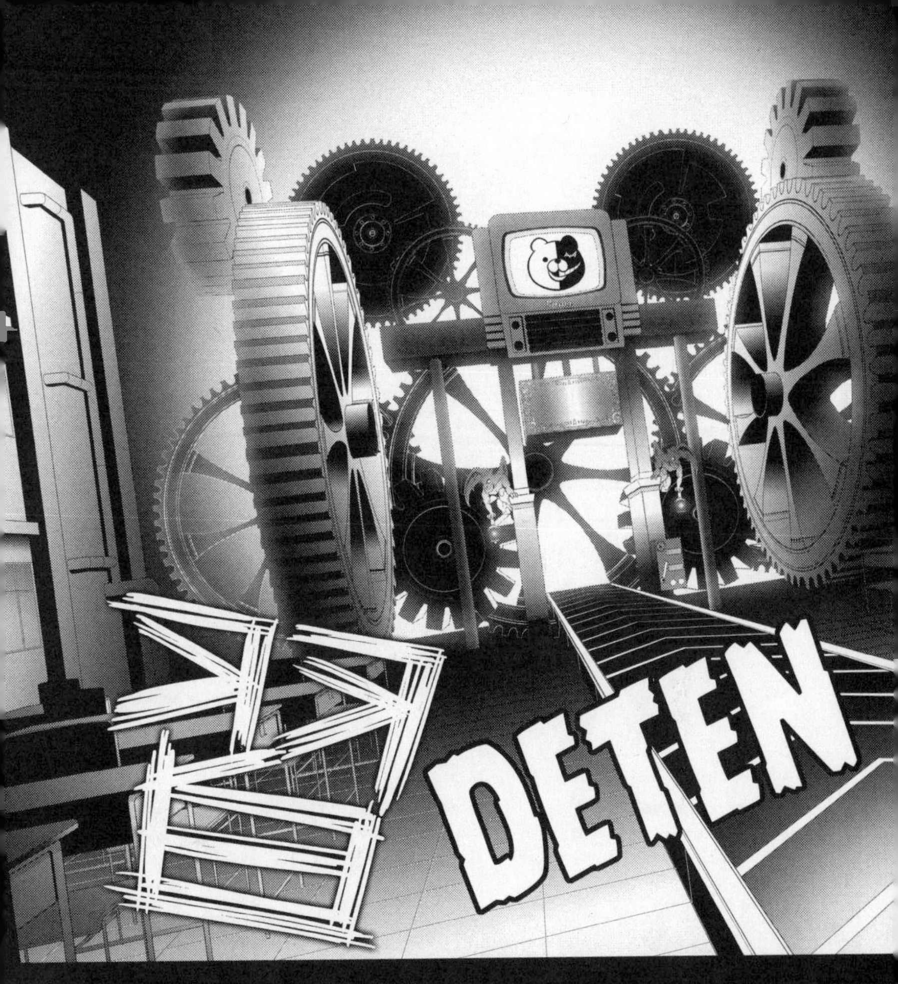
DETEN
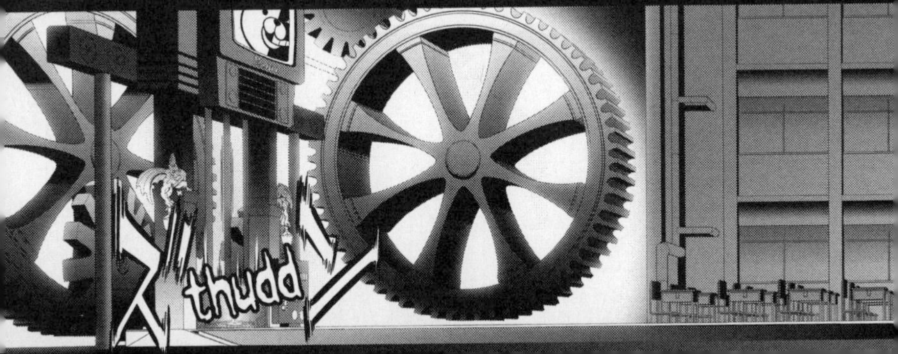
thudd

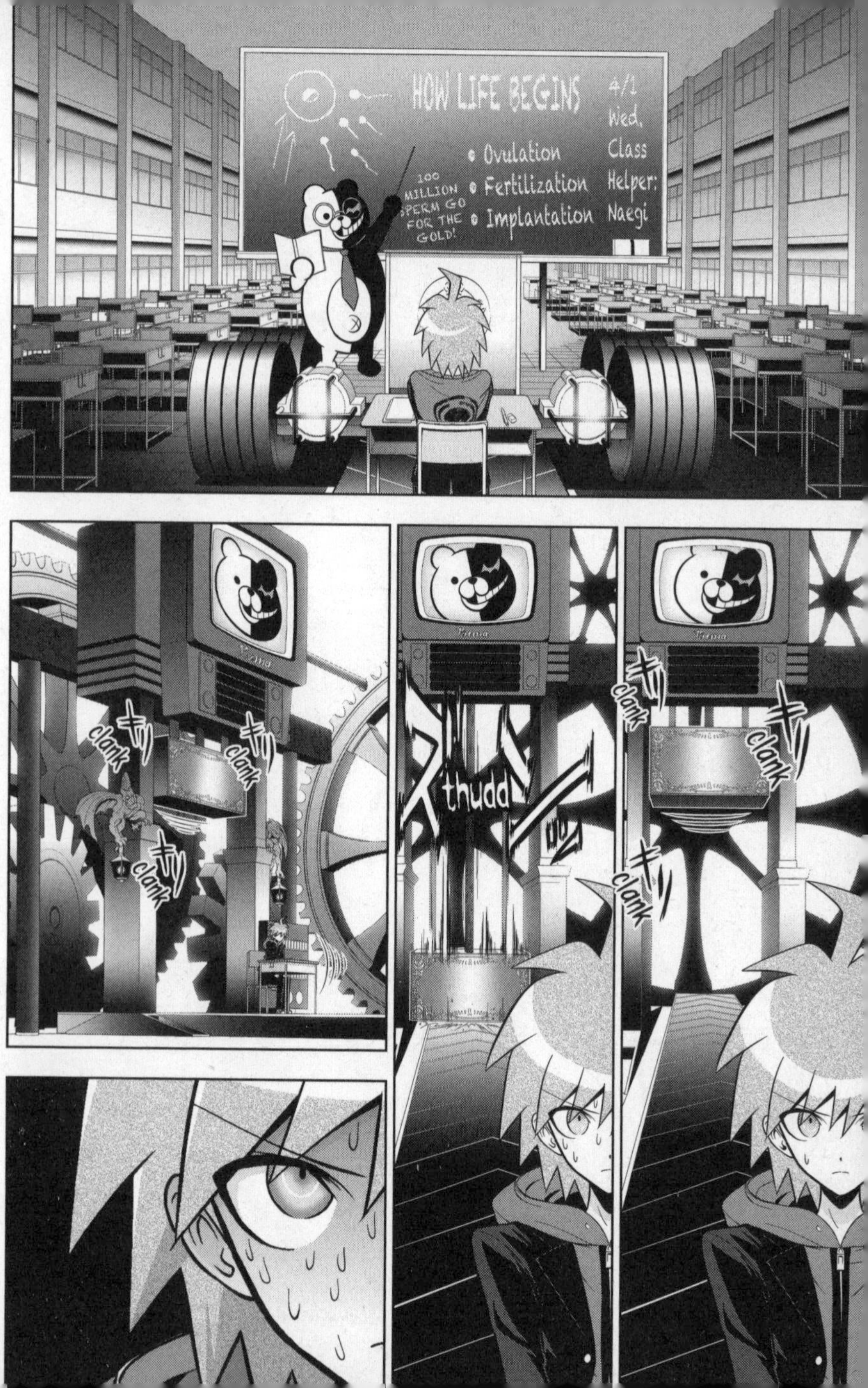
HOW LIFE BEGINS
4/1 Wed, Class Helper: Naegi
100 MILLION SPERM GO FOR THE GOLD!
Ovulation
Fertilization
Implantation
clank
clank
thudd
clank
clank
clank

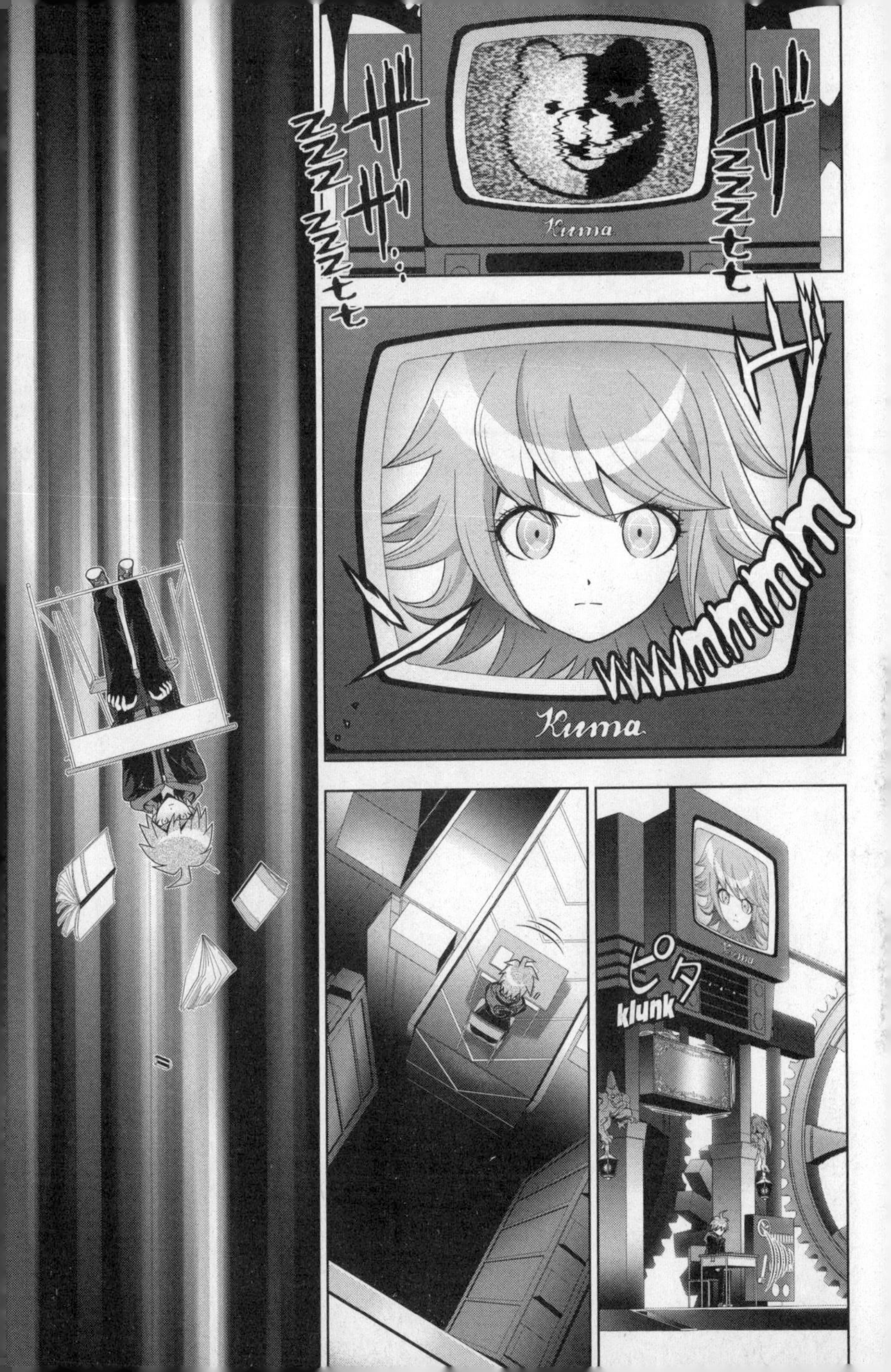
ザ
ZZZZtt
ザザ…
ZZZZZZZZtt
Kuma
WWMMMMMM
Kuma
ピタ
klunk

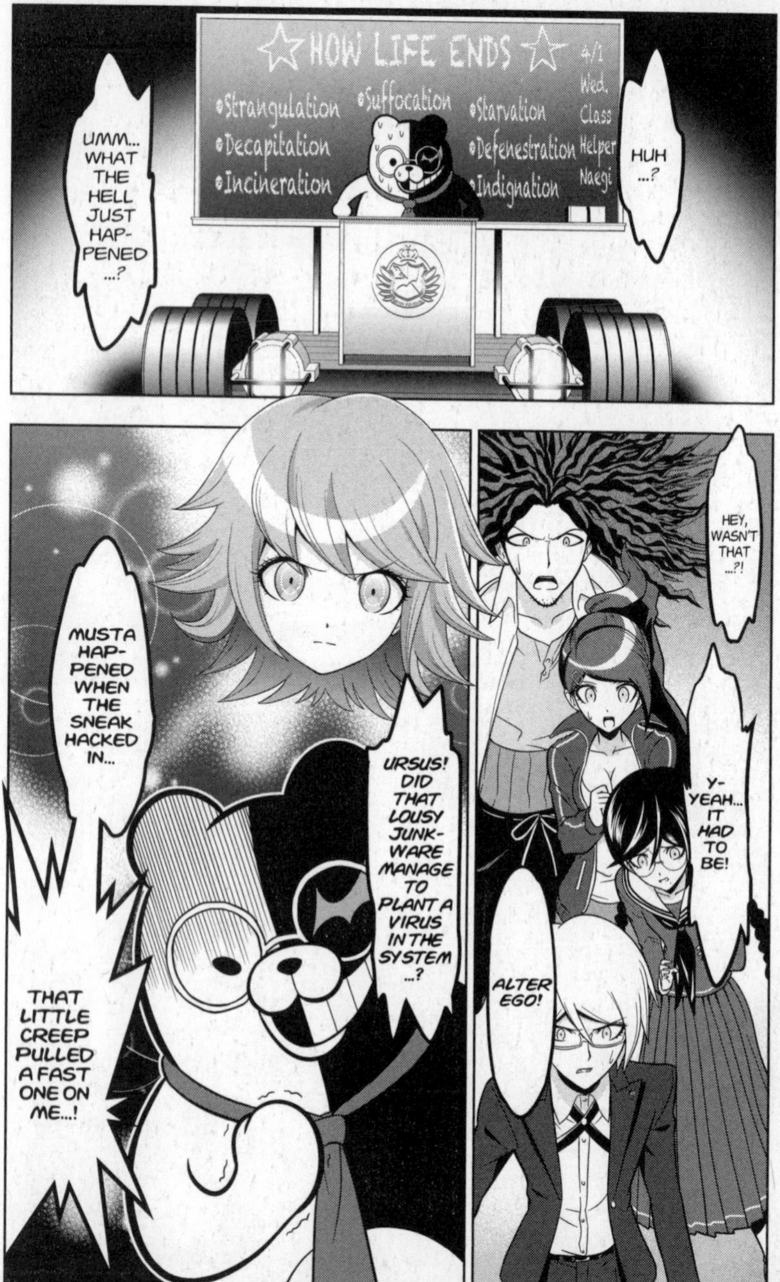
☆HOW LIFE ENDS☆
4/1 Wed. Class Helper Naegi
•Strangulation •Suffocation •Starvation
•Decapitation •Defenestration
•Incineration •Indignation
HUH ...?
UMM... WHAT THE HELL JUST HAPPENED ...?
HEY, WASN'T THAT ...?!
Y-YEAH... IT HAD TO BE!
ALTER EGO!
URSUS! DID THAT LOUSY JUNKWARE MANAGE TO PLANT A VIRUS IN THE SYSTEM ...?
MUSTA HAPPENED WHEN THE SNEAK HACKED IN...
THAT LITTLE CREEP PULLED A FAST ONE ON ME...!

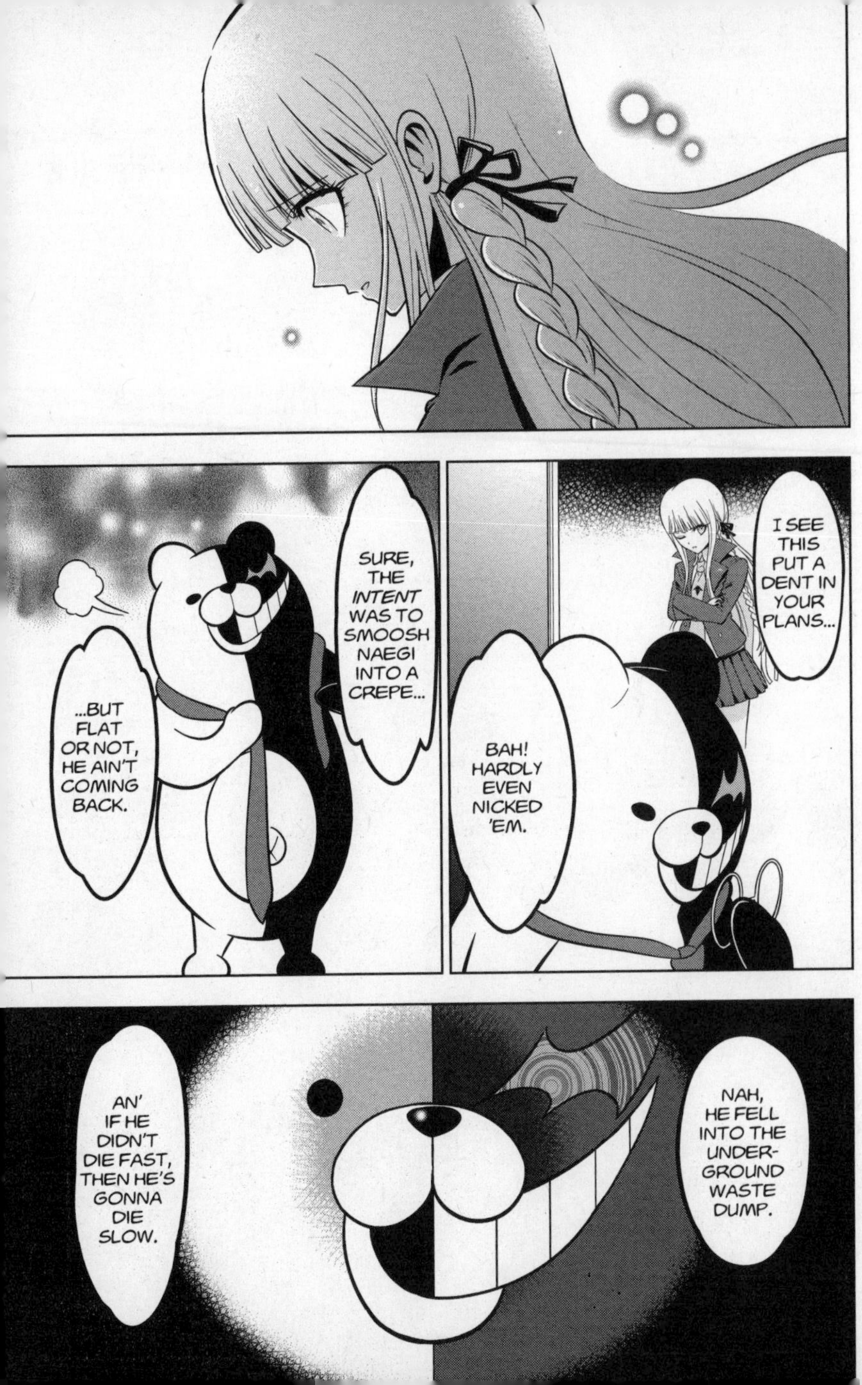
I SEE THIS PUT A DENT IN YOUR PLANS...
BAH! HARDLY EVEN NICKED 'EM.
SURE, THE *INTENT* WAS TO SMOOSH NAEGI INTO A CREPE...
...BUT FLAT OR NOT, HE AIN'T COMING BACK.
NAH, HE FELL INTO THE UNDER-GROUND WASTE DUMP.
AN' IF HE DIDN'T DIE FAST, THEN HE'S GONNA DIE SLOW.

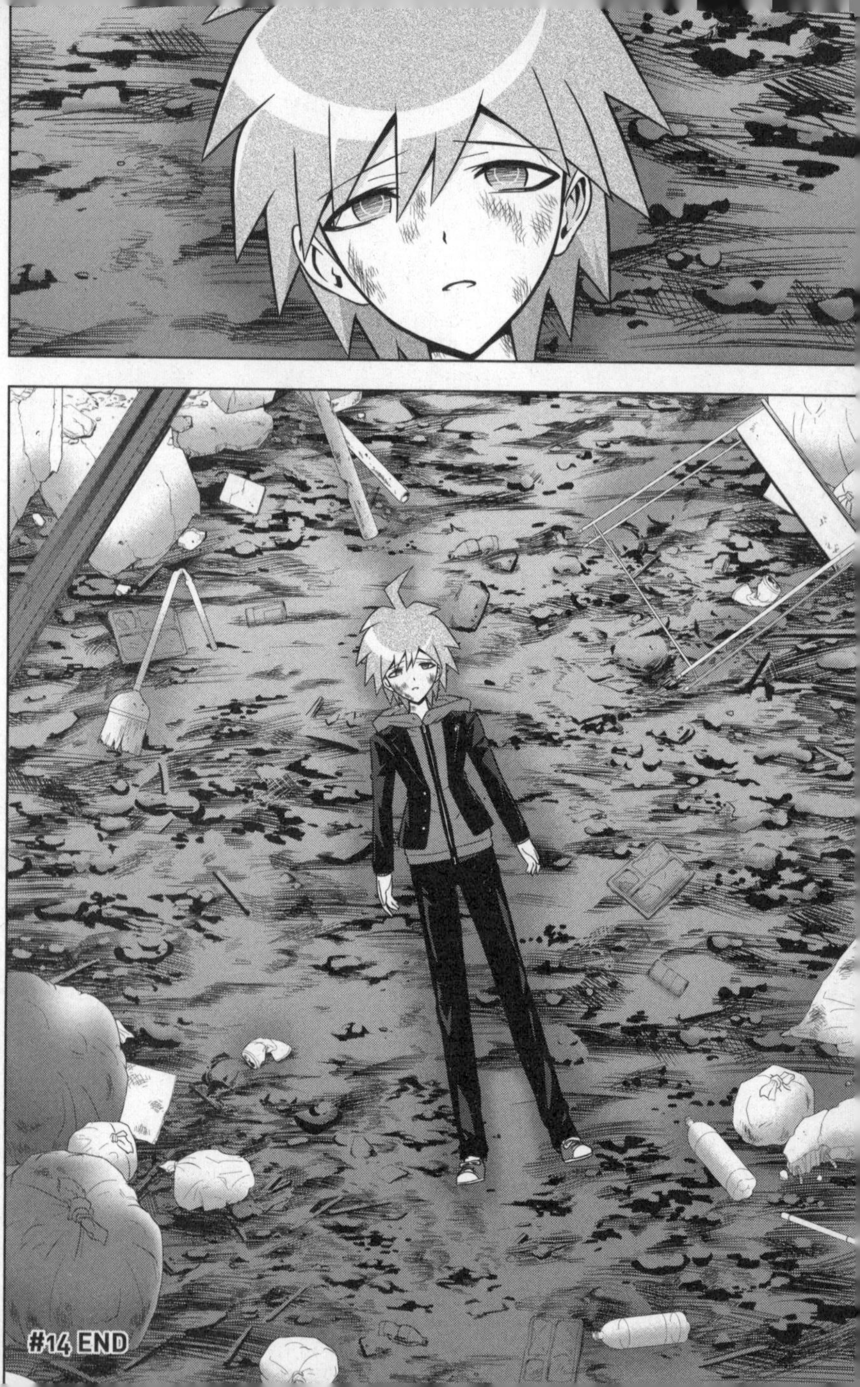
#14 END

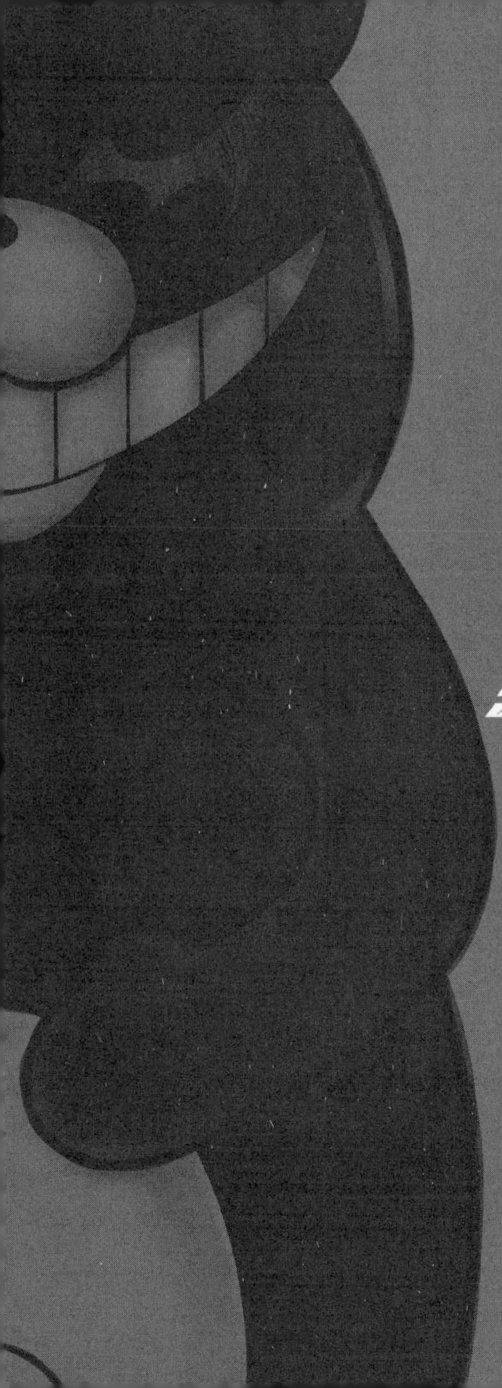

DANGANRONPA
A SCHOOL OF HOPE . . . WITH STUDENTS OF DESPAIR!
THE ANIMATION

DANGANRONPA

A SCHOOL OF HOPE . . . WITH STUDENTS OF DESPAIR!

THE ANIMATION

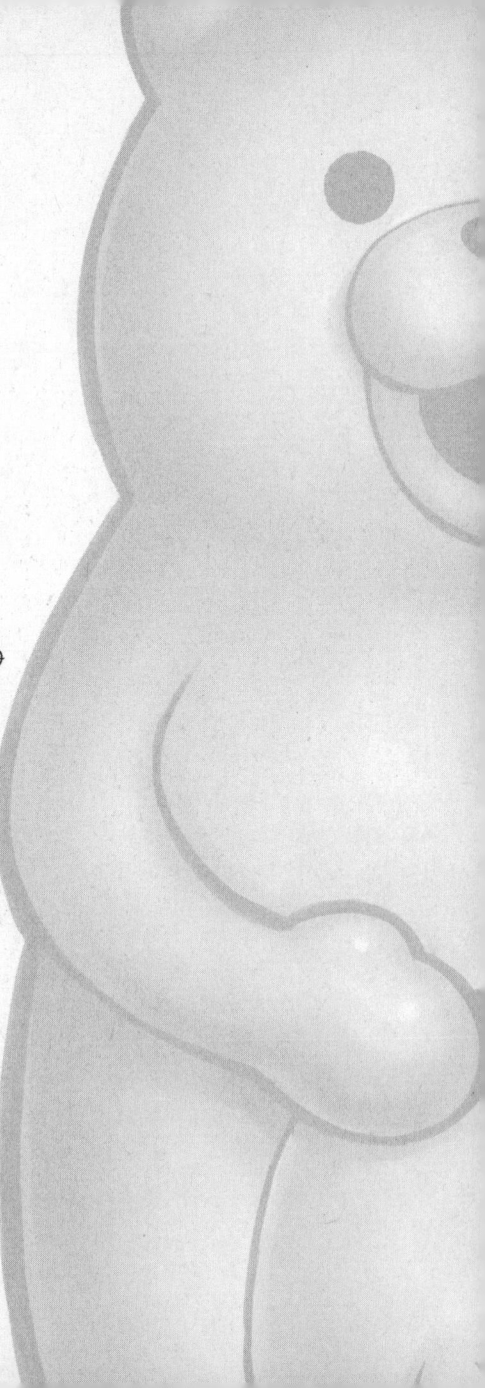

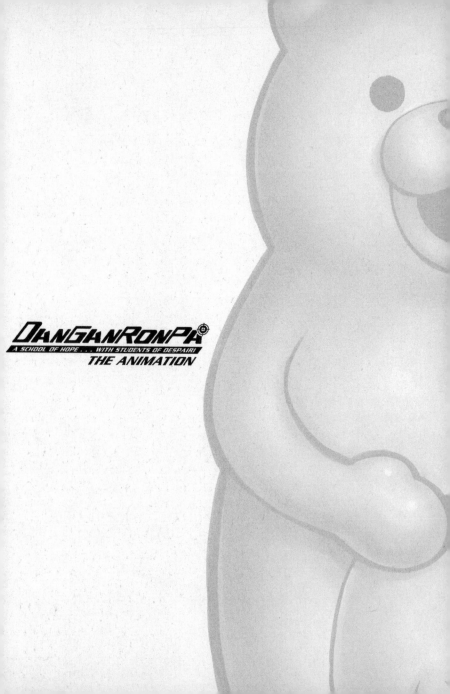

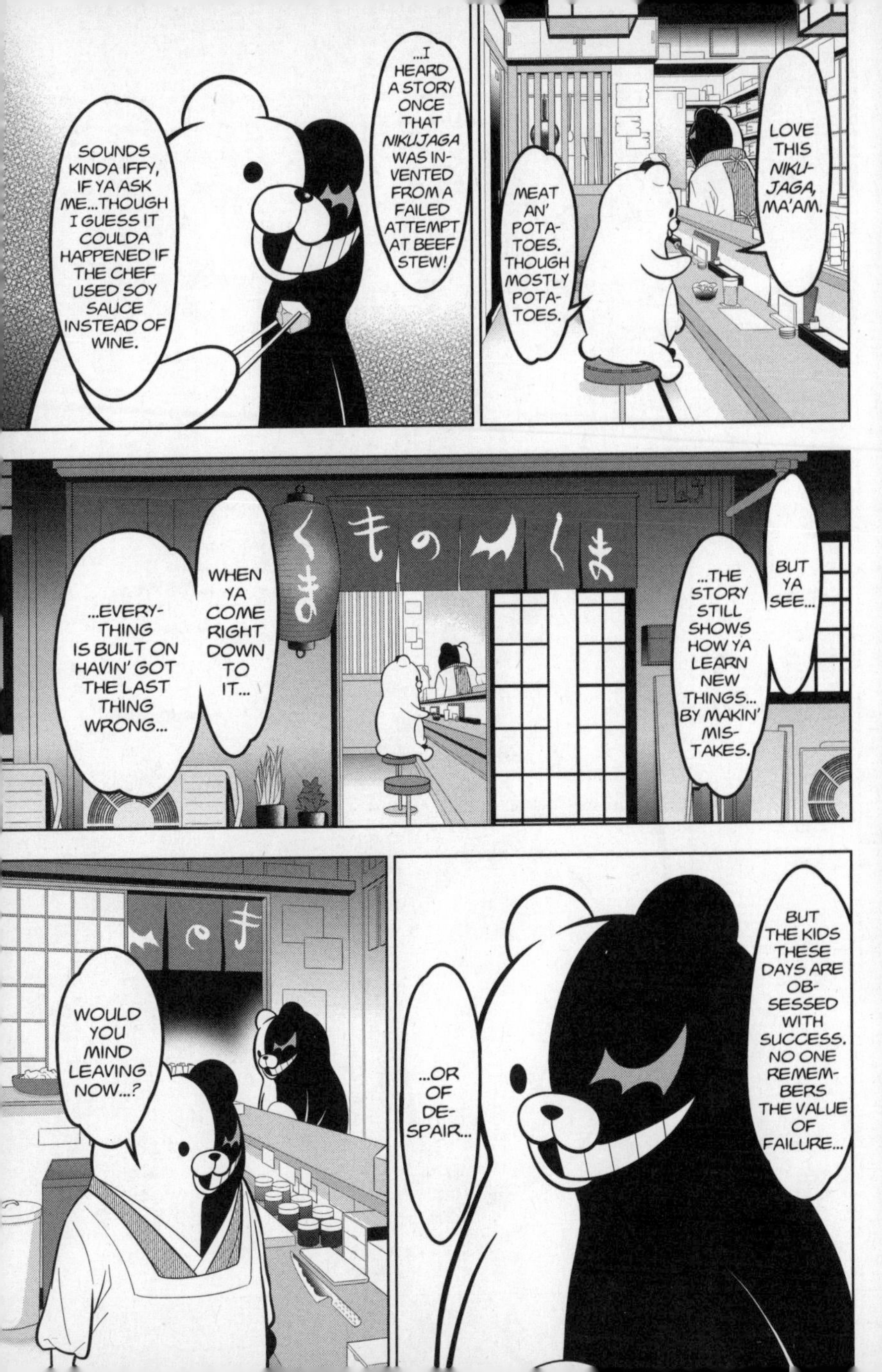
LOVE THIS NIKUJAGA, MA'AM.
MEAT AN' POTATOES. THOUGH MOSTLY POTATOES.
...I HEARD A STORY ONCE THAT NIKUJAGA WAS INVENTED FROM A FAILED ATTEMPT AT BEEF STEW!
SOUNDS KINDA IFFY, IF YA ASK ME...THOUGH I GUESS IT COULDA HAPPENED IF THE CHEF USED SOY SAUCE INSTEAD OF WINE.
BUT YA SEE...
...THE STORY STILL SHOWS HOW YA LEARN NEW THINGS... BY MAKIN' MISTAKES.
WHEN YA COME RIGHT DOWN TO IT...
...EVERYTHING IS BUILT ON HAVIN' GOT THE LAST THING WRONG...
BUT THE KIDS THESE DAYS ARE OBSESSED WITH SUCCESS. NO ONE REMEMBERS THE VALUE OF FAILURE...
...OR OF DESPAIR...
WOULD YOU MIND LEAVING NOW...?

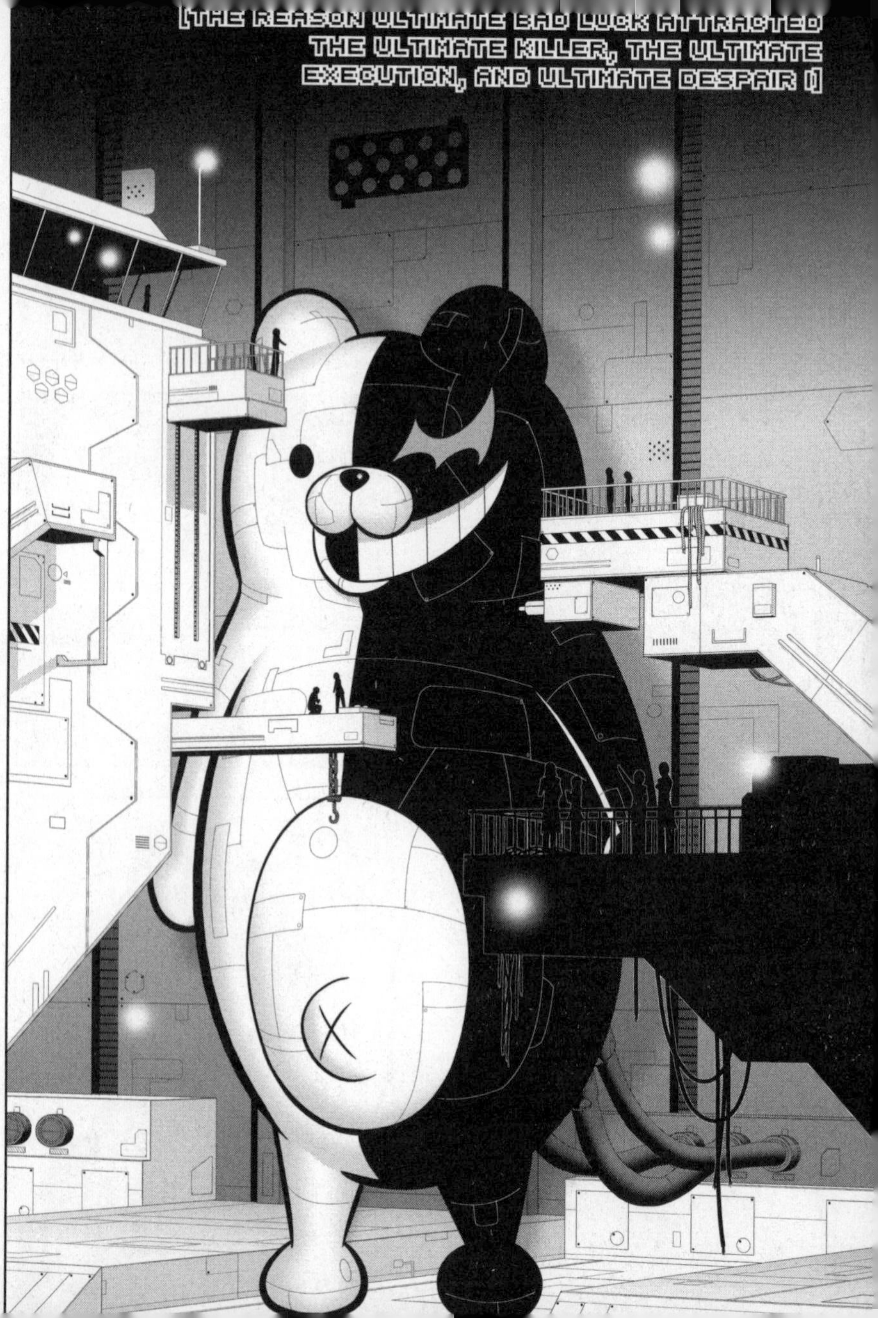
[THE REASON ULTIMATE BAD LUCK ATTRACTED THE ULTIMATE KILLER, THE ULTIMATE EXECUTION, AND ULTIMATE DESPAIR!]

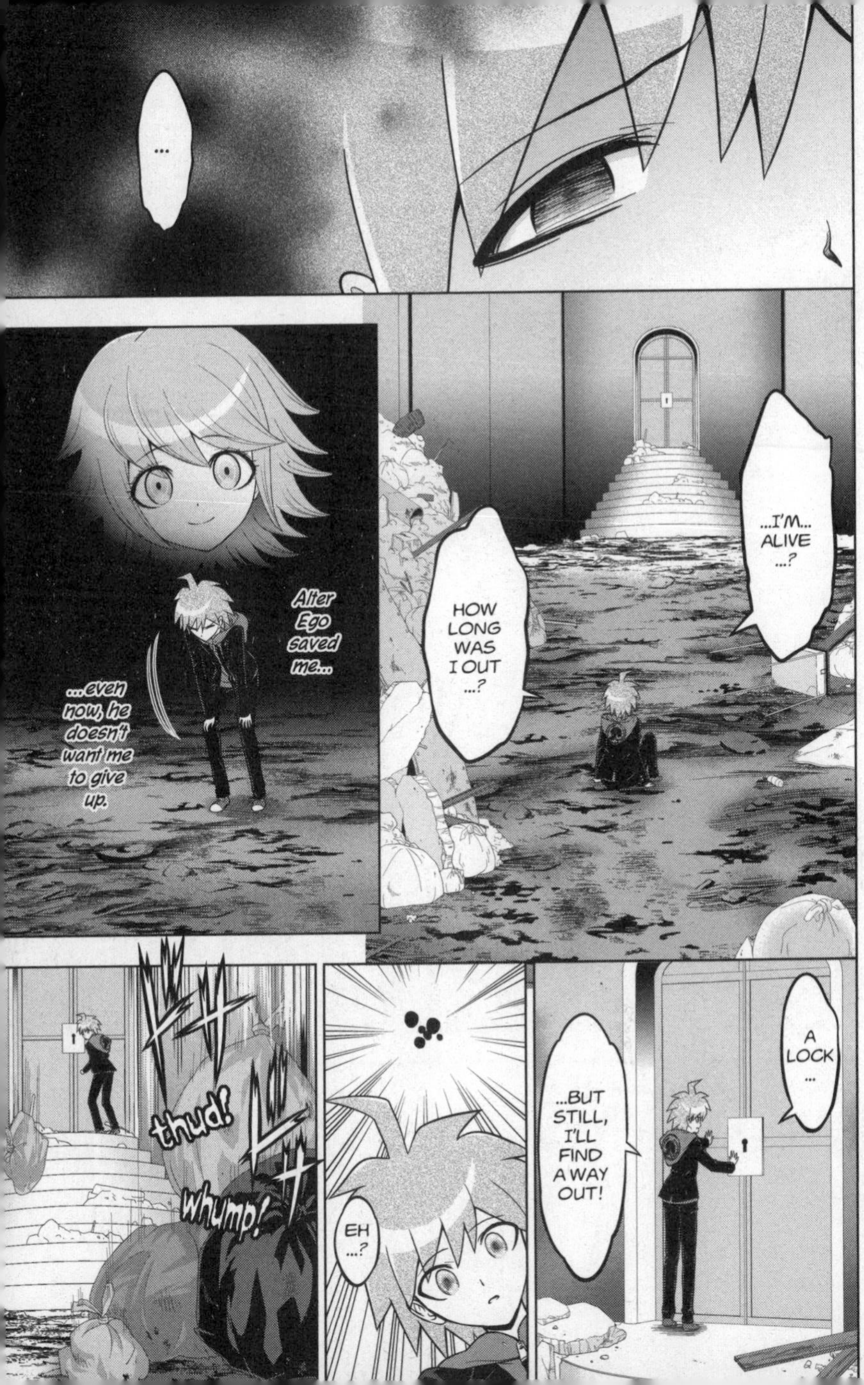
...
...I'M... ALIVE ...?
HOW LONG WAS I OUT ...?
Alter Ego saved me...
...even now, he doesn't want me to give up.
A LOCK ...
...BUT STILL, I'LL FIND A WAY OUT!
EH ...?
thud!
whump!

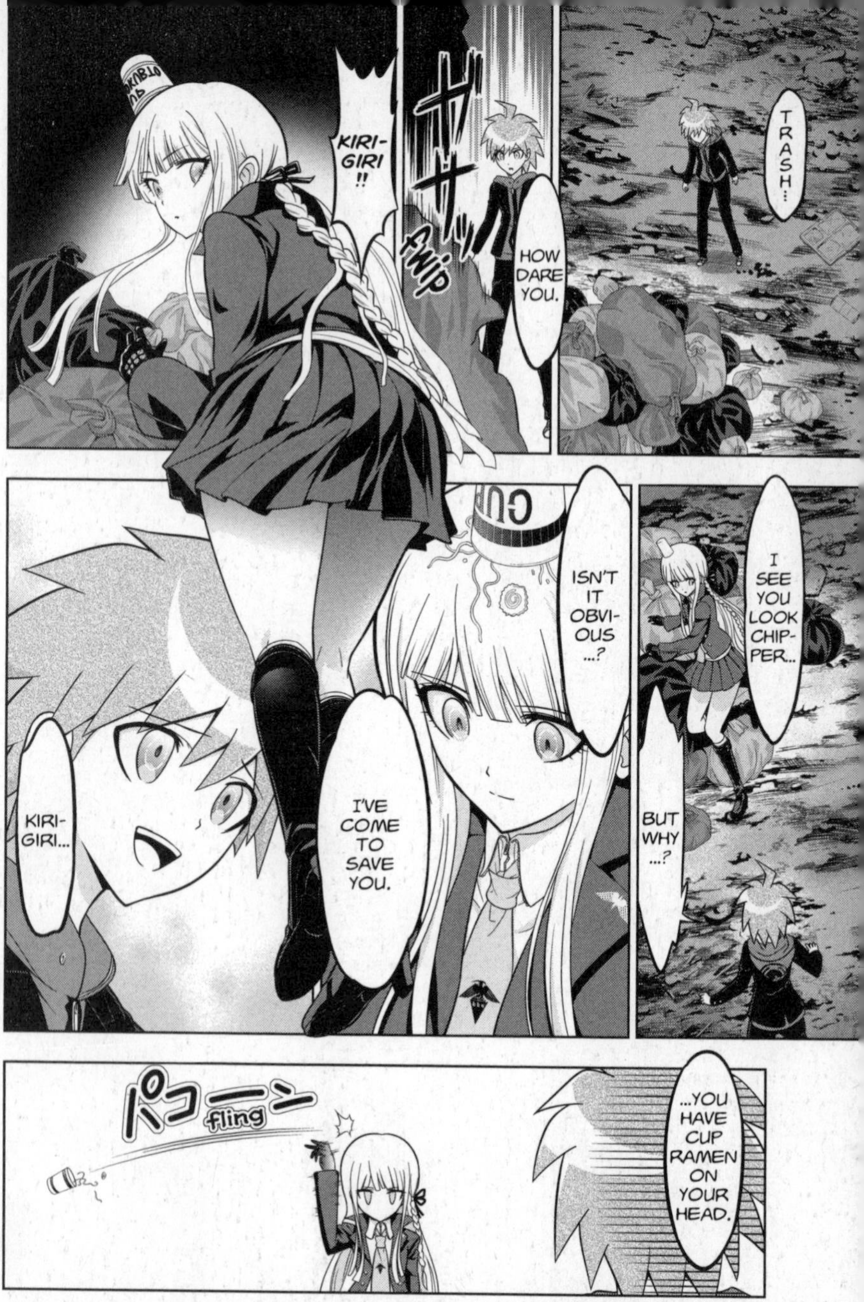
TRASH...
HOW DARE YOU.
ザザッ
FWIP
KIRI-GIRI!!
I SEE YOU LOOK CHIPPER...
BUT WHY...?
ISN'T IT OBVIOUS...?
I'VE COME TO SAVE YOU.
KIRI-GIRI...
...YOU HAVE CUP RAMEN ON YOUR HEAD.
パコーン
fling

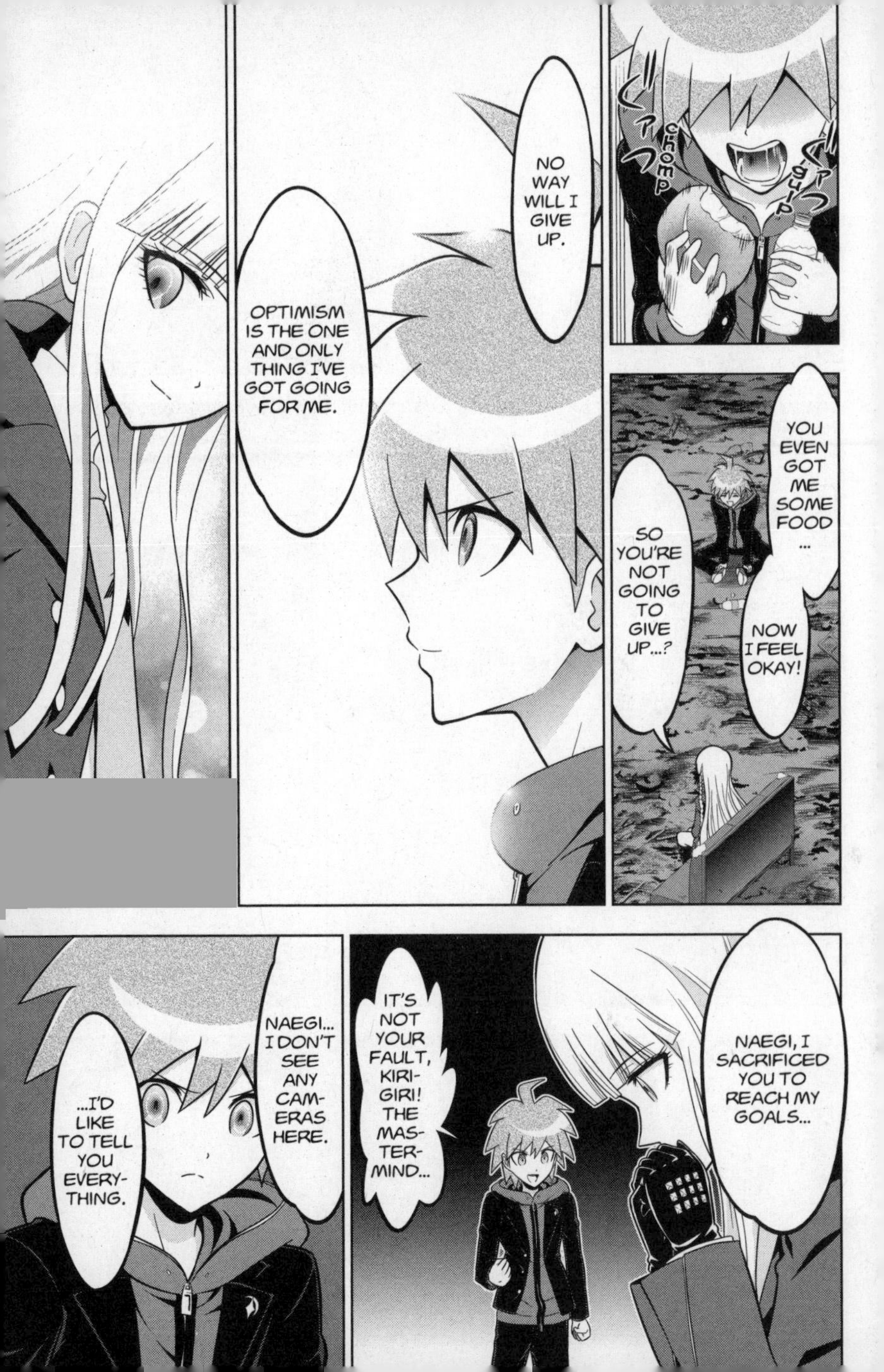
CHOMP
GULP
YOU EVEN GOT ME SOME FOOD...
NOW I FEEL OKAY!
SO YOU'RE NOT GOING TO GIVE UP...?
NO WAY WILL I GIVE UP.
OPTIMISM IS THE ONE AND ONLY THING I'VE GOT GOING FOR ME.
NAEGI, I SACRIFICED YOU TO REACH MY GOALS...
IT'S NOT YOUR FAULT, KIRI-GIRI! THE MAS-TER-MIND...
NAEGI... I DON'T SEE ANY CAM-ERAS HERE.
...I'D LIKE TO TELL YOU EVERY-THING.

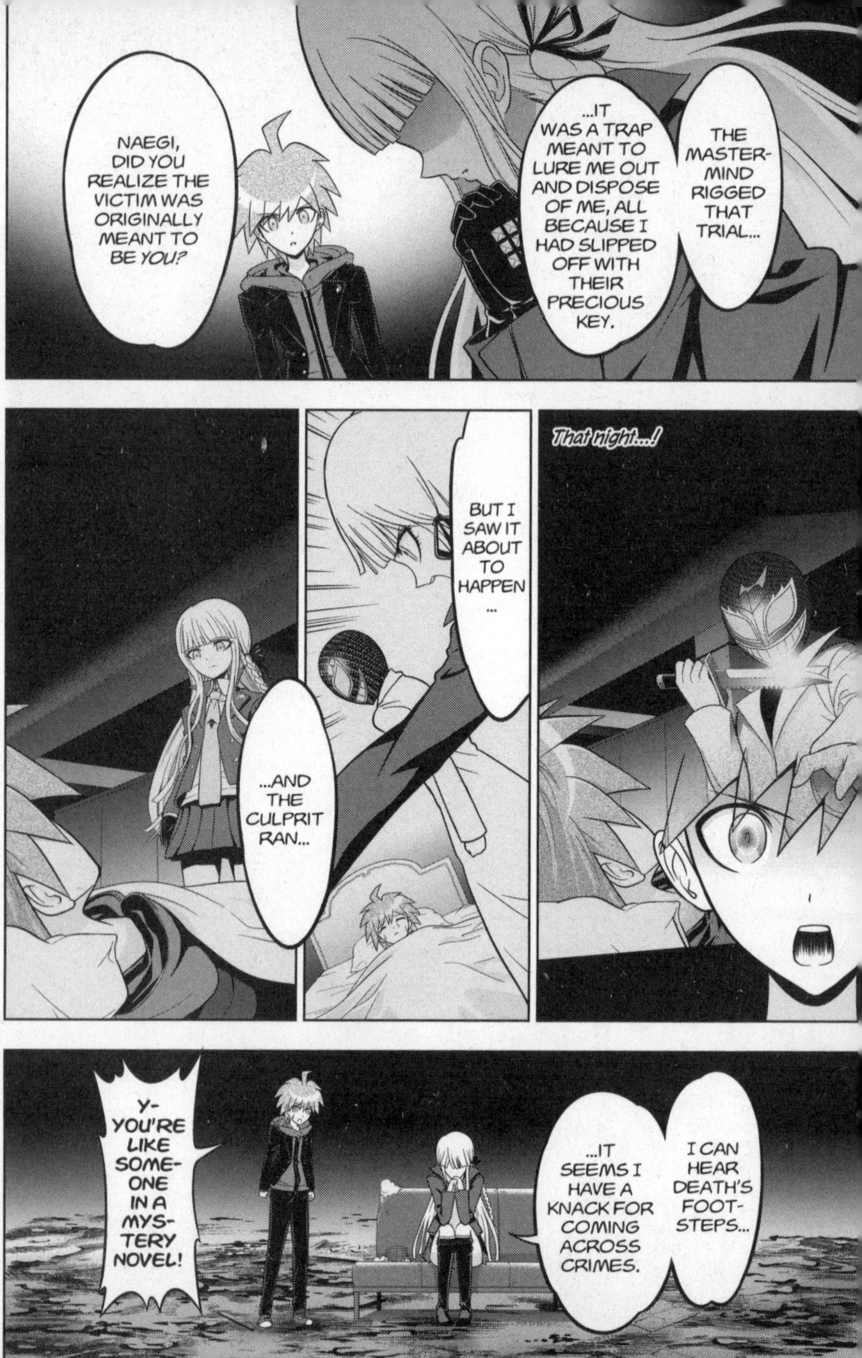
THE MASTERMIND RIGGED THAT TRIAL...
...IT WAS A TRAP MEANT TO LURE ME OUT AND DISPOSE OF ME, ALL BECAUSE I HAD SLIPPED OFF WITH THEIR PRECIOUS KEY.
NAEGI, DID YOU REALIZE THE VICTIM WAS ORIGINALLY MEANT TO BE YOU?
That night...!
BUT I SAW IT ABOUT TO HAPPEN...
...AND THE CULPRIT RAN...
I CAN HEAR DEATH'S FOOTSTEPS...
...IT SEEMS I HAVE A KNACK FOR COMING ACROSS CRIMES.
Y-YOU'RE LIKE SOMEONE IN A MYSTERY NOVEL!

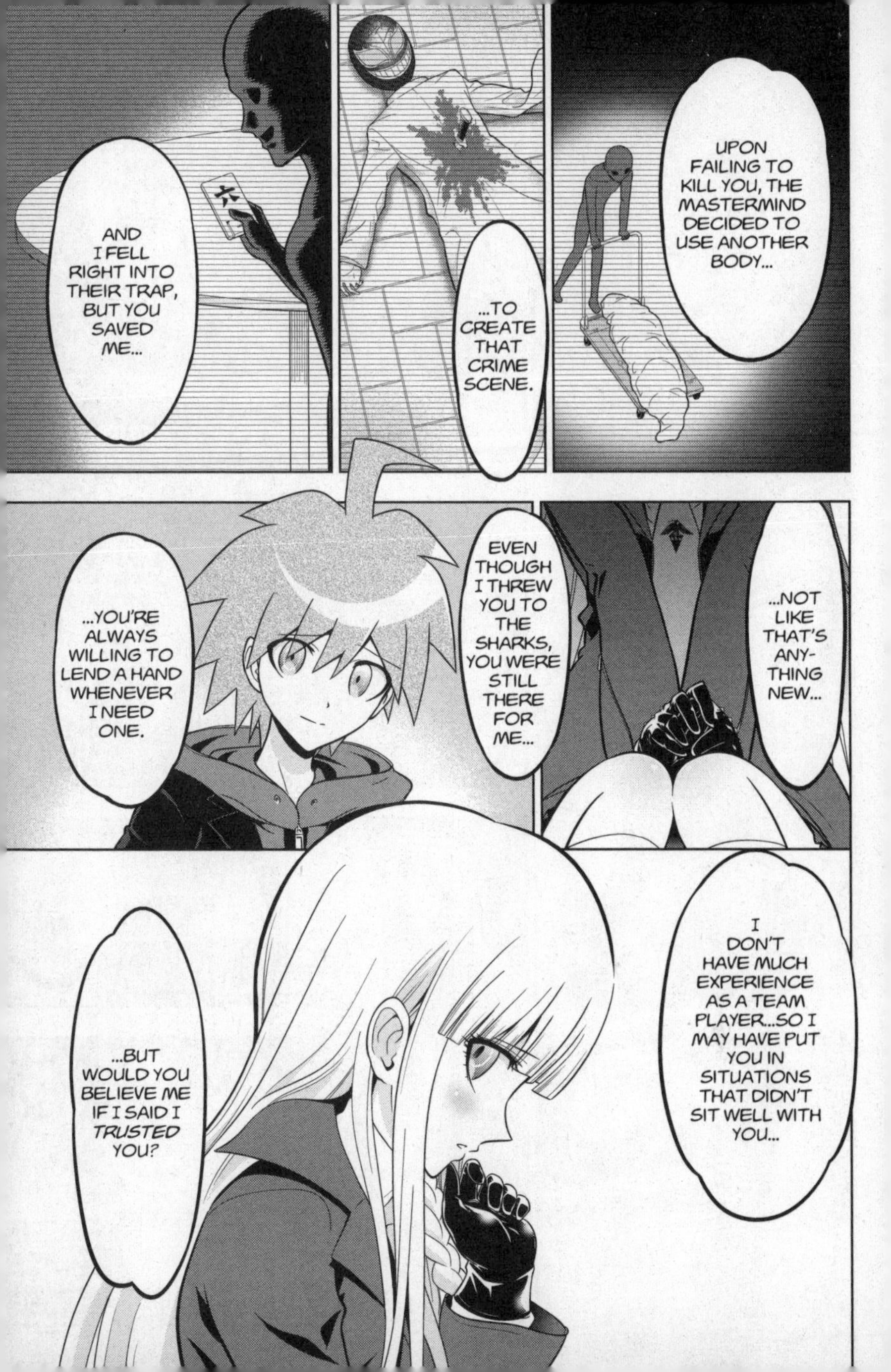
UPON FAILING TO KILL YOU, THE MASTERMIND DECIDED TO USE ANOTHER BODY...
...TO CREATE THAT CRIME SCENE.
AND I FELL RIGHT INTO THEIR TRAP, BUT YOU SAVED ME...
...NOT LIKE THAT'S ANY-THING NEW...
EVEN THOUGH I THREW YOU TO THE SHARKS, YOU WERE STILL THERE FOR ME...
...YOU'RE ALWAYS WILLING TO LEND A HAND WHENEVER I NEED ONE.
I DON'T HAVE MUCH EXPERIENCE AS A TEAM PLAYER...SO I MAY HAVE PUT YOU IN SITUATIONS THAT DIDN'T SIT WELL WITH YOU...
...BUT WOULD YOU BELIEVE ME IF I SAID I *TRUSTED* YOU?

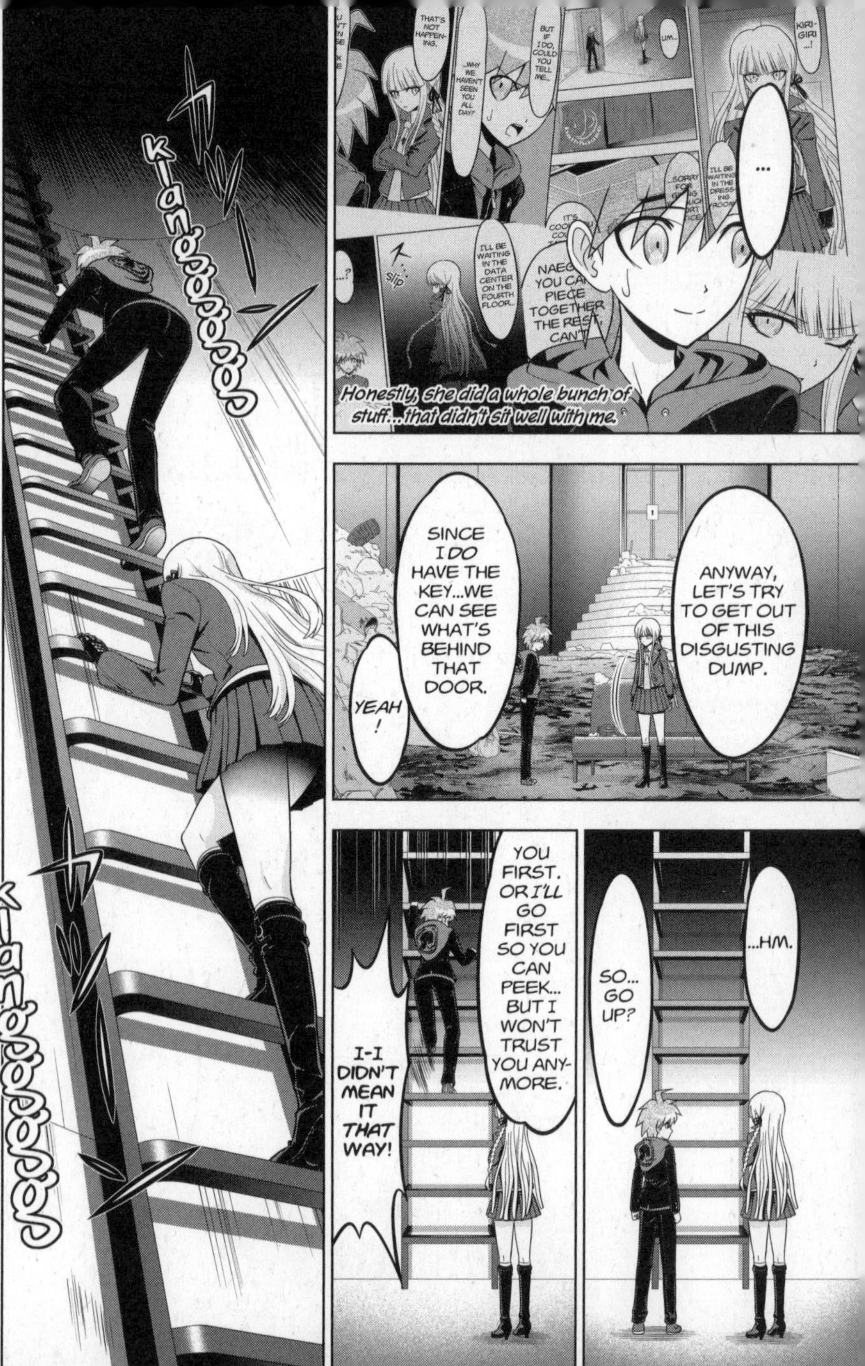
KIRI-GIRI ...!
...
I'LL BE WAITING IN THE DRESSING ROOM
UM...
BUT IF I DO, COULD YOU TELL ME...
...WHY WE HAVEN'T SEEN YOU ALL DAY?
THAT'S NOT HAPPENING.
I'LL BE WAITING IN THE DATA CENTER ON THE FOURTH FLOOR...
slip
...?
Honestly, she did a whole bunch of stuff...that didn't sit well with me.
ANYWAY, LET'S TRY TO GET OUT OF THIS DISGUSTING DUMP.
SINCE I DO HAVE THE KEY...WE CAN SEE WHAT'S BEHIND THAT DOOR.
YEAH!
...HM.
SO... GO UP?
YOU FIRST. OR I'LL GO FIRST SO YOU CAN PEEK... BUT I WON'T TRUST YOU ANYMORE.
I-I DIDN'T MEAN IT THAT WAY!
klangggg
klangggg

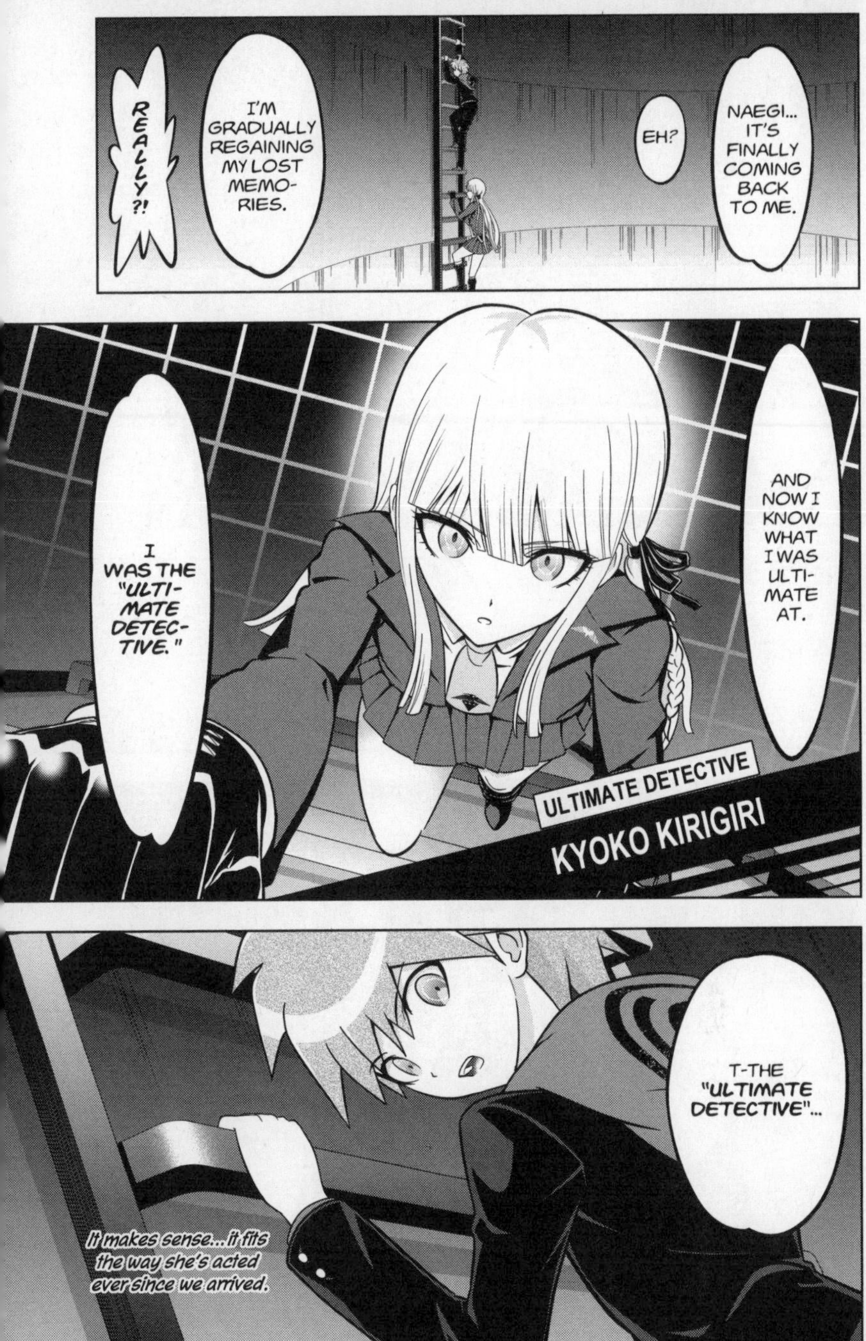
NAEGI... IT'S FINALLY COMING BACK TO ME.
EH?
I'M GRADUALLY REGAINING MY LOST MEMORIES.
REALLY?!
AND NOW I KNOW WHAT I WAS ULTIMATE AT.
I WAS THE "ULTIMATE DETECTIVE."
ULTIMATE DETECTIVE
KYOKO KIRIGIRI
T-THE "ULTIMATE DETECTIVE"...
It makes sense... it fits the way she's acted ever since we arrived.

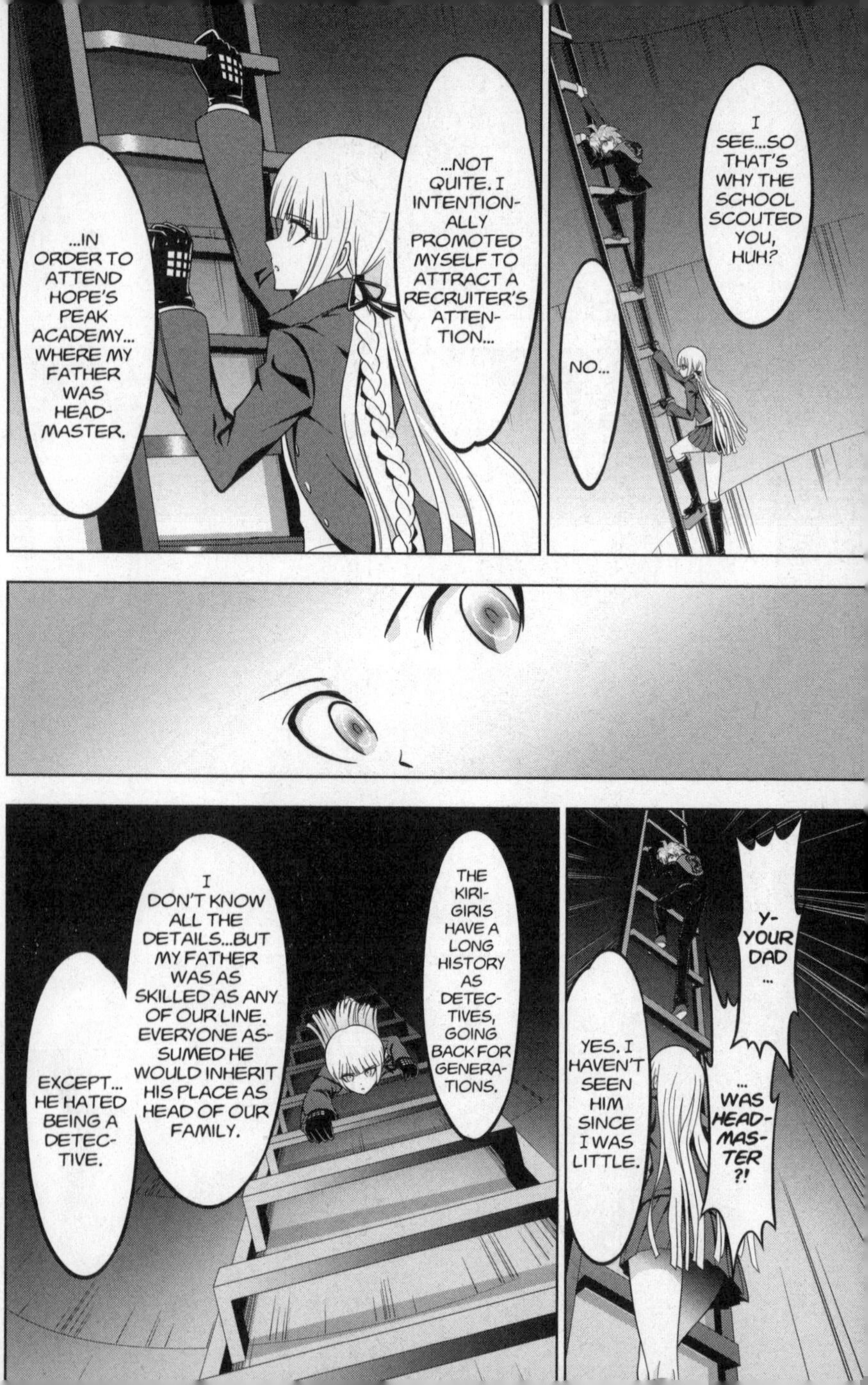
I SEE...SO THAT'S WHY THE SCHOOL SCOUTED YOU, HUH?
NO...
...NOT QUITE. I INTENTIONALLY PROMOTED MYSELF TO ATTRACT A RECRUITER'S ATTENTION...
...IN ORDER TO ATTEND HOPE'S PEAK ACADEMY... WHERE MY FATHER WAS HEADMASTER.
Y-YOUR DAD...
...WAS HEADMASTER?!
YES. I HAVEN'T SEEN HIM SINCE I WAS LITTLE.
THE KIRIGIRIS HAVE A LONG HISTORY AS DETECTIVES, GOING BACK FOR GENERATIONS.
I DON'T KNOW ALL THE DETAILS...BUT MY FATHER WAS AS SKILLED AS ANY OF OUR LINE. EVERYONE ASSUMED HE WOULD INHERIT HIS PLACE AS HEAD OF OUR FAMILY.
EXCEPT... HE HATED BEING A DETECTIVE.

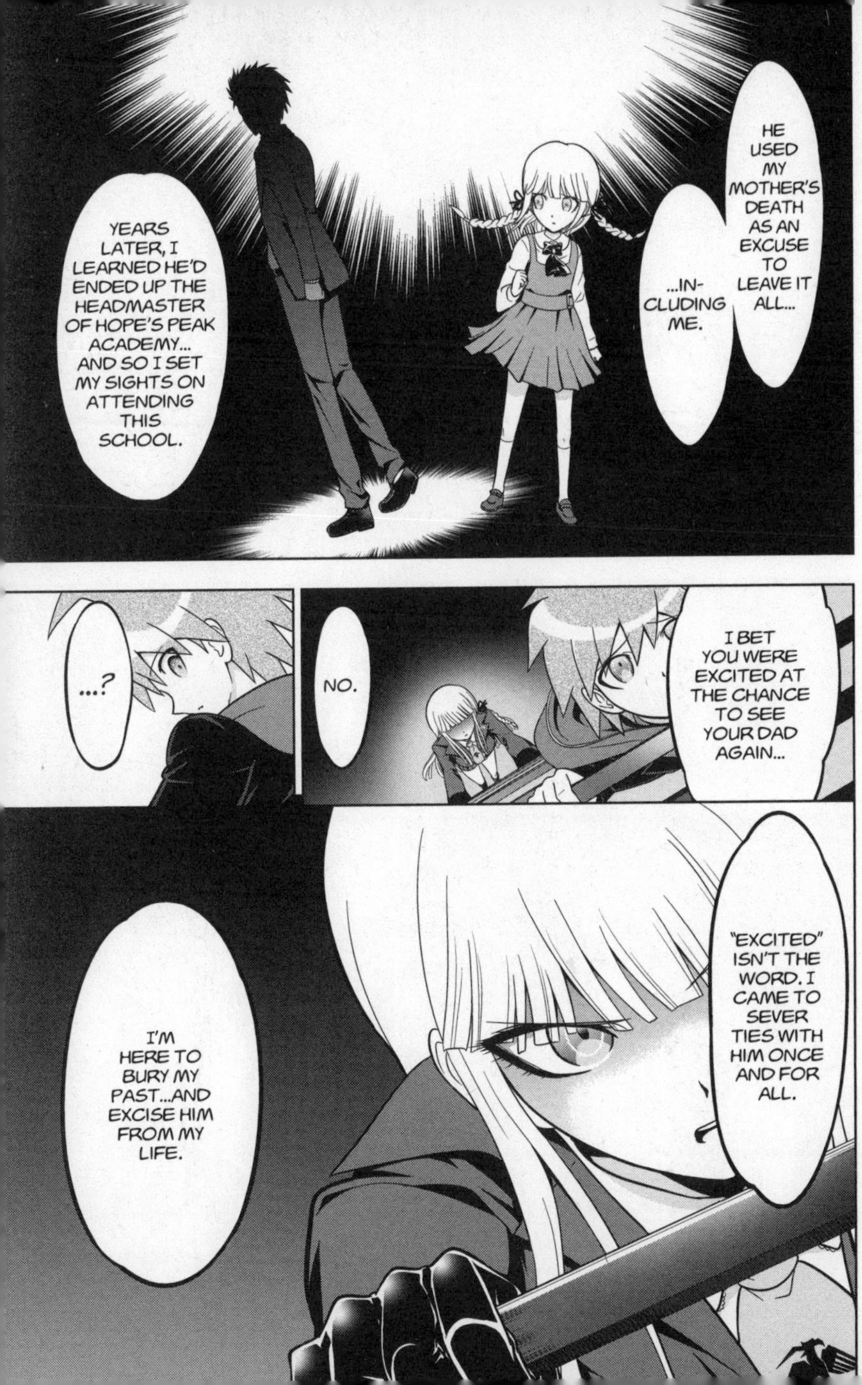
HE USED MY MOTHER'S DEATH AS AN EXCUSE TO LEAVE IT ALL...
...IN-CLUDING ME.
YEARS LATER, I LEARNED HE'D ENDED UP THE HEADMASTER OF HOPE'S PEAK ACADEMY... AND SO I SET MY SIGHTS ON ATTENDING THIS SCHOOL.
I BET YOU WERE EXCITED AT THE CHANCE TO SEE YOUR DAD AGAIN...
NO.
...?
"EXCITED" ISN'T THE WORD. I CAME TO SEVER TIES WITH HIM ONCE AND FOR ALL.
I'M HERE TO BURY MY PAST...AND EXCISE HIM FROM MY LIFE.

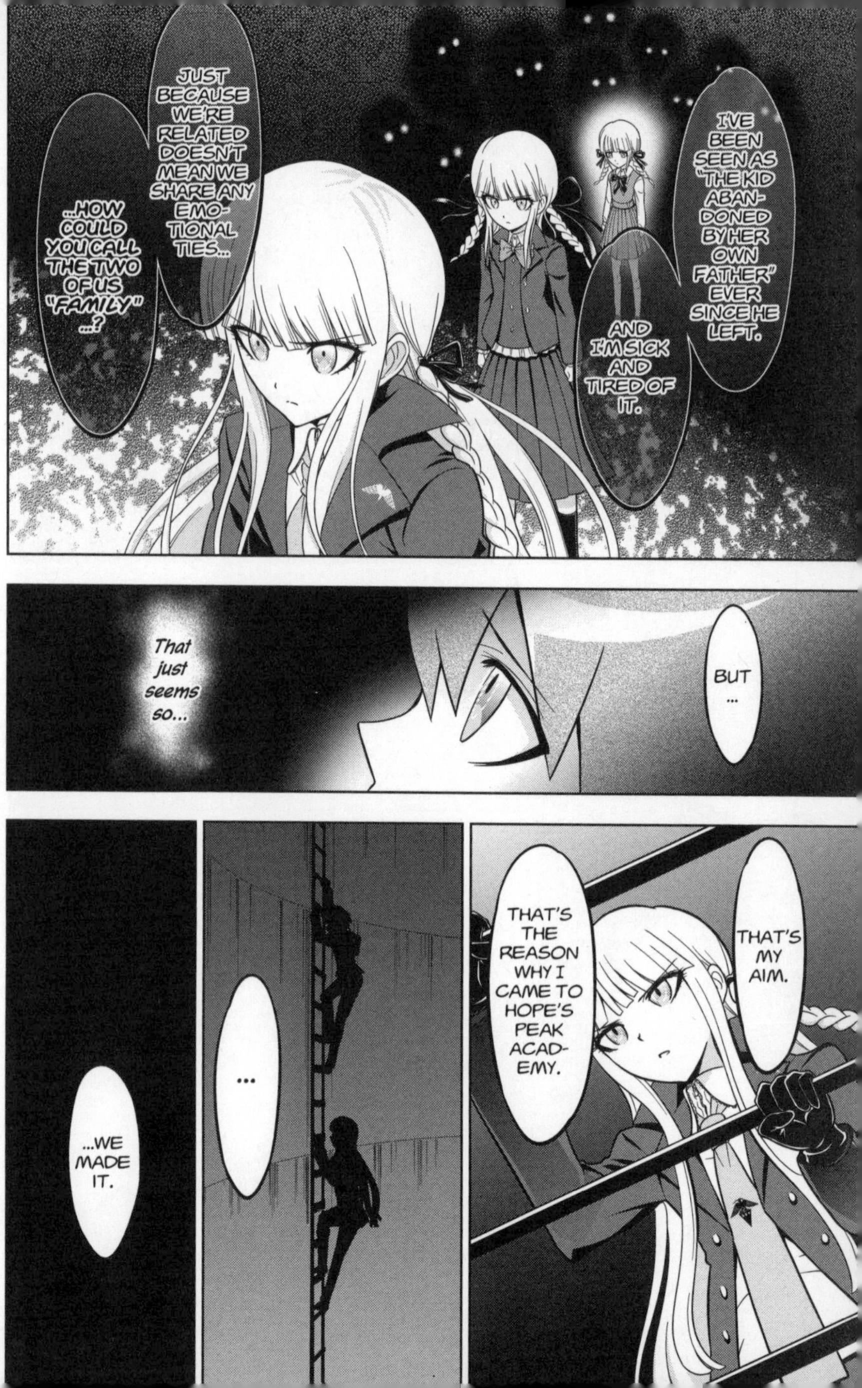
I'VE BEEN SEEN AS "THE KID ABANDONED BY HER OWN FATHER" EVER SINCE HE LEFT.
AND I'M SICK AND TIRED OF IT.
JUST BECAUSE WE'RE RELATED DOESN'T MEAN WE SHARE ANY EMOTIONAL TIES...
...HOW COULD YOU CALL THE TWO OF US "FAMILY" ...?
BUT ...
That just seems so...
THAT'S MY AIM.
THAT'S THE REASON WHY I CAME TO HOPE'S PEAK ACADEMY.
...
...WE MADE IT.

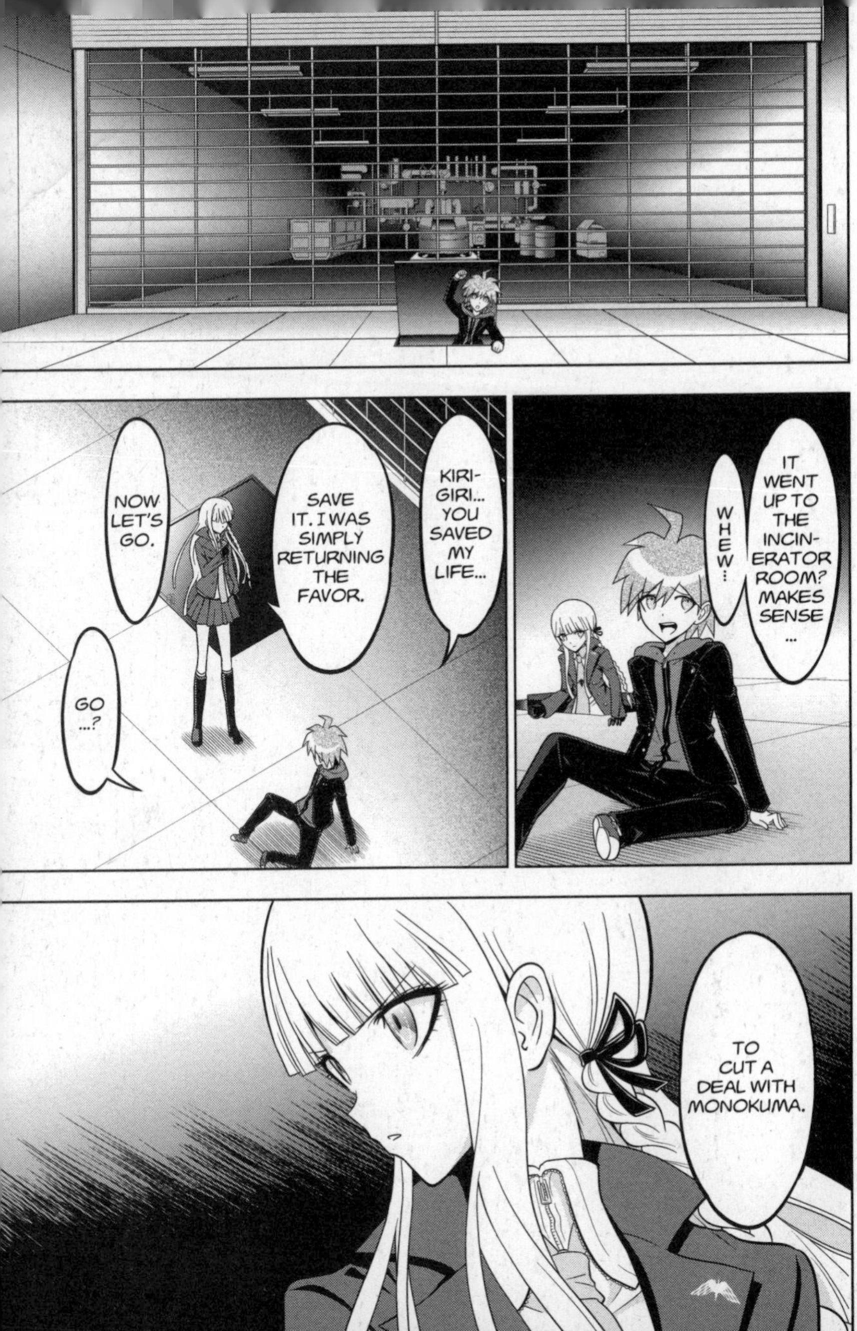
IT WENT UP TO THE INCIN-ERATOR ROOM? MAKES SENSE ...
WHEW...
KIRI-GIRI... YOU SAVED MY LIFE...
SAVE IT. I WAS SIMPLY RETURNING THE FAVOR.
NOW LET'S GO.
GO ...?
TO CUT A DEAL WITH MONOKUMA.

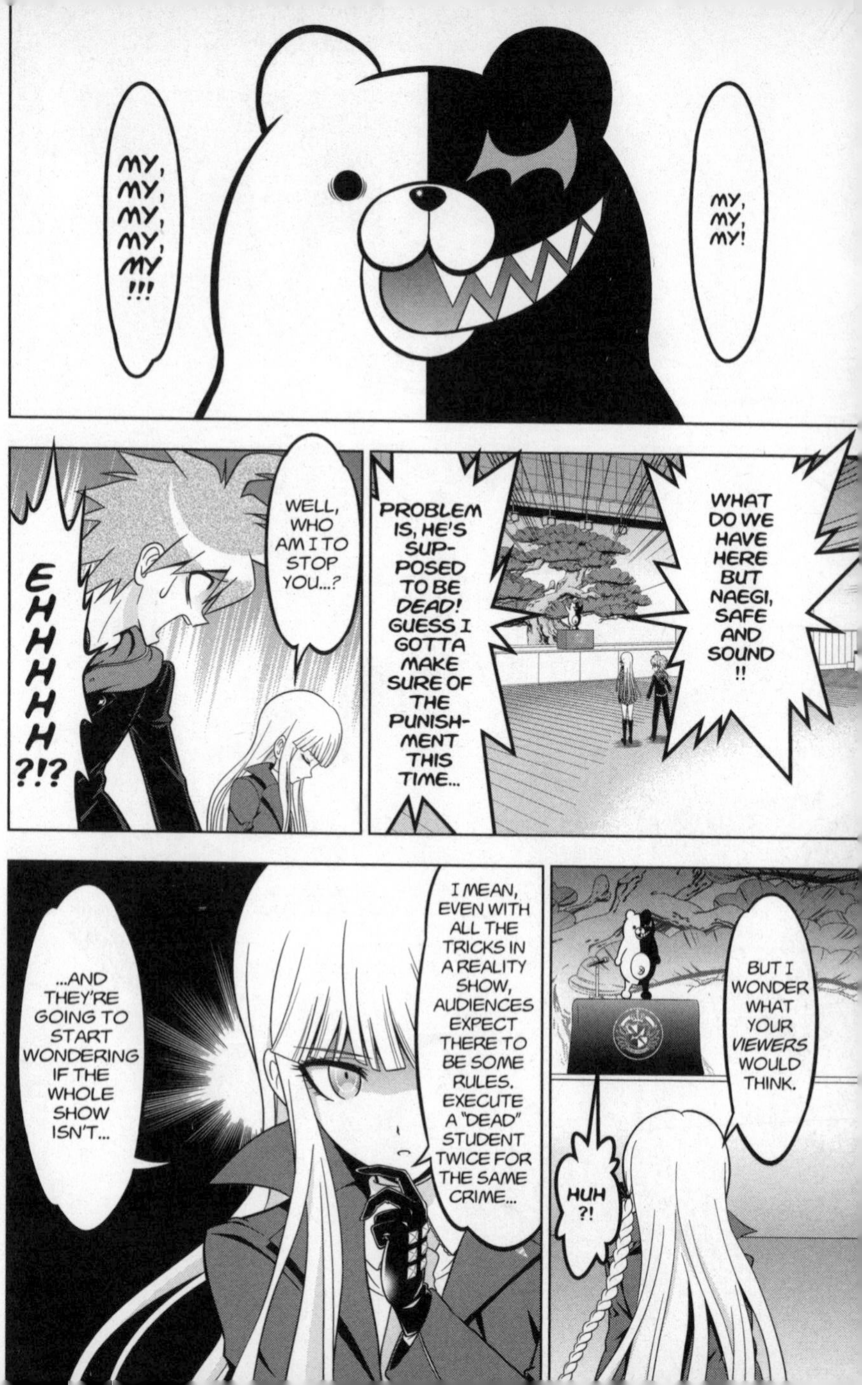
MY, MY, MY!
MY, MY, MY, MY, MY!!!
WHAT DO WE HAVE HERE BUT NAEGI, SAFE AND SOUND!!
PROBLEM IS, HE'S SUP-POSED TO BE DEAD! GUESS I GOTTA MAKE SURE OF THE PUNISH-MENT THIS TIME...
WELL, WHO AM I TO STOP YOU...?
EHHHHHH?!?
BUT I WONDER WHAT YOUR VIEWERS WOULD THINK.
HUH?!
I MEAN, EVEN WITH ALL THE TRICKS IN A REALITY SHOW, AUDIENCES EXPECT THERE TO BE SOME RULES. EXECUTE A "DEAD" STUDENT TWICE FOR THE SAME CRIME...
...AND THEY'RE GOING TO START WONDERING IF THE WHOLE SHOW ISN'T...

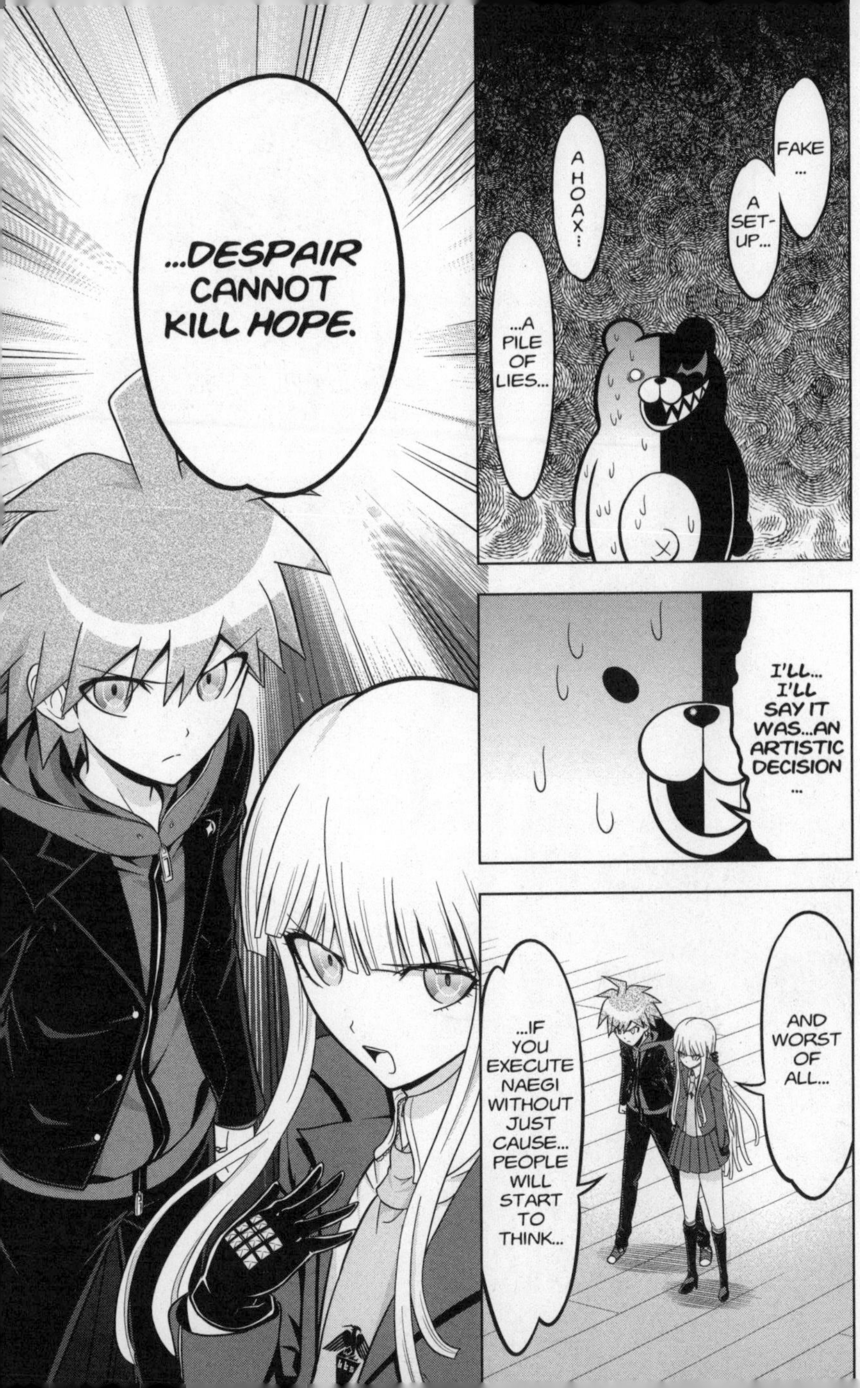
FAKE...
A SET-UP...
A HOAX...
...A PILE OF LIES...
I'LL... I'LL SAY IT WAS...AN ARTISTIC DECISION...
AND WORST OF ALL...
...IF YOU EXECUTE NAEGI WITHOUT JUST CAUSE... PEOPLE WILL START TO THINK...
...DESPAIR CANNOT KILL HOPE.

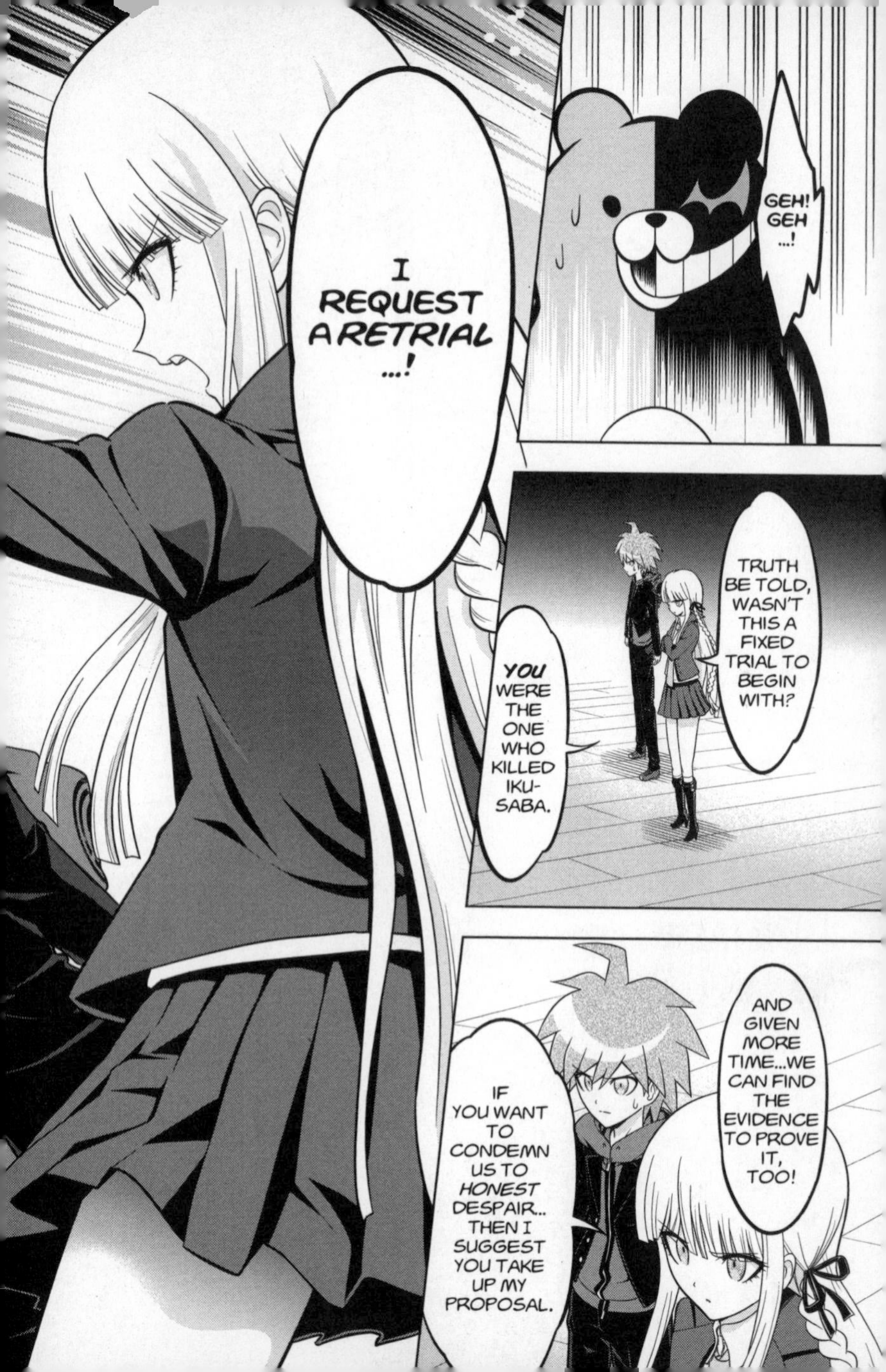
GEH! GEH ...!
TRUTH BE TOLD, WASN'T THIS A FIXED TRIAL TO BEGIN WITH?
YOU WERE THE ONE WHO KILLED IKU-SABA.
AND GIVEN MORE TIME...WE CAN FIND THE EVIDENCE TO PROVE IT, TOO!
IF YOU WANT TO CONDEMN US TO HONEST DESPAIR... THEN I SUGGEST YOU TAKE UP MY PROPOSAL.
I REQUEST A RETRIAL ...!

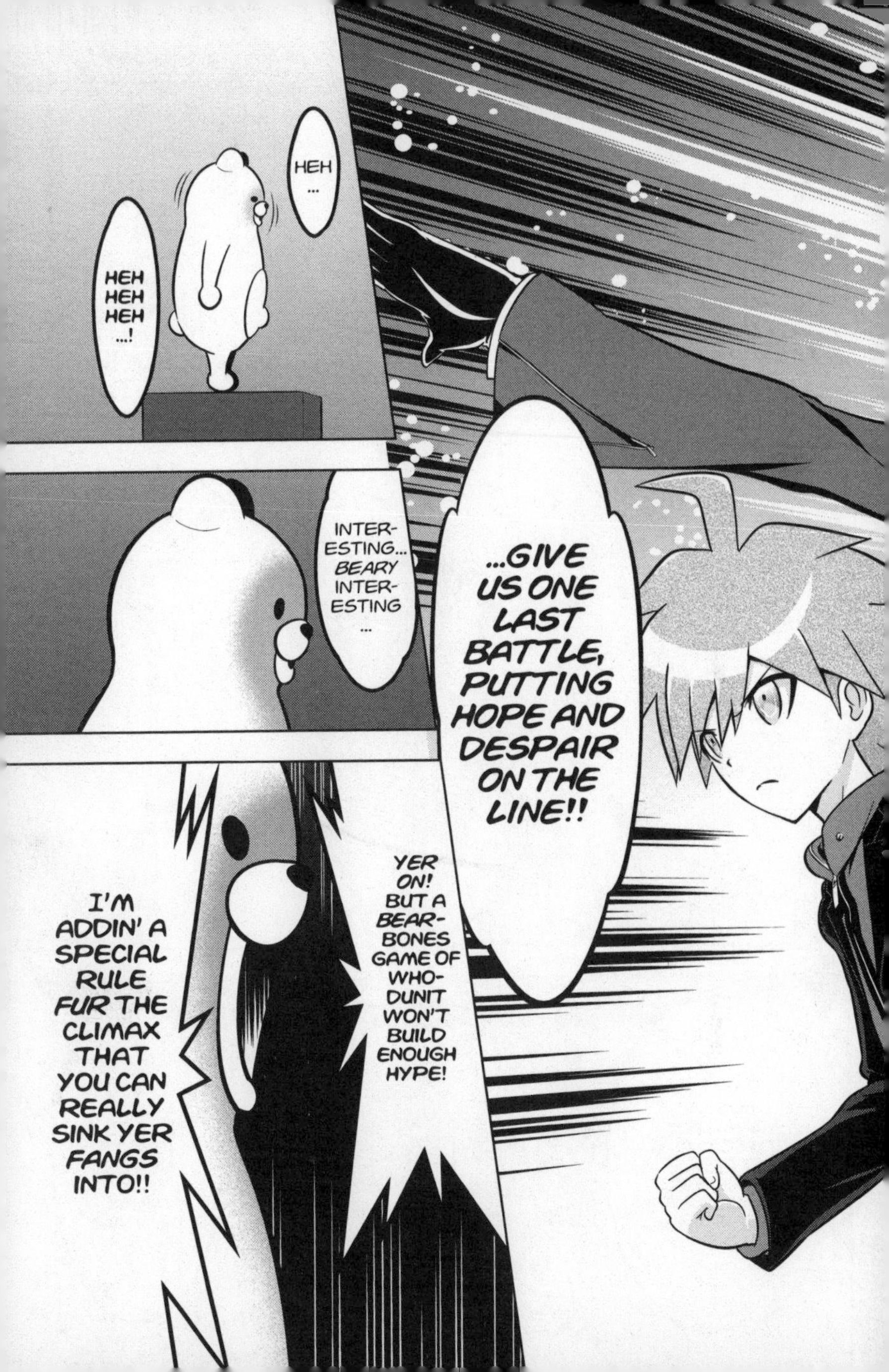
...GIVE US ONE LAST BATTLE, PUTTING HOPE AND DESPAIR ON THE LINE!!
HEH ...
HEH HEH HEH ...!
INTER-ESTING... BEARY INTER-ESTING ...
YER ON! BUT A BEAR-BONES GAME OF WHO-DUNIT WON'T BUILD ENOUGH HYPE!
I'M ADDIN' A SPECIAL RULE FUR THE CLIMAX THAT YOU CAN REALLY SINK YER FANGS INTO!!

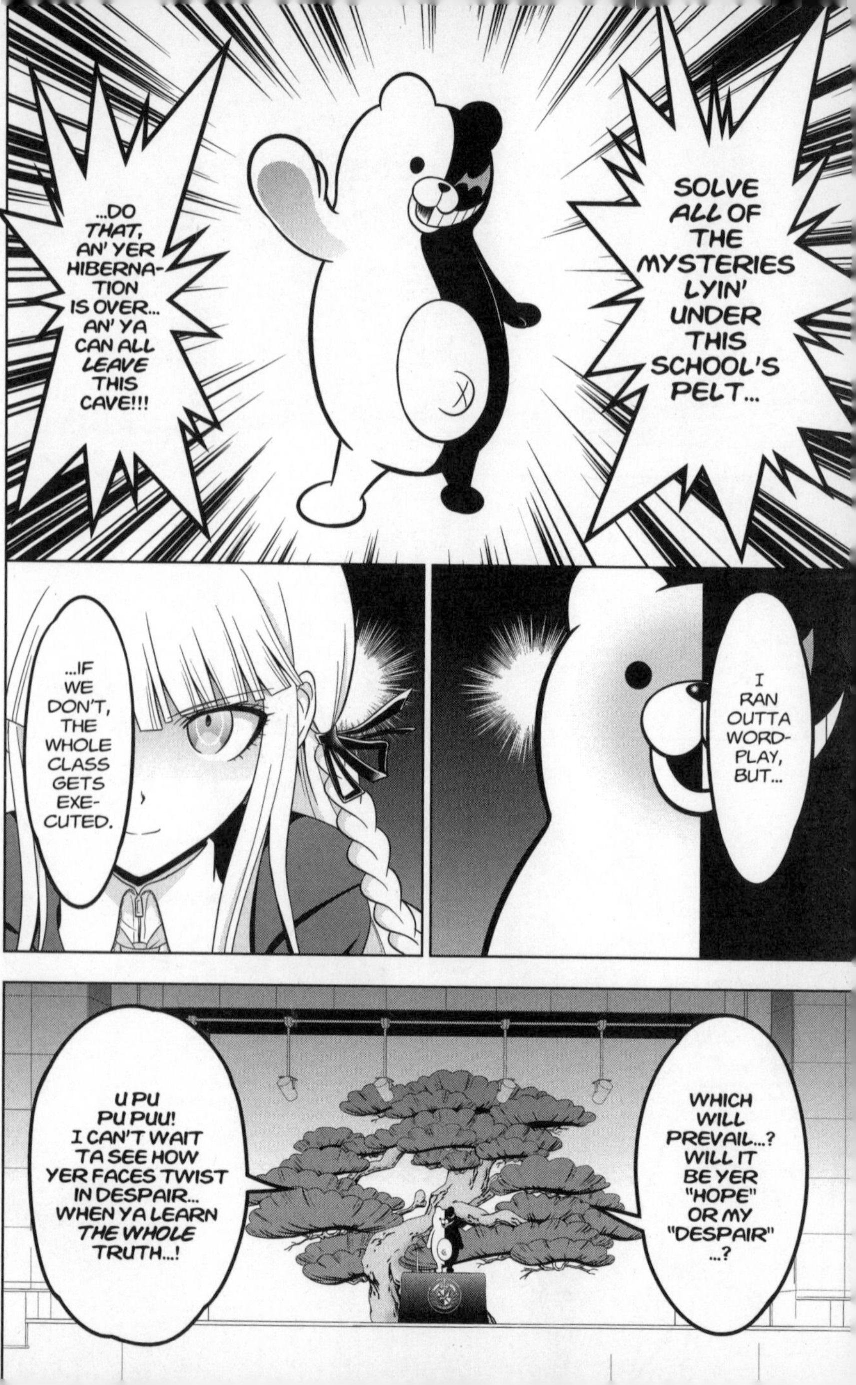
SOLVE ALL OF THE MYSTERIES LYIN' UNDER THIS SCHOOL'S PELT...
...DO THAT, AN' YER HIBERNATION IS OVER... AN' YA CAN ALL LEAVE THIS CAVE!!!
I RAN OUTTA WORDPLAY, BUT...
...IF WE DON'T, THE WHOLE CLASS GETS EXECUTED.
WHICH WILL PREVAIL...? WILL IT BE YER "HOPE" OR MY "DESPAIR" ...?
U PU PU PUU! I CAN'T WAIT TA SEE HOW YER FACES TWIST IN DESPAIR... WHEN YA LEARN THE WHOLE TRUTH...!

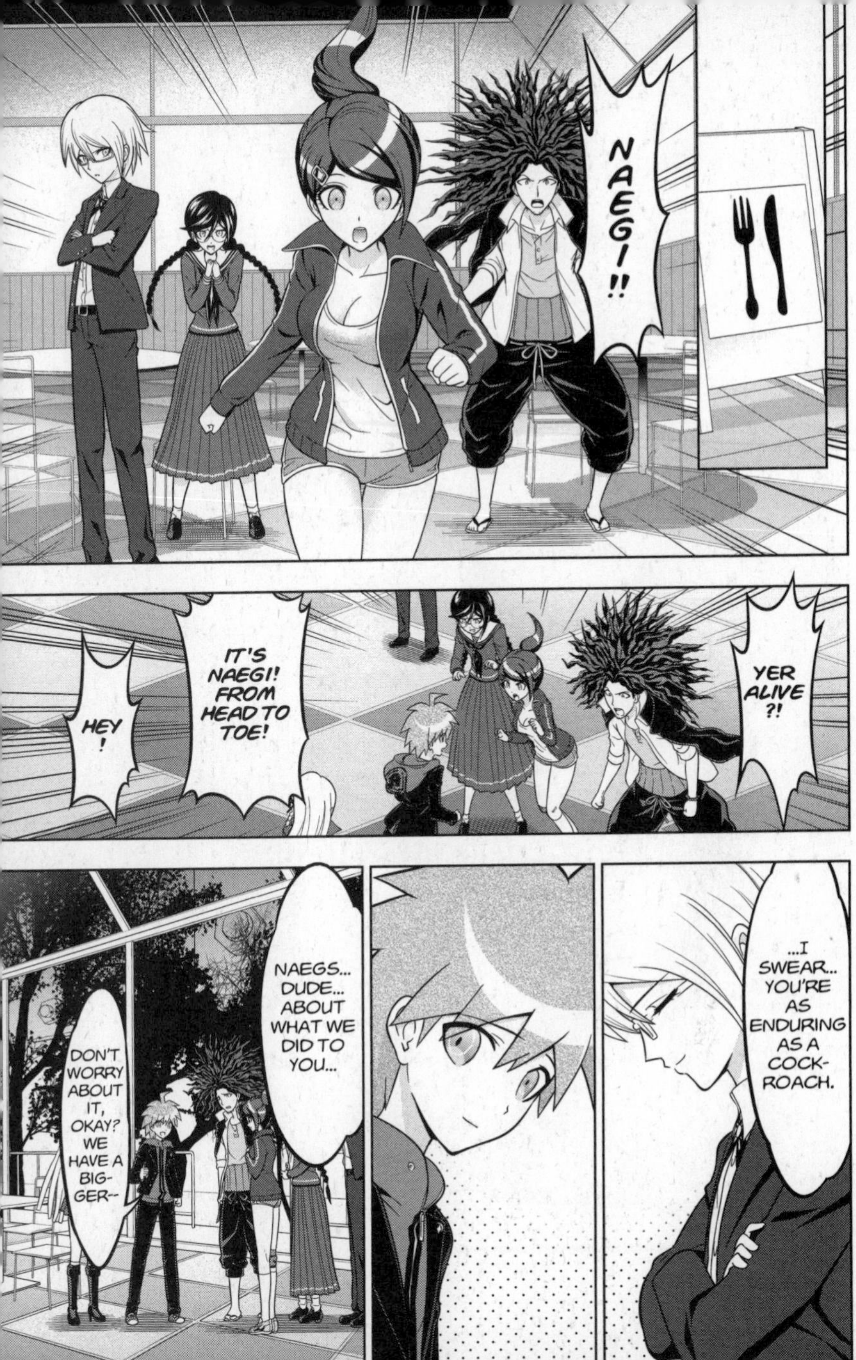
NAEGI!!
YER ALIVE ?!
IT'S NAEGI! FROM HEAD TO TOE!
HEY!
...I SWEAR... YOU'RE AS ENDURING AS A COCK-ROACH.
NAEGS... DUDE... ABOUT WHAT WE DID TO YOU...
DON'T WORRY ABOUT IT, OKAY? WE HAVE A BIG-GER--

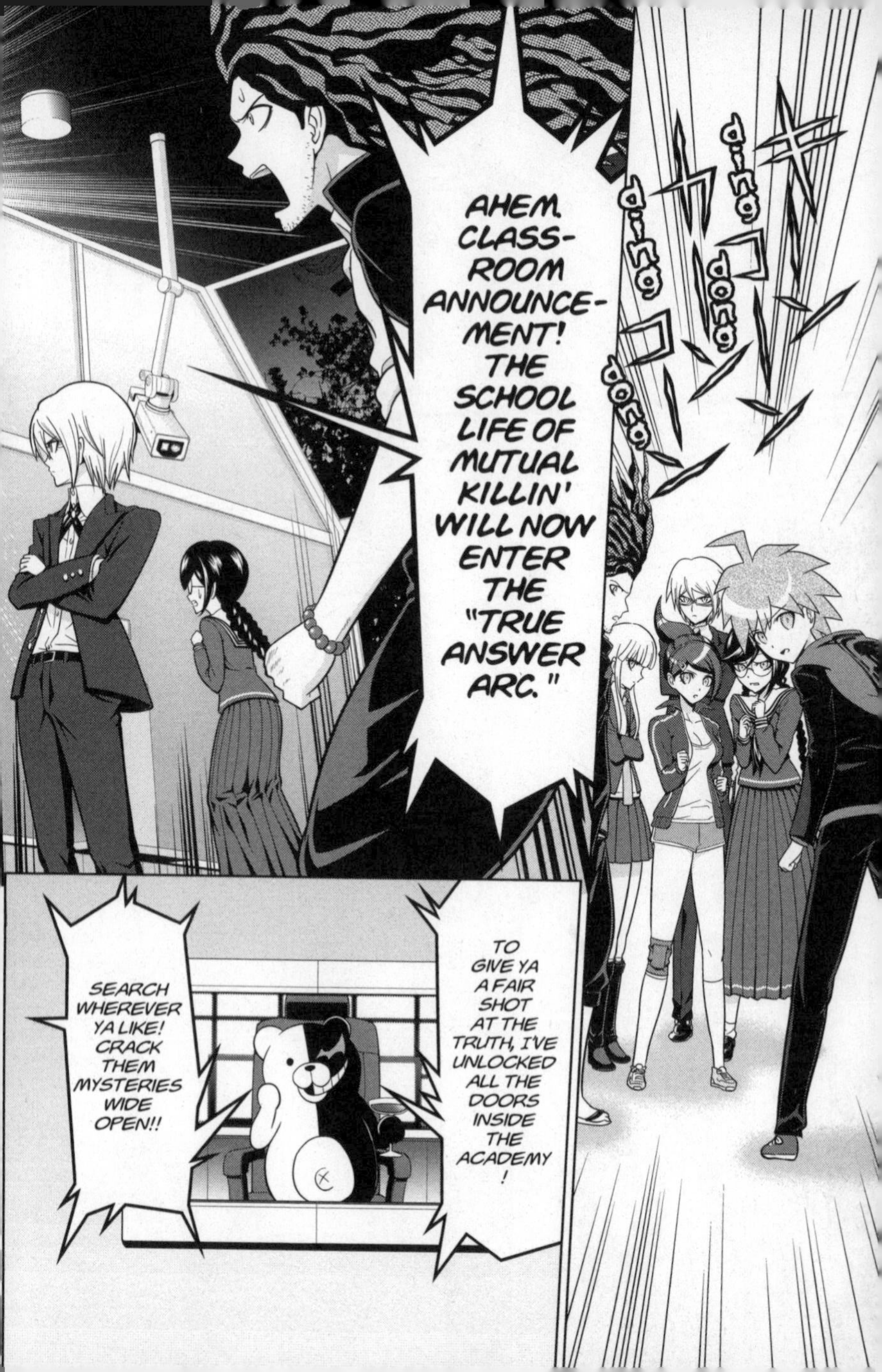
ding dong
ding dong
AHEM. CLASS-ROOM ANNOUNCE-MENT! THE SCHOOL LIFE OF MUTUAL KILLIN' WILL NOW ENTER THE "TRUE ANSWER ARC."
TO GIVE YA A FAIR SHOT AT THE TRUTH, I'VE UNLOCKED ALL THE DOORS INSIDE THE ACADEMY!
SEARCH WHEREVER YA LIKE! CRACK THEM MYSTERIES WIDE OPEN!!

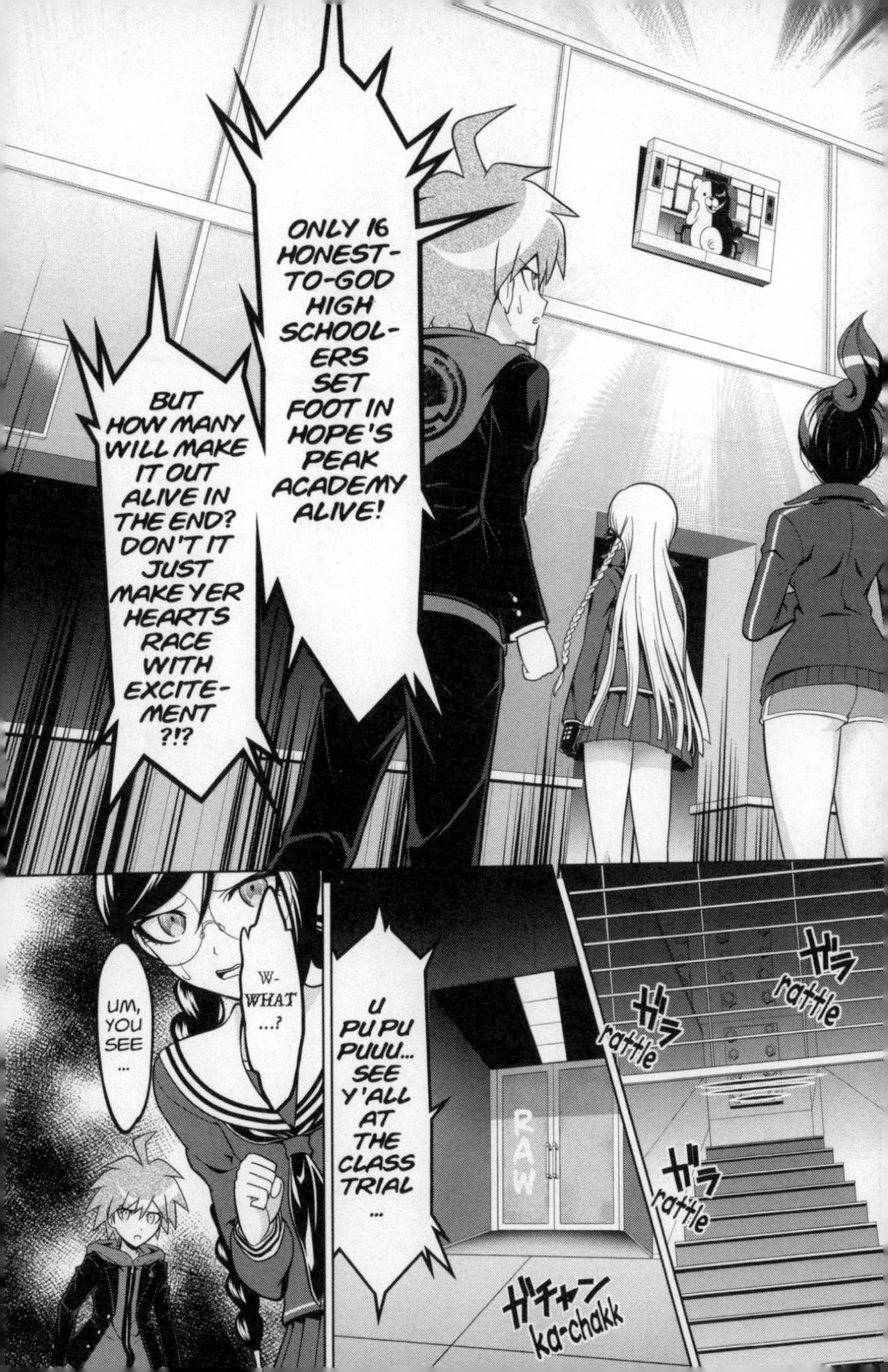
ONLY 16 HONEST-TO-GOD HIGH SCHOOLERS SET FOOT IN HOPE'S PEAK ACADEMY ALIVE!
BUT HOW MANY WILL MAKE IT OUT ALIVE IN THE END? DON'T IT JUST MAKE YER HEARTS RACE WITH EXCITEMENT?!?
ガラ rattle
ガラ rattle
U PUPU PUUU... SEE Y'ALL AT THE CLASS TRIAL...
RAW
ガラ rattle
ガチャン ka-chakk
W-WHAT ...?
UM, YOU SEE ...

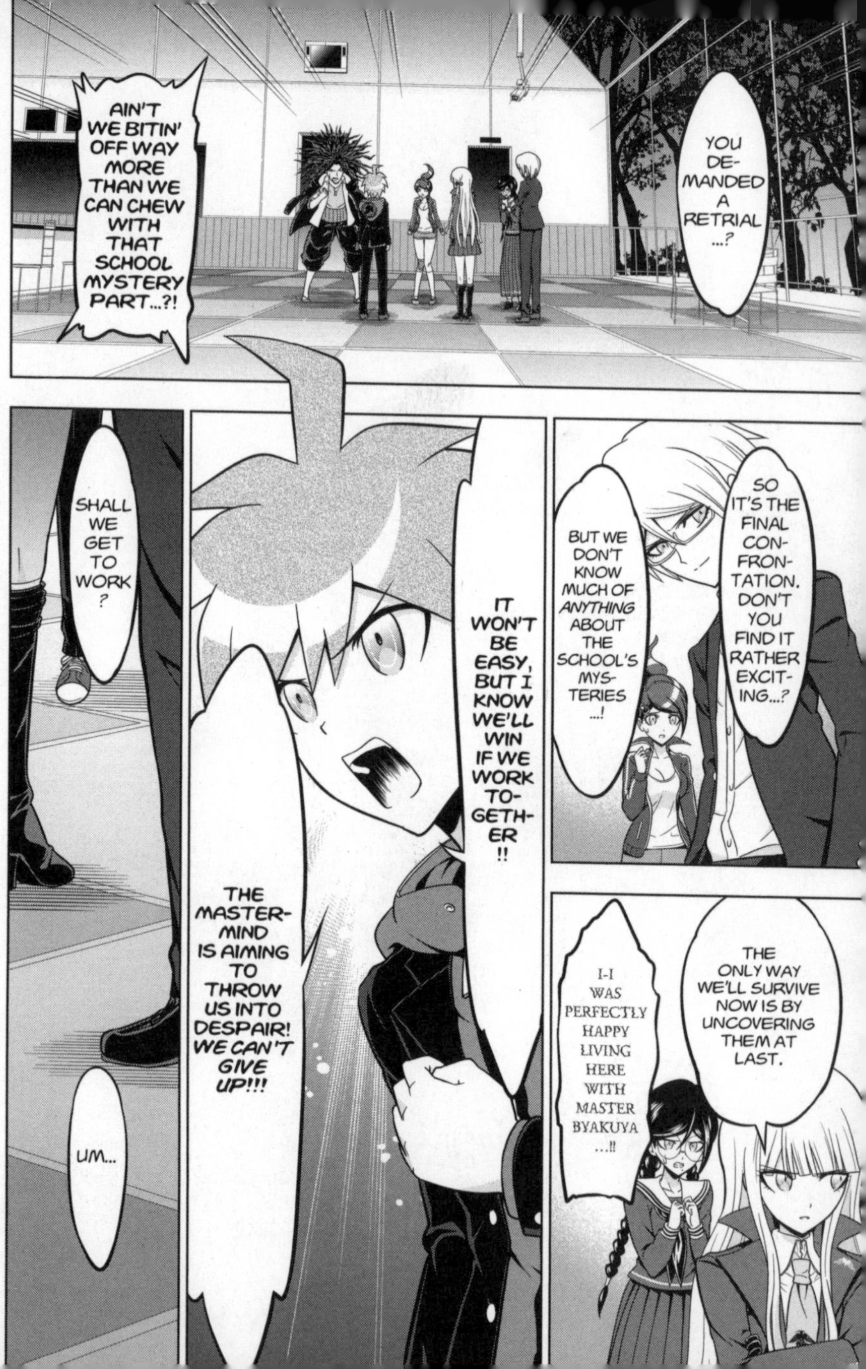

YOU DEMANDED A RETRIAL...?
AIN'T WE BITIN' OFF WAY MORE THAN WE CAN CHEW WITH THAT SCHOOL MYSTERY PART...?!
SO IT'S THE FINAL CONFRONTATION. DON'T YOU FIND IT RATHER EXCITING...?
BUT WE DON'T KNOW MUCH OF *ANYTHING* ABOUT THE SCHOOL'S MYSTERIES...!
THE ONLY WAY WE'LL SURVIVE NOW IS BY UNCOVERING THEM AT LAST.
I-I WAS PERFECTLY HAPPY LIVING HERE WITH MASTER BYAKUYA...!!
IT WON'T BE EASY, BUT I KNOW WE'LL WIN IF WE WORK TOGETHER!!
THE MASTERMIND IS AIMING TO THROW US INTO DESPAIR! WE CAN'T GIVE UP!!!
SHALL WE GET TO WORK?
UM...

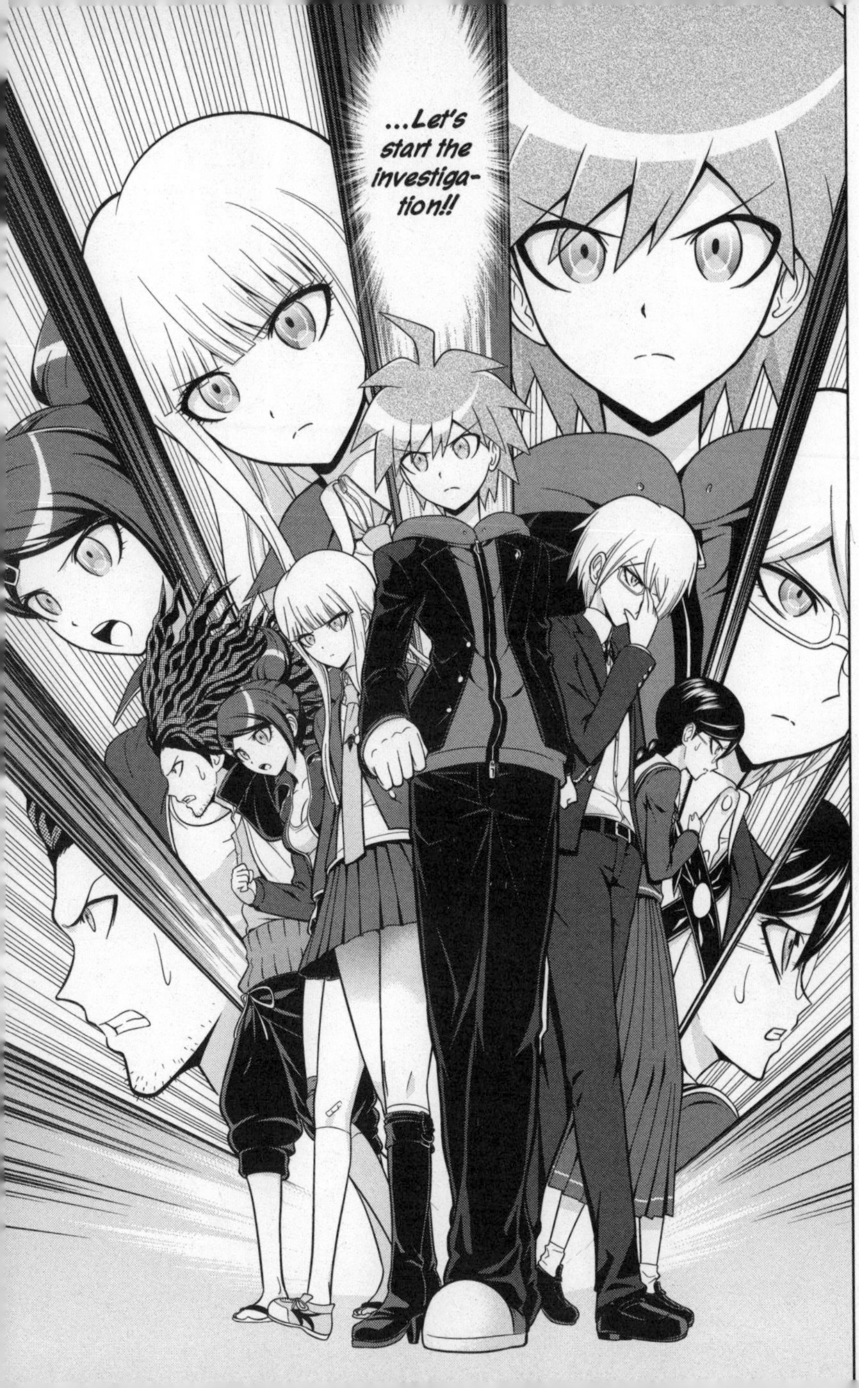
...Let's start the investiga-tion!!

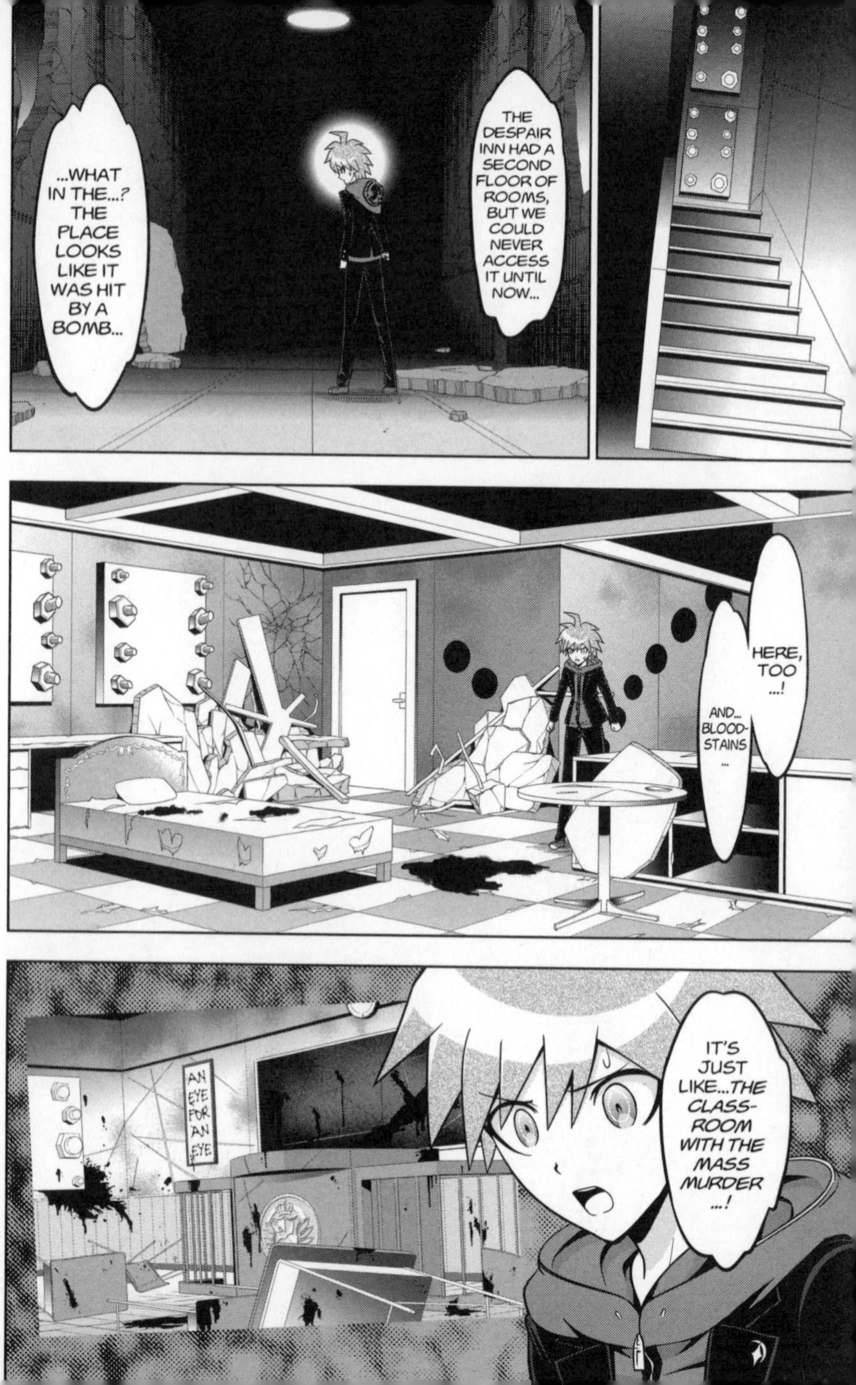
THE DESPAIR INN HAD A SECOND FLOOR OF ROOMS, BUT WE COULD NEVER ACCESS IT UNTIL NOW...
...WHAT IN THE...? THE PLACE LOOKS LIKE IT WAS HIT BY A BOMB...
HERE, TOO ...!
AND... BLOOD-STAINS ...
AN EYE FOR AN EYE
IT'S JUST LIKE...THE CLASS-ROOM WITH THE MASS MURDER ...!

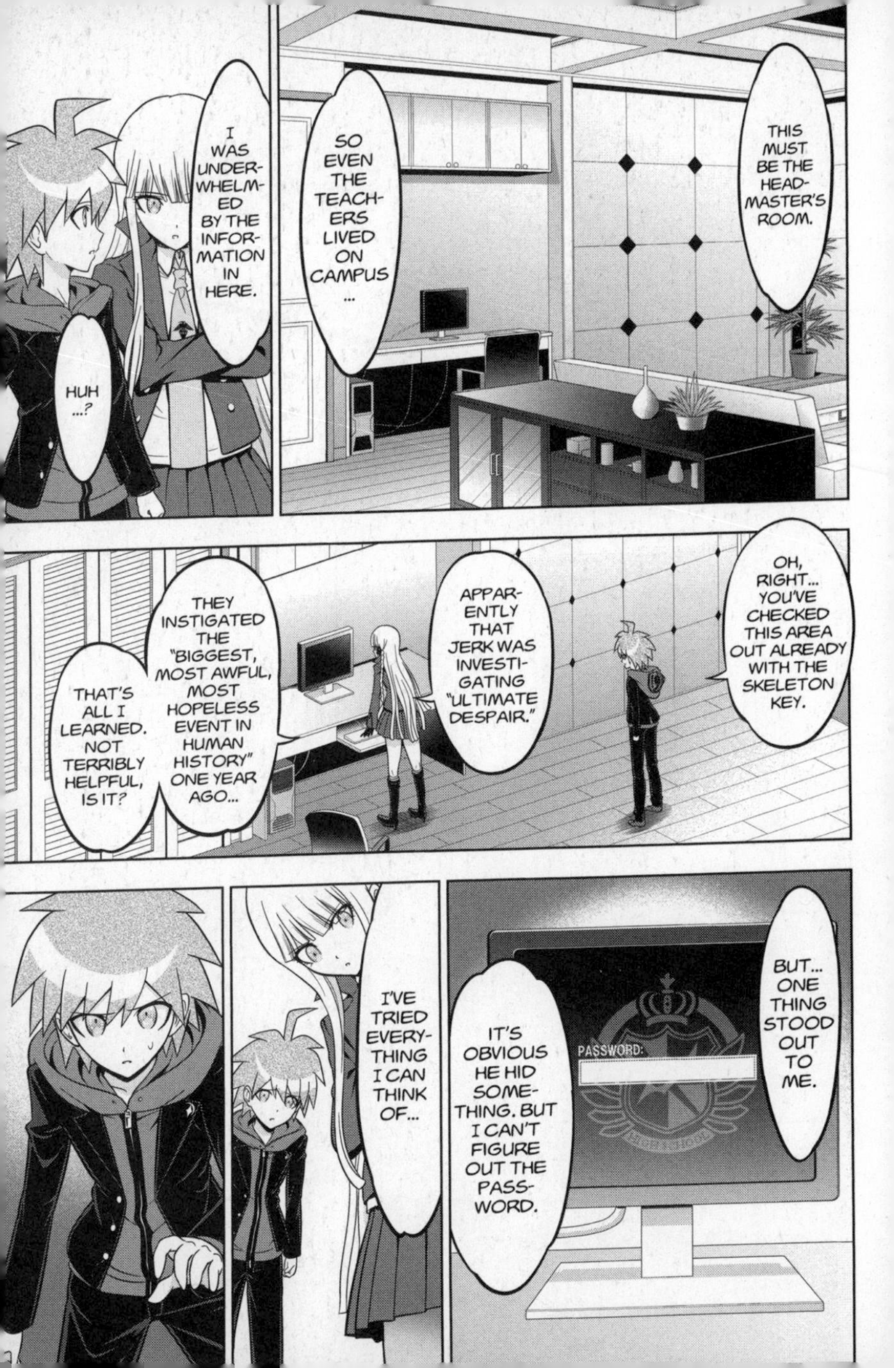
THIS MUST BE THE HEADMASTER'S ROOM.
SO EVEN THE TEACHERS LIVED ON CAMPUS...
I WAS UNDERWHELMED BY THE INFORMATION IN HERE.
HUH...?
OH, RIGHT... YOU'VE CHECKED THIS AREA OUT ALREADY WITH THE SKELETON KEY.
APPARENTLY THAT JERK WAS INVESTIGATING "ULTIMATE DESPAIR."
THEY INSTIGATED THE "BIGGEST, MOST AWFUL, MOST HOPELESS EVENT IN HUMAN HISTORY" ONE YEAR AGO...
THAT'S ALL I LEARNED. NOT TERRIBLY HELPFUL, IS IT?
BUT... ONE THING STOOD OUT TO ME.
PASSWORD:
IT'S OBVIOUS HE HID SOMETHING. BUT I CAN'T FIGURE OUT THE PASSWORD.
I'VE TRIED EVERYTHING I CAN THINK OF...

PASSWORD:
KYOKO

takka

...WHY?

YOUR *NAME* WAS THE PASS-WORD...

A HID-DEN DOOR!

chakk

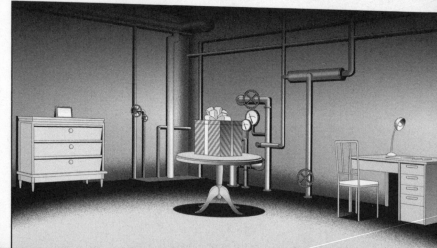

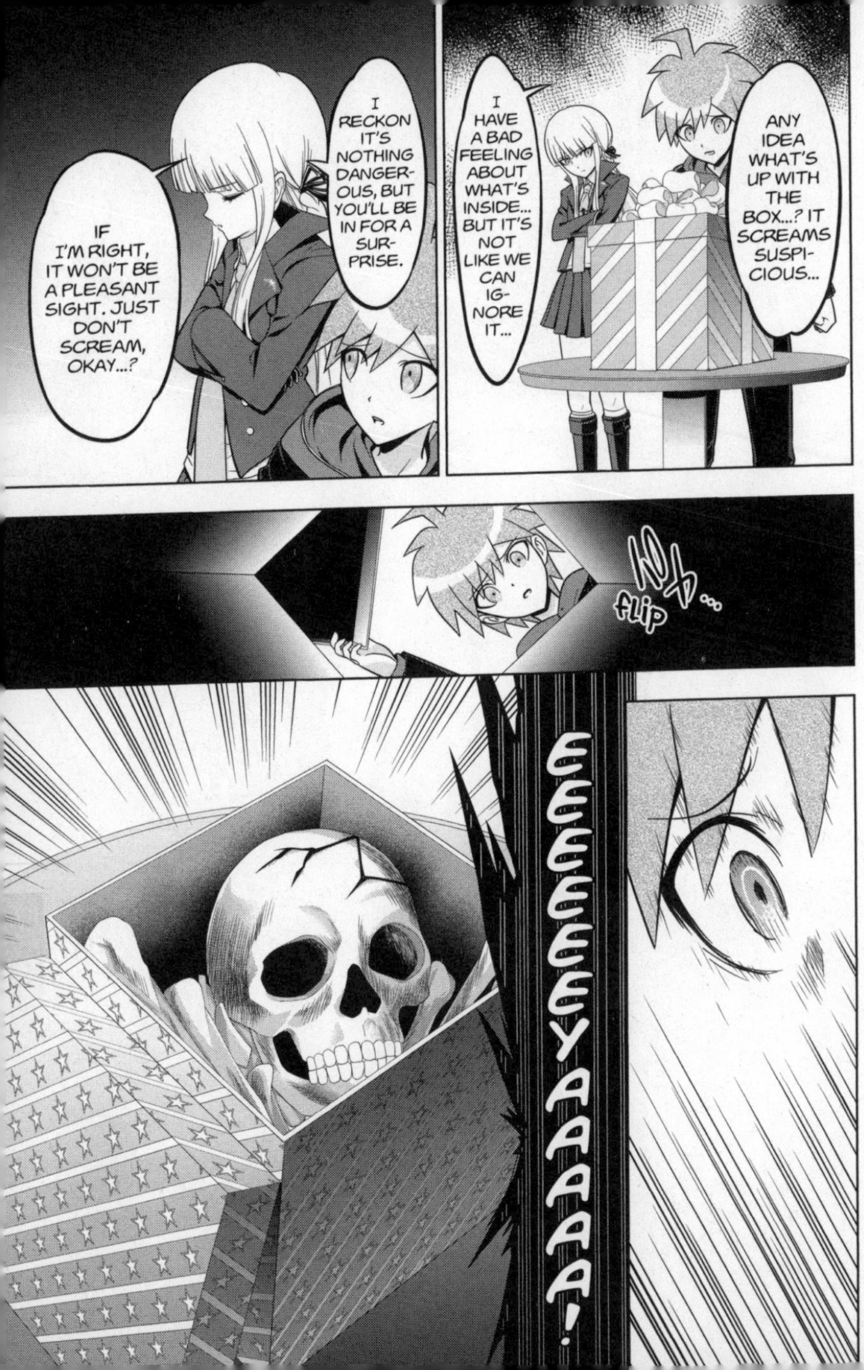
ANY IDEA WHAT'S UP WITH THE BOX...? IT SCREAMS SUSPICIOUS...
I HAVE A BAD FEELING ABOUT WHAT'S INSIDE... BUT IT'S NOT LIKE WE CAN IGNORE IT...
I RECKON IT'S NOTHING DANGEROUS, BUT YOU'LL BE IN FOR A SURPRISE.
IF I'M RIGHT, IT WON'T BE A PLEASANT SIGHT. JUST DON'T SCREAM, OKAY...?
FLIP...
EEEEEEYAAAAAA!

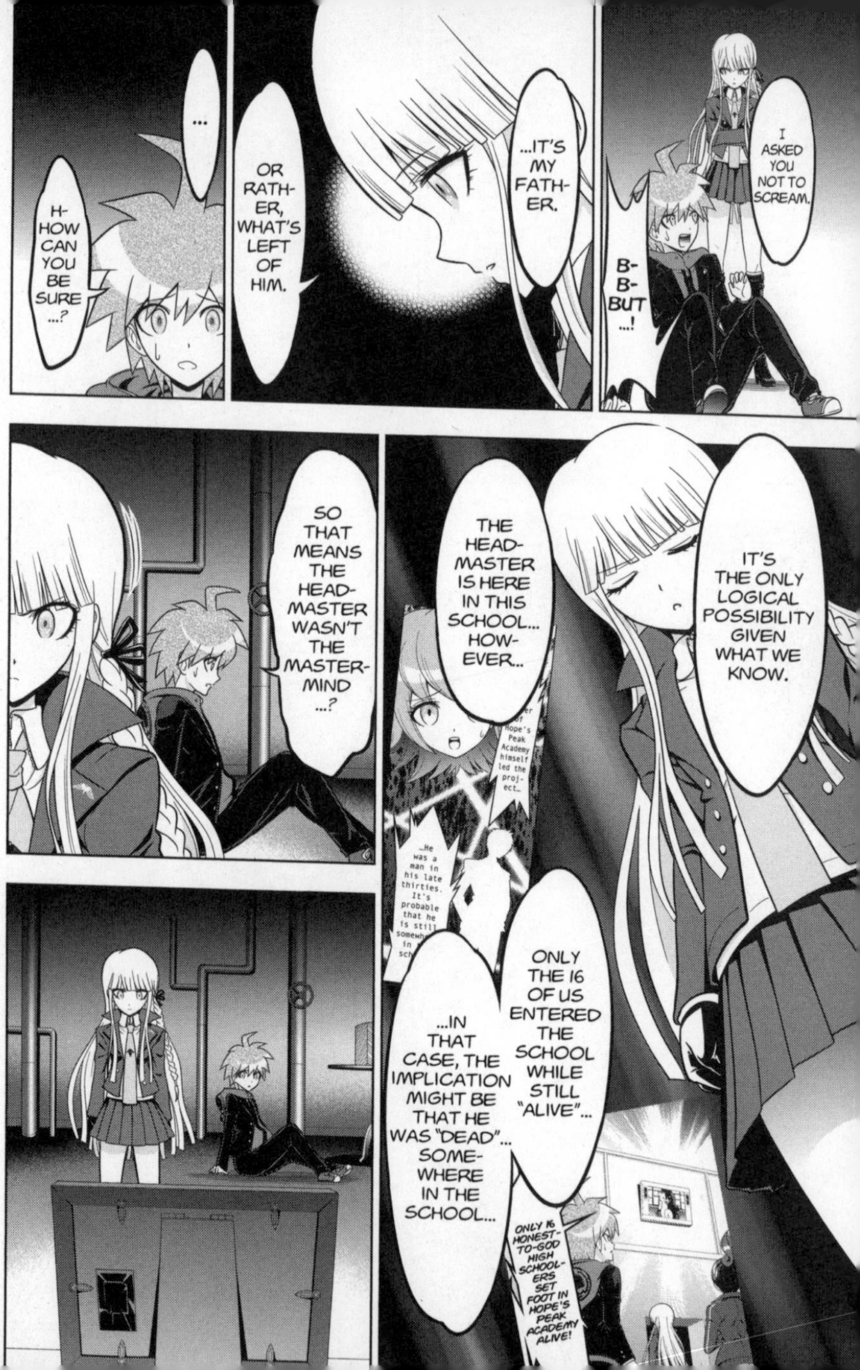
I ASKED YOU NOT TO SCREAM.
B-B-BUT...!
...IT'S MY FATHER.
OR RATHER, WHAT'S LEFT OF HIM.
...
H-HOW CAN YOU BE SURE...?
IT'S THE ONLY LOGICAL POSSIBILITY GIVEN WHAT WE KNOW.
THE HEADMASTER IS HERE IN THIS SCHOOL... HOWEVER...
Hope's Peak Academy himself led the project...
...He was a man in his late thirties. It's probable that he is still
ONLY THE 16 OF US ENTERED THE SCHOOL WHILE STILL "ALIVE"...
...IN THAT CASE, THE IMPLICATION MIGHT BE THAT HE WAS "DEAD"... SOMEWHERE IN THE SCHOOL...
ONLY 16 HONEST-TO-GOD HIGH SCHOOLERS SET FOOT IN HOPE'S PEAK ACADEMY ALIVE!
SO THAT MEANS THE HEADMASTER WASN'T THE MASTERMIND...?

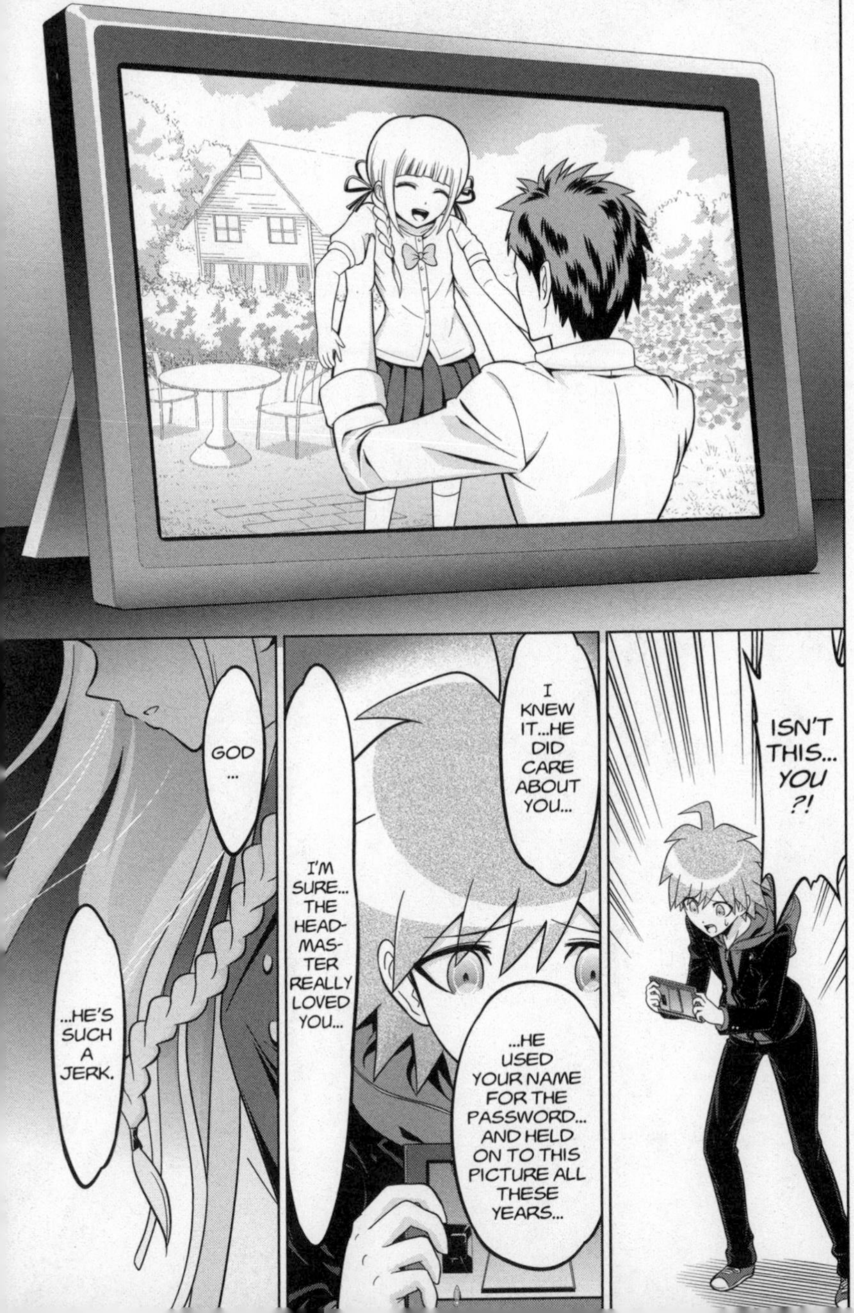
ISN'T THIS... YOU?!
I KNEW IT...HE DID CARE ABOUT YOU...
I'M SURE... THE HEAD-MAS-TER REALLY LOVED YOU...
...HE USED YOUR NAME FOR THE PASSWORD... AND HELD ON TO THIS PICTURE ALL THESE YEARS...
GOD...
...HE'S SUCH A JERK.

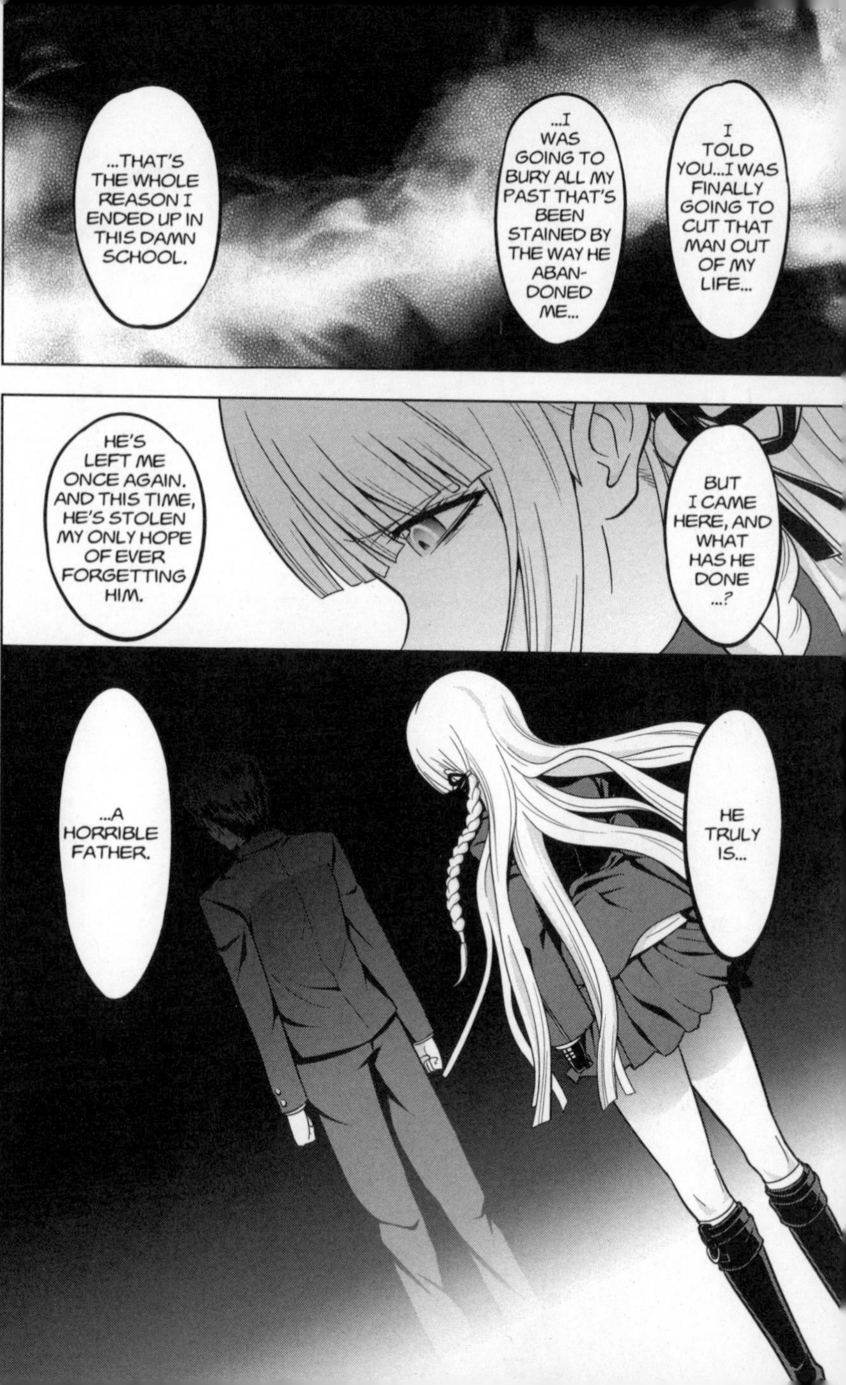
I TOLD YOU...I WAS FINALLY GOING TO CUT THAT MAN OUT OF MY LIFE...
...I WAS GOING TO BURY ALL MY PAST THAT'S BEEN STAINED BY THE WAY HE ABAN-DONED ME...
...THAT'S THE WHOLE REASON I ENDED UP IN THIS DAMN SCHOOL.
BUT I CAME HERE, AND WHAT HAS HE DONE ...?
HE'S LEFT ME ONCE AGAIN. AND THIS TIME, HE'S STOLEN MY ONLY HOPE OF EVER FORGETTING HIM.
HE TRULY IS...
...A HORRIBLE FATHER.

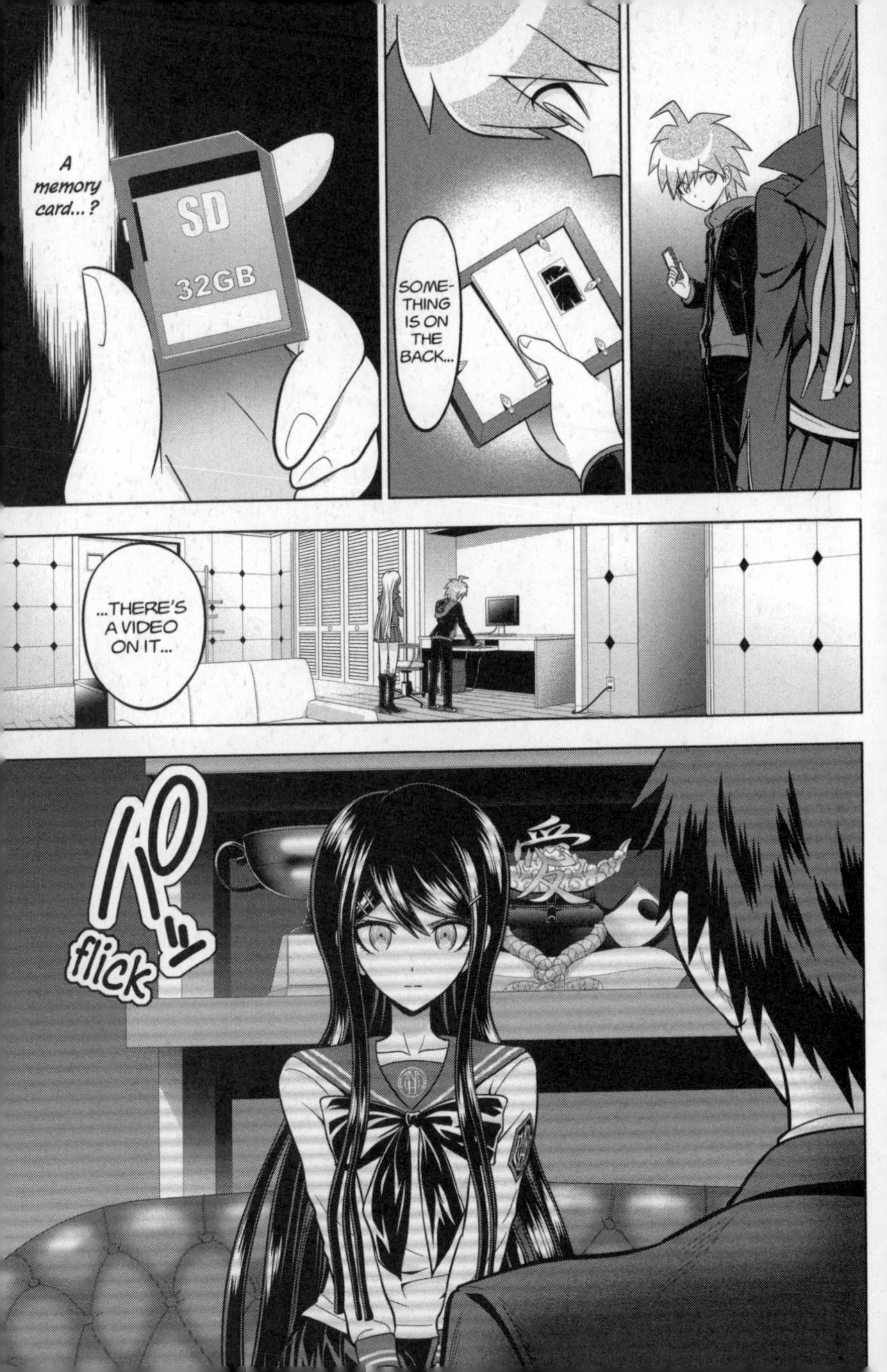
SOME-THING IS ON THE BACK...
A memory card...?
SD
32GB
...THERE'S A VIDEO ON IT...
flick

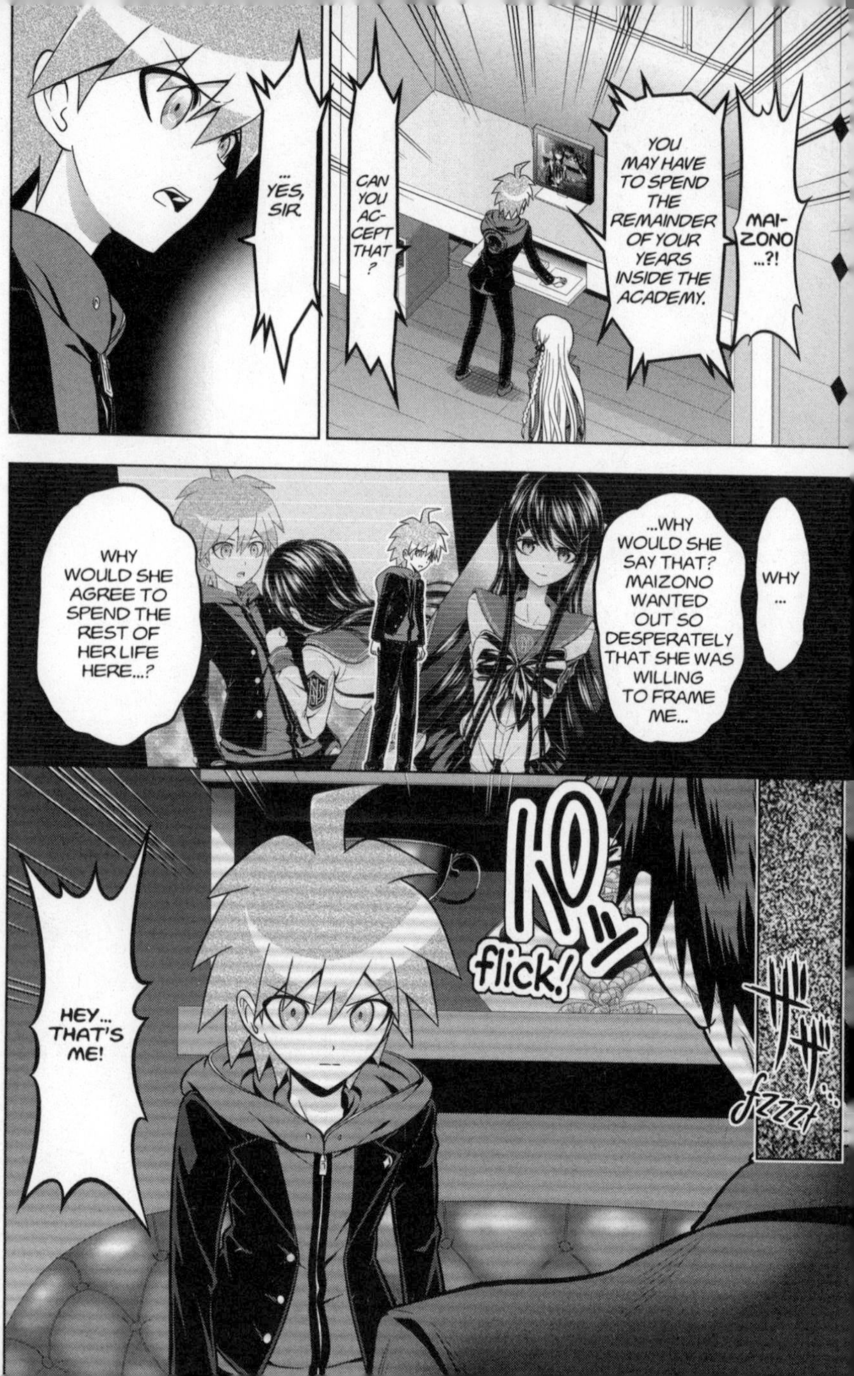
MAI-ZONO ...?!
YOU MAY HAVE TO SPEND THE REMAINDER OF YOUR YEARS INSIDE THE ACADEMY.
CAN YOU AC-CEPT THAT?
... YES, SIR.
WHY ...
...WHY WOULD SHE SAY THAT? MAIZONO WANTED OUT SO DESPERATELY THAT SHE WAS WILLING TO FRAME ME...
WHY WOULD SHE AGREE TO SPEND THE REST OF HER LIFE HERE...?
flick!
fzzzt
HEY... THAT'S ME!

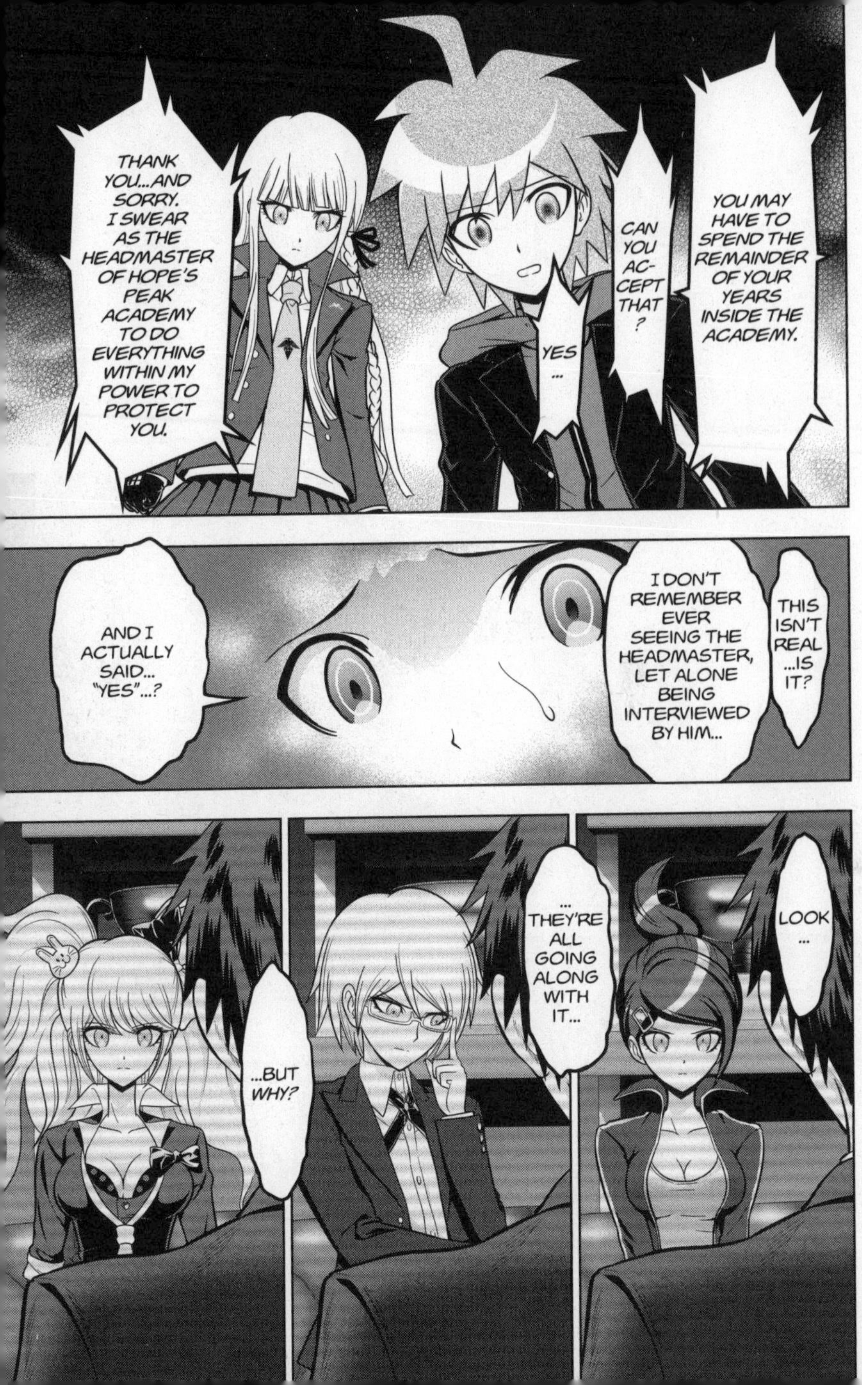
YOU MAY HAVE TO SPEND THE REMAINDER OF YOUR YEARS INSIDE THE ACADEMY.
CAN YOU ACCEPT THAT?
YES...
THANK YOU...AND SORRY. I SWEAR AS THE HEADMASTER OF HOPE'S PEAK ACADEMY TO DO EVERYTHING WITHIN MY POWER TO PROTECT YOU.
THIS ISN'T REAL ...IS IT?
I DON'T REMEMBER EVER SEEING THE HEADMASTER, LET ALONE BEING INTERVIEWED BY HIM...
AND I ACTUALLY SAID... "YES"...?
LOOK...
...THEY'RE ALL GOING ALONG WITH IT...
...BUT WHY?

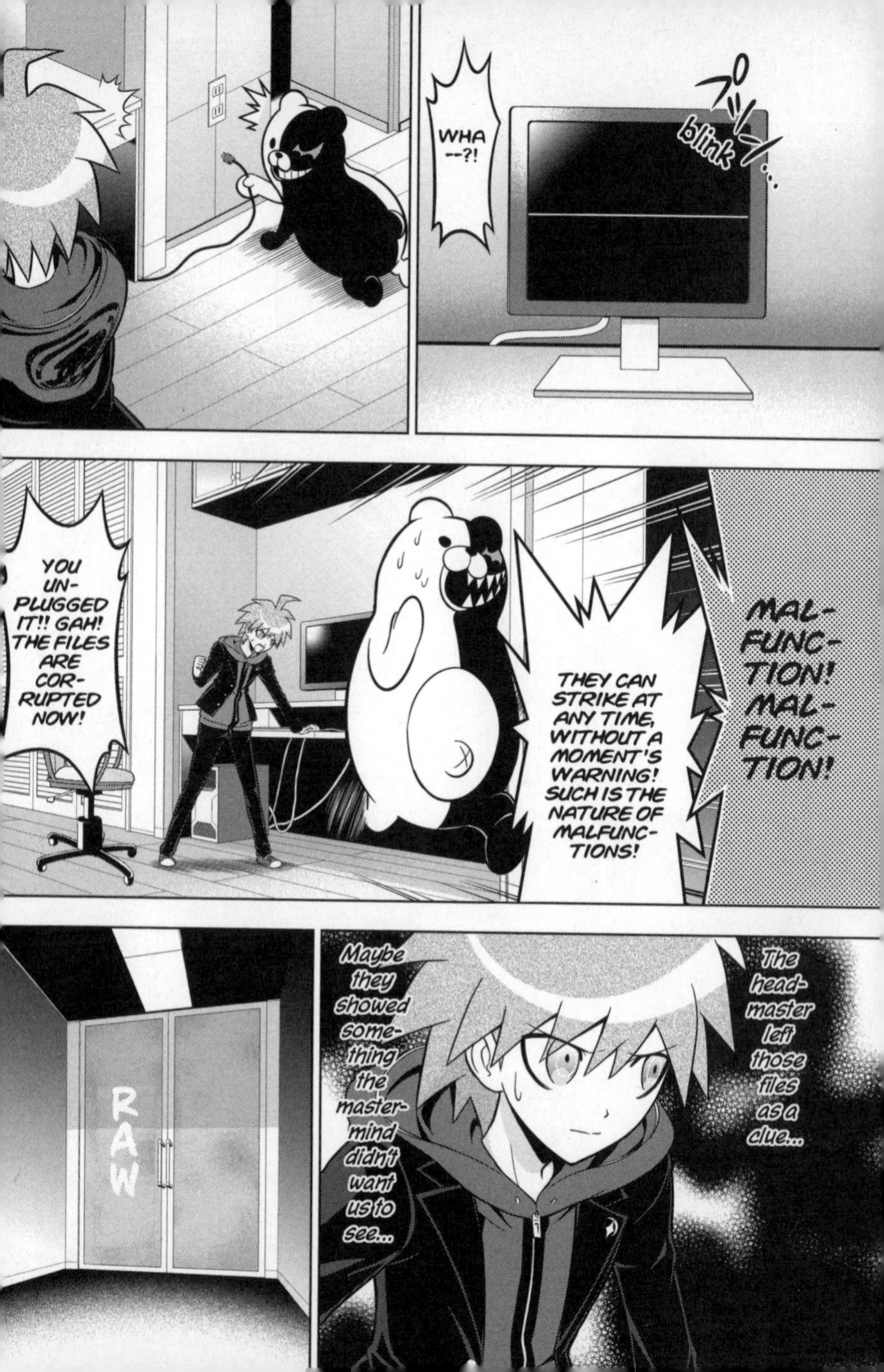
blink
WHA --?!
MAL-FUNCTION! MAL-FUNCTION!
THEY CAN STRIKE AT ANY TIME, WITHOUT A MOMENT'S WARNING! SUCH IS THE NATURE OF MALFUNCTIONS!
YOU UNPLUGGED IT!! GAH! THE FILES ARE CORRUPTED NOW!
The headmaster left those files as a clue...
Maybe they showed something the mastermind didn't want us to see...
RAW

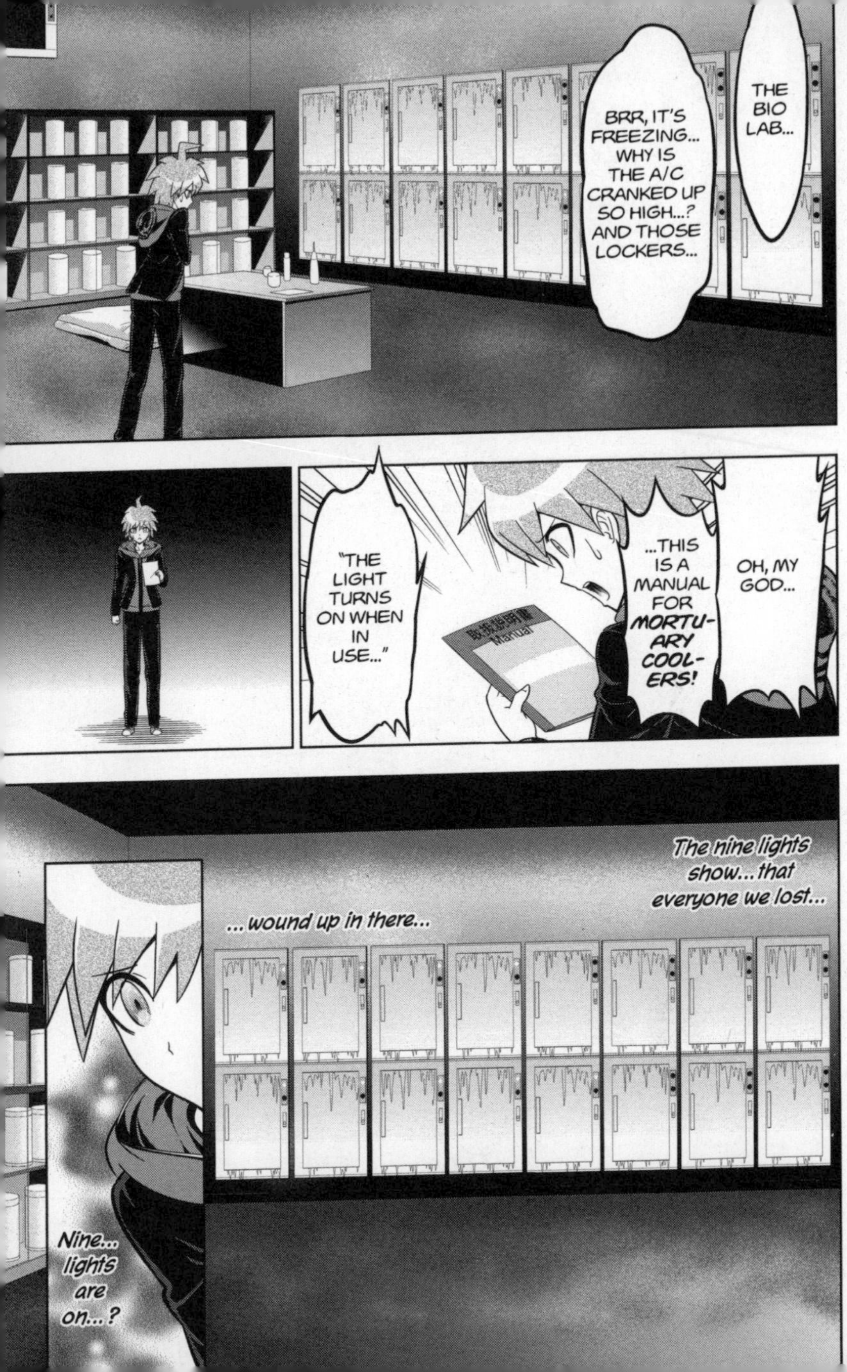
THE BIO LAB...
BRR, IT'S FREEZING... WHY IS THE A/C CRANKED UP SO HIGH...? AND THOSE LOCKERS...
OH, MY GOD...
...THIS IS A MANUAL FOR MORTUARY COOLERS!
"THE LIGHT TURNS ON WHEN IN USE..."
取扱説明書
Manual
The nine lights show... that everyone we lost...
... wound up in there...
Nine... lights are on...?

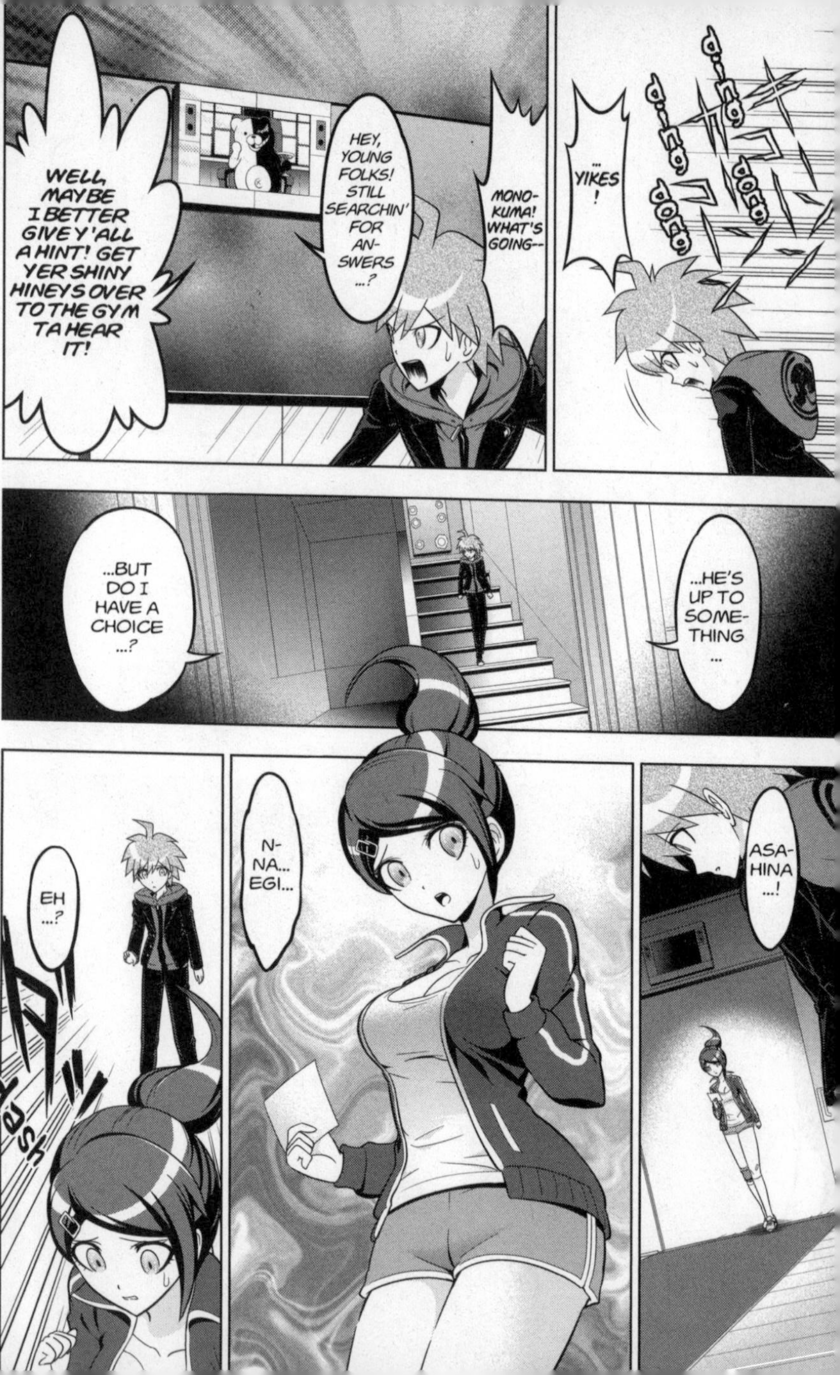
ding dong ding dong
...YIKES!
MONOKUMA! WHAT'S GOING--
HEY, YOUNG FOLKS! STILL SEARCHIN' FOR ANSWERS...?
WELL, MAYBE I BETTER GIVE Y'ALL A HINT! GET YER SHINY HINEYS OVER TO THE GYM TA HEAR IT!
...HE'S UP TO SOMETHING...
...BUT DO I HAVE A CHOICE...?
ASAHINA...!
N-NA...EGI...
EH...?
dash

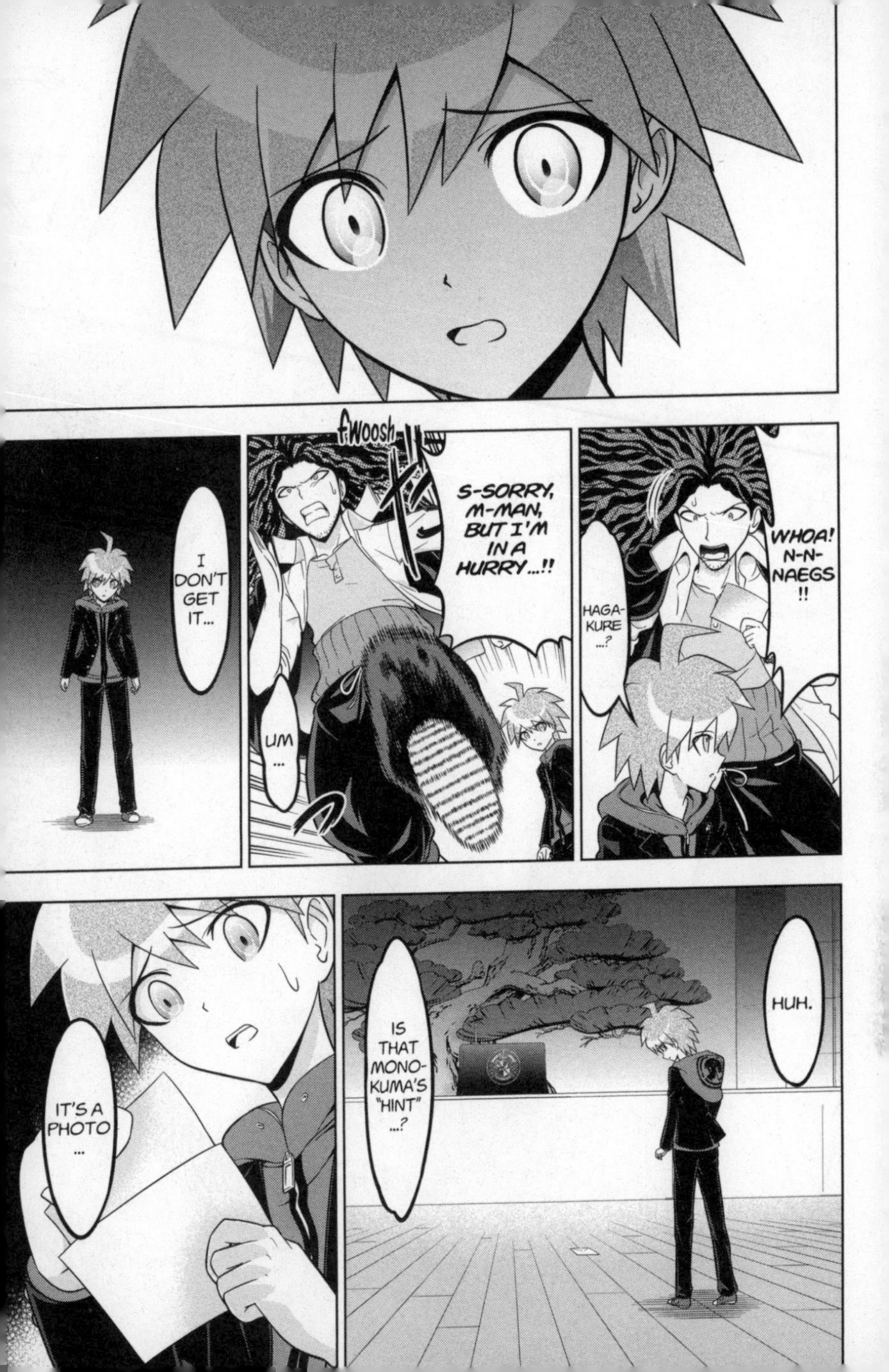
WHOA! N-N-NAEGS!!
HAGA-KURE...?
fwoosh
S-SORRY, M-MAN, BUT I'M IN A HURRY...!!
UM...
I DON'T GET IT...
HUH.
IS THAT MONO-KUMA'S "HINT"...?
IT'S A PHOTO...

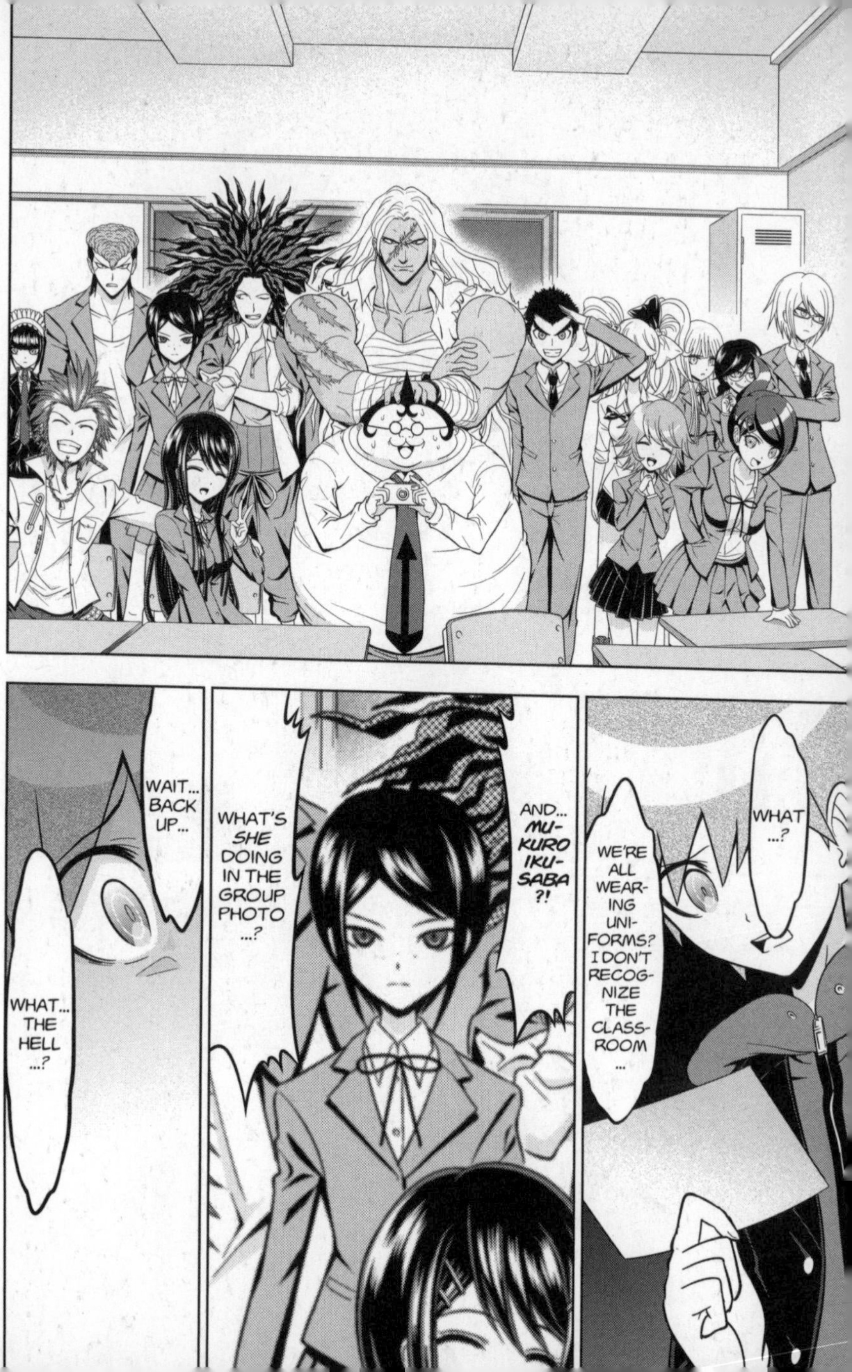
WHAT ...?
WE'RE ALL WEARING UNIFORMS? I DON'T RECOGNIZE THE CLASSROOM ...
AND... MUKURO IKUSABA?!
WHAT'S SHE DOING IN THE GROUP PHOTO ...?
WAIT... BACK UP...
WHAT... THE HELL ...?

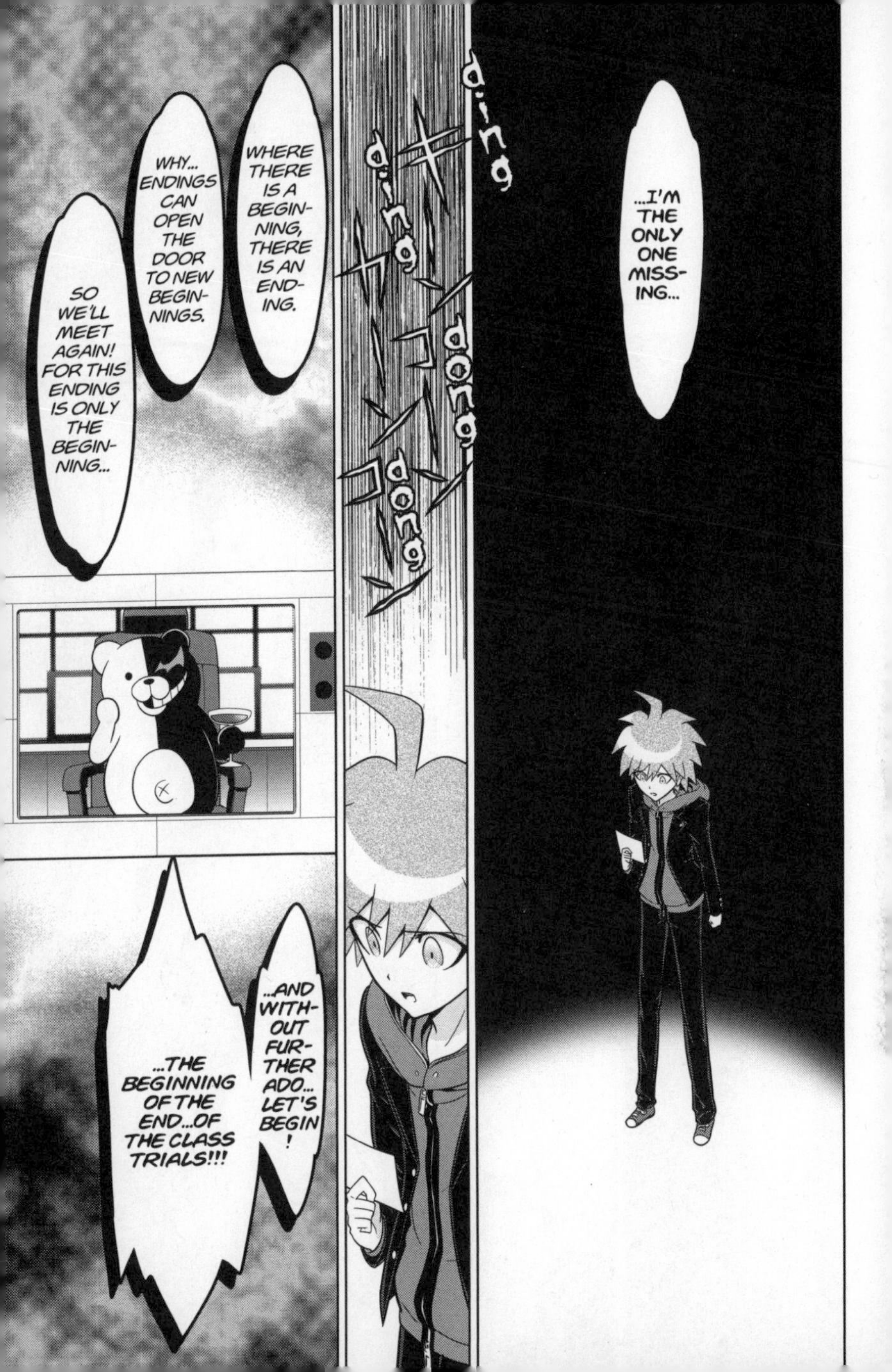
...I'M THE ONLY ONE MISSING...
ding
ding
dong
dong
WHERE THERE IS A BEGINNING, THERE IS AN ENDING.
WHY... ENDINGS CAN OPEN THE DOOR TO NEW BEGINNINGS.
SO WE'LL MEET AGAIN! FOR THIS ENDING IS ONLY THE BEGINNING...
...AND WITHOUT FURTHER ADO... LET'S BEGIN!
...THE BEGINNING OF THE END...OF THE CLASS TRIALS!!!

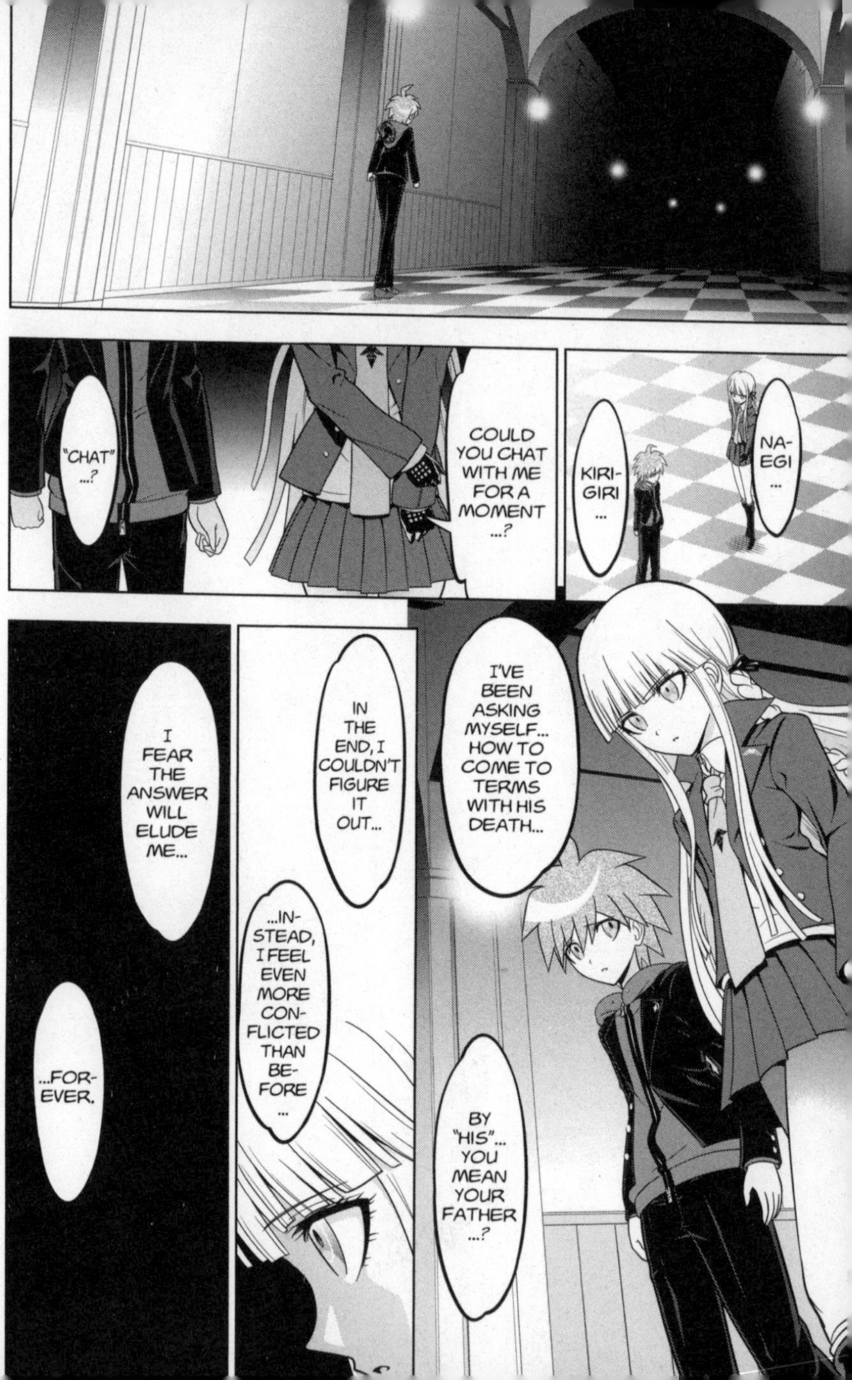
NA-EGI...
KIRI-GIRI...
COULD YOU CHAT WITH ME FOR A MOMENT...?
"CHAT"...?
I'VE BEEN ASKING MYSELF... HOW TO COME TO TERMS WITH HIS DEATH...
BY "HIS"... YOU MEAN YOUR FATHER...?
IN THE END, I COULDN'T FIGURE IT OUT...
...IN-STEAD, I FEEL EVEN MORE CON-FLICTED THAN BE-FORE...
I FEAR THE ANSWER WILL ELUDE ME...
...FOR-EVER.

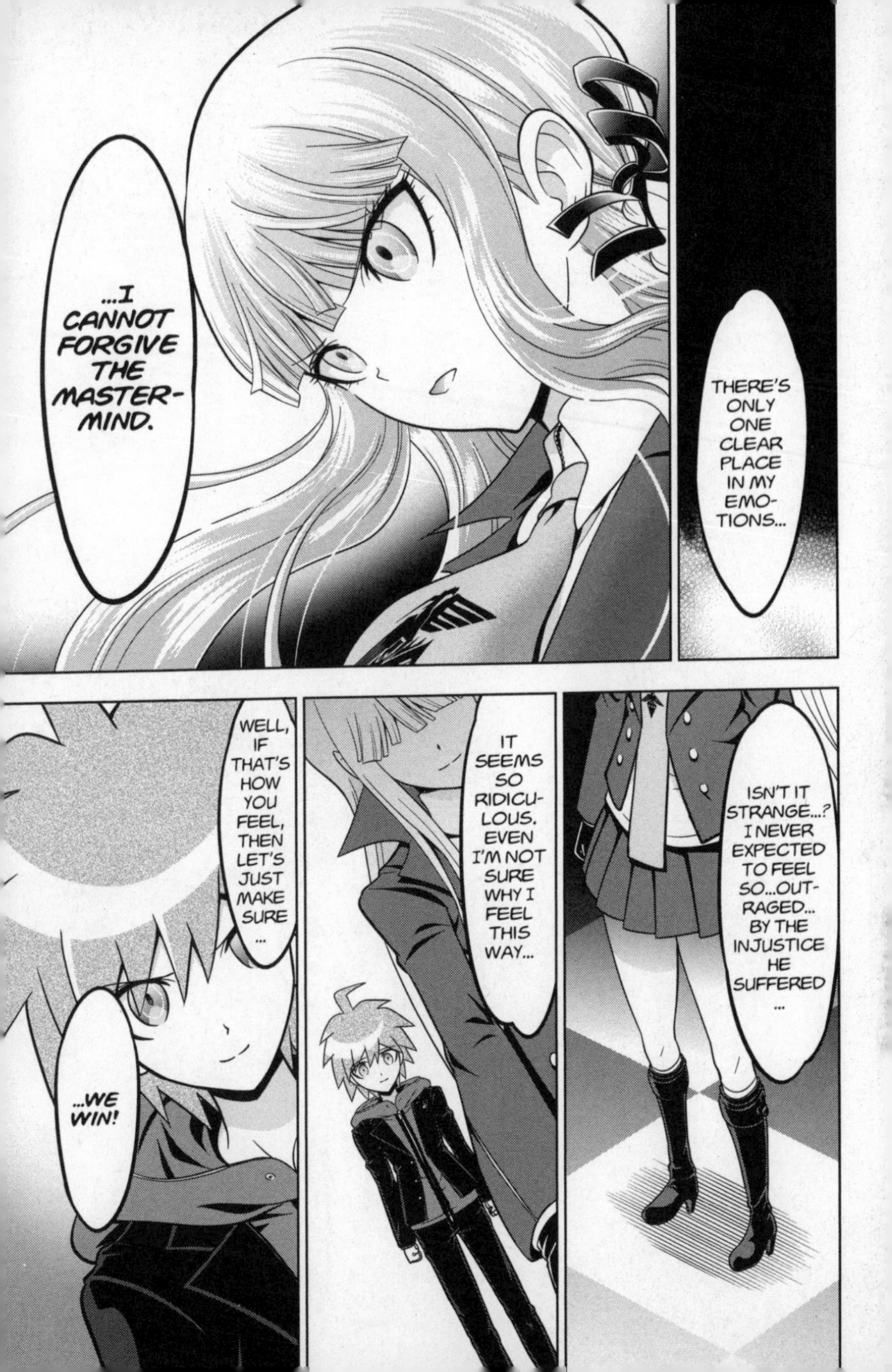
THERE'S ONLY ONE CLEAR PLACE IN MY EMOTIONS...
...I CANNOT FORGIVE THE MASTER-MIND.
ISN'T IT STRANGE...? I NEVER EXPECTED TO FEEL SO...OUT-RAGED... BY THE INJUSTICE HE SUFFERED...
IT SEEMS SO RIDICULOUS. EVEN I'M NOT SURE WHY I FEEL THIS WAY...
WELL, IF THAT'S HOW YOU FEEL, THEN LET'S JUST MAKE SURE...
...WE WIN!

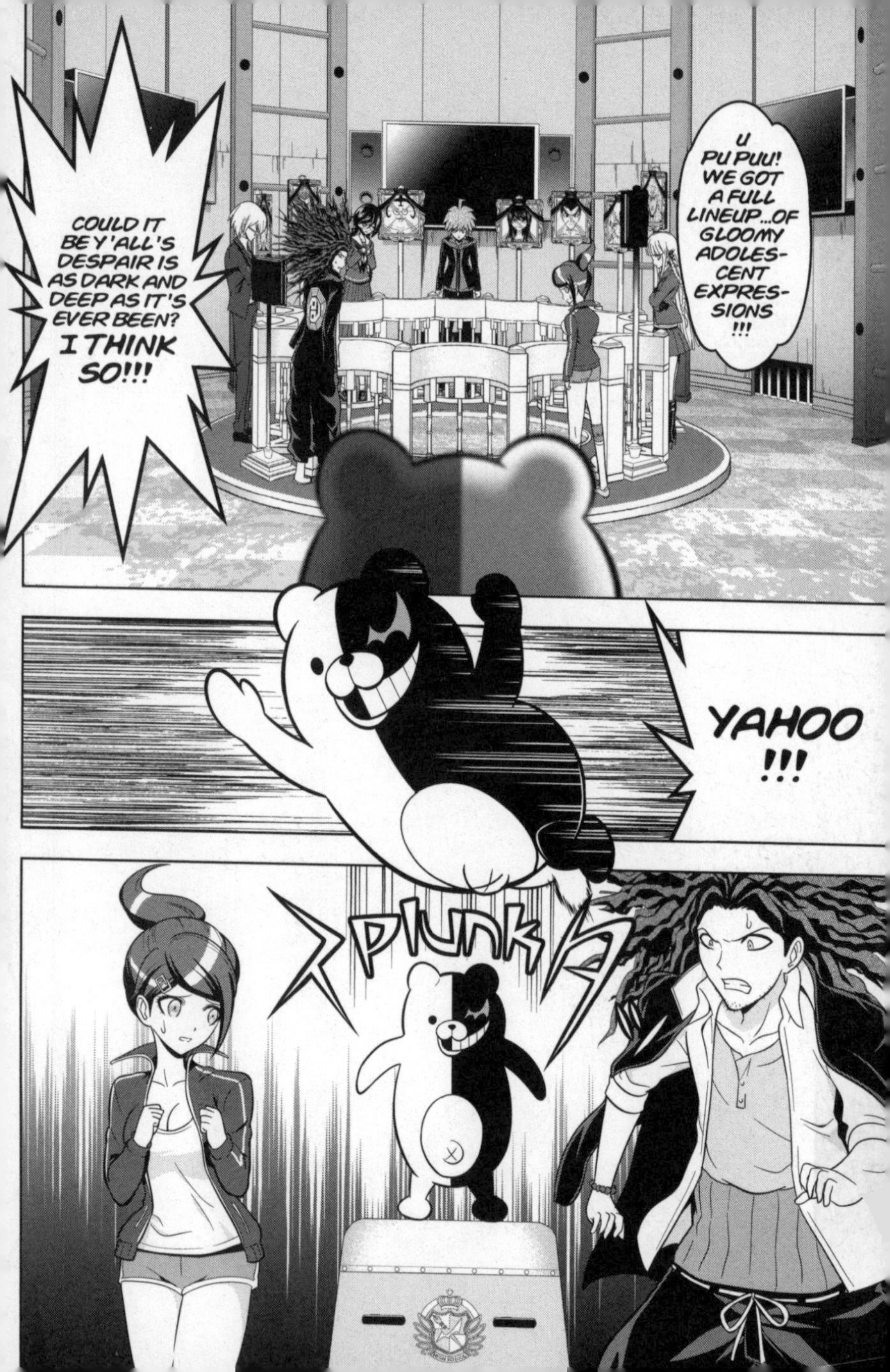
U PUPUU! WE GOT A FULL LINEUP...OF GLOOMY ADOLES-CENT EXPRES-SIONS !!!
COULD IT BE Y'ALL'S DESPAIR IS AS DARK AND DEEP AS IT'S EVER BEEN? I THINK SO!!!
YAHOO !!!
PLUNK

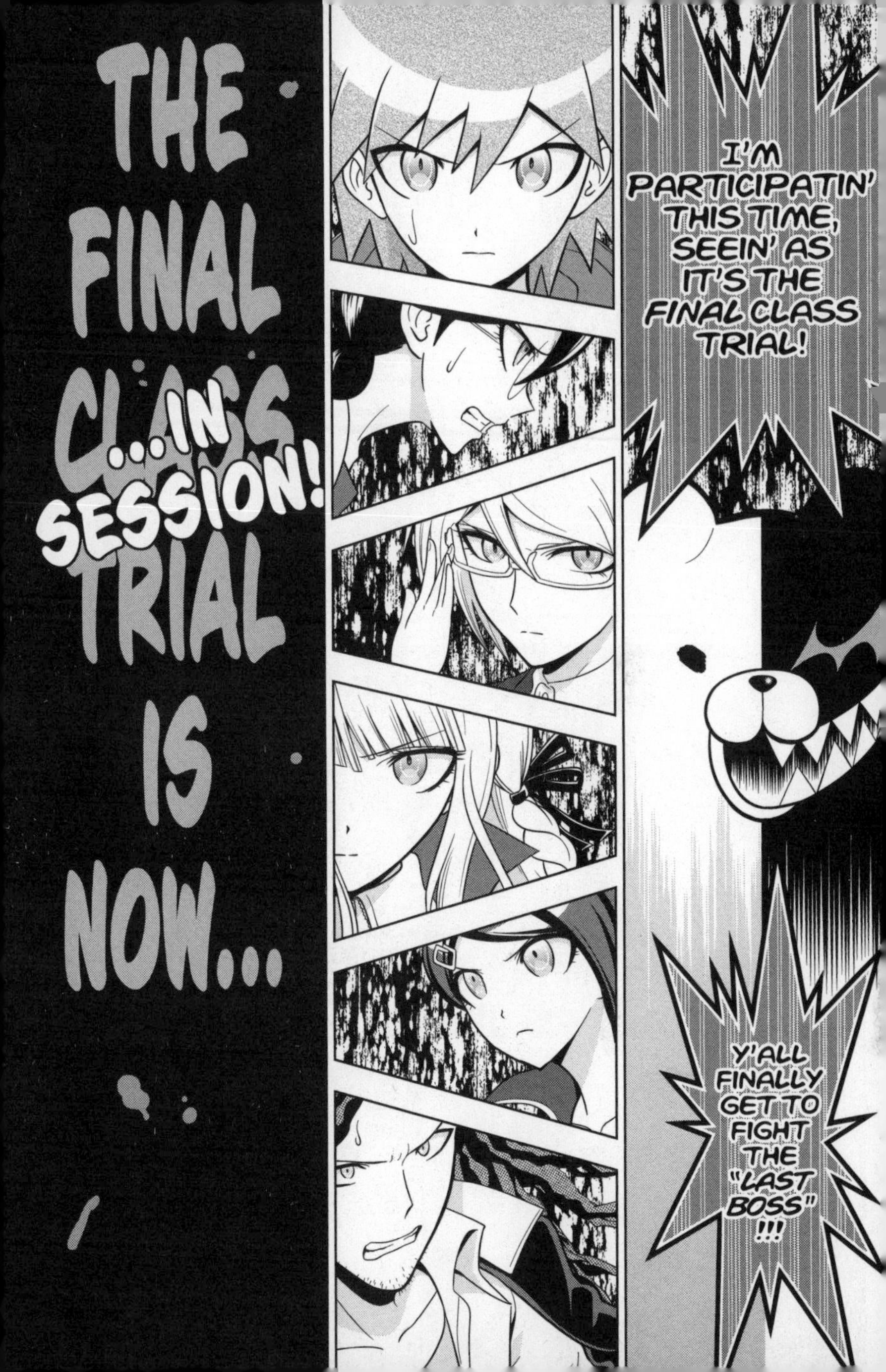
I'M PARTICIPATIN' THIS TIME, SEEIN' AS IT'S THE FINAL CLASS TRIAL!
Y'ALL FINALLY GET TO FIGHT THE "LAST BOSS"!!!
THE FINAL CLASS TRIAL IS NOW...
...IN SESSION!

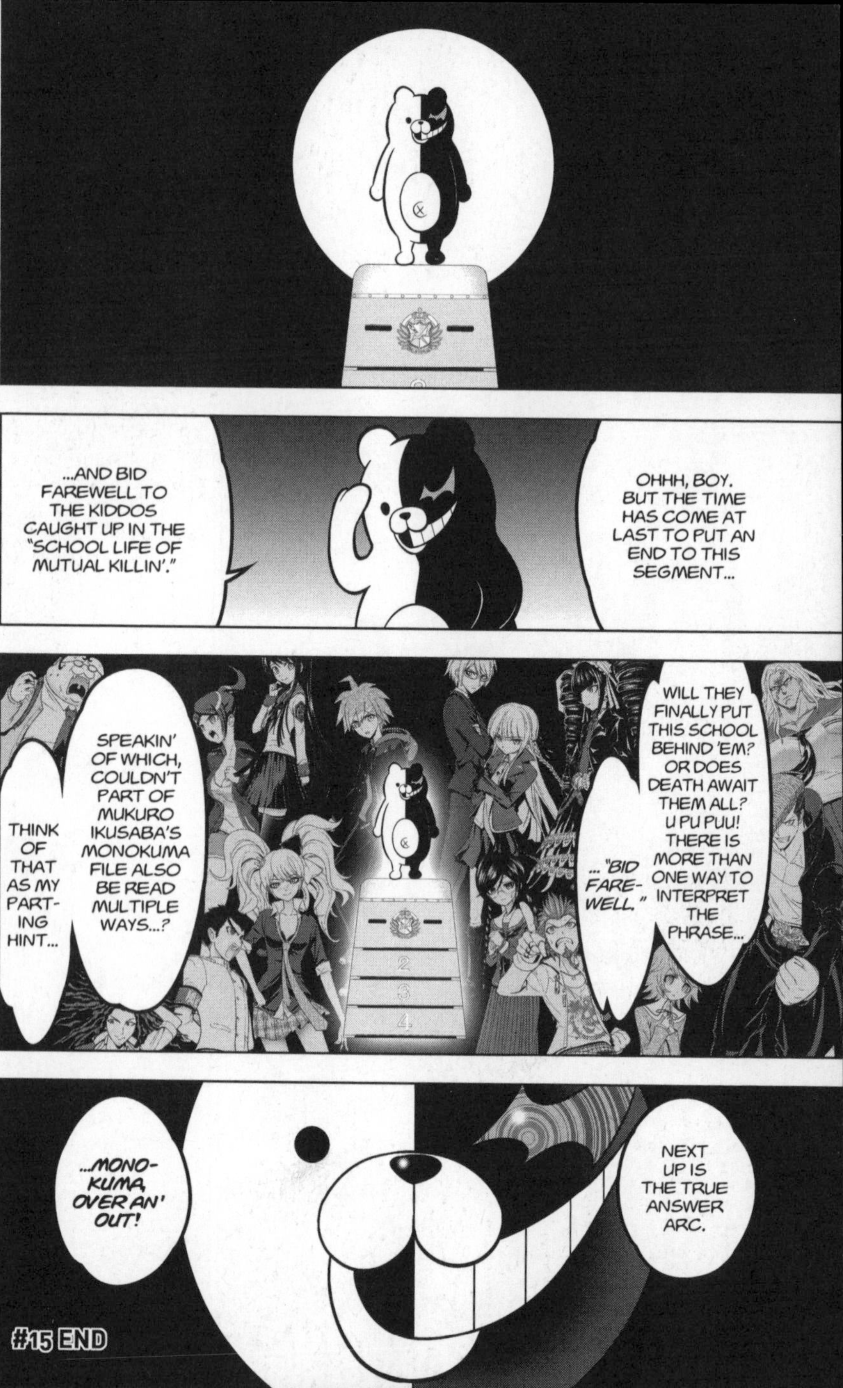
OHHH, BOY. BUT THE TIME HAS COME AT LAST TO PUT AN END TO THIS SEGMENT...
...AND BID FAREWELL TO THE KIDDOS CAUGHT UP IN THE "SCHOOL LIFE OF MUTUAL KILLIN'."
WILL THEY FINALLY PUT THIS SCHOOL BEHIND 'EM? OR DOES DEATH AWAIT THEM ALL? U PU PUU! THERE IS MORE THAN ONE WAY TO INTERPRET THE PHRASE...
... "BID FARE-WELL."
SPEAKIN' OF WHICH, COULDN'T PART OF MUKURO IKUSABA'S MONOKUMA FILE ALSO BE READ MULTIPLE WAYS...?
THINK OF THAT AS MY PART-ING HINT...
NEXT UP IS THE TRUE ANSWER ARC.
...MONO-KUMA, OVER AN' OUT!
#15 END

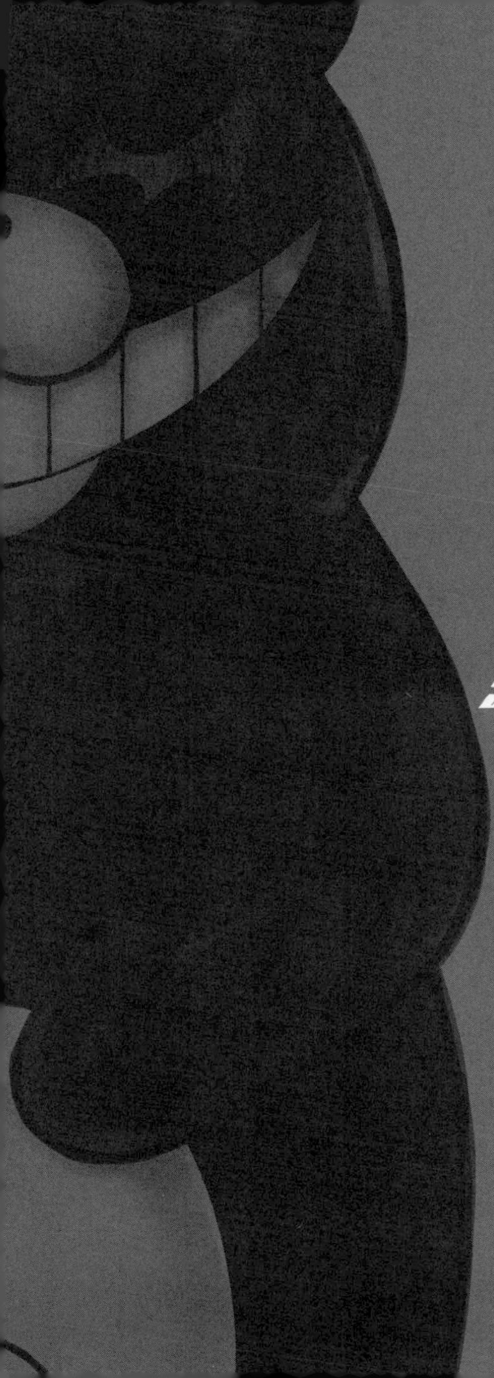

DANGANRONPA

A SCHOOL OF HOPE . . . WITH STUDENTS OF DESPAIR!

THE ANIMATION

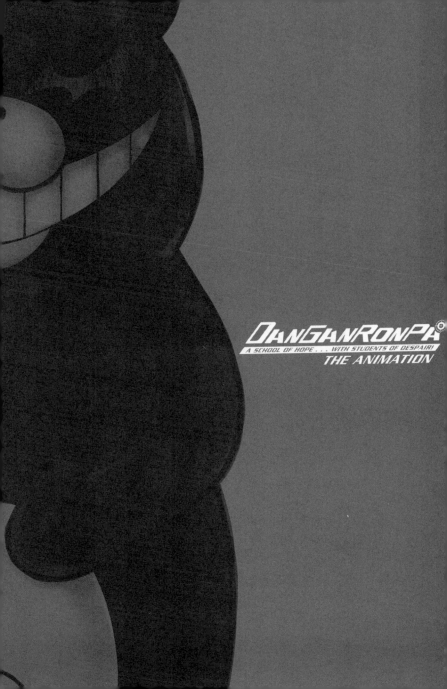

DANGANRONPA
A SCHOOL OF HOPE . . . WITH STUDENTS OF DESPAIR!
THE ANIMATION

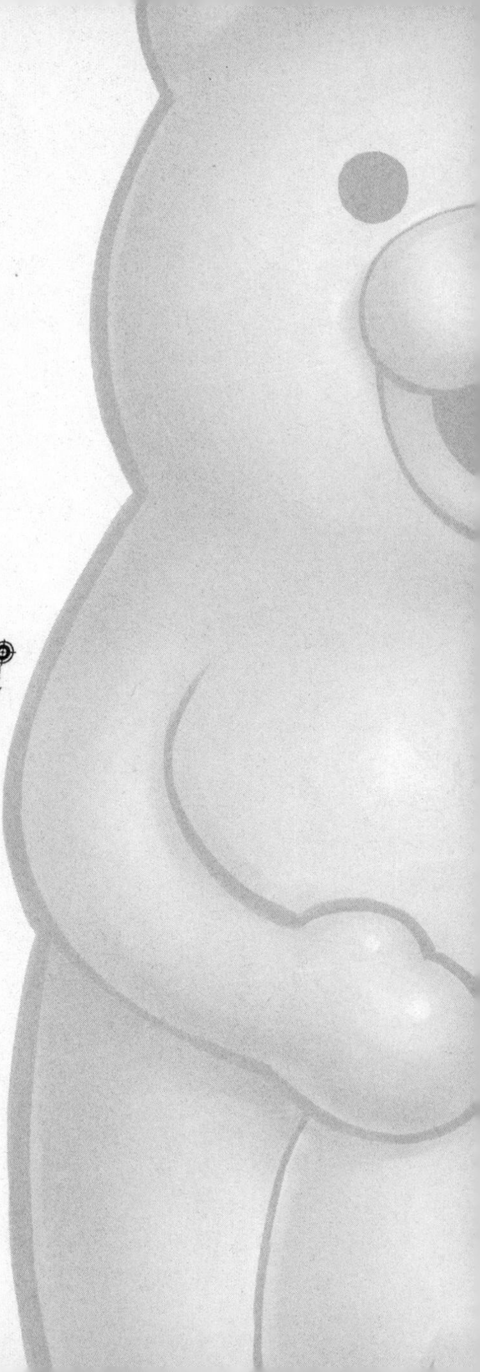

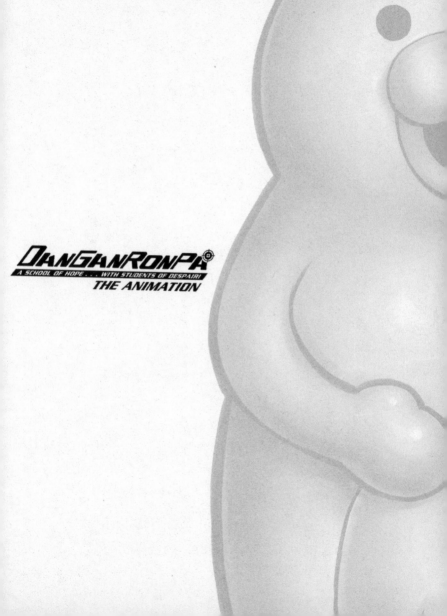

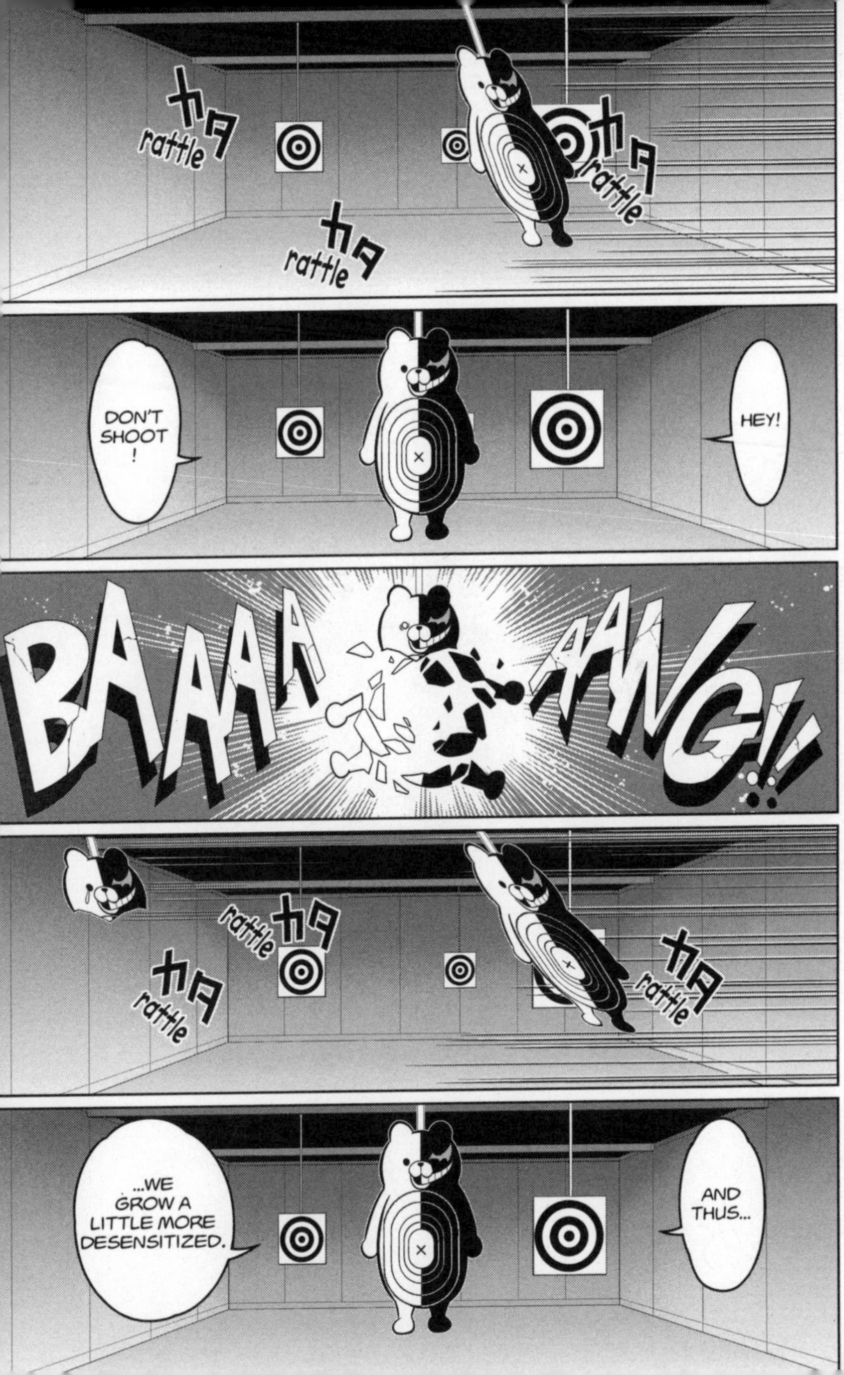
カタ rattle
カタ rattle
カタ rattle
HEY!
DON'T SHOOT!
BAAAA AANG!!
カタ rattle
カタ rattle
カタ rattle
AND THUS...
...WE GROW A LITTLE MORE DESENSITIZED.

#16
[THE REASON ULTIMATE BAD LUCK ATTRACTED THE ULTIMATE KILLER, THE ULTIMATE EXECUTION, AND ULTIMATE DESPAIR II]

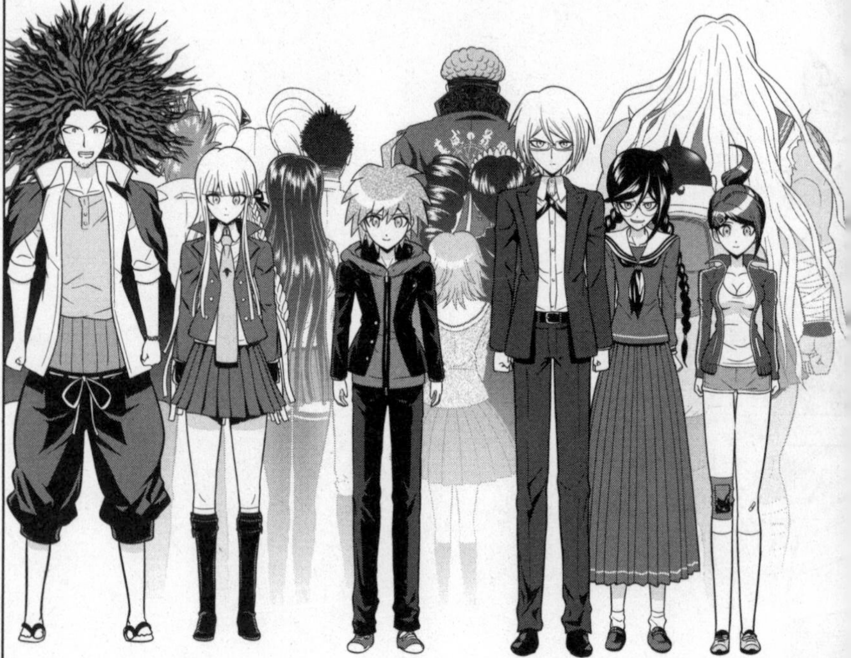

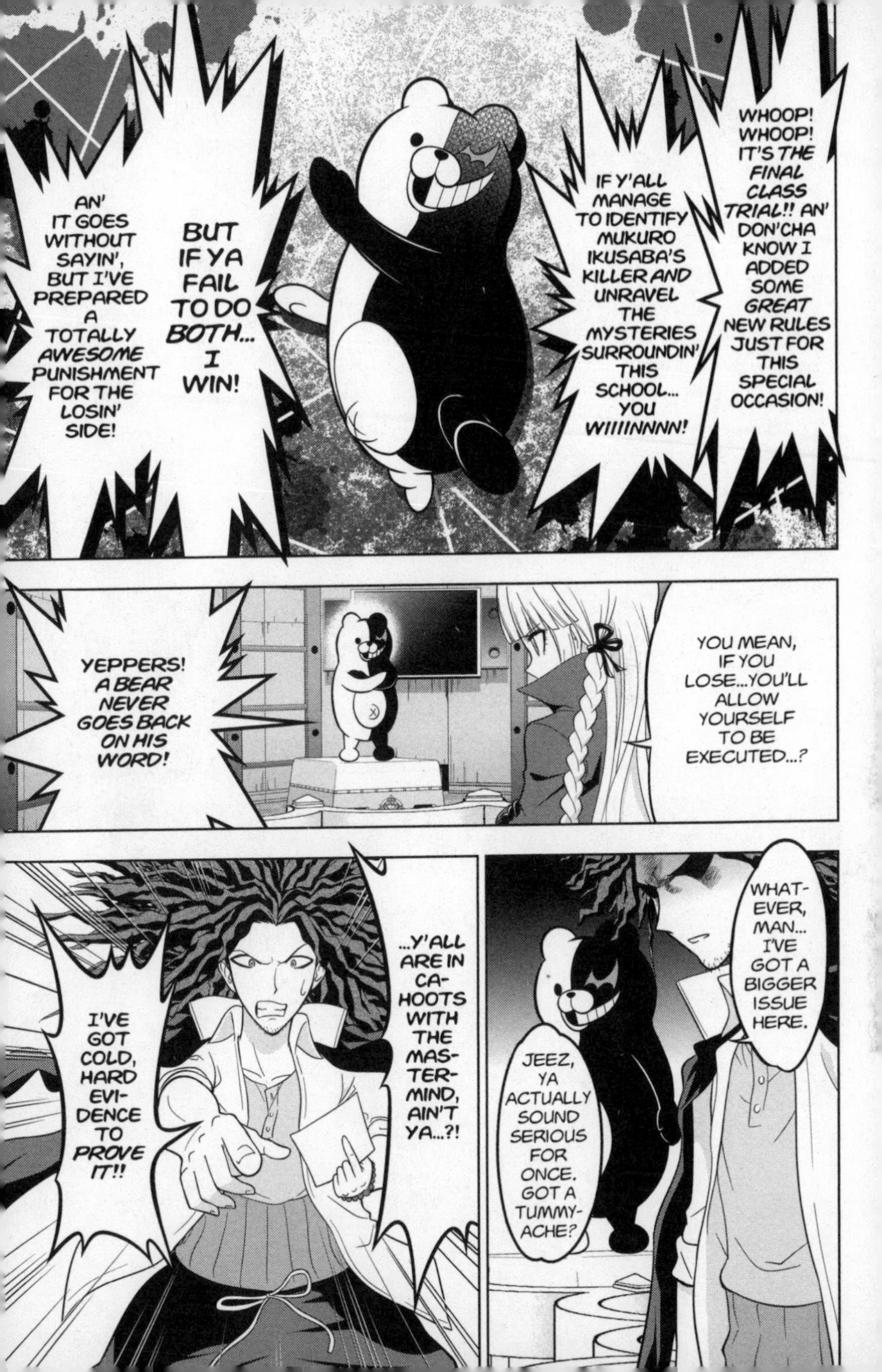
WHOOP! WHOOP! IT'S THE FINAL CLASS TRIAL!! AN' DON'CHA KNOW I ADDED SOME GREAT NEW RULES JUST FOR THIS SPECIAL OCCASION!
IF Y'ALL MANAGE TO IDENTIFY MUKURO IKUSABA'S KILLER AND UNRAVEL THE MYSTERIES SURROUNDIN' THIS SCHOOL... YOU WIIIINNNN!
BUT IF YA FAIL TO DO BOTH... I WIN!
AN' IT GOES WITHOUT SAYIN', BUT I'VE PREPARED A TOTALLY AWESOME PUNISHMENT FOR THE LOSIN' SIDE!
YOU MEAN, IF YOU LOSE...YOU'LL ALLOW YOURSELF TO BE EXECUTED...?
YEPPERS! A BEAR NEVER GOES BACK ON HIS WORD!
WHAT-EVER, MAN... I'VE GOT A BIGGER ISSUE HERE.
JEEZ, YA ACTUALLY SOUND SERIOUS FOR ONCE. GOT A TUMMY-ACHE?
...Y'ALL ARE IN CA-HOOTS WITH THE MAS-TER-MIND, AIN'T YA...?!
I'VE GOT COLD, HARD EVI-DENCE TO PROVE IT!!

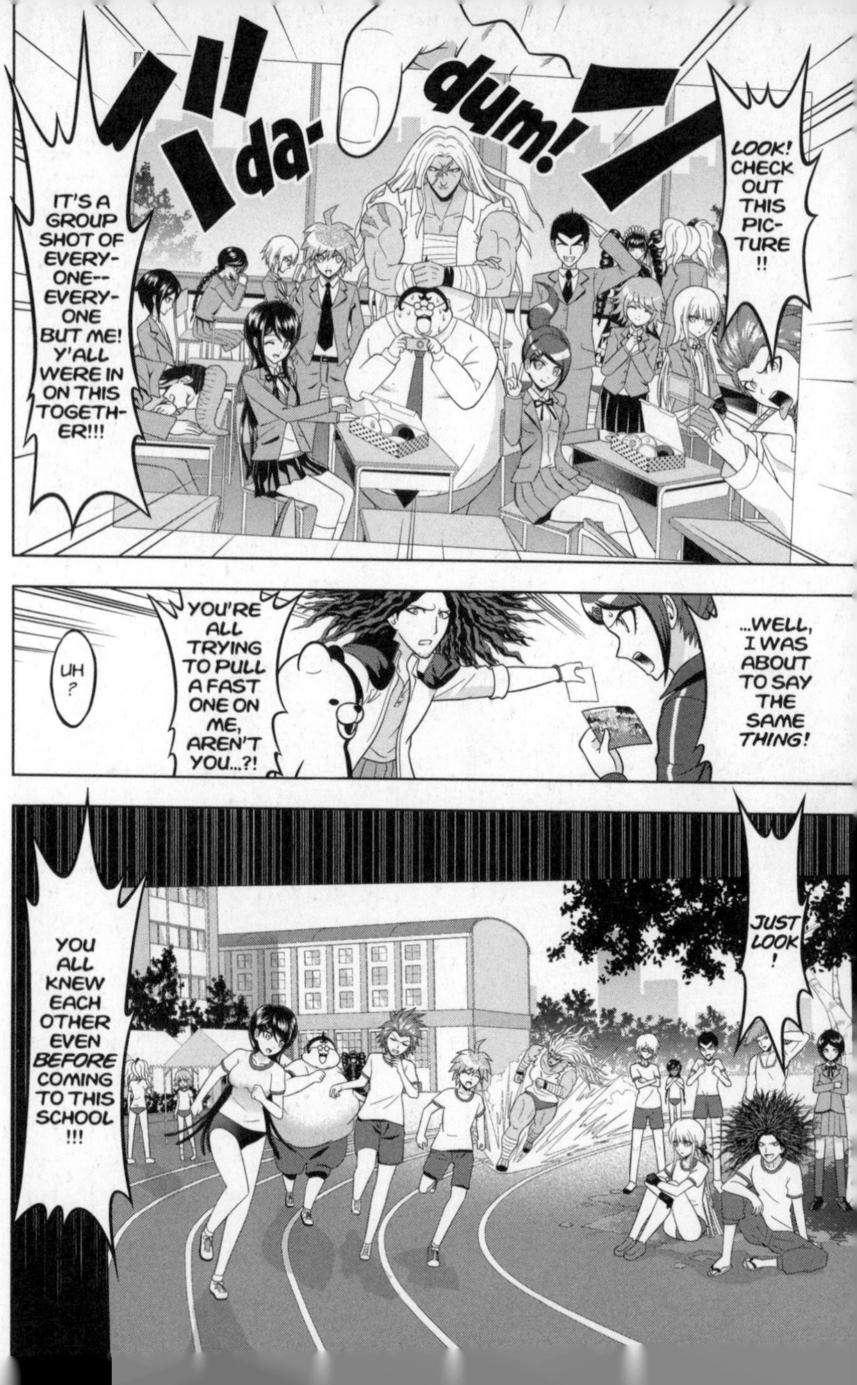
LOOK! CHECK OUT THIS PICTURE!!
da-dum!
IT'S A GROUP SHOT OF EVERYONE--EVERYONE BUT ME! Y'ALL WERE IN ON THIS TOGETHER!!!
...WELL, I WAS ABOUT TO SAY THE SAME THING!
YOU'RE ALL TRYING TO PULL A FAST ONE ON ME, AREN'T YOU...?!
UH?
JUST LOOK!
YOU ALL KNEW EACH OTHER EVEN BEFORE COMING TO THIS SCHOOL!!!

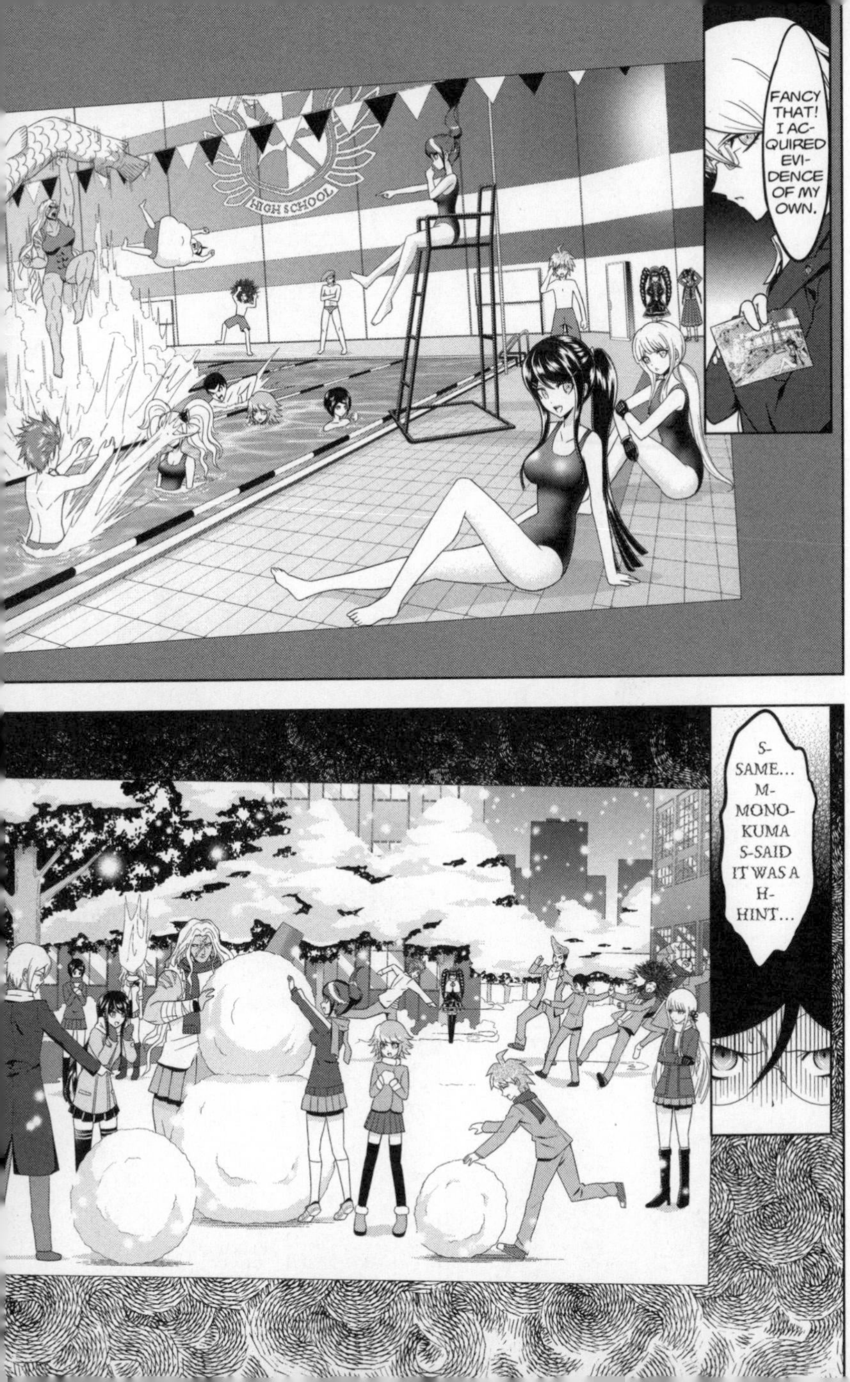
FANCY THAT! I AC-QUIRED EVI-DENCE OF MY OWN.
HIGH SCHOOL
S-SAME... M-MONO-KUMA S-SAID IT WAS A H-HINT...

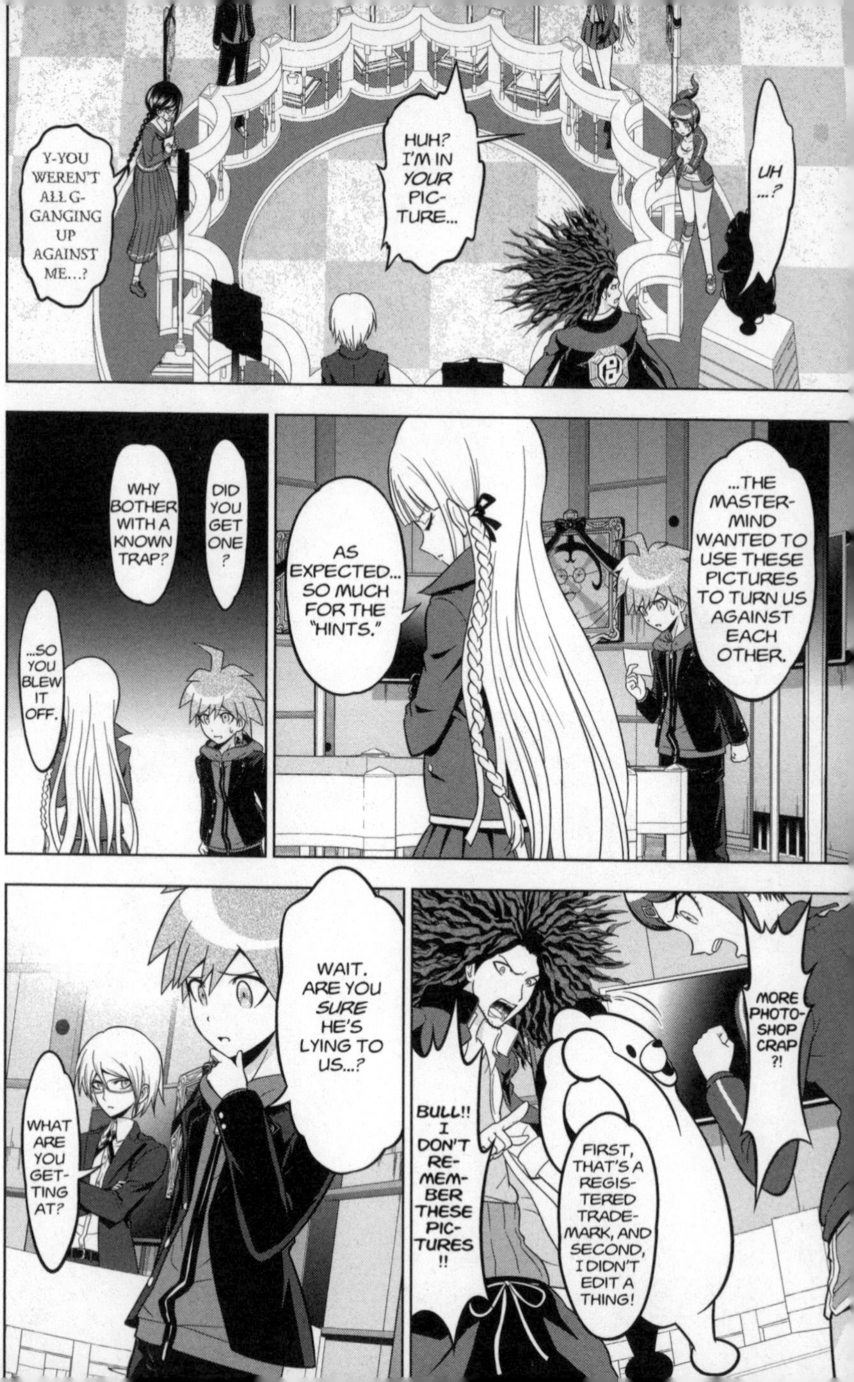
UH ...?
HUH? I'M IN *YOUR* PICTURE...
Y-YOU WEREN'T ALL G-GANGING UP AGAINST ME...?
...THE MASTERMIND WANTED TO USE THESE PICTURES TO TURN US AGAINST EACH OTHER.
AS EXPECTED... SO MUCH FOR THE "HINTS."
DID YOU GET ONE?
WHY BOTHER WITH A KNOWN TRAP?
...SO YOU BLEW IT OFF.
MORE PHOTOSHOP CRAP?!
FIRST, THAT'S A REGISTERED TRADEMARK, AND SECOND, I DIDN'T EDIT A THING!
BULL!! I DON'T REMEMBER THESE PICTURES!!
WAIT. ARE YOU *SURE* HE'S LYING TO US...?
WHAT ARE YOU GETTING AT?

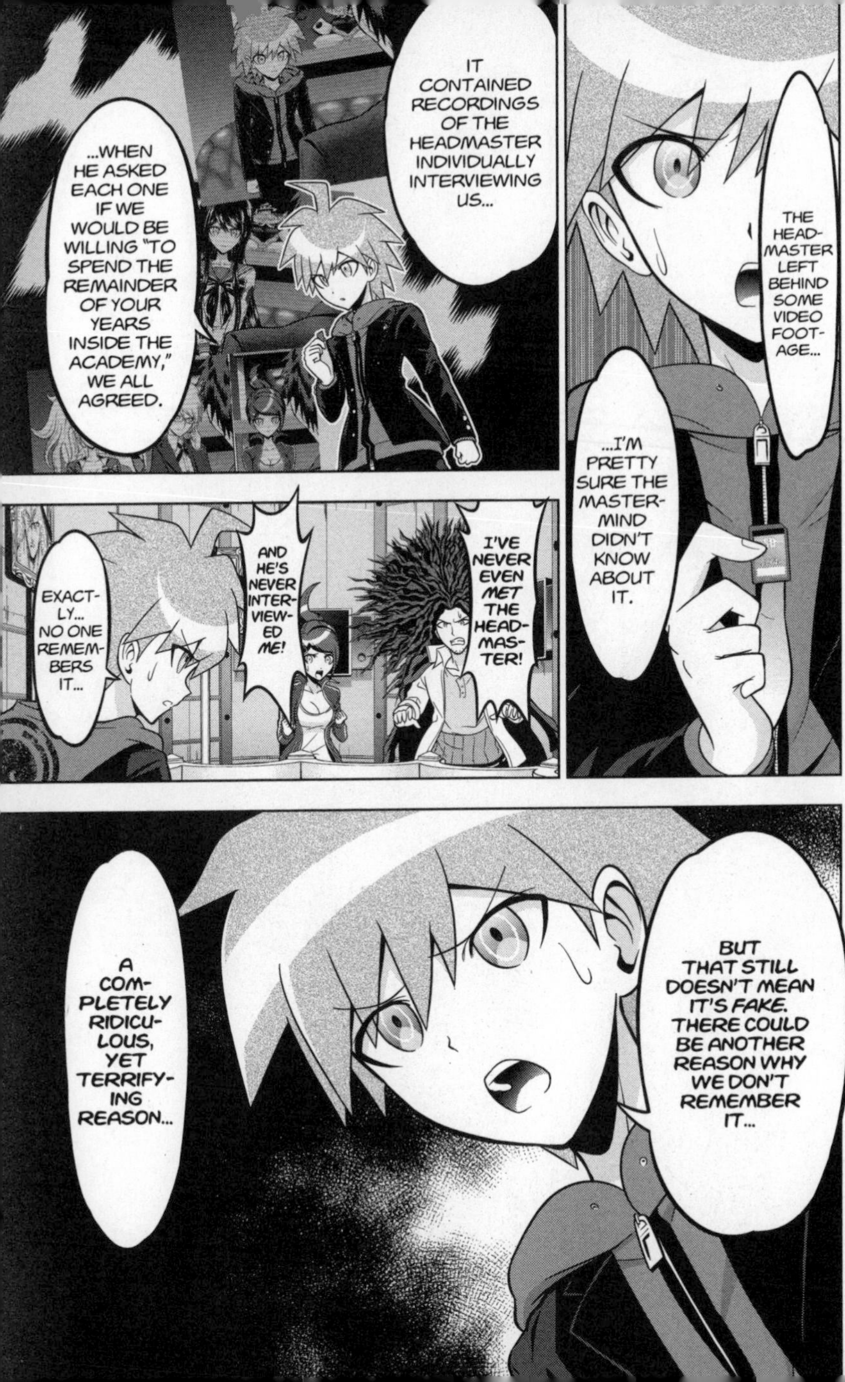
THE HEADMASTER LEFT BEHIND SOME VIDEO FOOTAGE...
...I'M PRETTY SURE THE MASTERMIND DIDN'T KNOW ABOUT IT.
IT CONTAINED RECORDINGS OF THE HEADMASTER INDIVIDUALLY INTERVIEWING US...
...WHEN HE ASKED EACH ONE IF WE WOULD BE WILLING "TO SPEND THE REMAINDER OF YOUR YEARS INSIDE THE ACADEMY," WE ALL AGREED.
I'VE NEVER EVEN *MET* THE HEADMASTER!
AND HE'S NEVER INTERVIEWED *ME*!
EXACTLY... NO ONE REMEMBERS IT...
BUT THAT STILL DOESN'T MEAN IT'S *FAKE*. THERE COULD BE ANOTHER REASON WHY WE DON'T REMEMBER IT...
A COMPLETELY RIDICULOUS, YET TERRIFYING REASON...

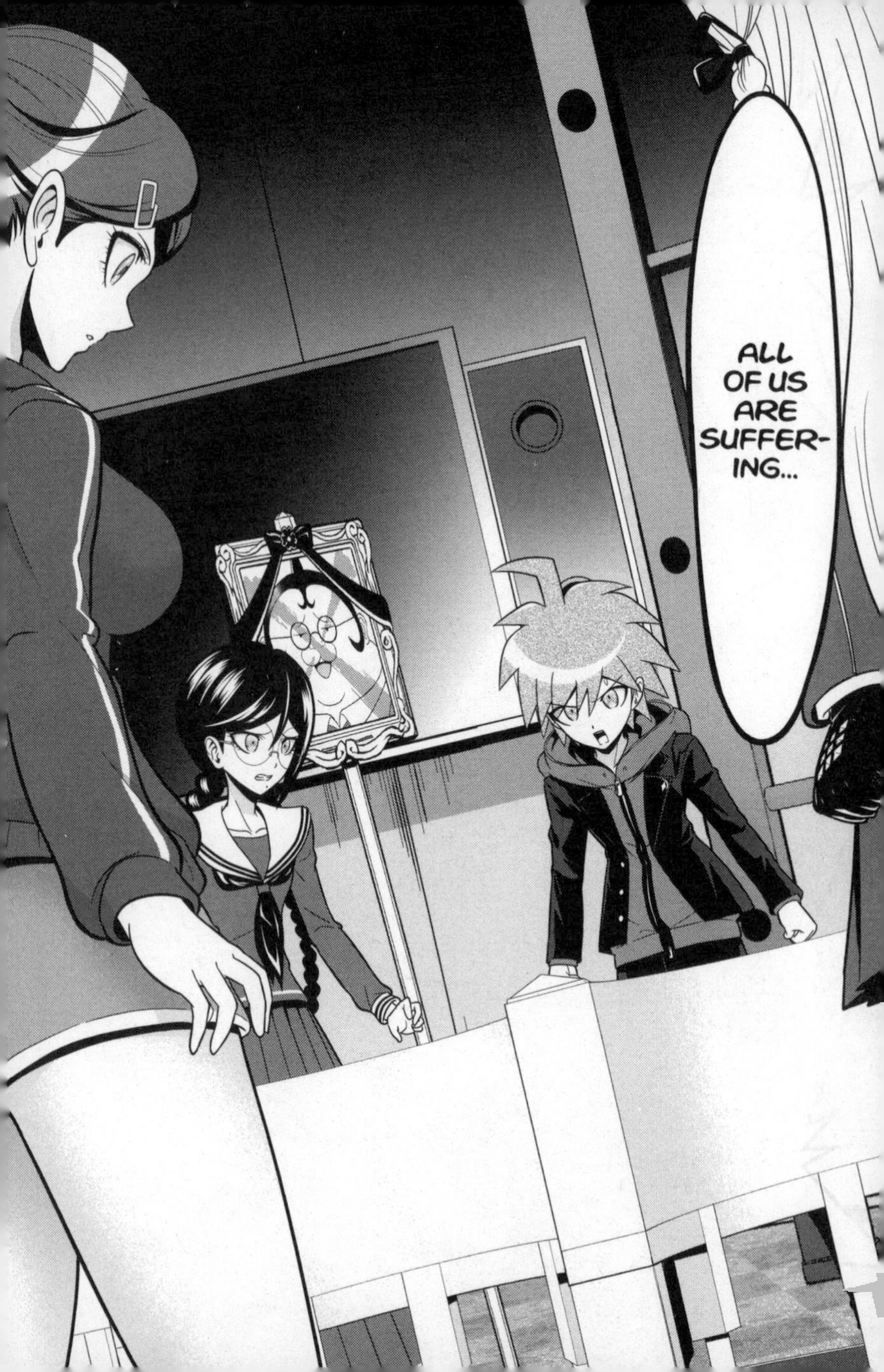
ALL OF US ARE SUFFER-ING...

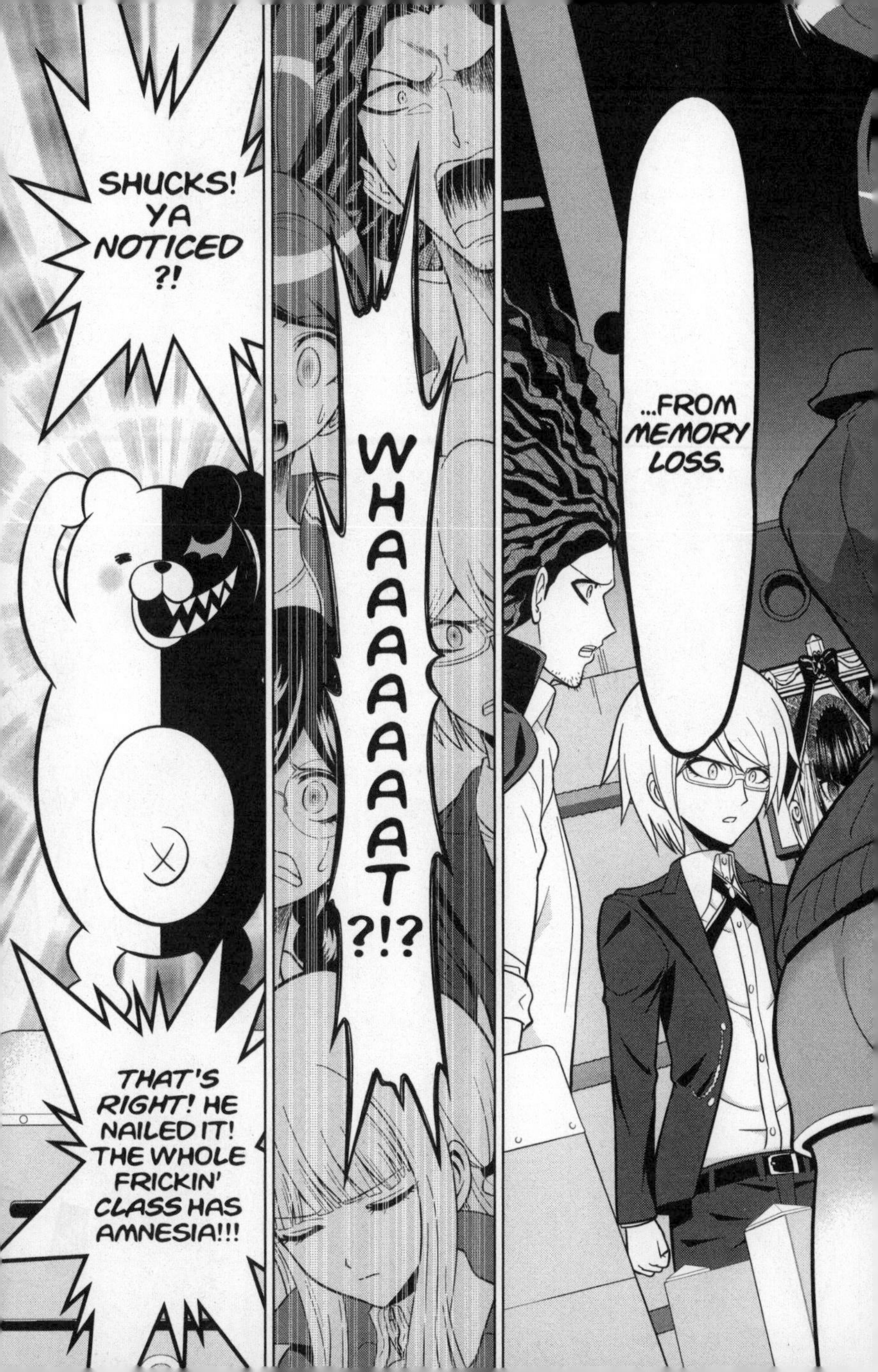
...FROM MEMORY LOSS.
WHAAAAAAAT?!?
SHUCKS! YA NOTICED?!
THAT'S RIGHT! HE NAILED IT! THE WHOLE FRICKIN' CLASS HAS AMNESIA!!!

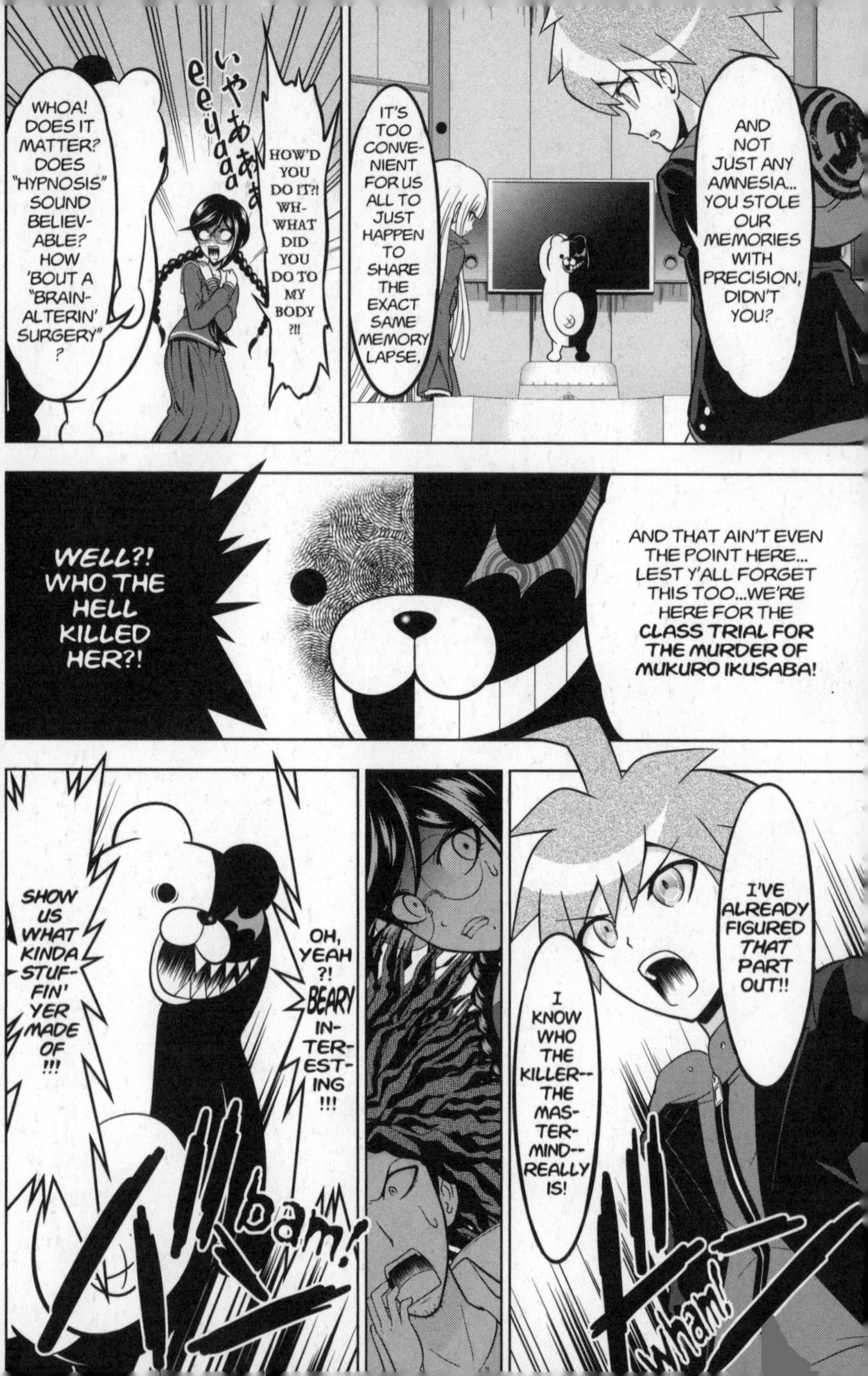
AND NOT JUST ANY AMNESIA... YOU STOLE OUR MEMORIES WITH PRECISION, DIDN'T YOU?
IT'S TOO CONVENIENT FOR US ALL TO JUST HAPPEN TO SHARE THE EXACT SAME MEMORY LAPSE.
いやあああ
eeyaaa
HOW'D YOU DO IT?! WH-WHAT DID YOU DO TO MY BODY?!!
WHOA! DOES IT MATTER? DOES "HYPNOSIS" SOUND BELIEVABLE? HOW 'BOUT A "BRAIN-ALTERIN' SURGERY"?
AND THAT AIN'T EVEN THE POINT HERE... LEST Y'ALL FORGET THIS TOO...WE'RE HERE FOR THE **CLASS TRIAL FOR THE MURDER OF MUKURO IKUSABA!**
WELL?! WHO THE HELL KILLED HER?!
I'VE ALREADY FIGURED THAT PART OUT!!
I KNOW WHO THE KILLER--THE MASTERMIND--REALLY IS!
Wham!
OH, YEAH?! BEARY INTERESTING!!!
SHOW US WHAT KINDA STUFFIN' YER MADE OF!!!
bam!

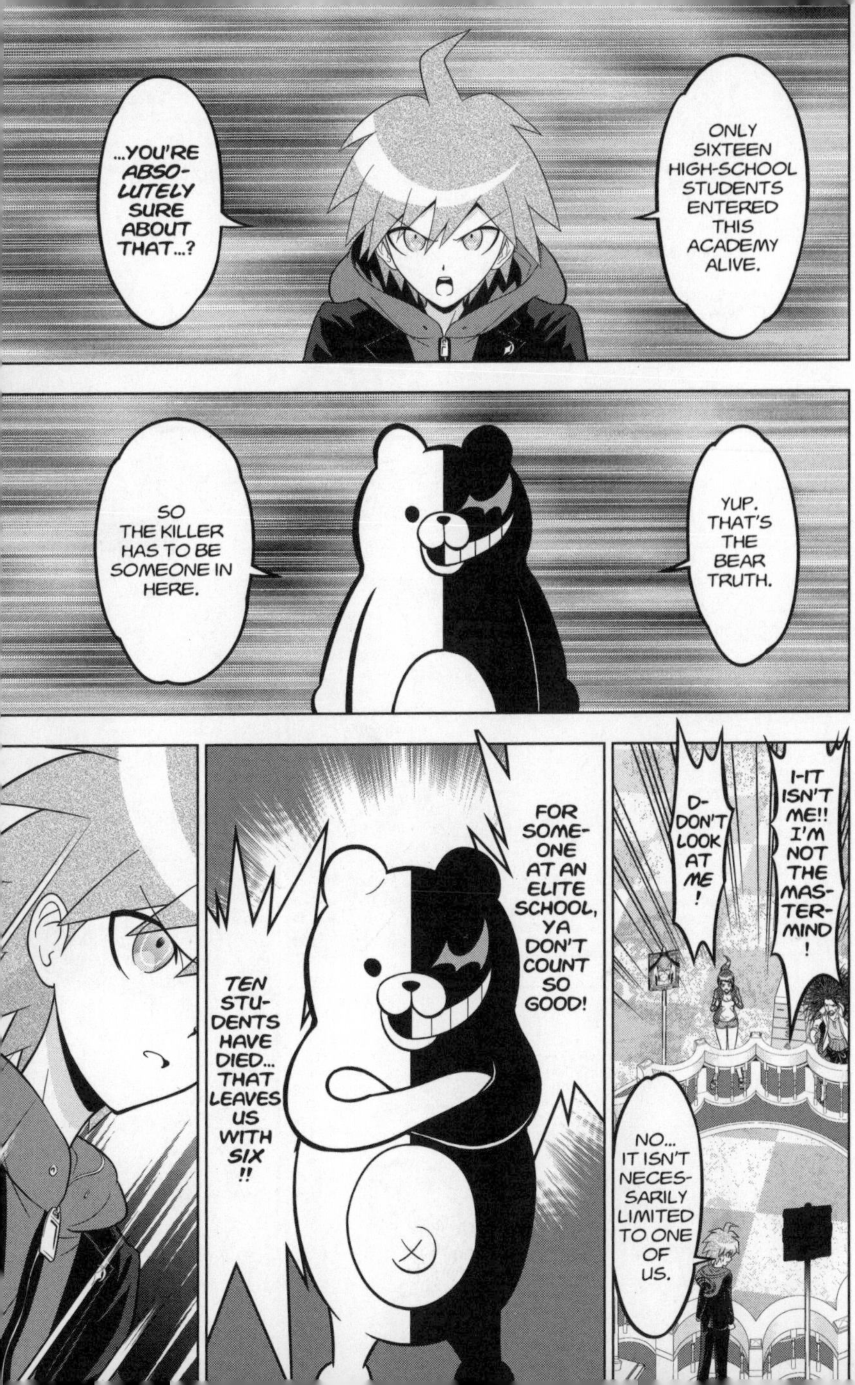
ONLY SIXTEEN HIGH-SCHOOL STUDENTS ENTERED THIS ACADEMY ALIVE.
...YOU'RE ABSOLUTELY SURE ABOUT THAT...?
YUP. THAT'S THE BEAR TRUTH.
SO THE KILLER HAS TO BE SOMEONE IN HERE.
I-IT ISN'T ME!! I'M NOT THE MASTERMIND!
D-DON'T LOOK AT ME!
NO... IT ISN'T NECESSARILY LIMITED TO ONE OF US.
FOR SOMEONE AT AN ELITE SCHOOL, YA DON'T COUNT SO GOOD!
TEN STUDENTS HAVE DIED... THAT LEAVES US WITH SIX!!

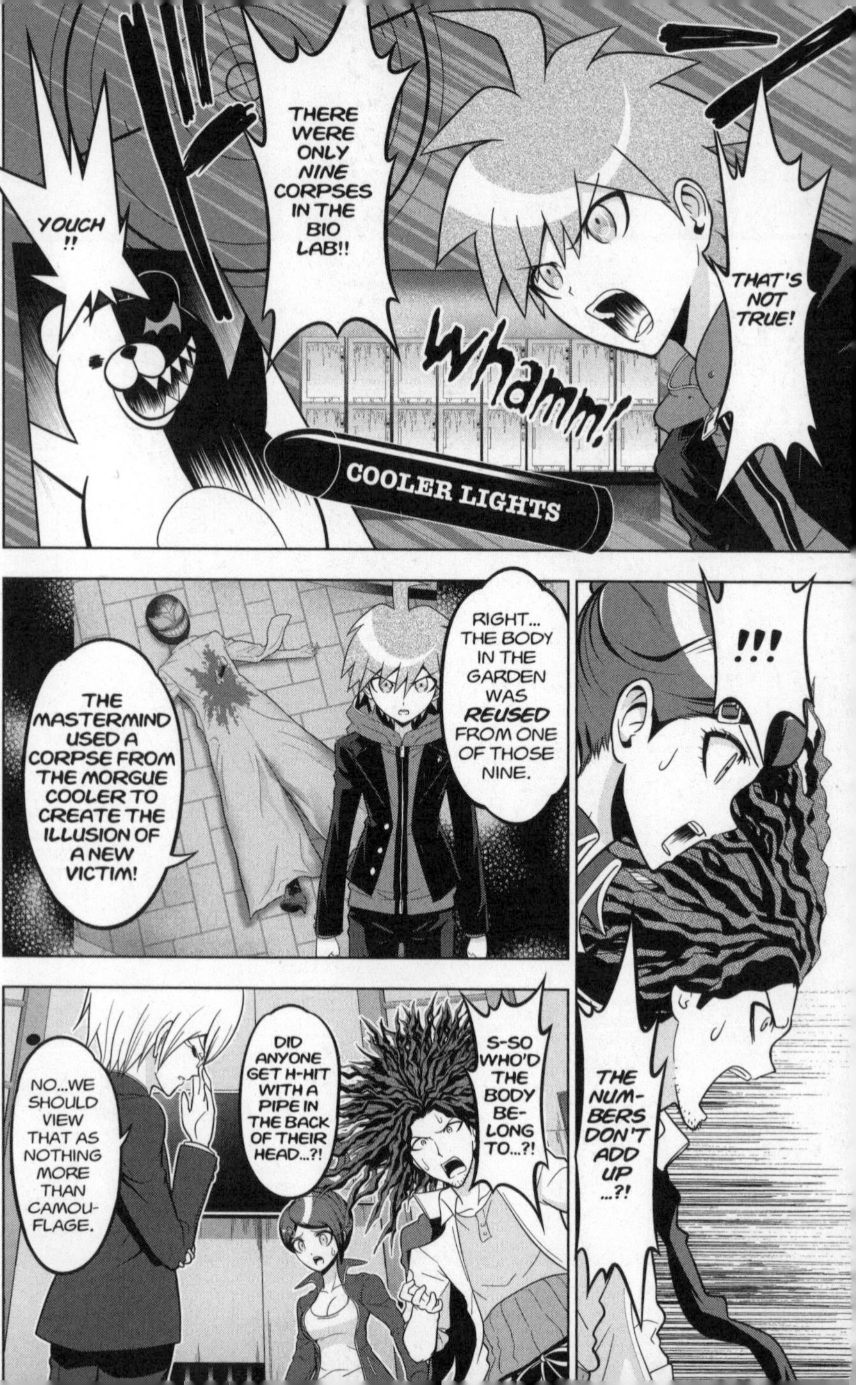
THAT'S NOT TRUE!
THERE WERE ONLY NINE CORPSES IN THE BIO LAB!!
Whamm!
YOUCH!!
COOLER LIGHTS
!!!
THE NUMBERS DON'T ADD UP...?!
RIGHT... THE BODY IN THE GARDEN WAS REUSED FROM ONE OF THOSE NINE.
THE MASTERMIND USED A CORPSE FROM THE MORGUE COOLER TO CREATE THE ILLUSION OF A NEW VICTIM!
S-SO WHO'D THE BODY BELONG TO...?!
DID ANYONE GET H-HIT WITH A PIPE IN THE BACK OF THEIR HEAD...?!
NO...WE SHOULD VIEW THAT AS NOTHING MORE THAN CAMOUFLAGE.

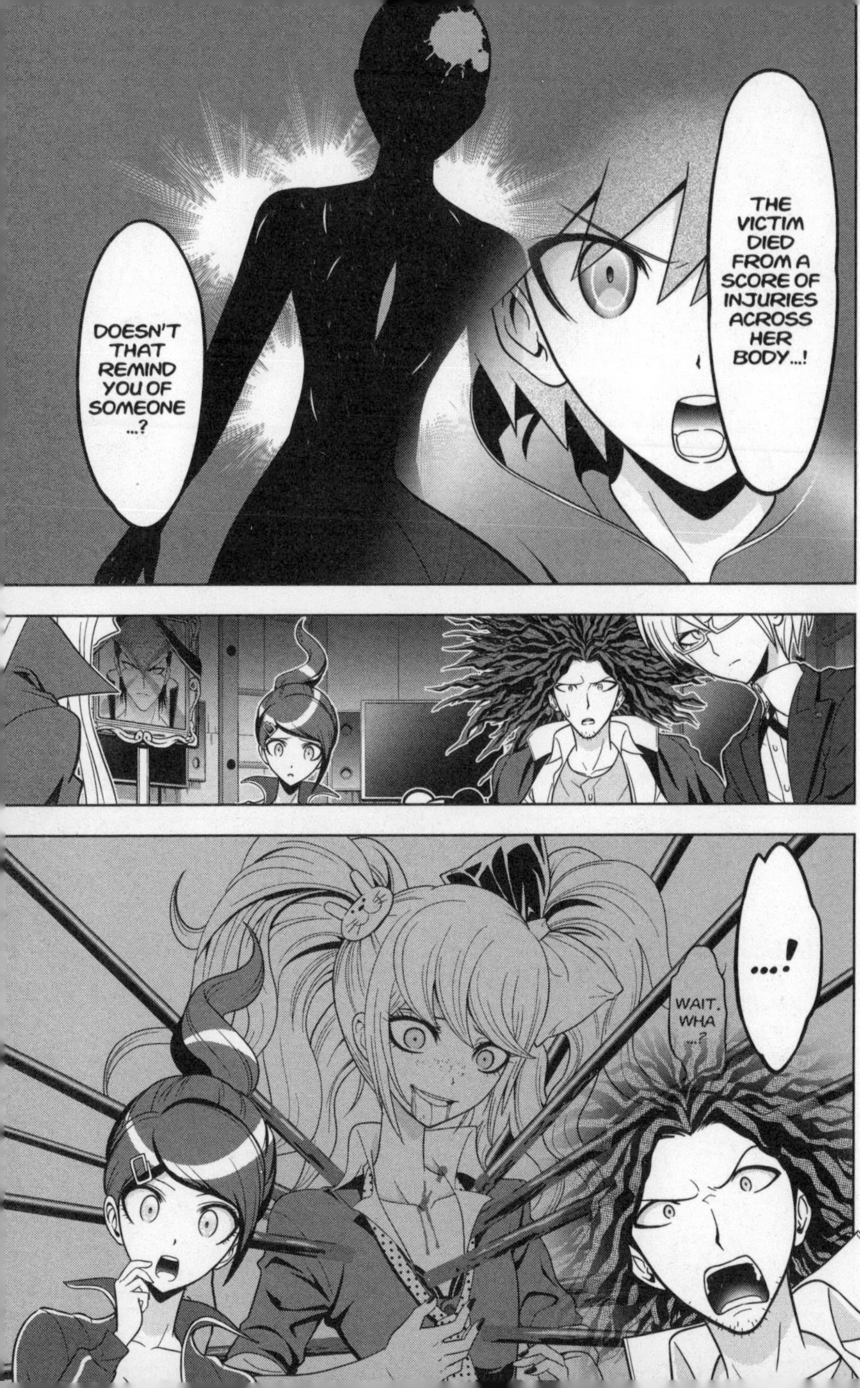
THE VICTIM DIED FROM A SCORE OF INJURIES ACROSS HER BODY...!
DOESN'T THAT REMIND YOU OF SOMEONE ...?
...!
WAIT, WHA ...?

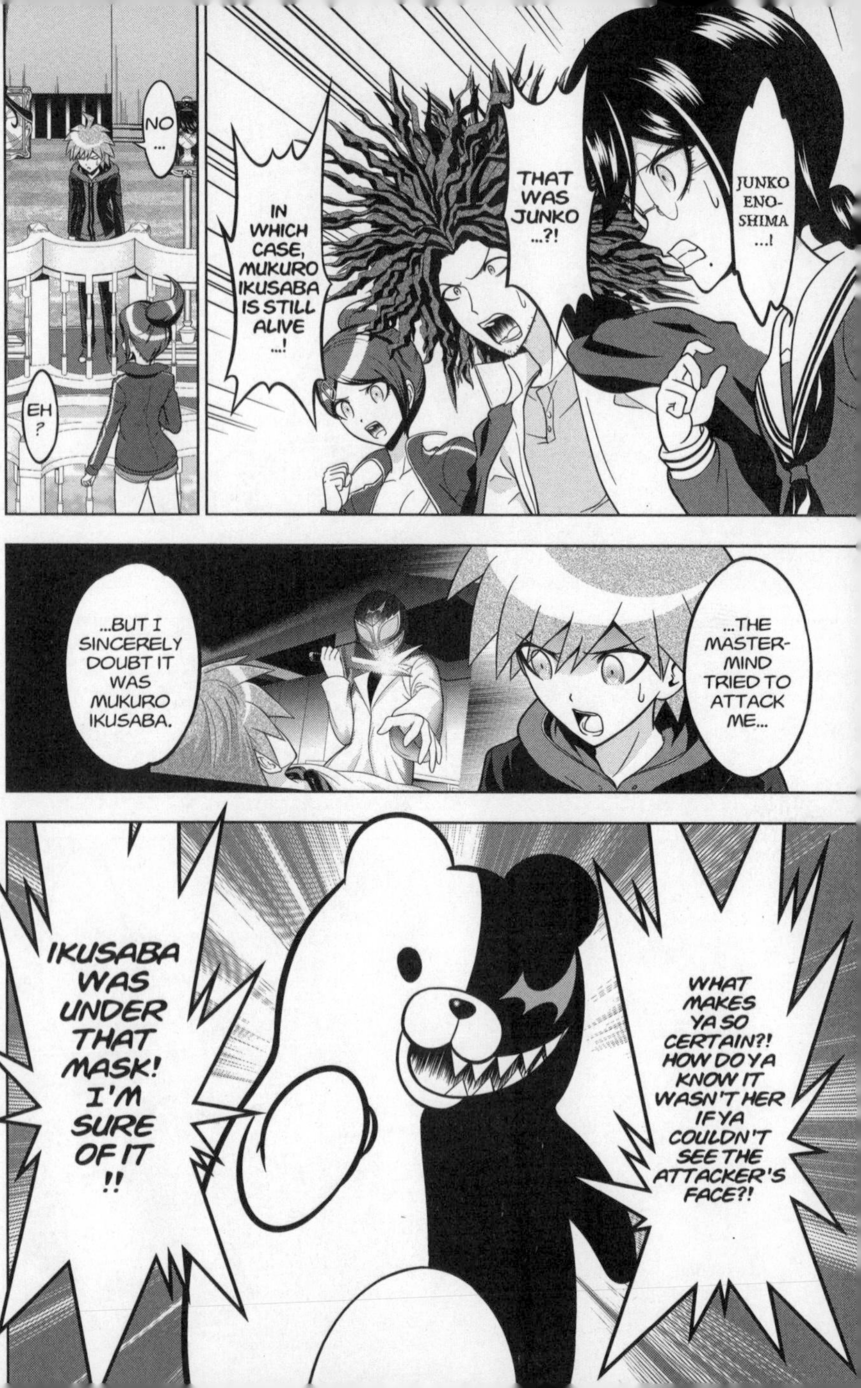
JUNKO ENO-SHIMA ...!
THAT WAS JUNKO ...?!
IN WHICH CASE, MUKURO IKUSABA IS STILL ALIVE ...!
NO ...
EH ?
...THE MASTER-MIND TRIED TO ATTACK ME...
...BUT I SINCERELY DOUBT IT WAS MUKURO IKUSABA.
WHAT MAKES YA SO CERTAIN?! HOW DO YA KNOW IT WASN'T HER IF YA COULDN'T SEE THE ATTACKER'S FACE?!
IKUSABA WAS UNDER THAT MASK! I'M SURE OF IT !!

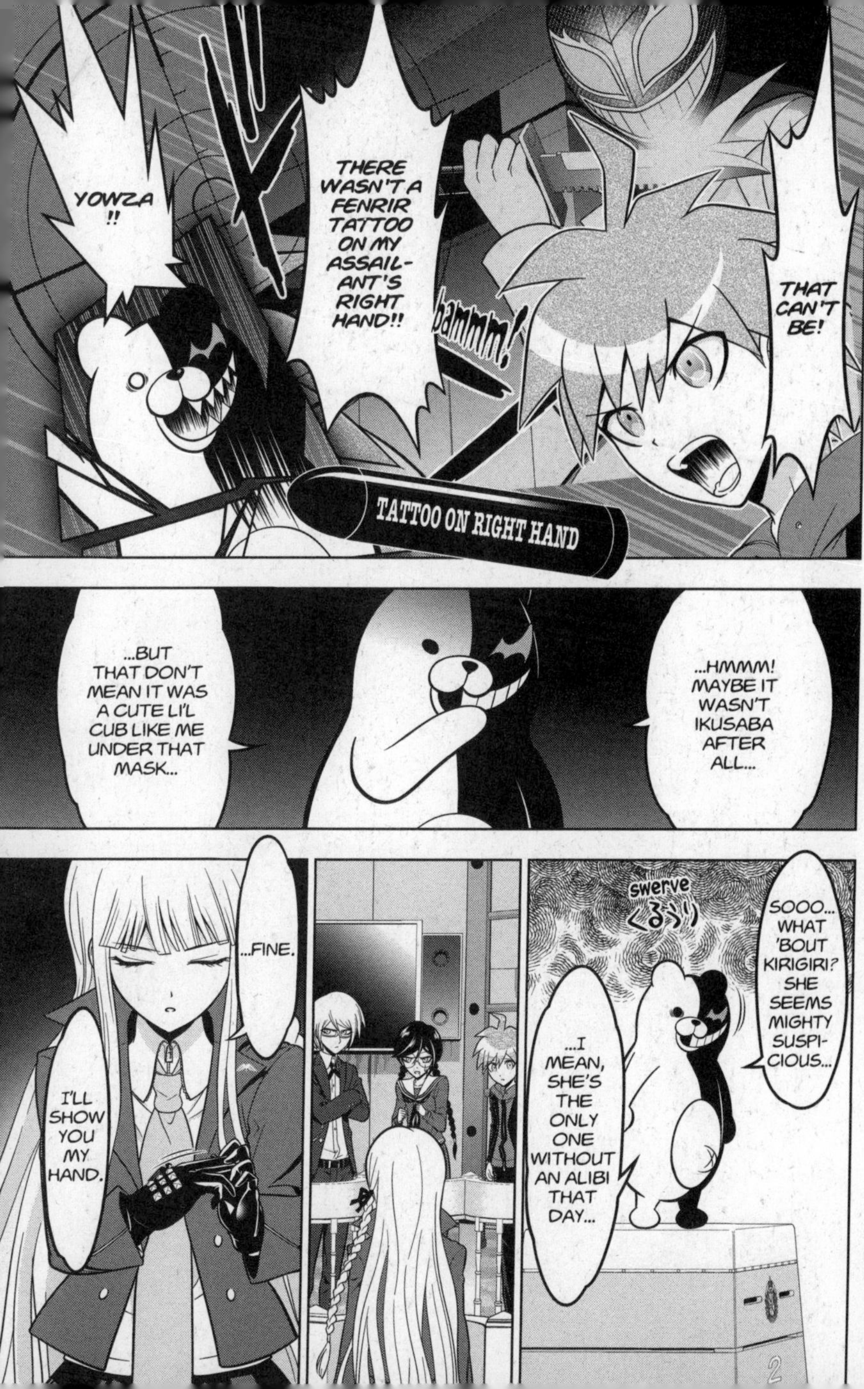

THAT CAN'T BE!
THERE WASN'T A FENRIR TATTOO ON MY ASSAILANT'S RIGHT HAND!!
bammm!
YOWZA!!
TATTOO ON RIGHT HAND
...HMMM! MAYBE IT WASN'T IKUSABA AFTER ALL...
...BUT THAT DON'T MEAN IT WAS A CUTE LI'L CUB LIKE ME UNDER THAT MASK...
swerve
くるっ
SOOO... WHAT 'BOUT KIRIGIRI? SHE SEEMS MIGHTY SUSPICIOUS...
...I MEAN, SHE'S THE ONLY ONE WITHOUT AN ALIBI THAT DAY...
...FINE.
I'LL SHOW YOU MY HAND.

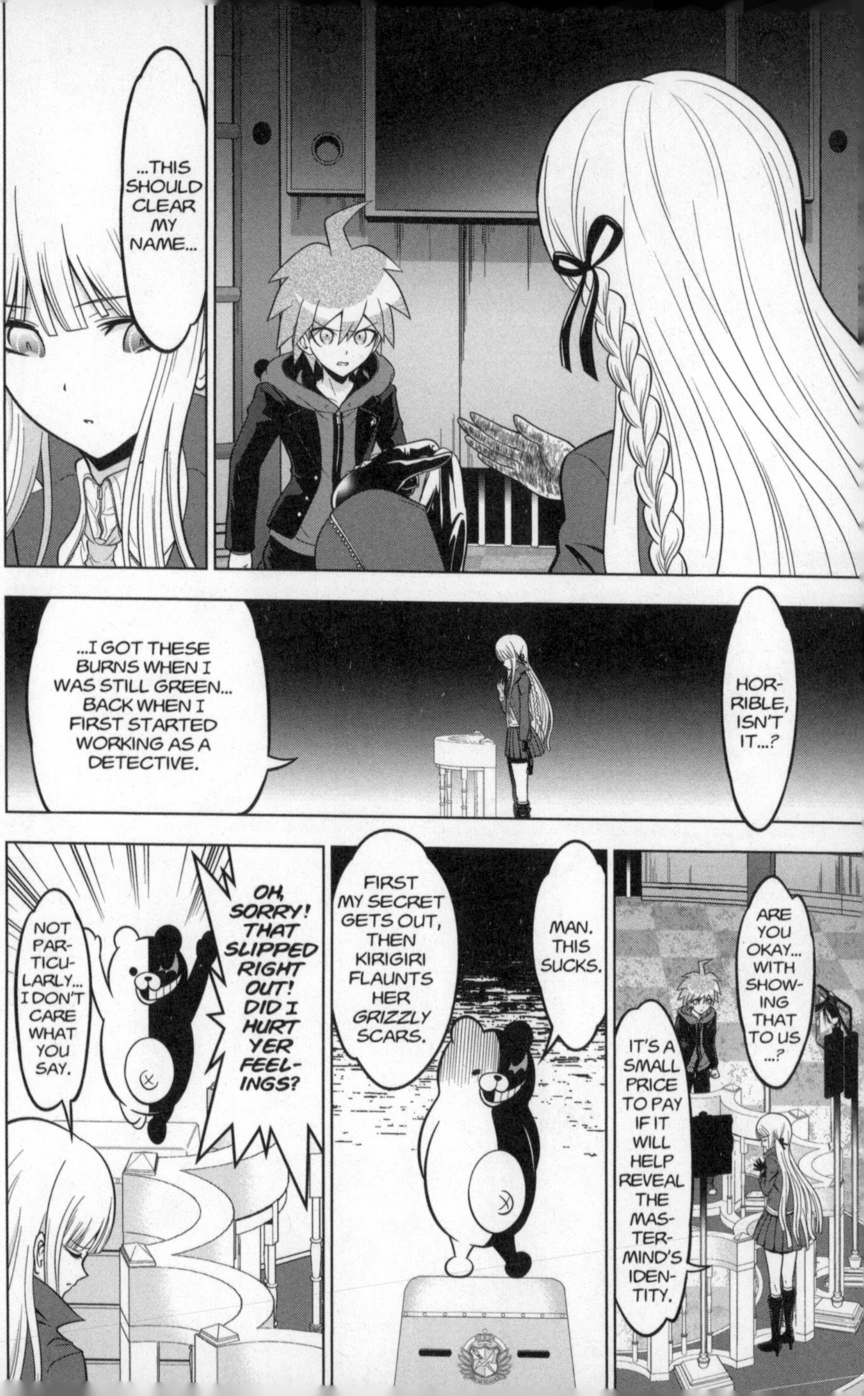
...THIS SHOULD CLEAR MY NAME...
HORRIBLE, ISN'T IT...?
...I GOT THESE BURNS WHEN I WAS STILL GREEN... BACK WHEN I FIRST STARTED WORKING AS A DETECTIVE.
ARE YOU OKAY... WITH SHOWING THAT TO US...?
IT'S A SMALL PRICE TO PAY IF IT WILL HELP REVEAL THE MASTERMIND'S IDENTITY.
MAN. THIS SUCKS.
FIRST MY SECRET GETS OUT, THEN KIRIGIRI FLAUNTS HER GRIZZLY SCARS.
OH, SORRY! THAT SLIPPED RIGHT OUT! DID I HURT YER FEELINGS?
NOT PARTICULARLY... I DON'T CARE WHAT YOU SAY.

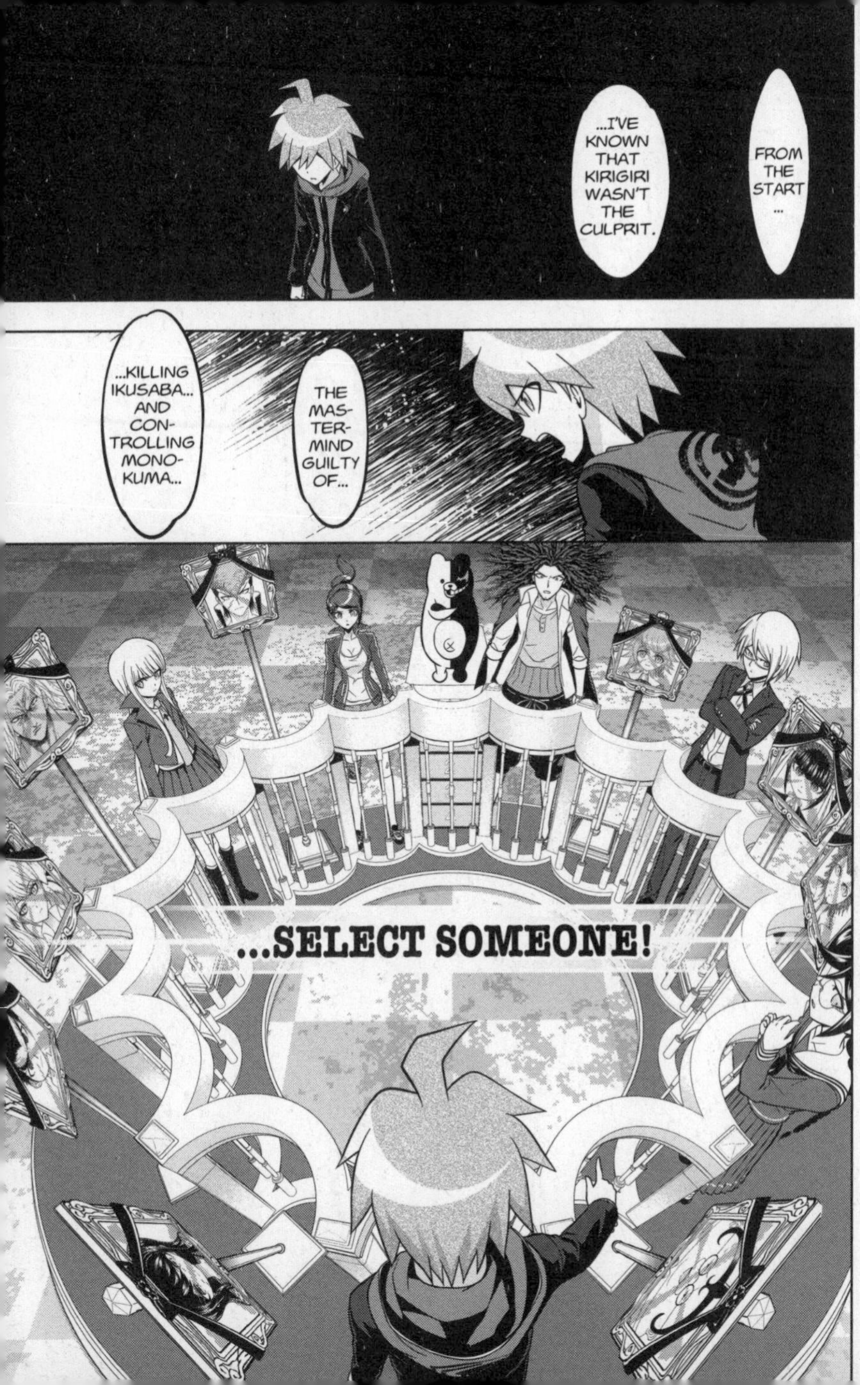
FROM THE START ...
...I'VE KNOWN THAT KIRIGIRI WASN'T THE CULPRIT.
THE MAS-TER-MIND GUILTY OF...
...KILLING IKUSABA... AND CON-TROLLING MONO-KUMA...
...SELECT SOMEONE!

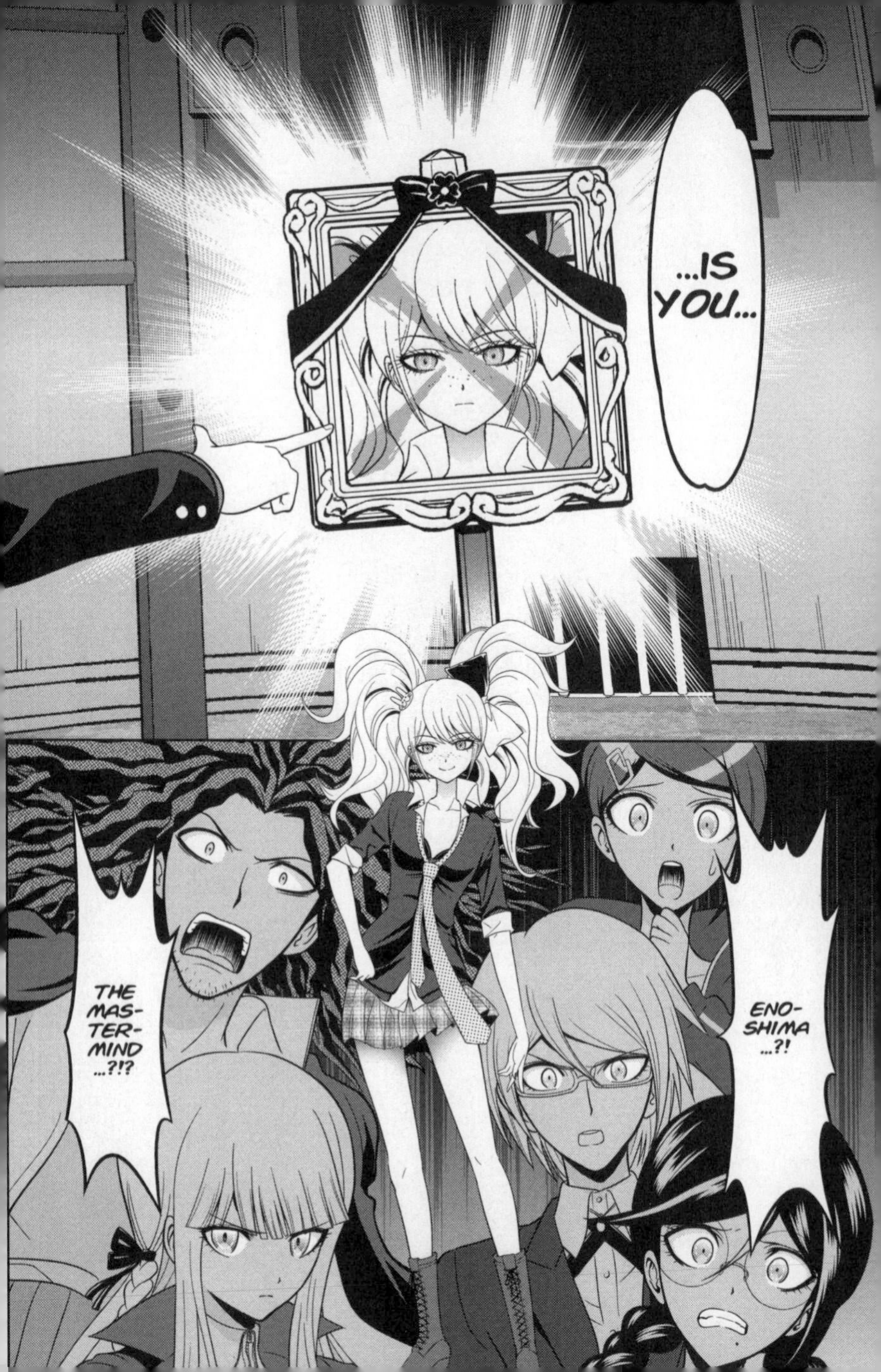
...IS YOU...
ENO-SHIMA ...?!
THE MAS-TER-MIND ...?!?

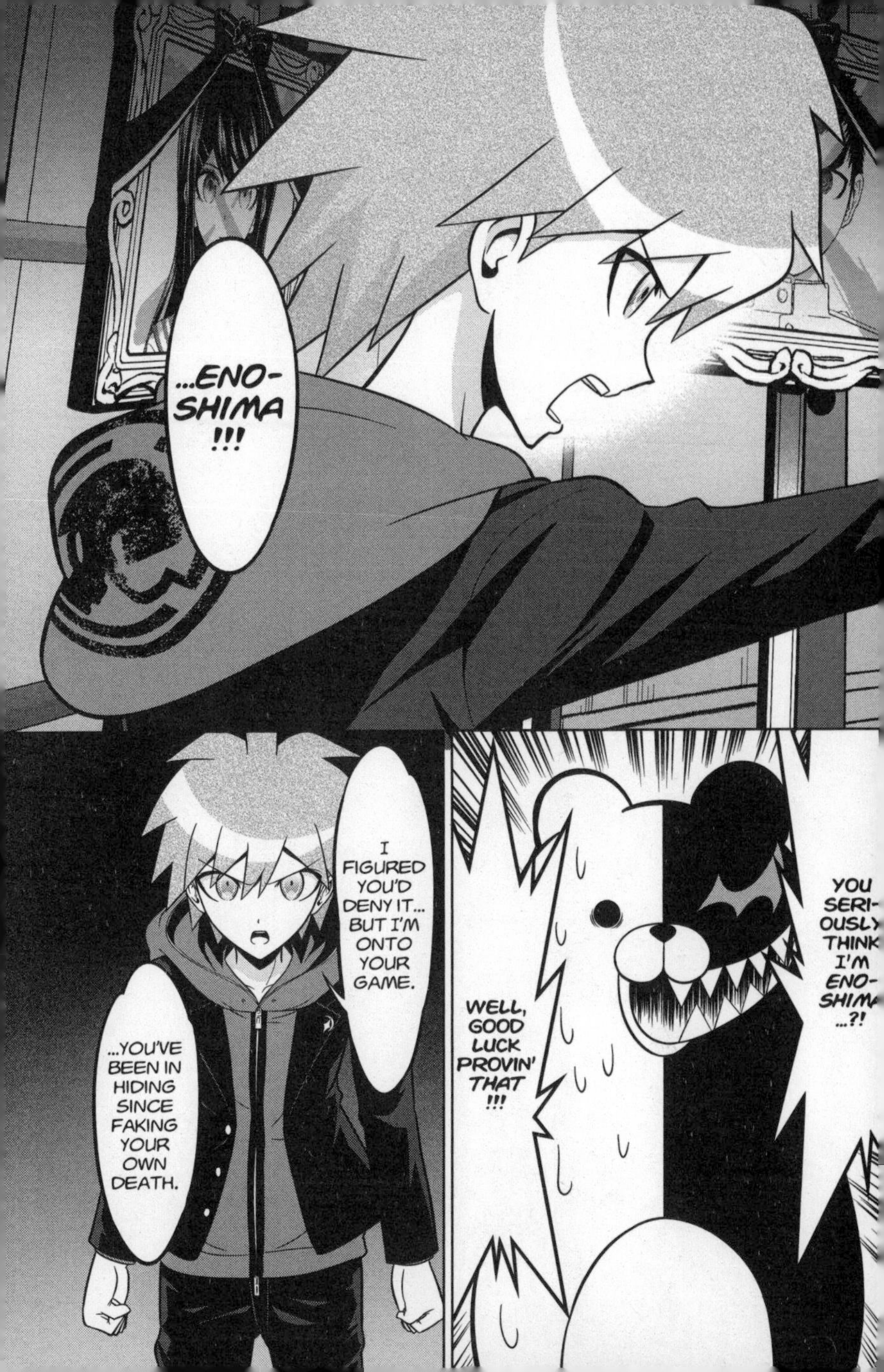
...ENO-SHIMA !!!
YOU SERI-OUSLY THINK I'M ENO-SHIMA ...?!
WELL, GOOD LUCK PROVIN' THAT !!!
I FIGURED YOU'D DENY IT... BUT I'M ONTO YOUR GAME.
...YOU'VE BEEN IN HIDING SINCE FAKING YOUR OWN DEATH.

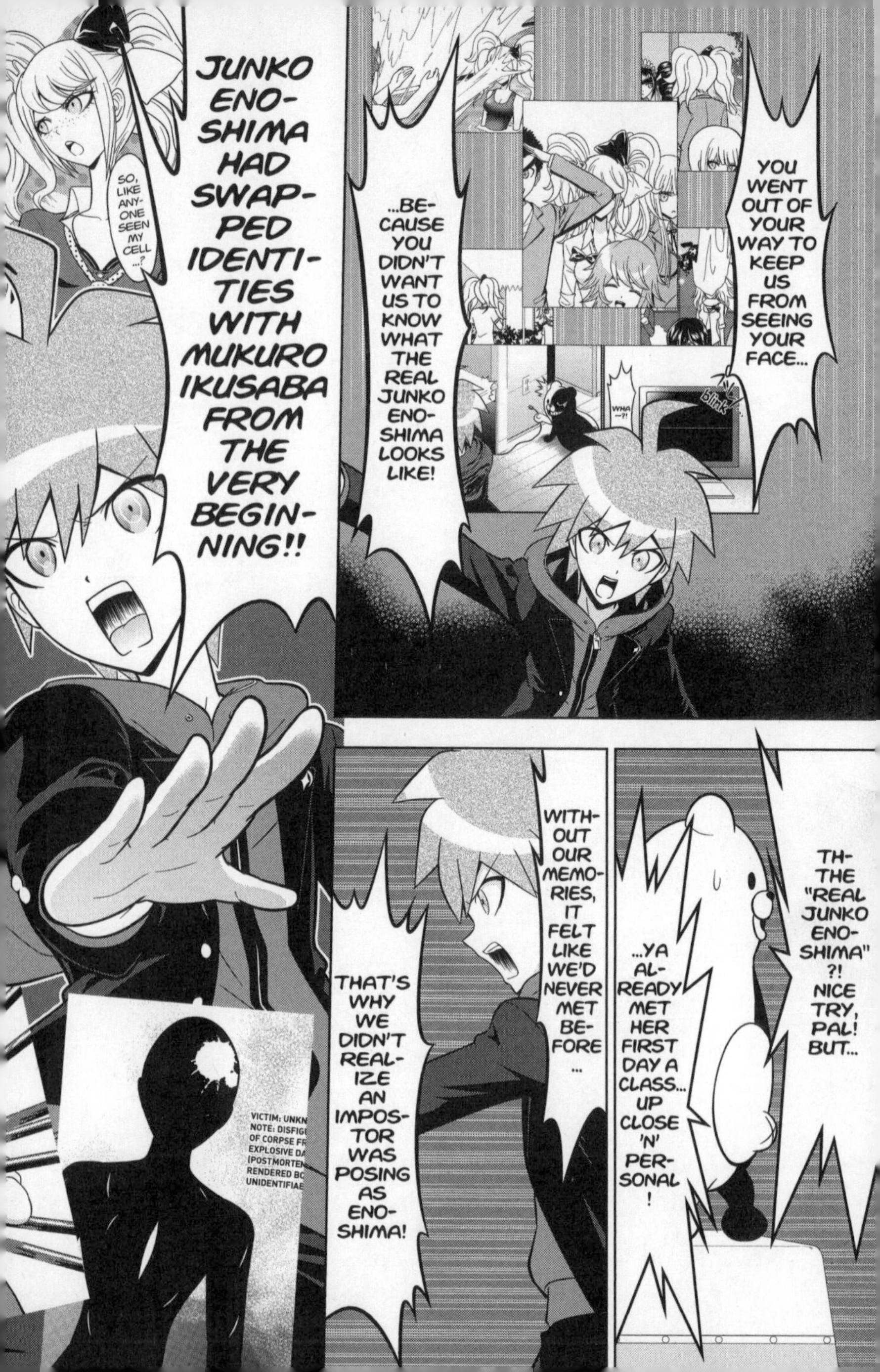
YOU WENT OUT OF YOUR WAY TO KEEP US FROM SEEING YOUR FACE...
blink
WHA—?!
...BECAUSE YOU DIDN'T WANT US TO KNOW WHAT THE REAL JUNKO ENOSHIMA LOOKS LIKE!
TH-THE "REAL JUNKO ENOSHIMA"?! NICE TRY, PAL! BUT...
...YA ALREADY MET HER FIRST DAY A CLASS... UP CLOSE 'N' PERSONAL!
WITHOUT OUR MEMORIES, IT FELT LIKE WE'D NEVER MET BEFORE...
THAT'S WHY WE DIDN'T REALIZE AN IMPOSTOR WAS POSING AS ENOSHIMA!
JUNKO ENOSHIMA HAD SWAPPED IDENTITIES WITH MUKURO IKUSABA FROM THE VERY BEGINNING!!
SO, LIKE ANYONE SEEN MY CELL...?

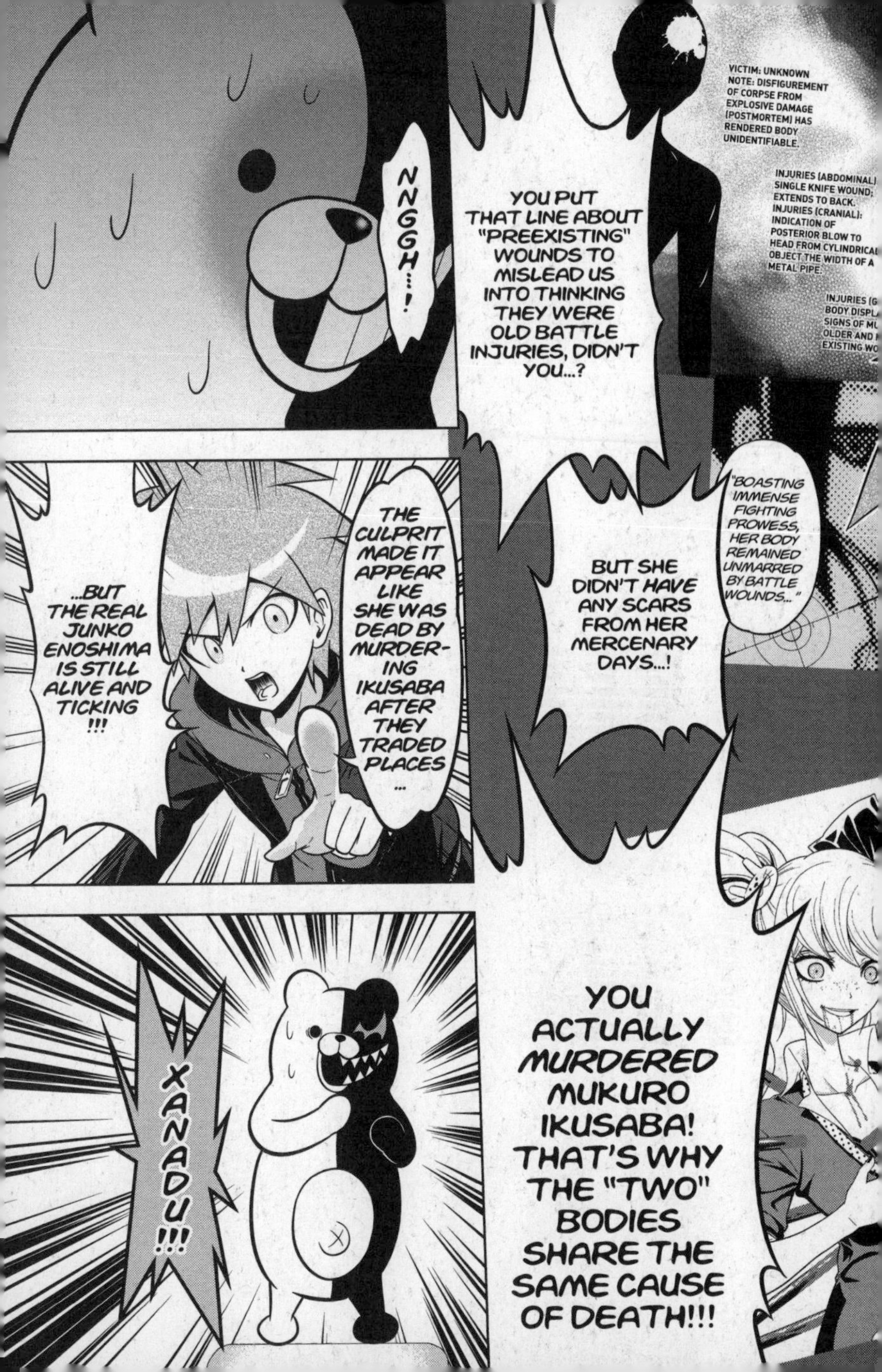
VICTIM: UNKNOWN
NOTE: DISFIGUREMENT OF CORPSE FROM EXPLOSIVE DAMAGE (POSTMORTEM) HAS RENDERED BODY UNIDENTIFIABLE.
INJURIES (ABDOMINAL) SINGLE KNIFE WOUND; EXTENDS TO BACK.
INJURIES (CRANIAL): INDICATION OF POSTERIOR BLOW TO HEAD FROM CYLINDRICAL OBJECT THE WIDTH OF A METAL PIPE.
INJURIES (G BODY DISPL SIGNS OF MU OLDER AND EXISTING WO
YOU PUT THAT LINE ABOUT "PREEXISTING" WOUNDS TO MISLEAD US INTO THINKING THEY WERE OLD BATTLE INJURIES, DIDN'T YOU...?
NNGGH...!
"BOASTING IMMENSE FIGHTING PROWESS, HER BODY REMAINED UNMARRED BY BATTLE WOUNDS..."
BUT SHE DIDN'T HAVE ANY SCARS FROM HER MERCENARY DAYS...!
THE CULPRIT MADE IT APPEAR LIKE SHE WAS DEAD BY MURDER-ING IKUSABA AFTER THEY TRADED PLACES...
...BUT THE REAL JUNKO ENOSHIMA IS STILL ALIVE AND TICKING!!!
YOU ACTUALLY MURDERED MUKURO IKUSABA! THAT'S WHY THE "TWO" BODIES SHARE THE SAME CAUSE OF DEATH!!!
XANADU!!!

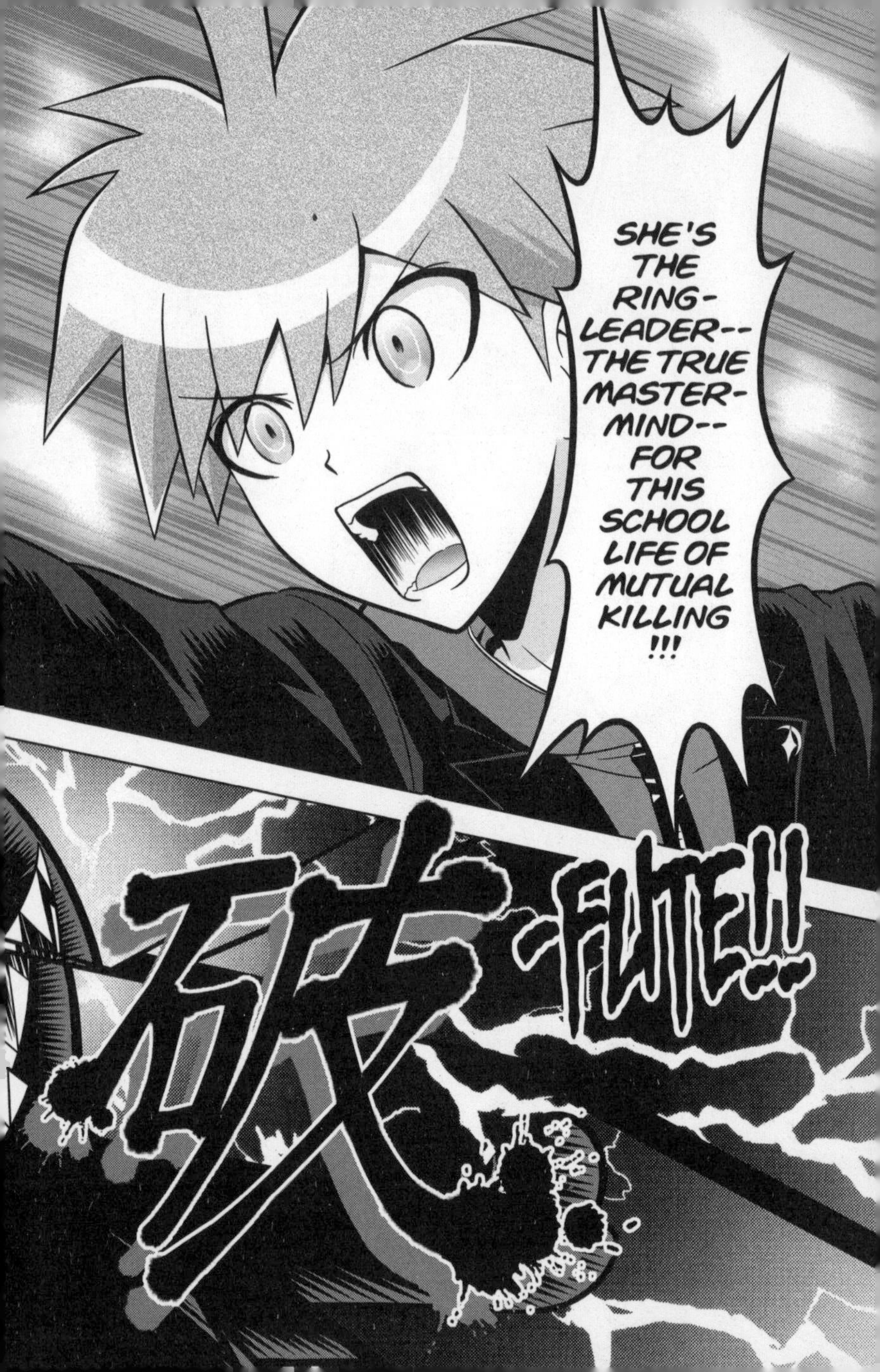
SHE'S THE RING-LEADER-- THE TRUE MASTER-MIND-- FOR THIS SCHOOL LIFE OF MUTUAL KILLING !!!
-FLUTE!!

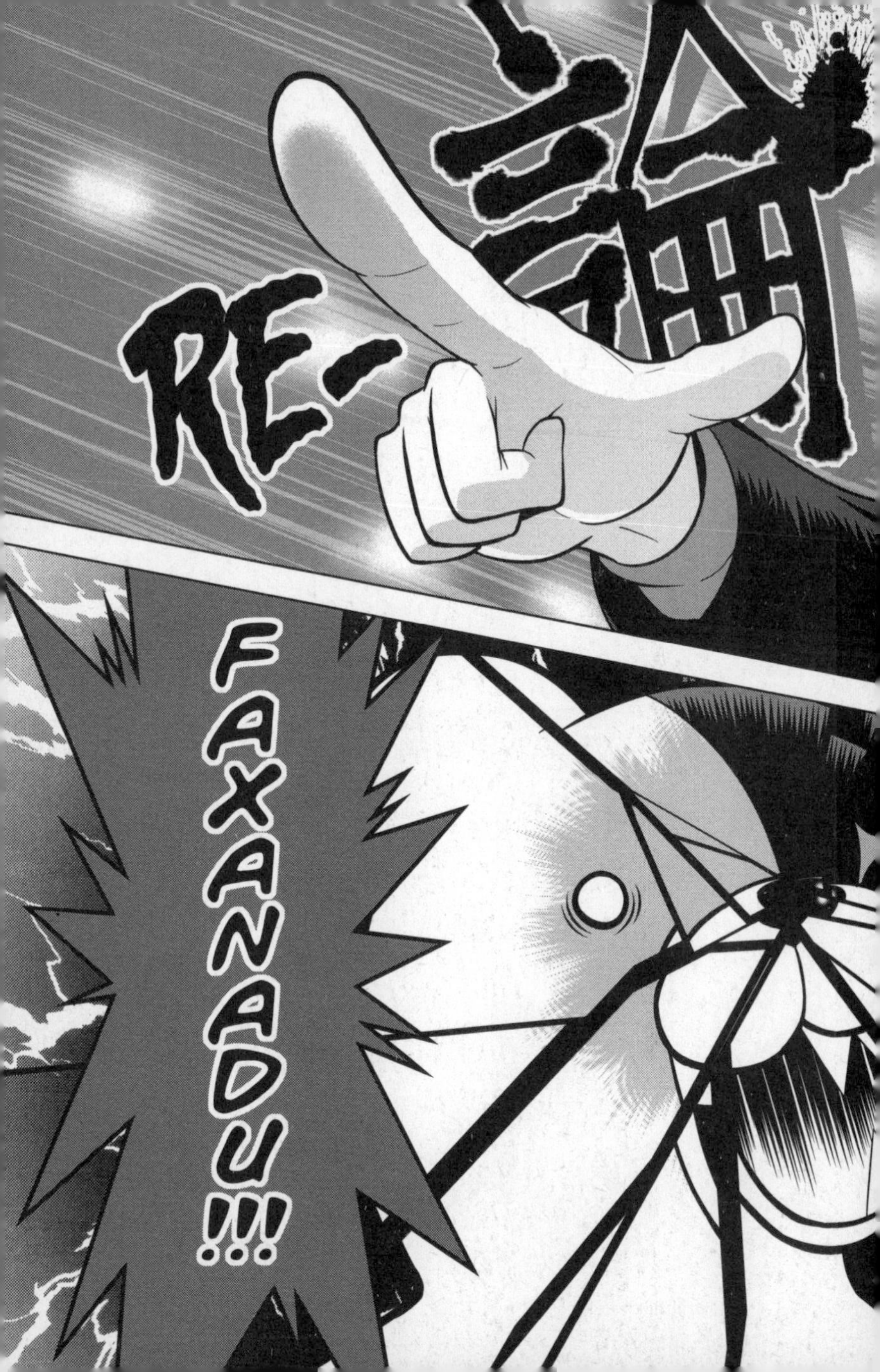
RE-
FAXANADU!!!

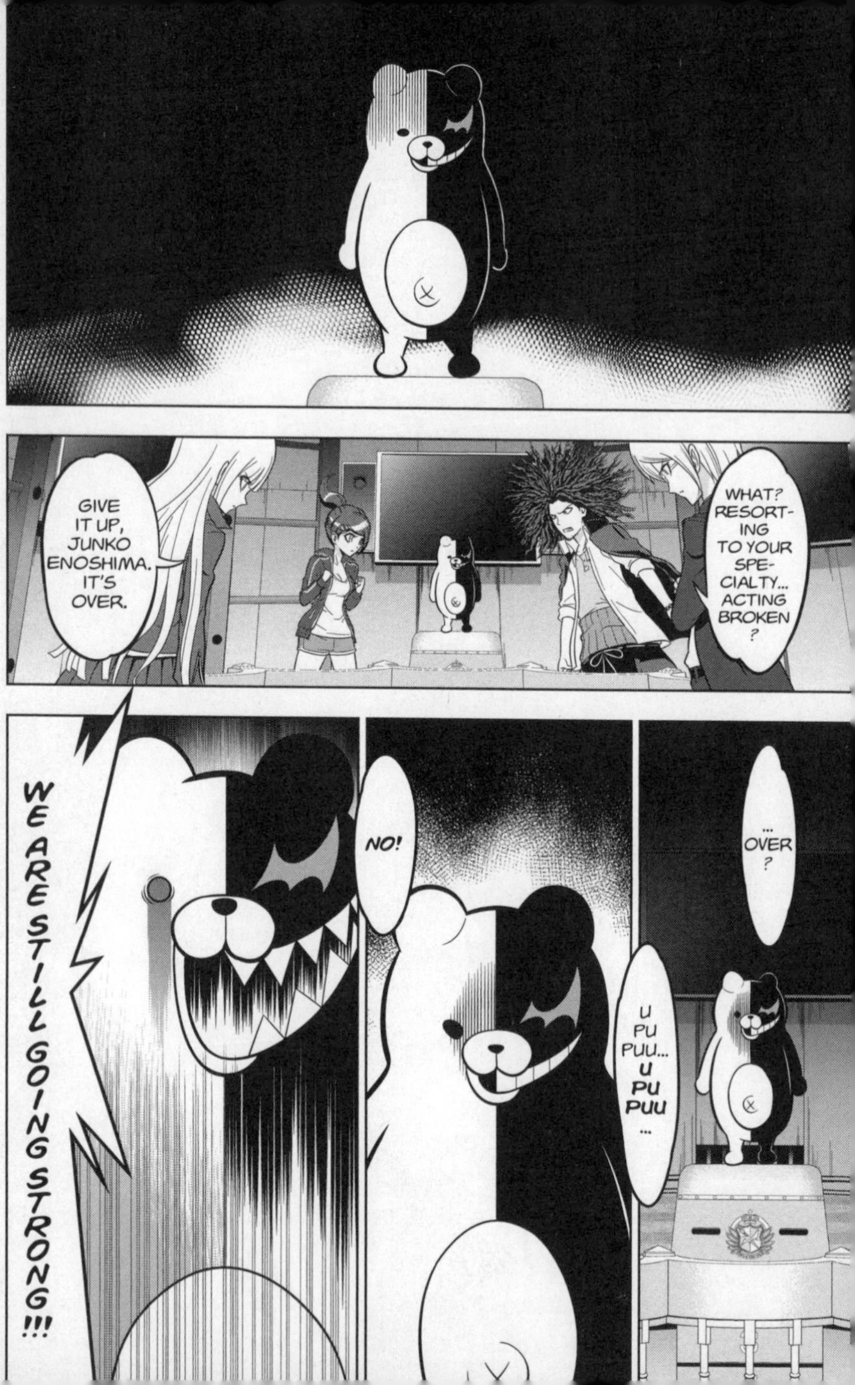
WHAT? RESORTING TO YOUR SPECIALTY... ACTING BROKEN?
GIVE IT UP, JUNKO ENOSHIMA. IT'S OVER.
... OVER?
U PU PUU... U PU PUU ...
NO!
WE ARE STILL GOING STRONG!!!

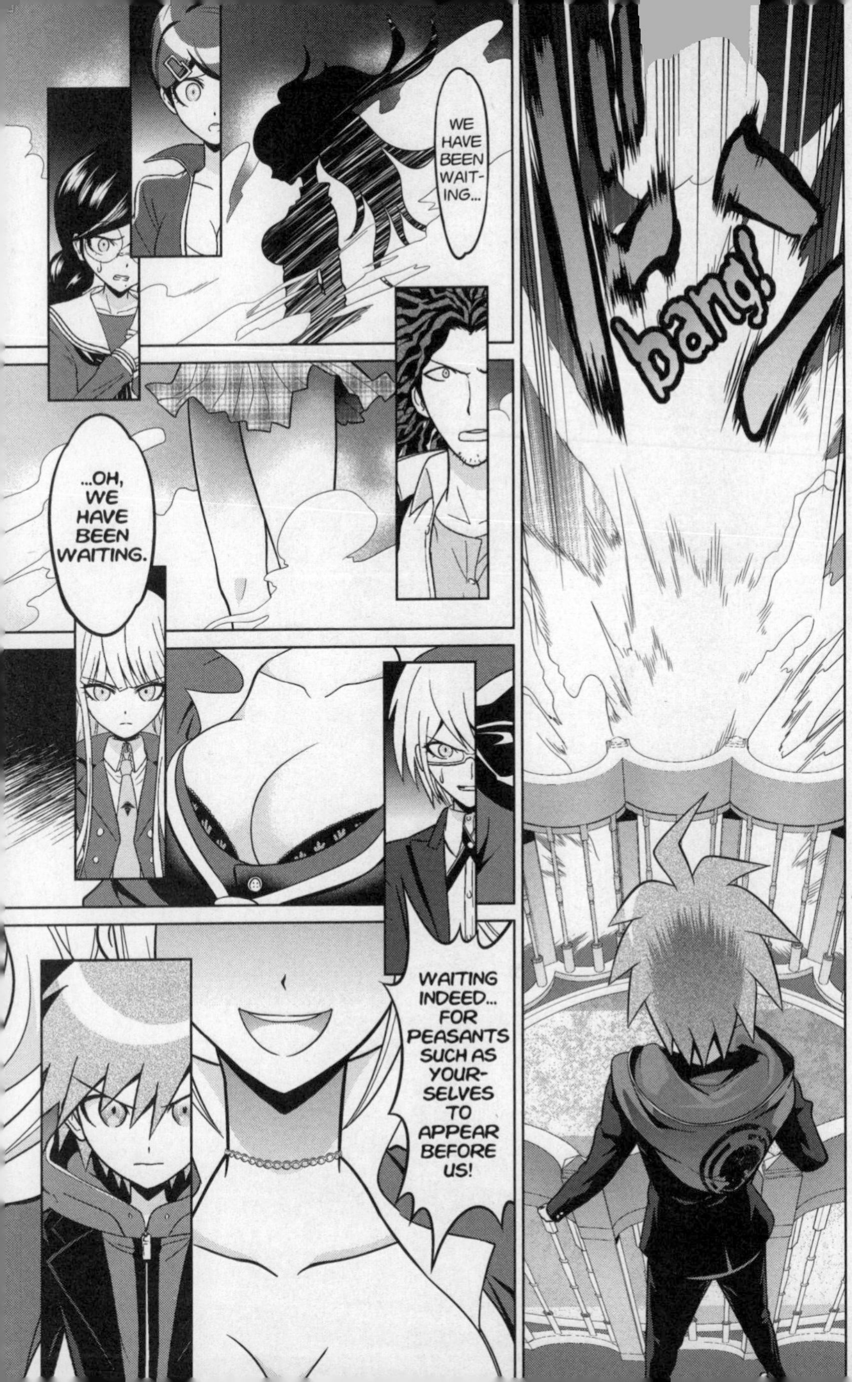
bang!
WE HAVE BEEN WAIT-ING...
...OH, WE HAVE BEEN WAITING.
WAITING INDEED... FOR PEASANTS SUCH AS YOUR-SELVES TO APPEAR BEFORE US!

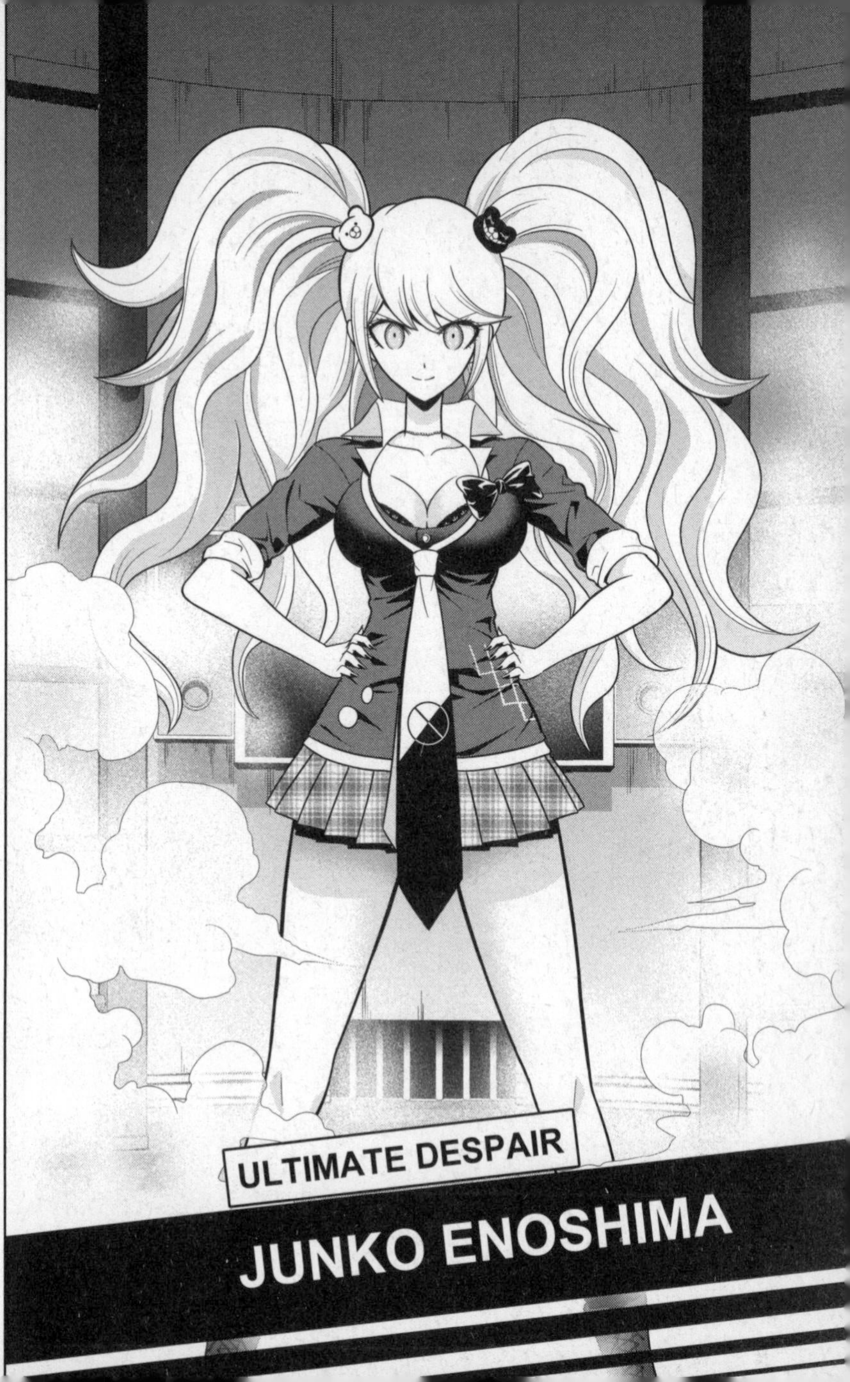
ULTIMATE DESPAIR
JUNKO ENOSHIMA

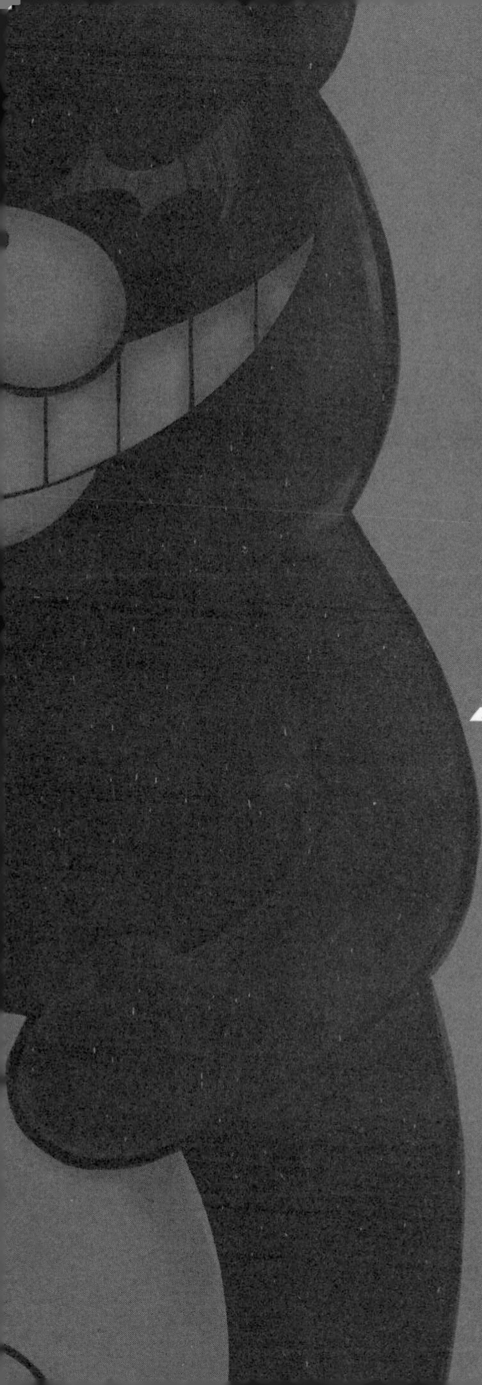

DANGANRONPA

A SCHOOL OF HOPE . . . WITH STUDENTS OF DESPAIR!

THE ANIMATION

DANGANRONPA

A SCHOOL OF HOPE . . . WITH STUDENTS OF DESPAIR!

THE ANIMATION

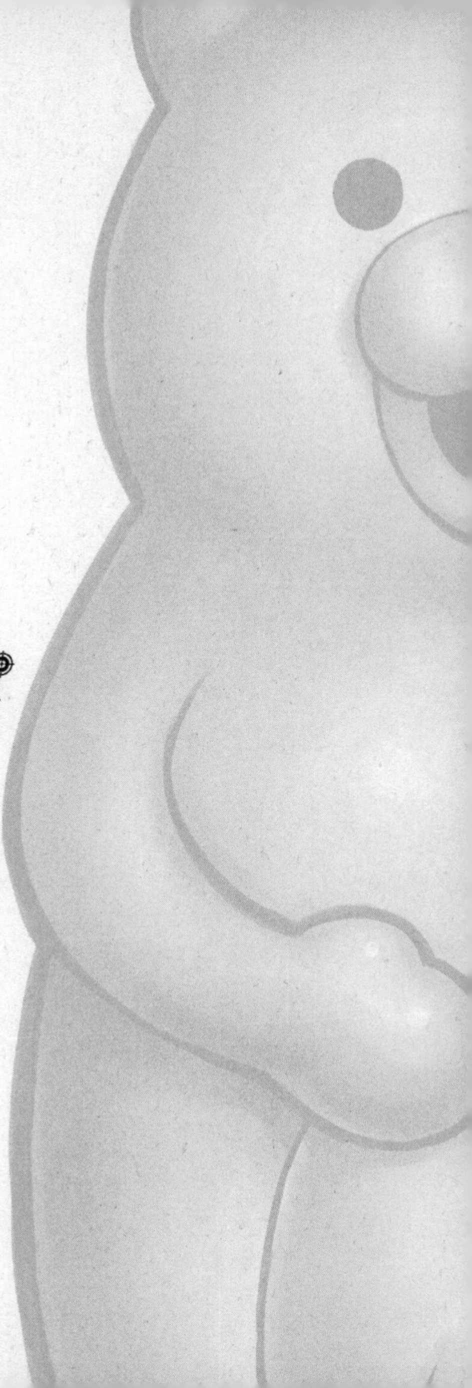

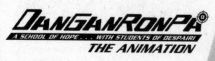

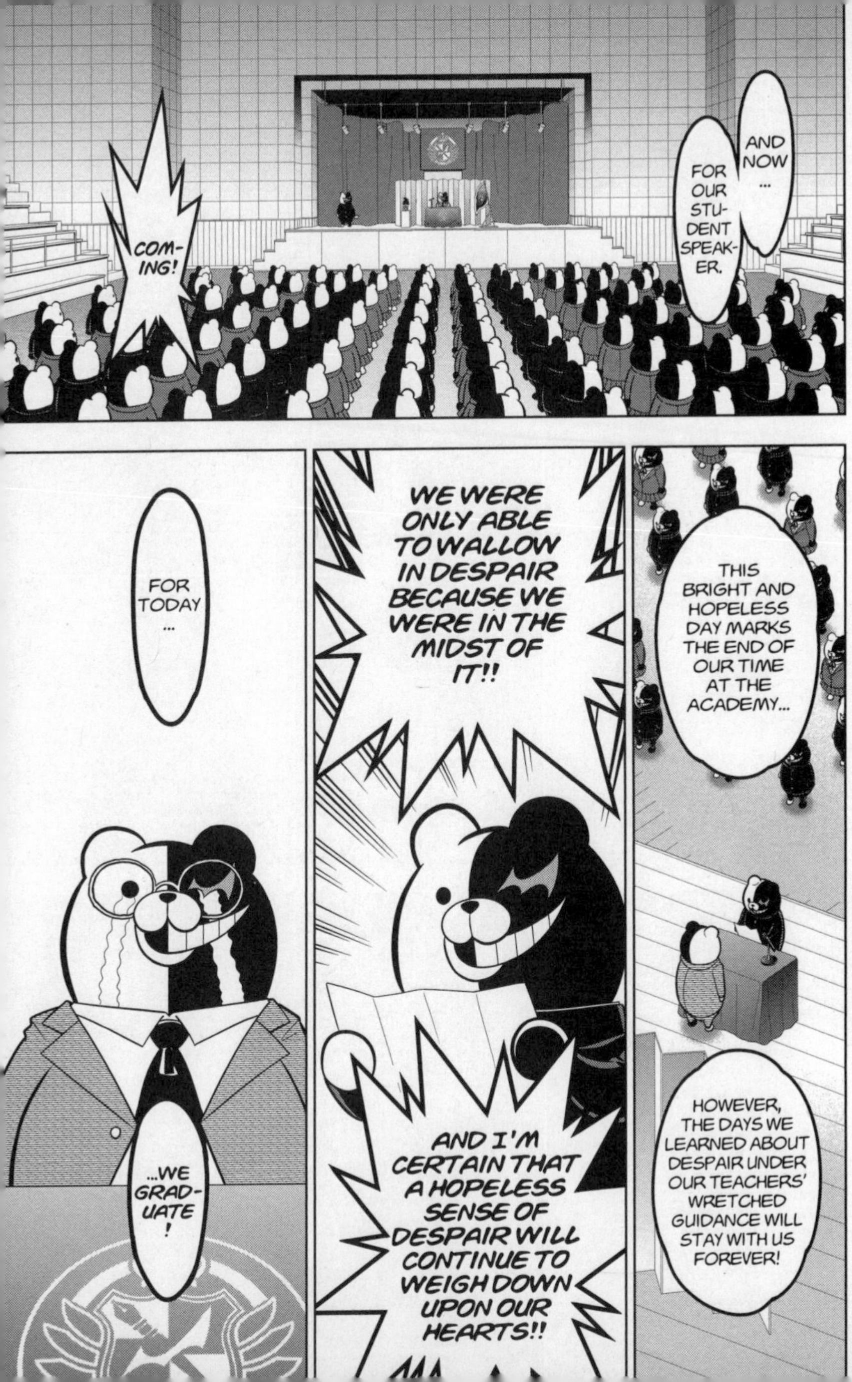
AND NOW ... FOR OUR STUDENT SPEAKER.
COMING!
THIS BRIGHT AND HOPELESS DAY MARKS THE END OF OUR TIME AT THE ACADEMY...
HOWEVER, THE DAYS WE LEARNED ABOUT DESPAIR UNDER OUR TEACHERS' WRETCHED GUIDANCE WILL STAY WITH US FOREVER!
WE WERE ONLY ABLE TO WALLOW IN DESPAIR BECAUSE WE WERE IN THE MIDST OF IT!!
AND I'M CERTAIN THAT A HOPELESS SENSE OF DESPAIR WILL CONTINUE TO WEIGH DOWN UPON OUR HEARTS!!
FOR TODAY ...
...WE GRADUATE!

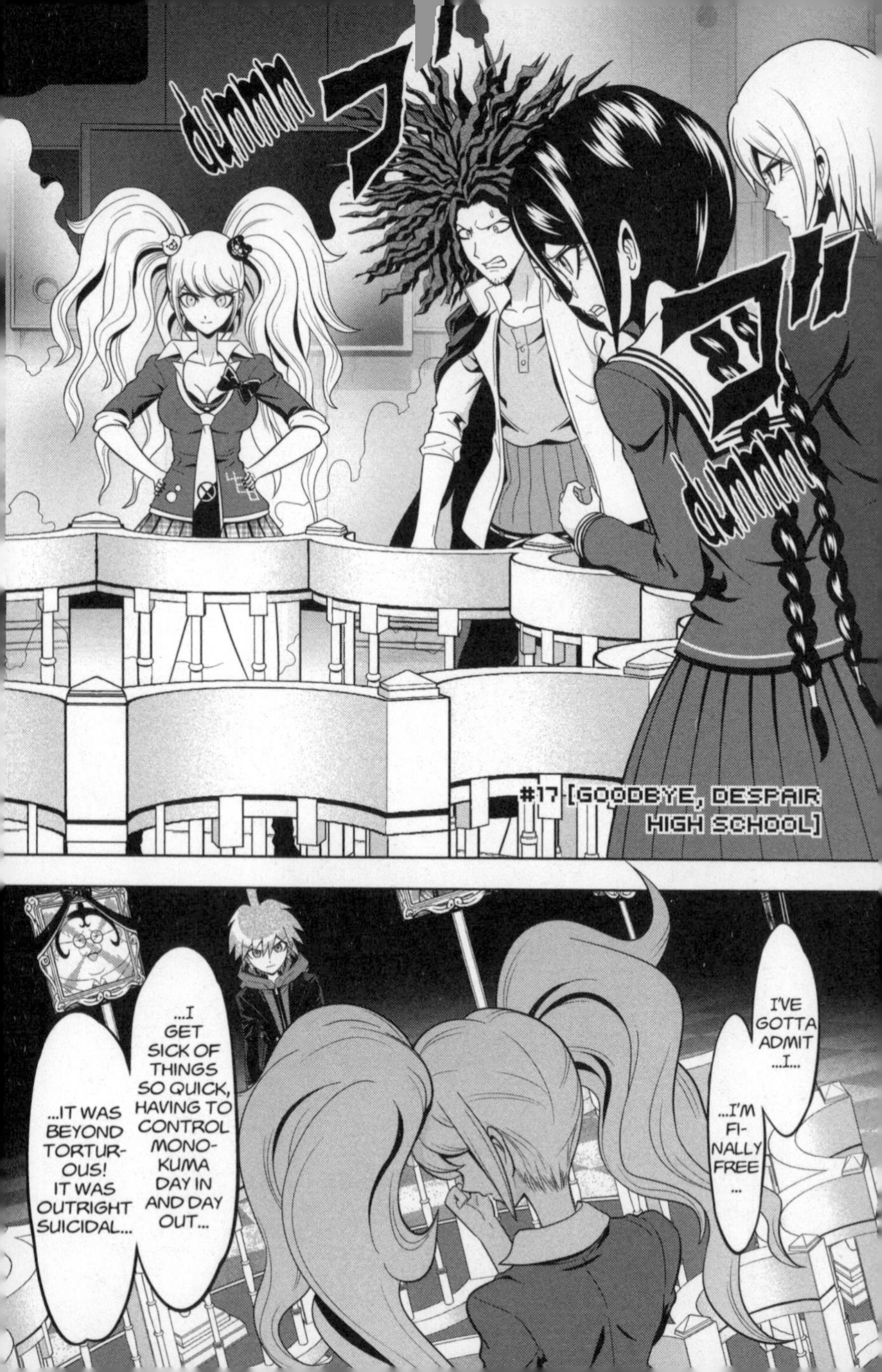
#17 [GOODBYE, DESPAIR HIGH SCHOOL]
I'VE GOTTA ADMIT ...I...
...I'M FI-NALLY FREE ...
...I GET SICK OF THINGS SO QUICK, HAVING TO CONTROL MONO-KUMA DAY IN AND DAY OUT...
...IT WAS BEYOND TORTUR-OUS! IT WAS OUTRIGHT SUICIDAL...

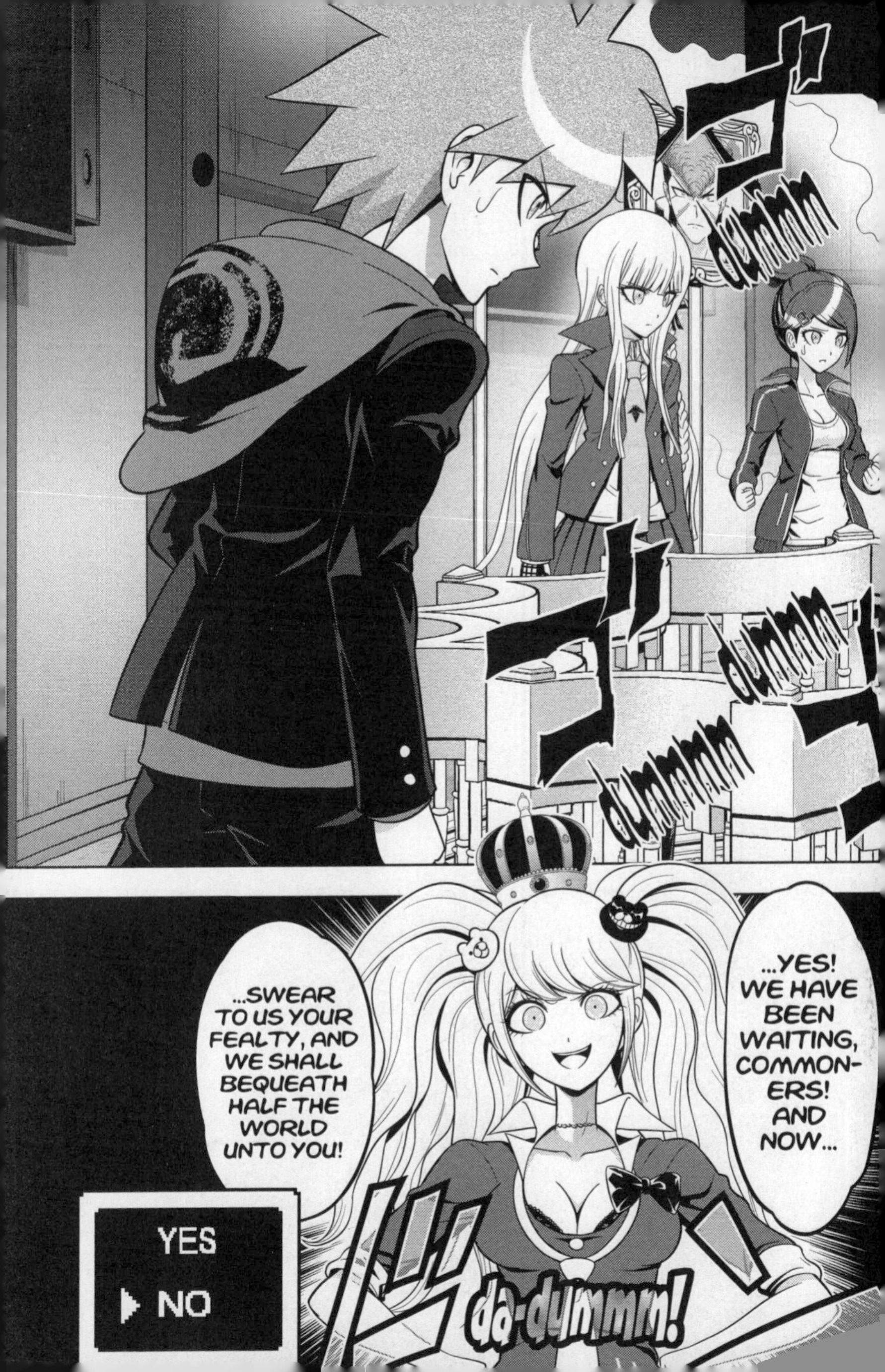
...YES! WE HAVE BEEN WAITING, COMMONERS! AND NOW...
...SWEAR TO US YOUR FEALTY, AND WE SHALL BEQUEATH HALF THE WORLD UNTO YOU!
YES
▶ NO
da-dummm!

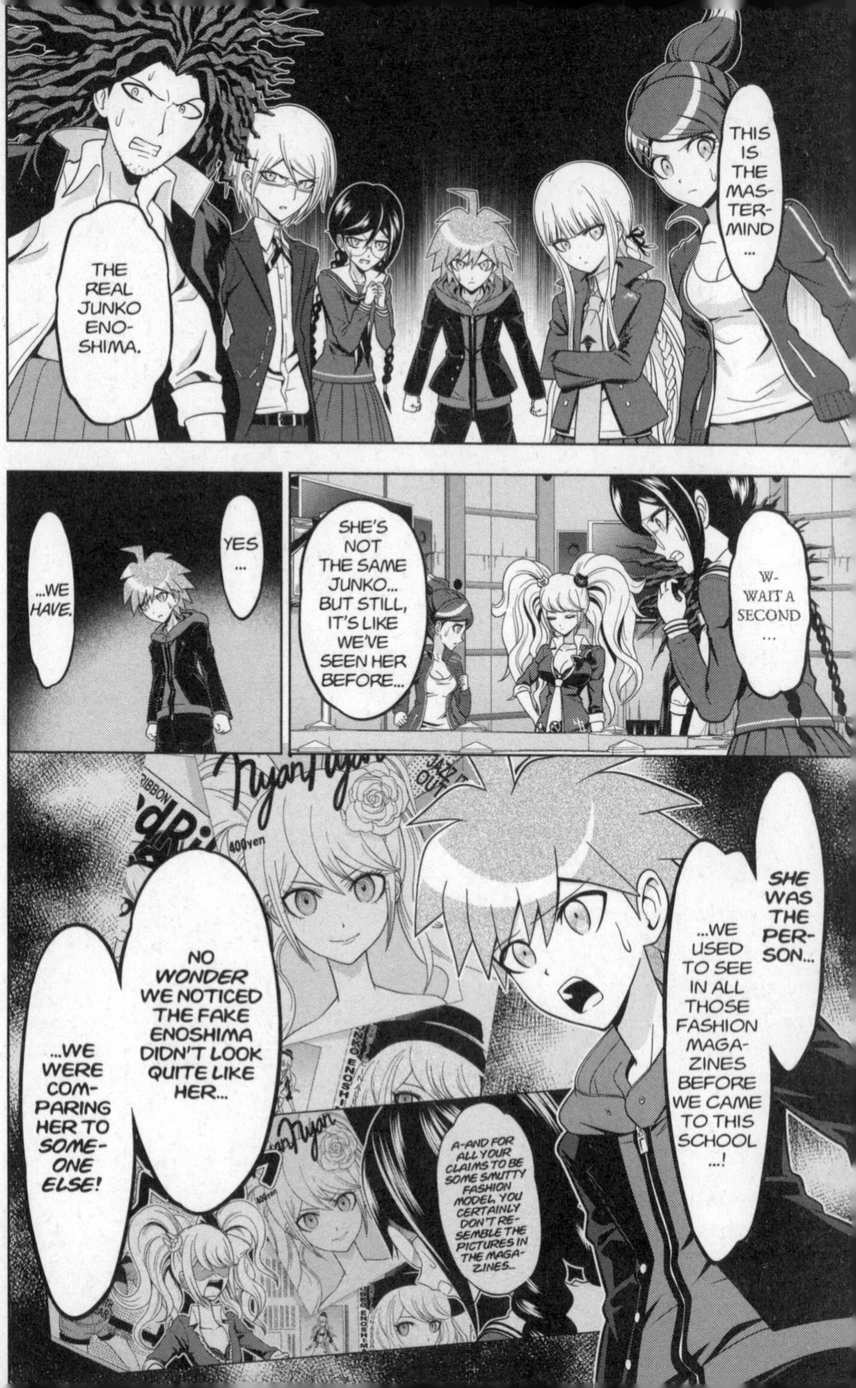
THIS IS THE MASTERMIND...
THE REAL JUNKO ENOSHIMA.
W-WAIT A SECOND...
SHE'S NOT THE SAME JUNKO... BUT STILL, IT'S LIKE WE'VE SEEN HER BEFORE...
YES...
...WE HAVE.
SHE WAS THE PERSON...
...WE USED TO SEE IN ALL THOSE FASHION MAGAZINES BEFORE WE CAME TO THIS SCHOOL...!
400yen
NO WONDER WE NOTICED THE FAKE ENOSHIMA DIDN'T LOOK QUITE LIKE HER...
...WE WERE COMPARING HER TO SOMEONE ELSE!
A-AND FOR ALL YOUR CLAIMS TO BE SOME SMUTTY FASHION MODEL, YOU CERTAINLY DON'T RESEMBLE THE PICTURES IN THE MAGAZINES...

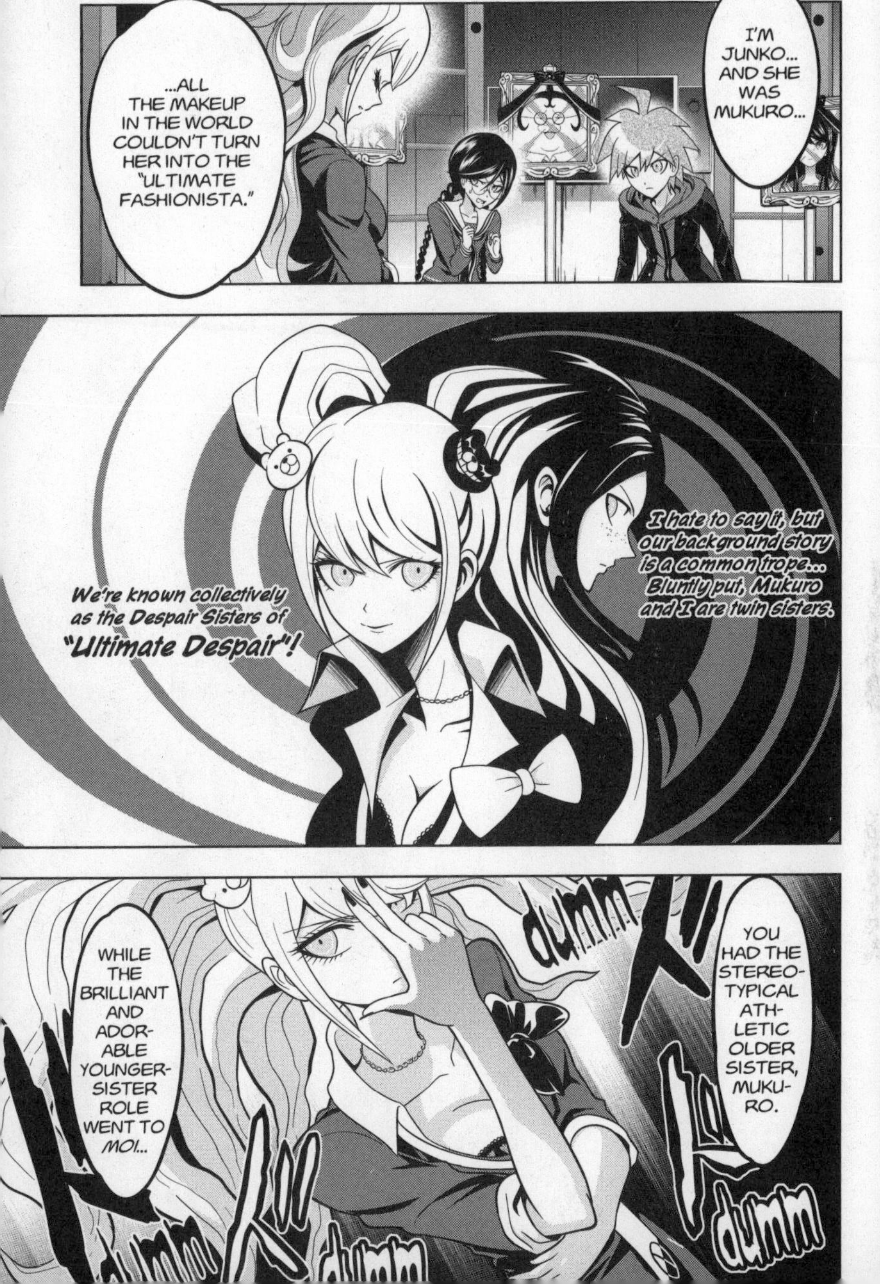
I'M JUNKO... AND SHE WAS MUKURO...
...ALL THE MAKEUP IN THE WORLD COULDN'T TURN HER INTO THE "ULTIMATE FASHIONISTA."
I hate to say it, but our background story is a common trope... Bluntly put, Mukuro and I are twin sisters.
We're known collectively as the Despair Sisters of "Ultimate Despair"!
YOU HAD THE STEREO-TYPICAL ATH-LETIC OLDER SISTER, MUKU-RO.
WHILE THE BRILLIANT AND ADOR-ABLE YOUNGER-SISTER ROLE WENT TO MOI...
dumm
dumm
dumm

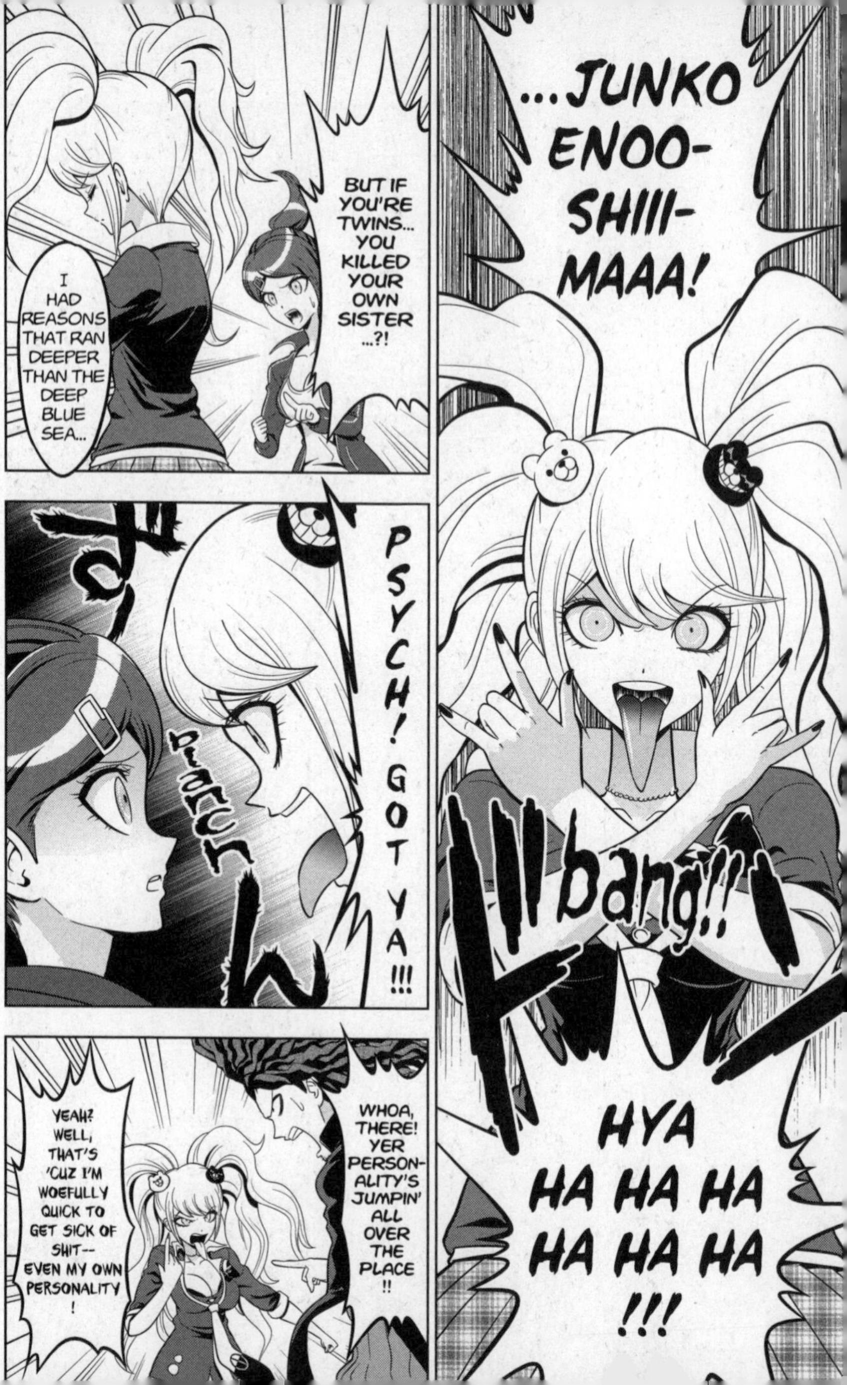
...JUNKO ENOO-SHIII-MAAA!
bang!!
HYA HA HA HA HA HA HA HA !!!
BUT IF YOU'RE TWINS... YOU KILLED YOUR OWN SISTER ...?!
I HAD REASONS THAT RAN DEEPER THAN THE DEEP BLUE SEA...
PSYCH! GOT YA !!!
blanch
WHOA, THERE! YER PERSON-ALITY'S JUMPIN' ALL OVER THE PLACE !!
YEAH? WELL, THAT'S 'CUZ I'M WOEFULLY QUICK TO GET SICK OF SHIT-- EVEN MY OWN PERSONALITY !

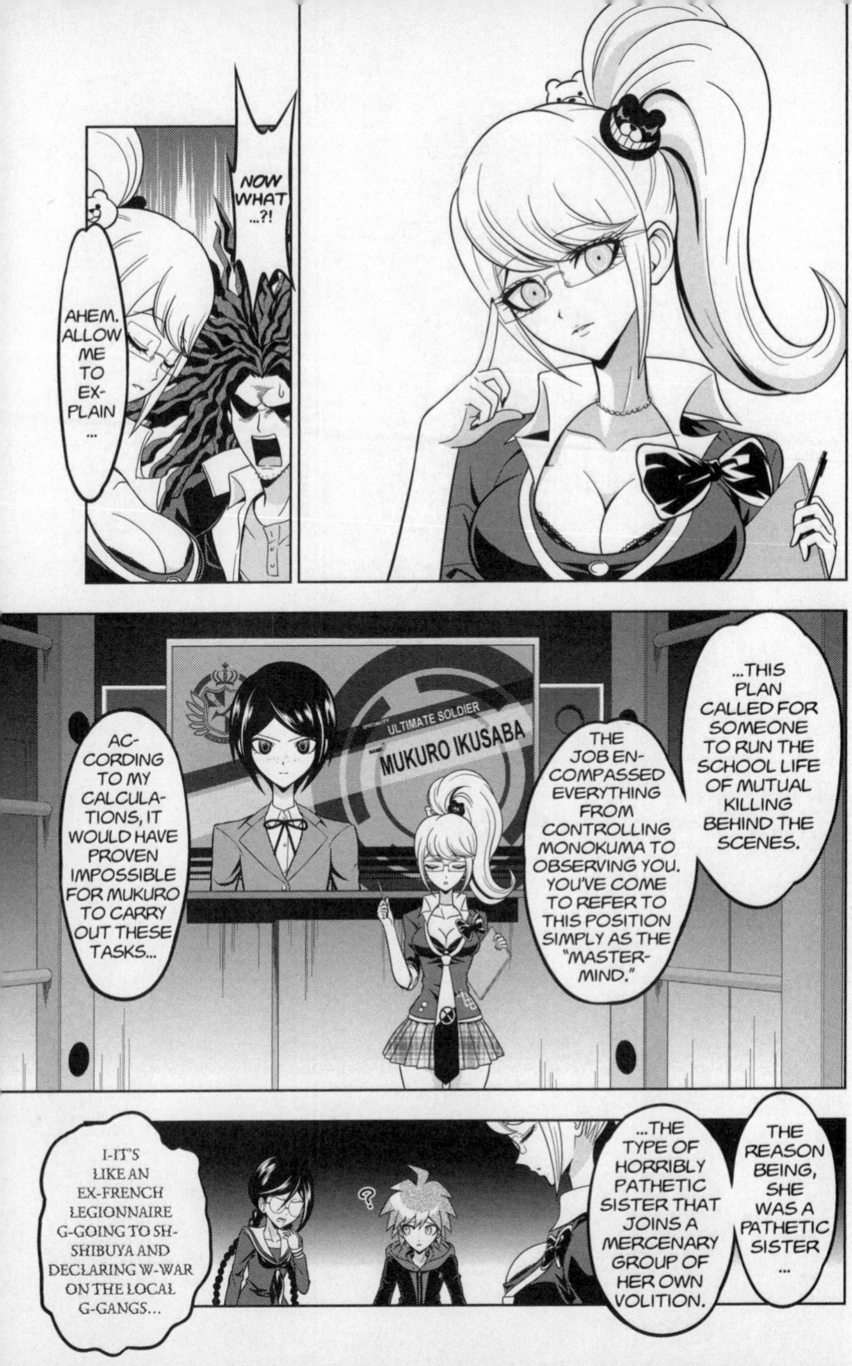
NOW WHAT ...?!
AHEM. ALLOW ME TO EX-PLAIN ...
...THIS PLAN CALLED FOR SOMEONE TO RUN THE SCHOOL LIFE OF MUTUAL KILLING BEHIND THE SCENES.
ULTIMATE SOLDIER
MUKURO IKUSABA
THE JOB EN-COMPASSED EVERYTHING FROM CONTROLLING MONOKUMA TO OBSERVING YOU. YOU'VE COME TO REFER TO THIS POSITION SIMPLY AS THE "MASTER-MIND."
AC-CORDING TO MY CALCULA-TIONS, IT WOULD HAVE PROVEN IMPOSSIBLE FOR MUKURO TO CARRY OUT THESE TASKS...
THE REASON BEING, SHE WAS A PATHETIC SISTER ...
...THE TYPE OF HORRIBLY PATHETIC SISTER THAT JOINS A MERCENARY GROUP OF HER OWN VOLITION.
I-IT'S LIKE AN EX-FRENCH LEGIONNAIRE G-GOING TO SH-SHIBUYA AND DECLARING W-WAR ON THE LOCAL G-GANGS...

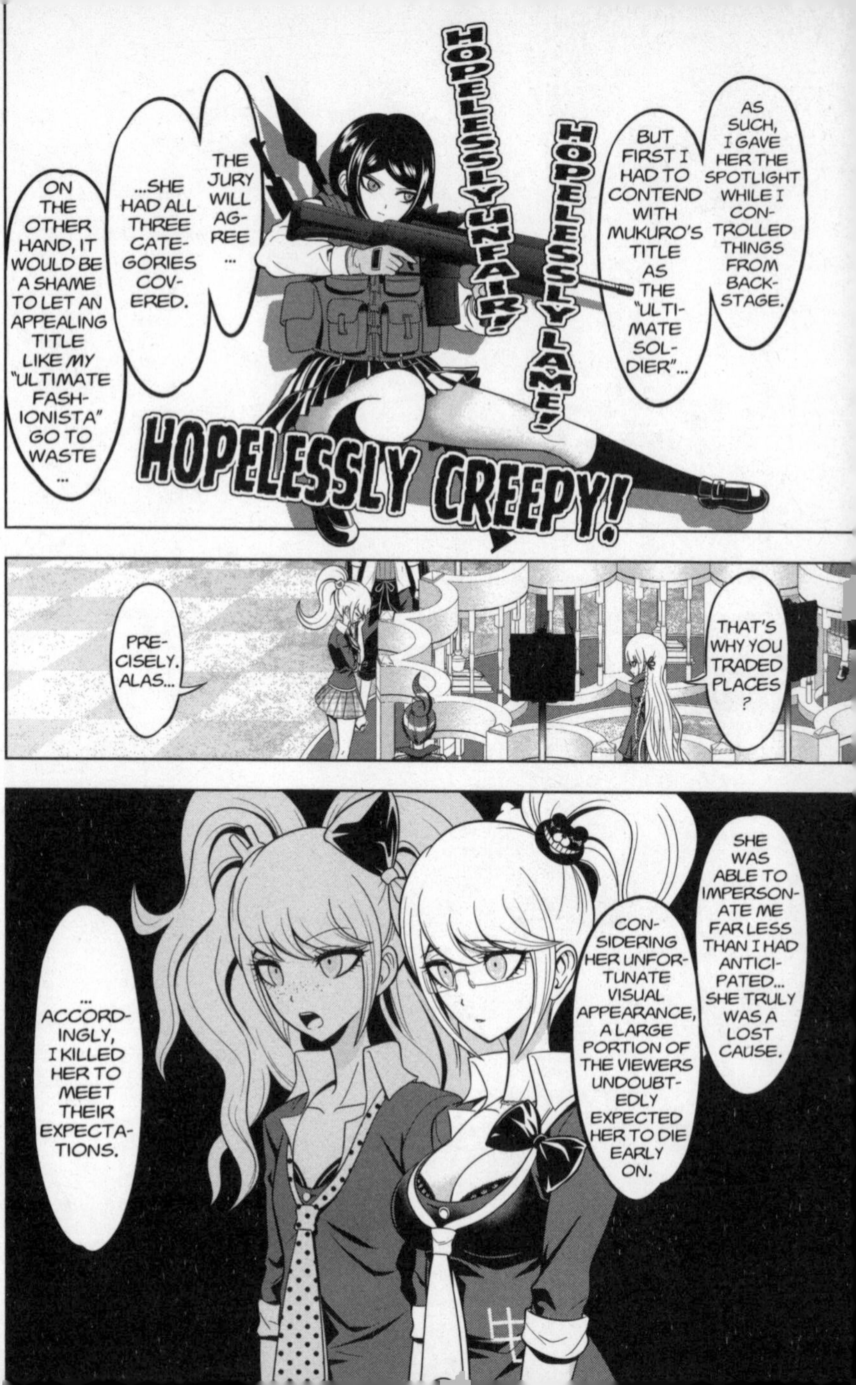
AS SUCH, I GAVE HER THE SPOTLIGHT WHILE I CONTROLLED THINGS FROM BACKSTAGE.
BUT FIRST I HAD TO CONTEND WITH MUKURO'S TITLE AS THE "ULTIMATE SOLDIER"...
HOPELESSLY LAME!
HOPELESSLY UNFAIR!
THE JURY WILL AGREE...
...SHE HAD ALL THREE CATEGORIES COVERED.
HOPELESSLY CREEPY!
ON THE OTHER HAND, IT WOULD BE A SHAME TO LET AN APPEALING TITLE LIKE *MY* "ULTIMATE FASHIONISTA" GO TO WASTE...
THAT'S WHY YOU TRADED PLACES?
PRECISELY. ALAS...
SHE WAS ABLE TO IMPERSONATE ME FAR LESS THAN I HAD ANTICIPATED... SHE TRULY WAS A LOST CAUSE.
CONSIDERING HER UNFORTUNATE VISUAL APPEARANCE, A LARGE PORTION OF THE VIEWERS UNDOUBTEDLY EXPECTED HER TO DIE EARLY ON.
...ACCORDINGLY, I KILLED HER TO MEET THEIR EXPECTATIONS.

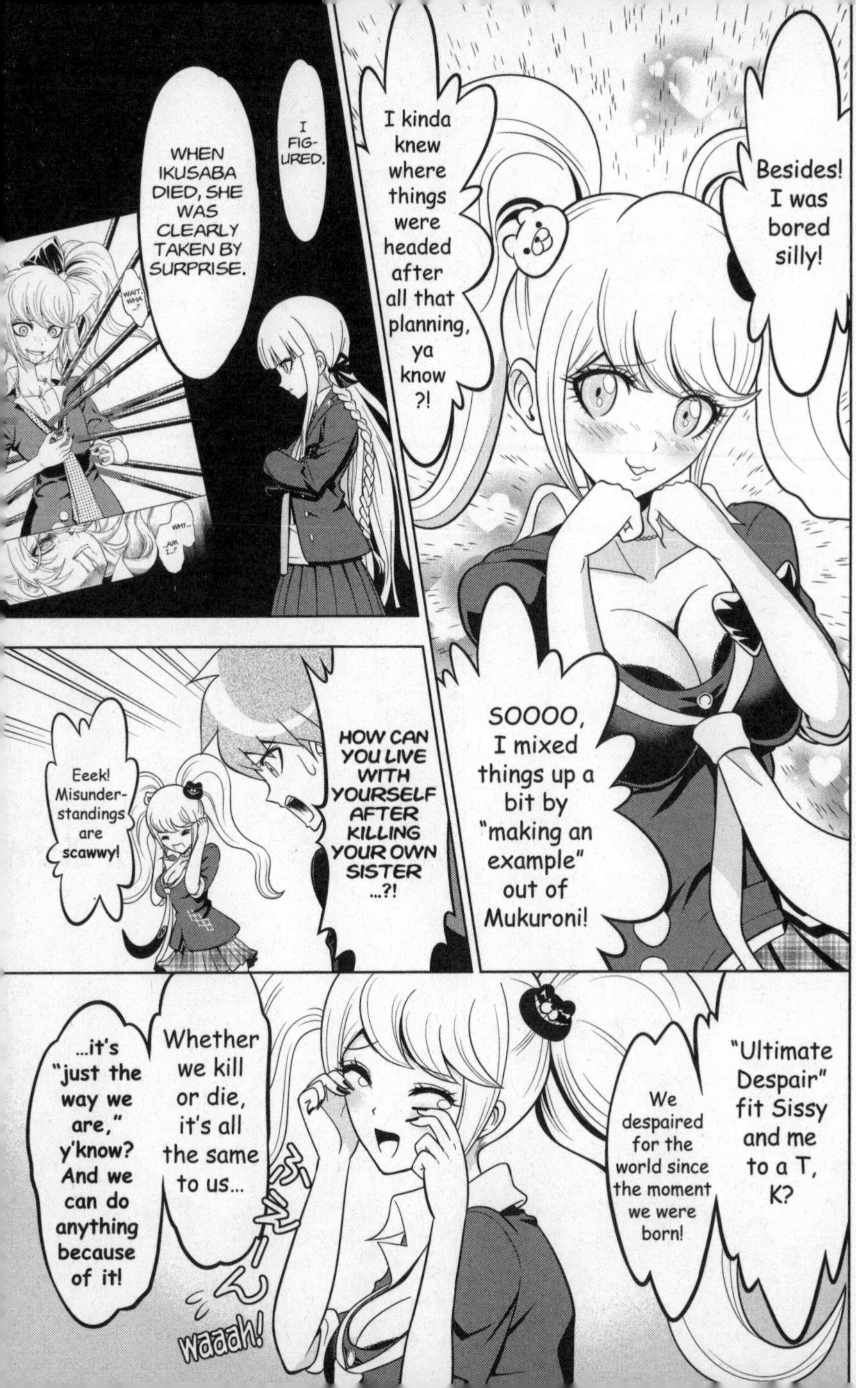
Besides! I was bored silly!
I kinda knew where things were headed after all that planning, ya know?!
SOOOO, I mixed things up a bit by "making an example" out of Mukuroni!
I FIGURED.
WHEN IKUSABA DIED, SHE WAS CLEARLY TAKEN BY SURPRISE.
WAIT. WHA...?
WHY... ...AM I...?
HOW CAN YOU LIVE WITH YOURSELF AFTER KILLING YOUR OWN SISTER ...?!
Eeek! Misunder-standings are scawwy!
"Ultimate Despair" fit Sissy and me to a T, K?
We despaired for the world since the moment we were born!
Whether we kill or die, it's all the same to us...
...it's "just the way we are," y'know? And we can do anything because of it!
Waaah!

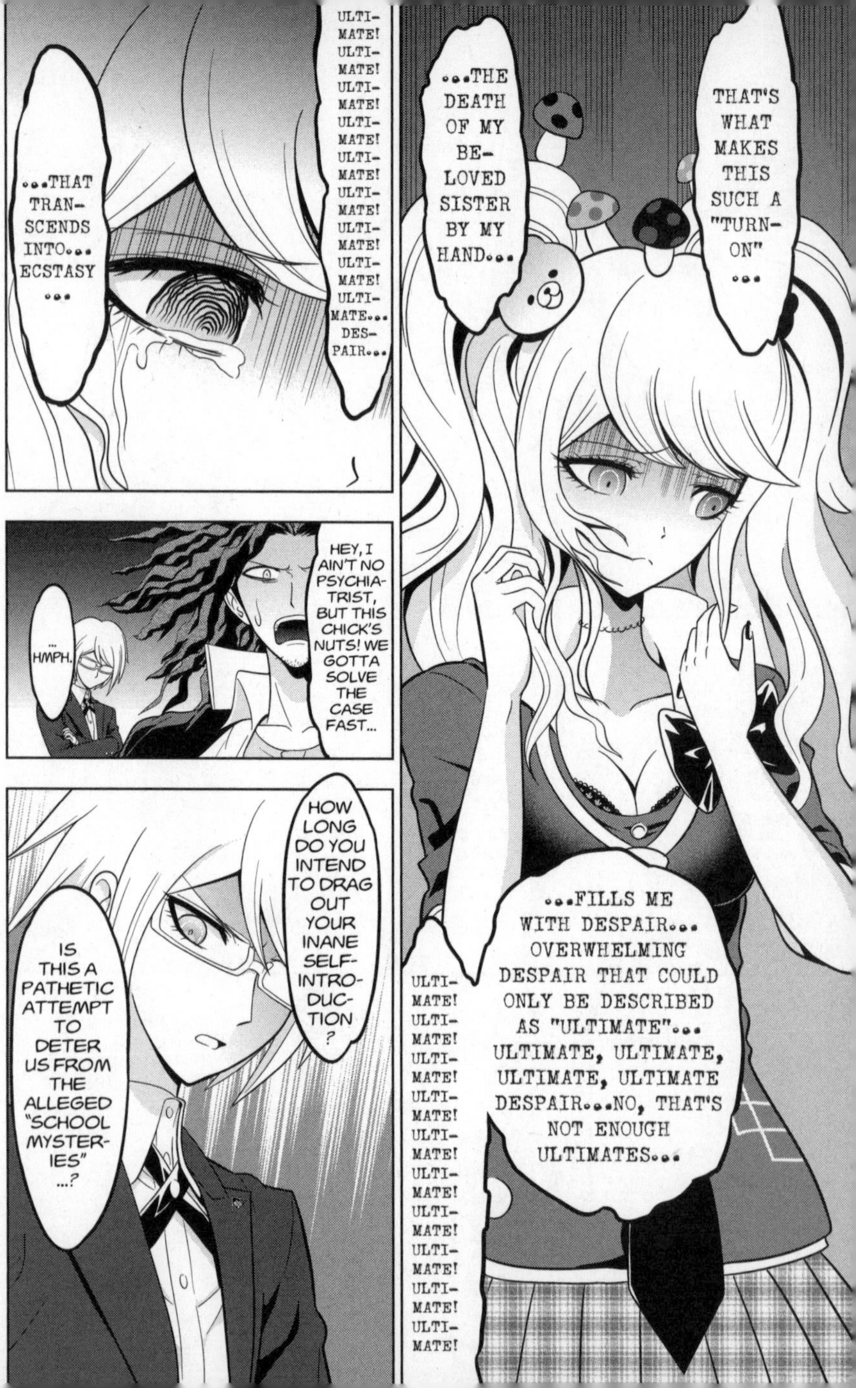
THAT'S WHAT MAKES THIS SUCH A "TURN-ON"...
...THE DEATH OF MY BELOVED SISTER BY MY HAND...
...FILLS ME WITH DESPAIR... OVERWHELMING DESPAIR THAT COULD ONLY BE DESCRIBED AS "ULTIMATE"... ULTIMATE, ULTIMATE, ULTIMATE, ULTIMATE DESPAIR...NO, THAT'S NOT ENOUGH ULTIMATES...
ULTIMATE! ULTIMATE! ULTIMATE! ULTIMATE! ULTIMATE! ULTIMATE! ULTIMATE! ULTIMATE! ULTIMATE! ULTIMATE!
ULTIMATE! ULTIMATE! ULTIMATE! ULTIMATE! ULTIMATE! ULTIMATE! ULTIMATE! ULTIMATE! ULTIMATE... DESPAIR...
...THAT TRANSCENDS INTO... ECSTASY ...
HEY, I AIN'T NO PSYCHIATRIST, BUT THIS CHICK'S NUTS! WE GOTTA SOLVE THE CASE FAST...
... HMPH.
HOW LONG DO YOU INTEND TO DRAG OUT YOUR INANE SELF-INTRODUCTION?
IS THIS A PATHETIC ATTEMPT TO DETER US FROM THE ALLEGED "SCHOOL MYSTERIES" ...?

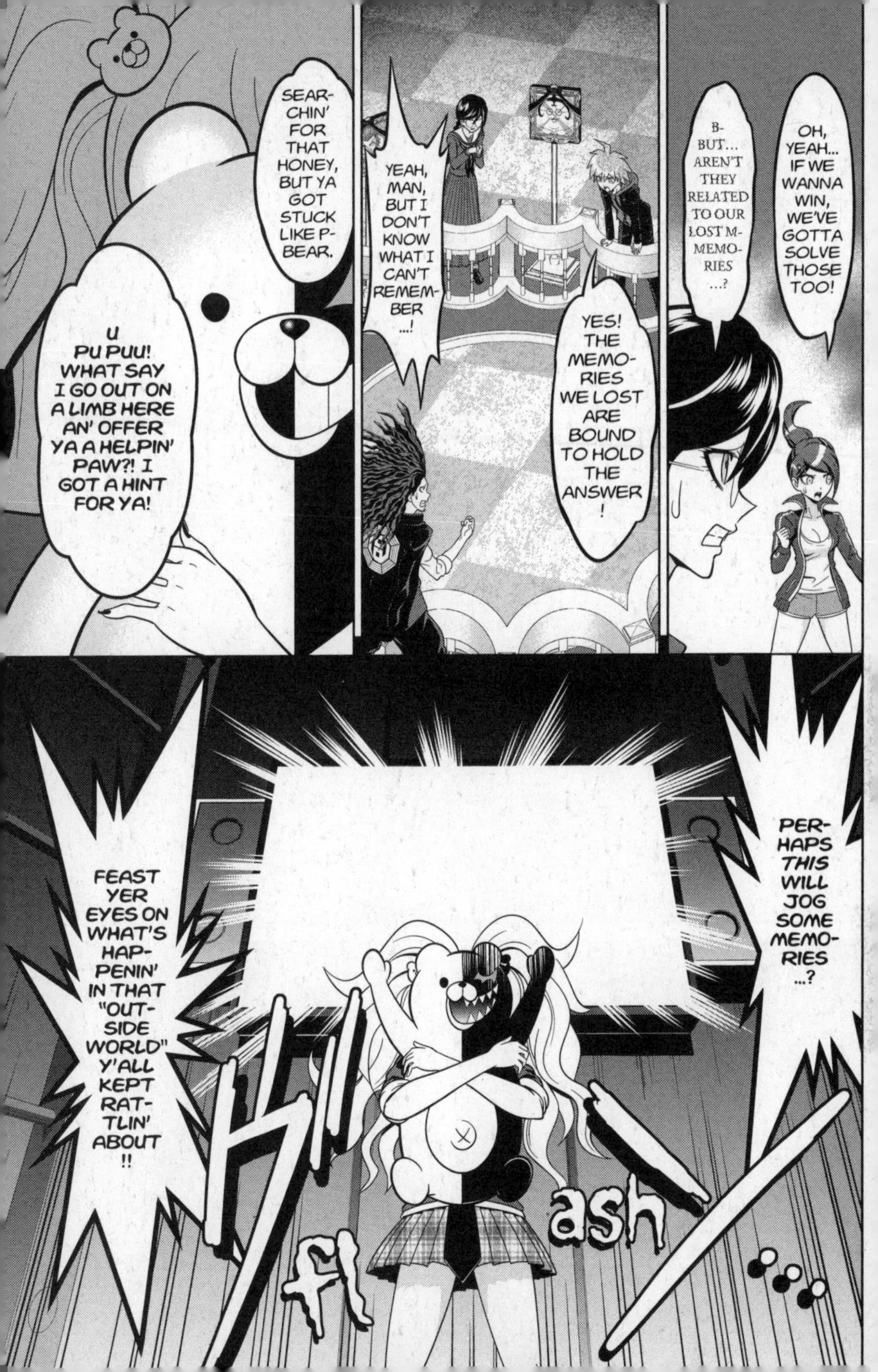
OH, YEAH... IF WE WANNA WIN, WE'VE GOTTA SOLVE THOSE TOO!
B-BUT... AREN'T THEY RELATED TO OUR LOST M-MEMORIES ...?
YEAH, MAN, BUT I DON'T KNOW WHAT I CAN'T REMEMBER ...!
YES! THE MEMORIES WE LOST ARE BOUND TO HOLD THE ANSWER!
SEARCHIN' FOR THAT HONEY, BUT YA GOT STUCK LIKE P-BEAR.
U PU PUU! WHAT SAY I GO OUT ON A LIMB HERE AN' OFFER YA A HELPIN' PAW?! I GOT A HINT FOR YA!
PERHAPS THIS WILL JOG SOME MEMORIES ...?
FEAST YER EYES ON WHAT'S HAPPENIN' IN THAT "OUTSIDE WORLD" Y'ALL KEPT RATTLIN' ABOUT !!
flash

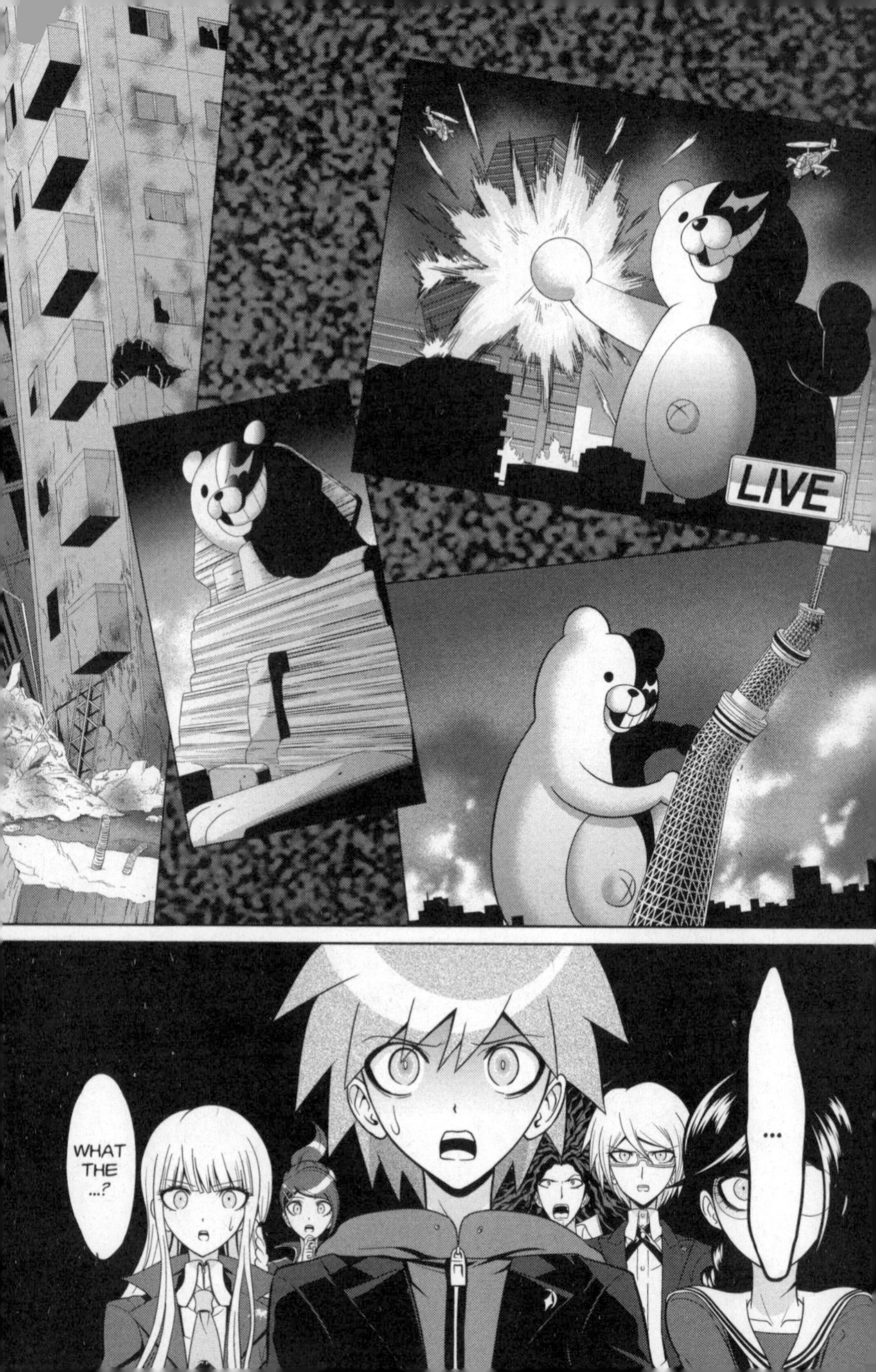
LIVE
...
WHAT THE ...?

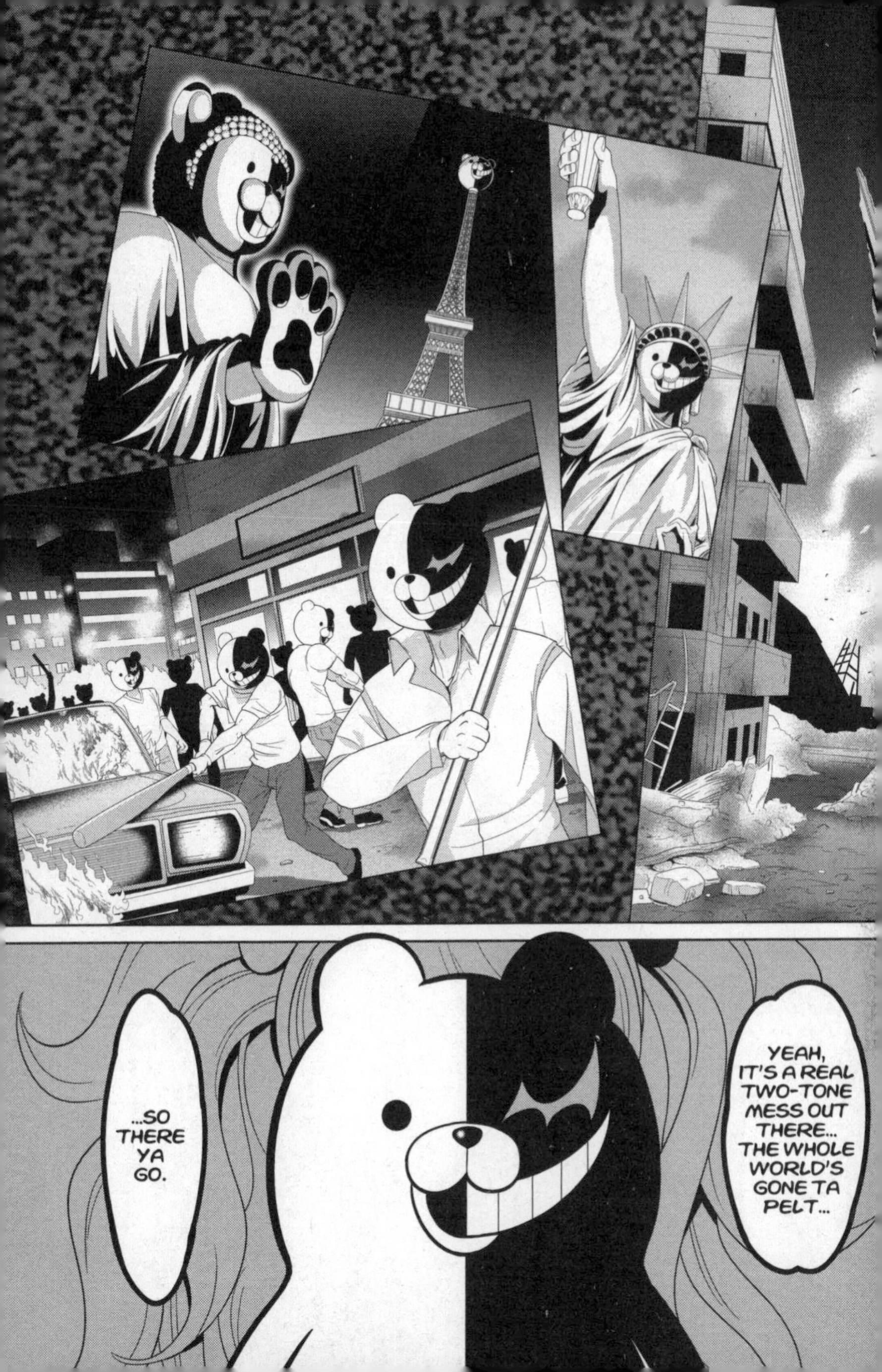
YEAH, IT'S A REAL TWO-TONE MESS OUT THERE... THE WHOLE WORLD'S GONE TA PELT...
...SO THERE YA GO.

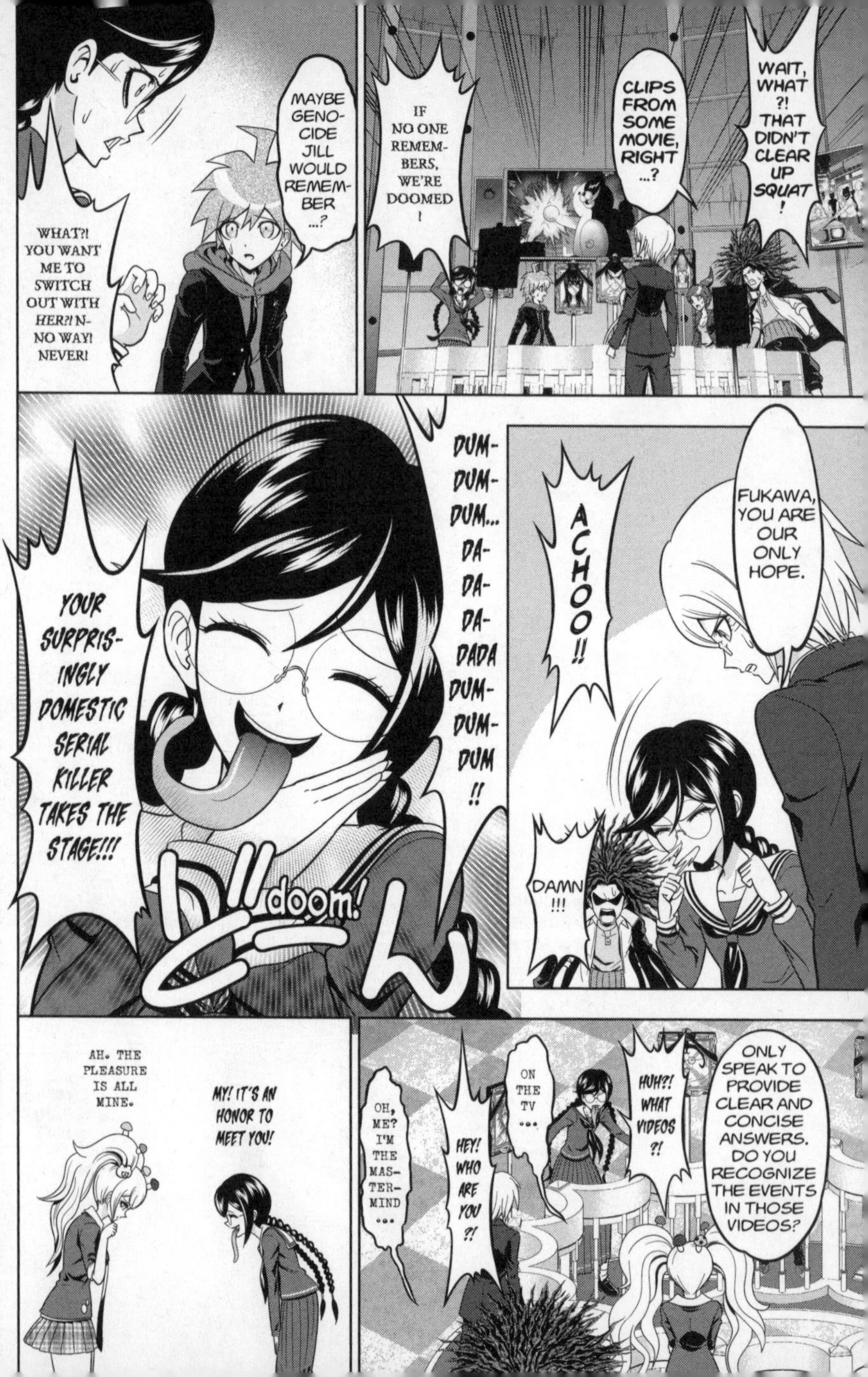
WAIT, WHAT?! THAT DIDN'T CLEAR UP SQUAT!
CLIPS FROM SOME MOVIE, RIGHT...?
IF NO ONE REMEMBERS, WE'RE DOOMED!
MAYBE GENOCIDE JILL WOULD REMEMBER...?
WHAT?! YOU WANT ME TO SWITCH OUT WITH HER?! N-NO WAY! NEVER!
FUKAWA, YOU ARE OUR ONLY HOPE.
ACHOO!!
DAMN!!!
DUM-DUM-DUM... DA-DA-DA-DADA DUM-DUM-DUM!!
YOUR SURPRISINGLY DOMESTIC SERIAL KILLER TAKES THE STAGE!!!
doom!
どーん
ONLY SPEAK TO PROVIDE CLEAR AND CONCISE ANSWERS. DO YOU RECOGNIZE THE EVENTS IN THOSE VIDEOS?
HUH?! WHAT VIDEOS?!
ON THE TV...
HEY! WHO ARE YOU?!
OH, ME? I'M THE MASTERMIND...
MY! IT'S AN HONOR TO MEET YOU!
AH. THE PLEASURE IS ALL MINE.

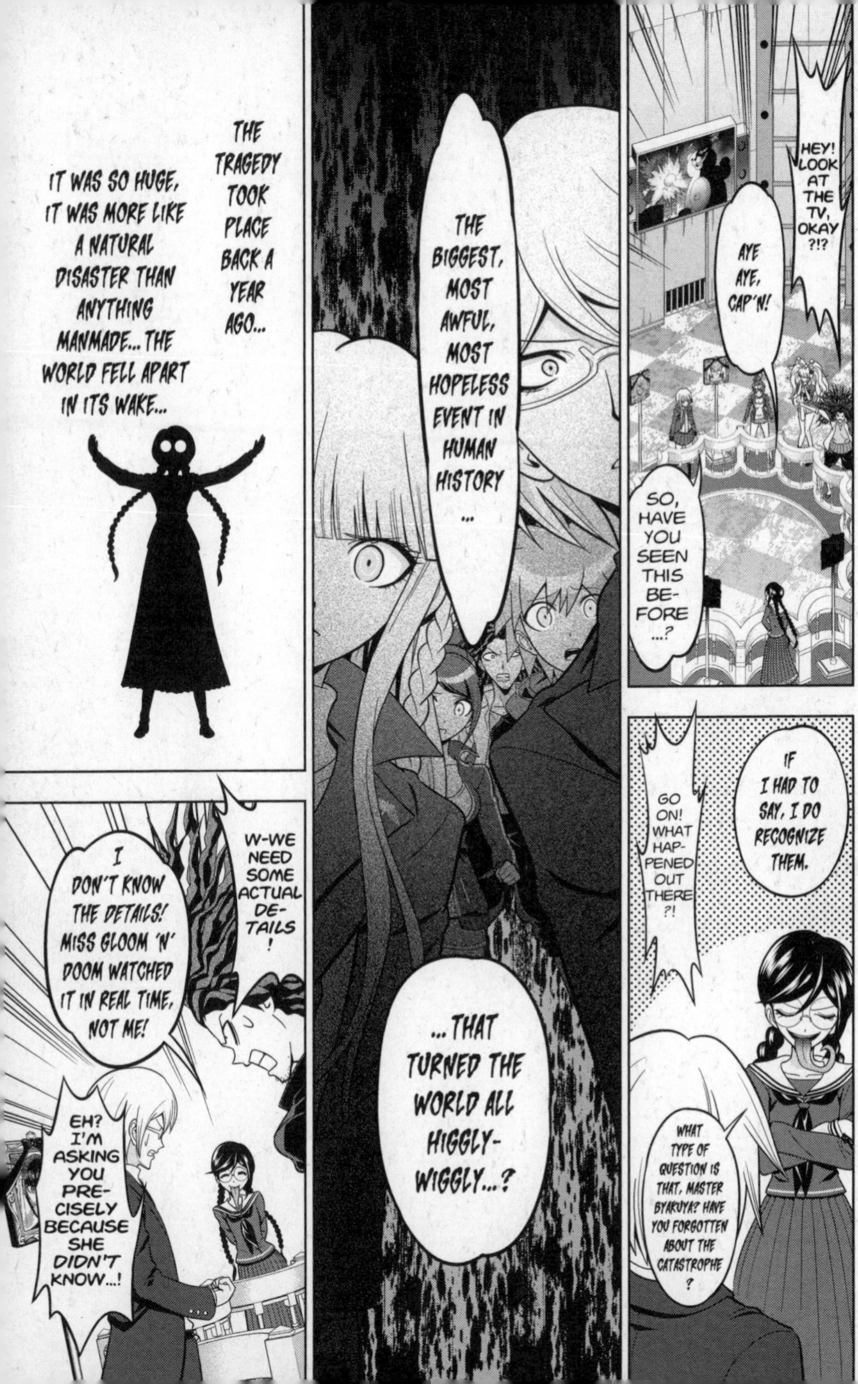
HEY! LOOK AT THE TV, OKAY?!?
AYE AYE, CAP'N!
SO, HAVE YOU SEEN THIS BE-FORE...?
IF I HAD TO SAY, I DO RECOGNIZE THEM.
GO ON! WHAT HAP-PENED OUT THERE?!
WHAT TYPE OF QUESTION IS THAT, MASTER BYAKUYA? HAVE YOU FORGOTTEN ABOUT THE CATASTROPHE?
W-WE NEED SOME ACTUAL DE-TAILS!
I DON'T KNOW THE DETAILS! MISS GLOOM 'N' DOOM WATCHED IT IN REAL TIME, NOT ME!
EH? I'M ASKING YOU PRE-CISELY BECAUSE SHE DIDN'T KNOW...!
THE TRAGEDY TOOK PLACE BACK A YEAR AGO...
IT WAS SO HUGE, IT WAS MORE LIKE A NATURAL DISASTER THAN ANYTHING MANMADE... THE WORLD FELL APART IN ITS WAKE...
THE BIGGEST, MOST AWFUL, MOST HOPELESS EVENT IN HUMAN HISTORY...
...THAT TURNED THE WORLD ALL HIGGLY-WIGGLY...?

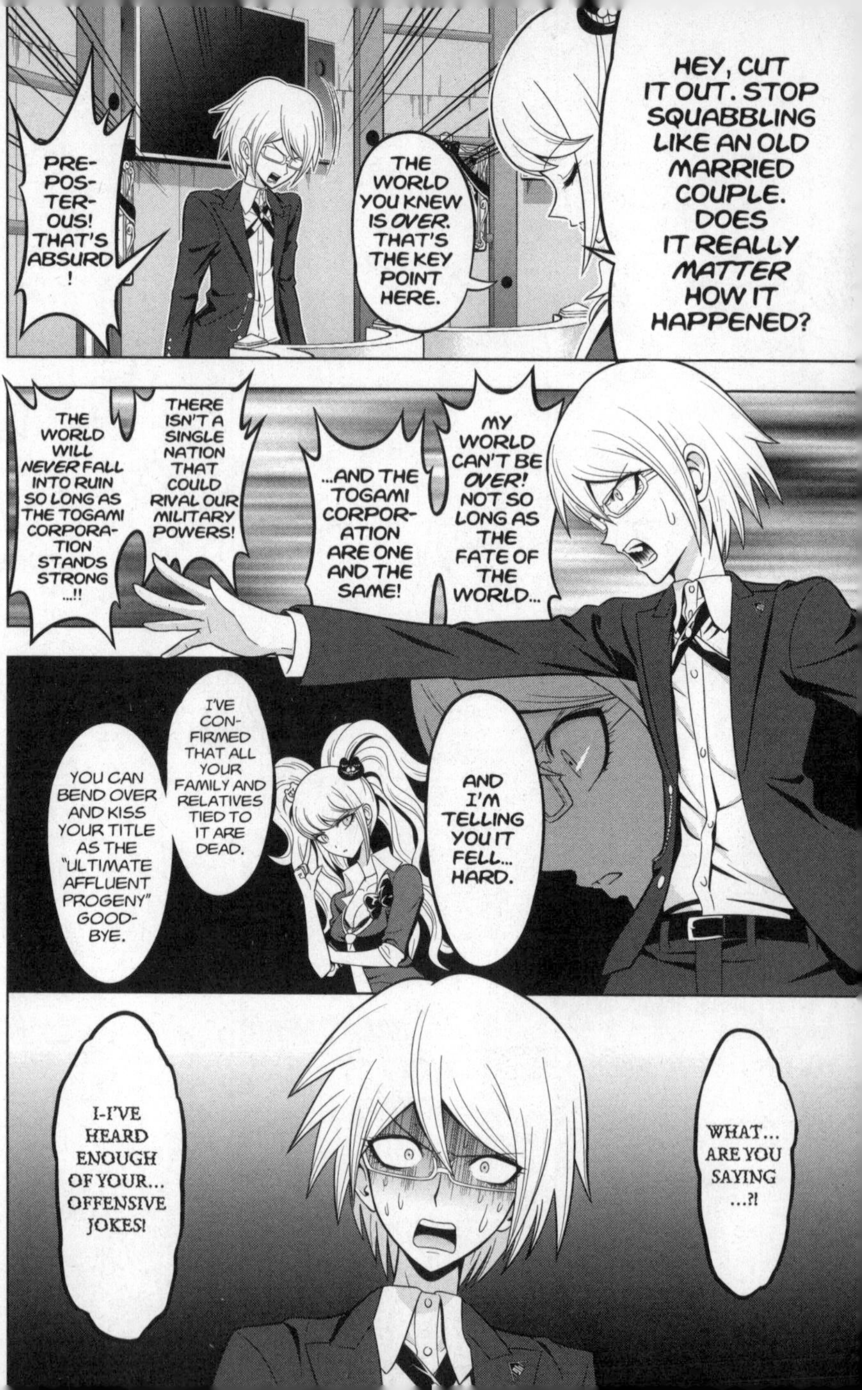
HEY, CUT IT OUT. STOP SQUABBLING LIKE AN OLD MARRIED COUPLE. DOES IT REALLY *MATTER* HOW IT HAPPENED?
THE WORLD YOU KNEW IS *OVER*. THAT'S THE KEY POINT HERE.
PRE-POS-TER-OUS! THAT'S ABSURD!
MY WORLD CAN'T BE *OVER*! NOT SO LONG AS THE FATE OF THE WORLD...
...AND THE TOGAMI CORPOR-ATION ARE ONE AND THE SAME!
THERE ISN'T A SINGLE NATION THAT COULD RIVAL OUR MILITARY POWERS!
THE WORLD WILL *NEVER* FALL INTO RUIN SO LONG AS THE TOGAMI CORPORA-TION STANDS STRONG ...!!
AND I'M TELLING YOU IT FELL... HARD.
I'VE CON-FIRMED THAT ALL YOUR FAMILY AND RELATIVES TIED TO IT ARE DEAD.
YOU CAN BEND OVER AND KISS YOUR TITLE AS THE "ULTIMATE AFFLUENT PROGENY" GOOD-BYE.
WHAT... ARE YOU SAYING ...?!
I-I'VE HEARD ENOUGH OF YOUR... OFFENSIVE JOKES!

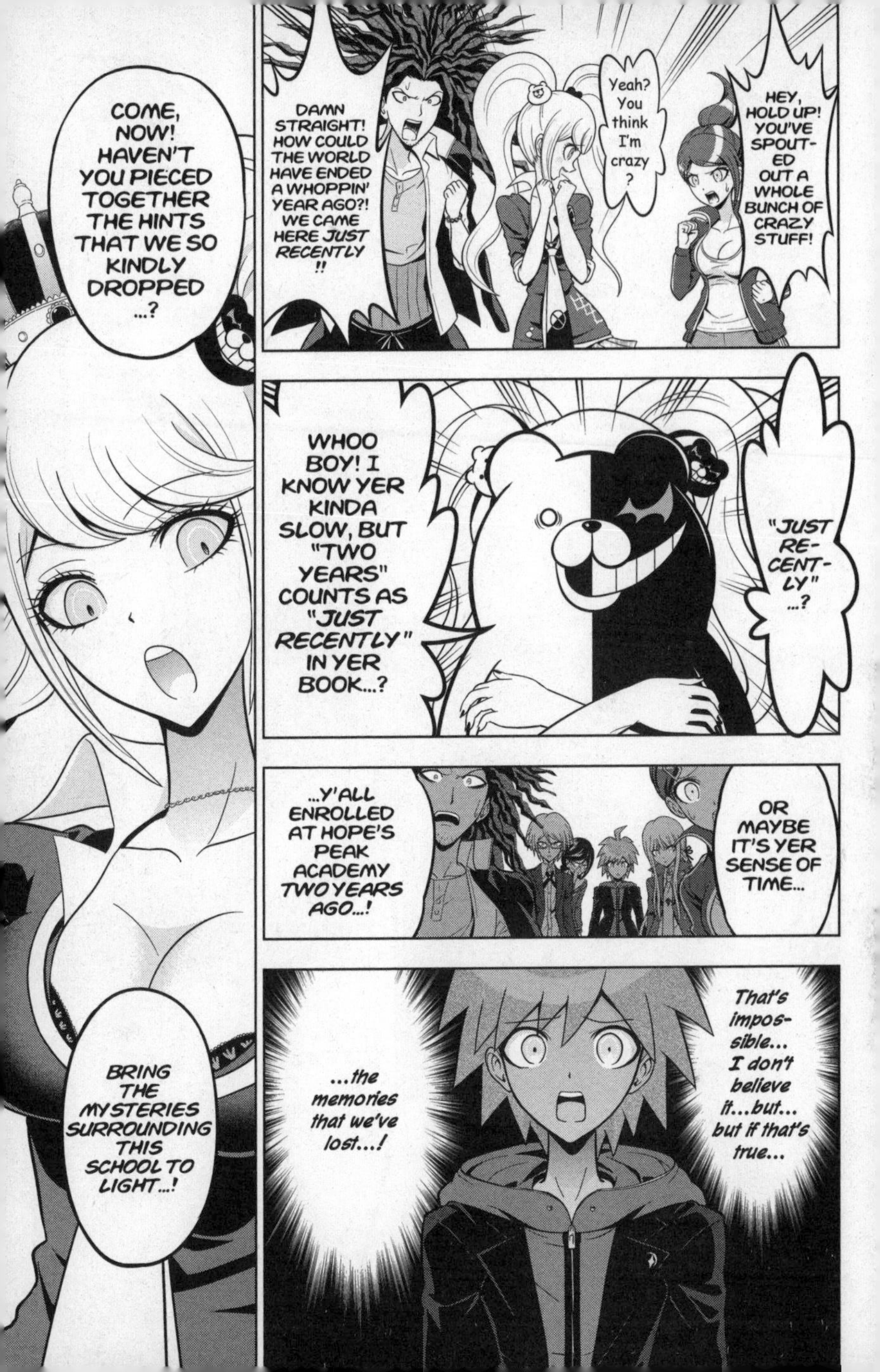
HEY, HOLD UP! YOU'VE SPOUTED OUT A WHOLE BUNCH OF CRAZY STUFF!
Yeah? You think I'm crazy?
DAMN STRAIGHT! HOW COULD THE WORLD HAVE ENDED A WHOPPIN' YEAR AGO?! WE CAME HERE JUST RECENTLY!!
"JUST RECENTLY"...?
WHOO BOY! I KNOW YER KINDA SLOW, BUT "TWO YEARS" COUNTS AS "JUST RECENTLY" IN YER BOOK...?
OR MAYBE IT'S YER SENSE OF TIME...
...Y'ALL ENROLLED AT HOPE'S PEAK ACADEMY TWO YEARS AGO...!
That's impossible... I don't believe it...but... but if that's true...
...the memories that we've lost...!
COME, NOW! HAVEN'T YOU PIECED TOGETHER THE HINTS THAT WE SO KINDLY DROPPED...?
BRING THE MYSTERIES SURROUNDING THIS SCHOOL TO LIGHT...!

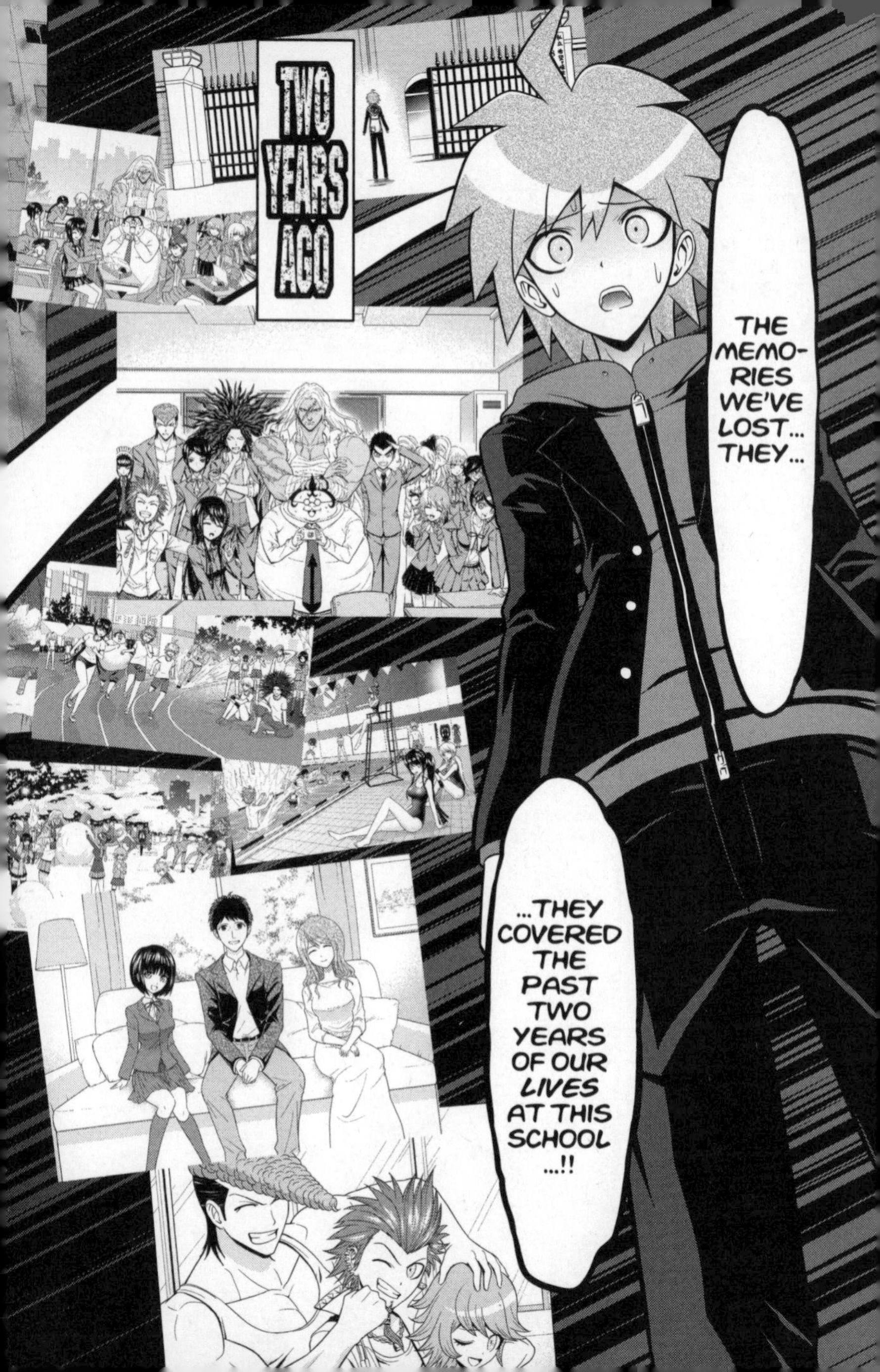
TWO YEARS AGO
THE MEMORIES WE'VE LOST... THEY...
...THEY COVERED THE PAST TWO YEARS OF OUR LIVES AT THIS SCHOOL ...!!

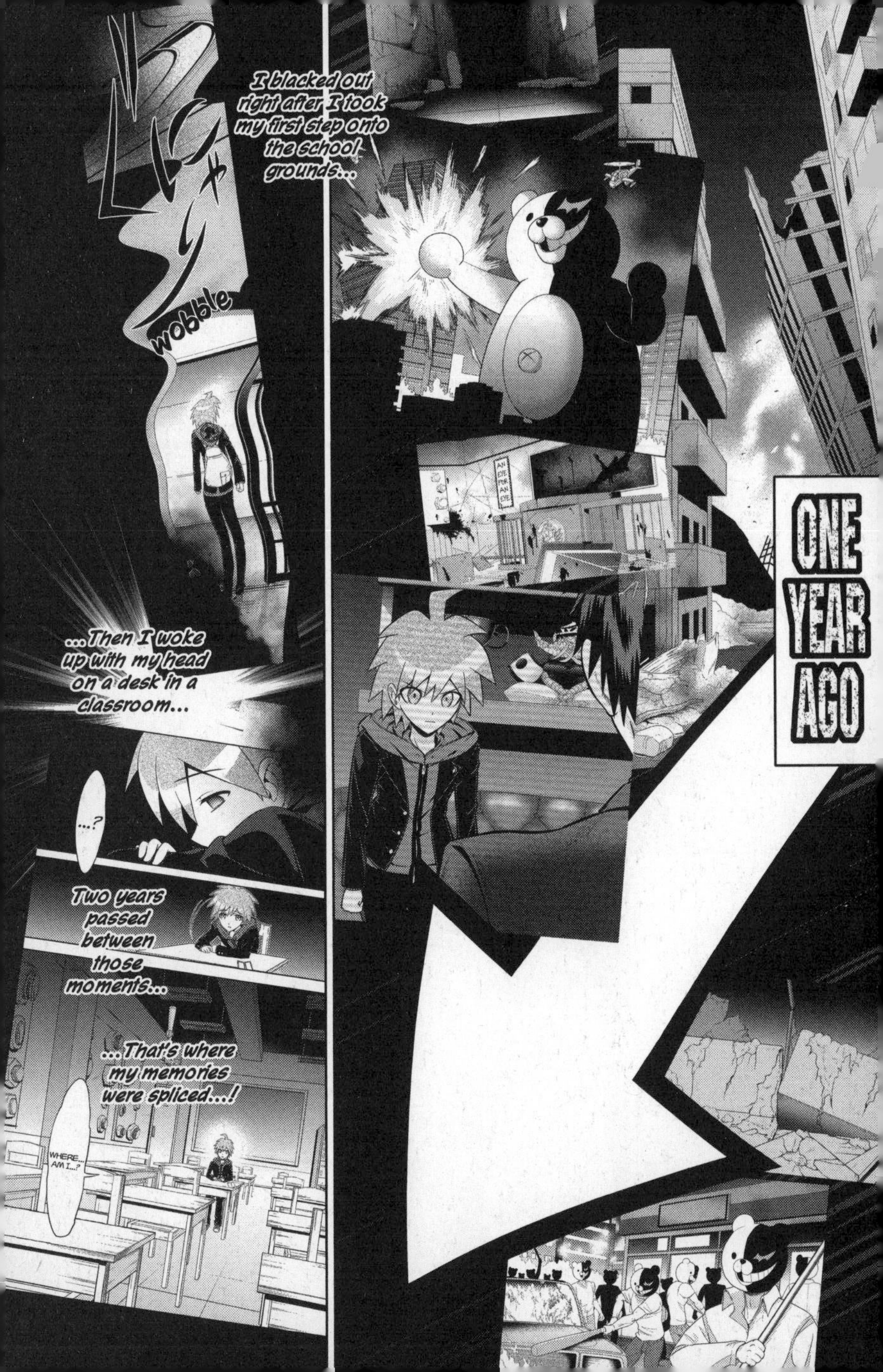
ONE YEAR AGO
I blacked out right after I took my first step onto the school grounds...
wobble
...Then I woke up with my head on a desk in a classroom...
...?
Two years passed between those moments...
...That's where my memories were spliced...!
WHERE... AM I...?

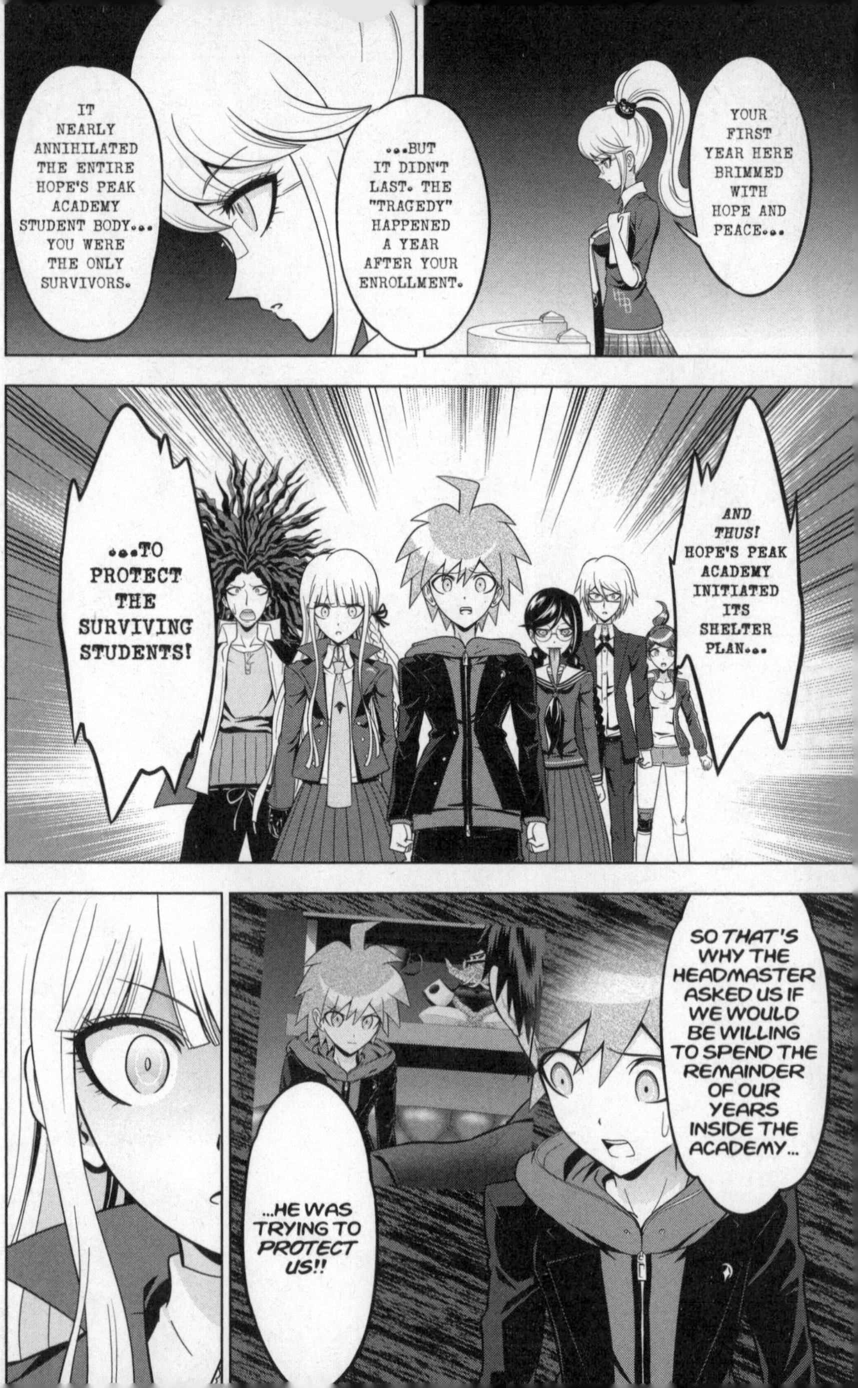
YOUR FIRST YEAR HERE BRIMMED WITH HOPE AND PEACE...
...BUT IT DIDN'T LAST. THE "TRAGEDY" HAPPENED A YEAR AFTER YOUR ENROLLMENT.
IT NEARLY ANNIHILATED THE ENTIRE HOPE'S PEAK ACADEMY STUDENT BODY... YOU WERE THE ONLY SURVIVORS.
AND THUS! HOPE'S PEAK ACADEMY INITIATED ITS SHELTER PLAN...
...TO PROTECT THE SURVIVING STUDENTS!
SO THAT'S WHY THE HEADMASTER ASKED US IF WE WOULD BE WILLING TO SPEND THE REMAINDER OF OUR YEARS INSIDE THE ACADEMY...
...HE WAS TRYING TO PROTECT US!!

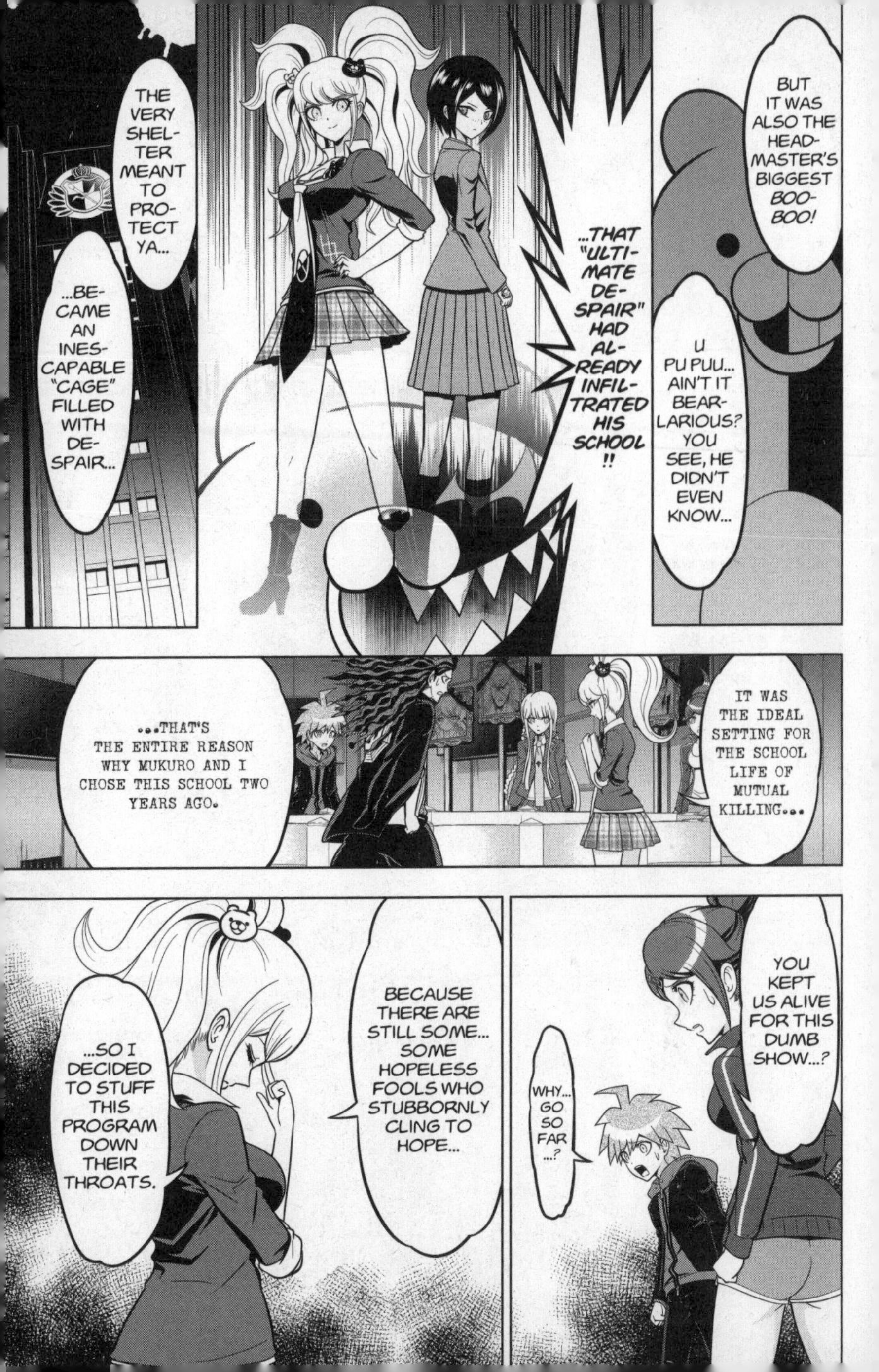
BUT IT WAS ALSO THE HEADMASTER'S BIGGEST BOO-BOO!
U PU PUU... AIN'T IT BEARLARIOUS? YOU SEE, HE DIDN'T EVEN KNOW...
...THAT "ULTIMATE DESPAIR" HAD ALREADY INFILTRATED HIS SCHOOL!!
THE VERY SHELTER MEANT TO PROTECT YA...
...BECAME AN INESCAPABLE "CAGE" FILLED WITH DESPAIR...
IT WAS THE IDEAL SETTING FOR THE SCHOOL LIFE OF MUTUAL KILLING...
...THAT'S THE ENTIRE REASON WHY MUKURO AND I CHOSE THIS SCHOOL TWO YEARS AGO.
YOU KEPT US ALIVE FOR THIS DUMB SHOW...?
WHY... GO SO FAR...?
BECAUSE THERE ARE STILL SOME... SOME HOPELESS FOOLS WHO STUBBORNLY CLING TO HOPE...
...SO I DECIDED TO STUFF THIS PROGRAM DOWN THEIR THROATS.

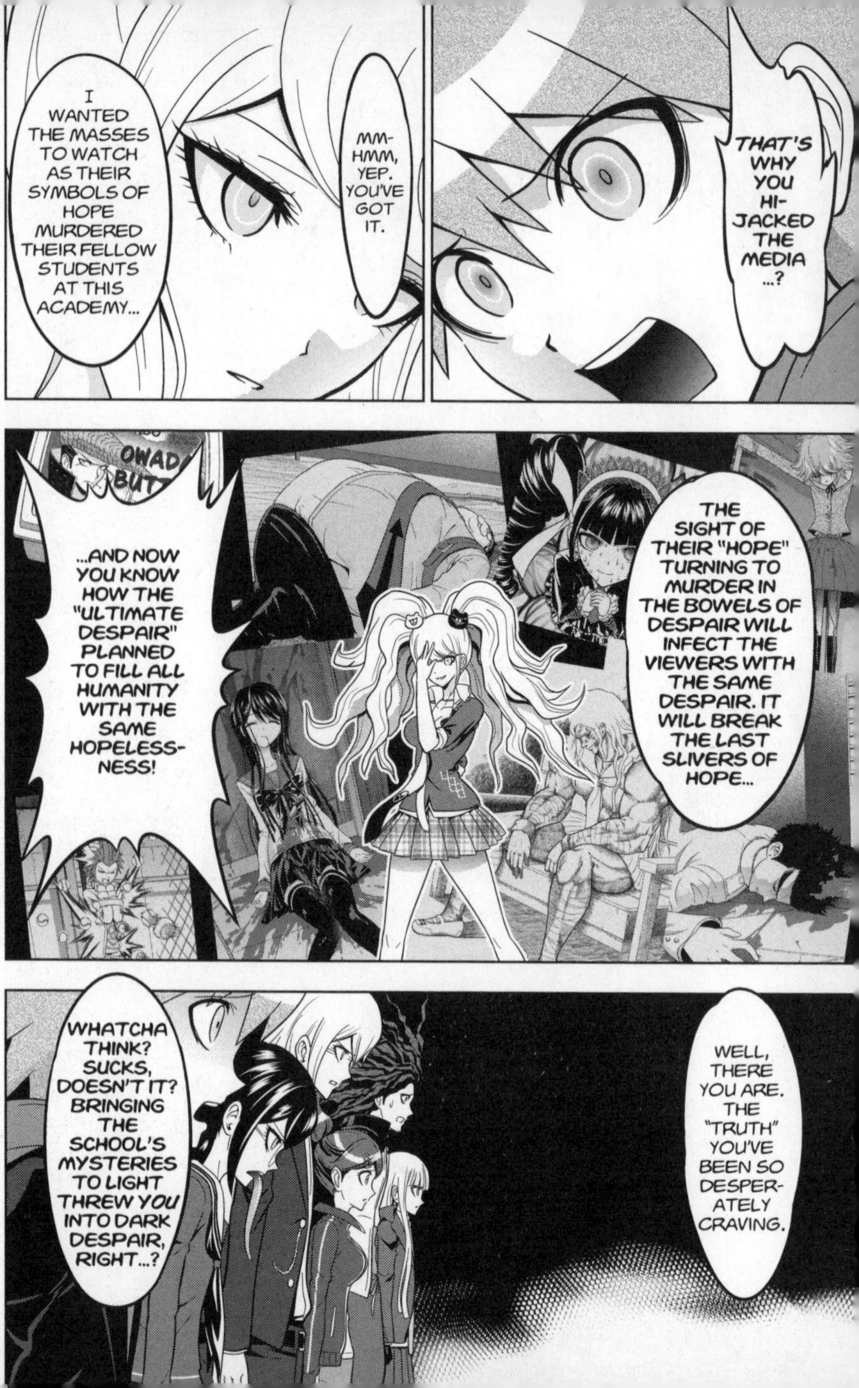
THAT'S WHY YOU HI-JACKED THE MEDIA ...?
MM-HMM, YEP. YOU'VE GOT IT.
I WANTED THE MASSES TO WATCH AS THEIR SYMBOLS OF HOPE MURDERED THEIR FELLOW STUDENTS AT THIS ACADEMY...
THE SIGHT OF THEIR "HOPE" TURNING TO MURDER IN THE BOWELS OF DESPAIR WILL INFECT THE VIEWERS WITH THE SAME DESPAIR. IT WILL BREAK THE LAST SLIVERS OF HOPE...
...AND NOW YOU KNOW HOW THE "ULTIMATE DESPAIR" PLANNED TO FILL ALL HUMANITY WITH THE SAME HOPELESS-NESS!
WELL, THERE YOU ARE. THE "TRUTH" YOU'VE BEEN SO DESPER-ATELY CRAVING.
WHATCHA THINK? SUCKS, DOESN'T IT? BRINGING THE SCHOOL'S MYSTERIES TO LIGHT THREW YOU INTO DARK DESPAIR, RIGHT...?

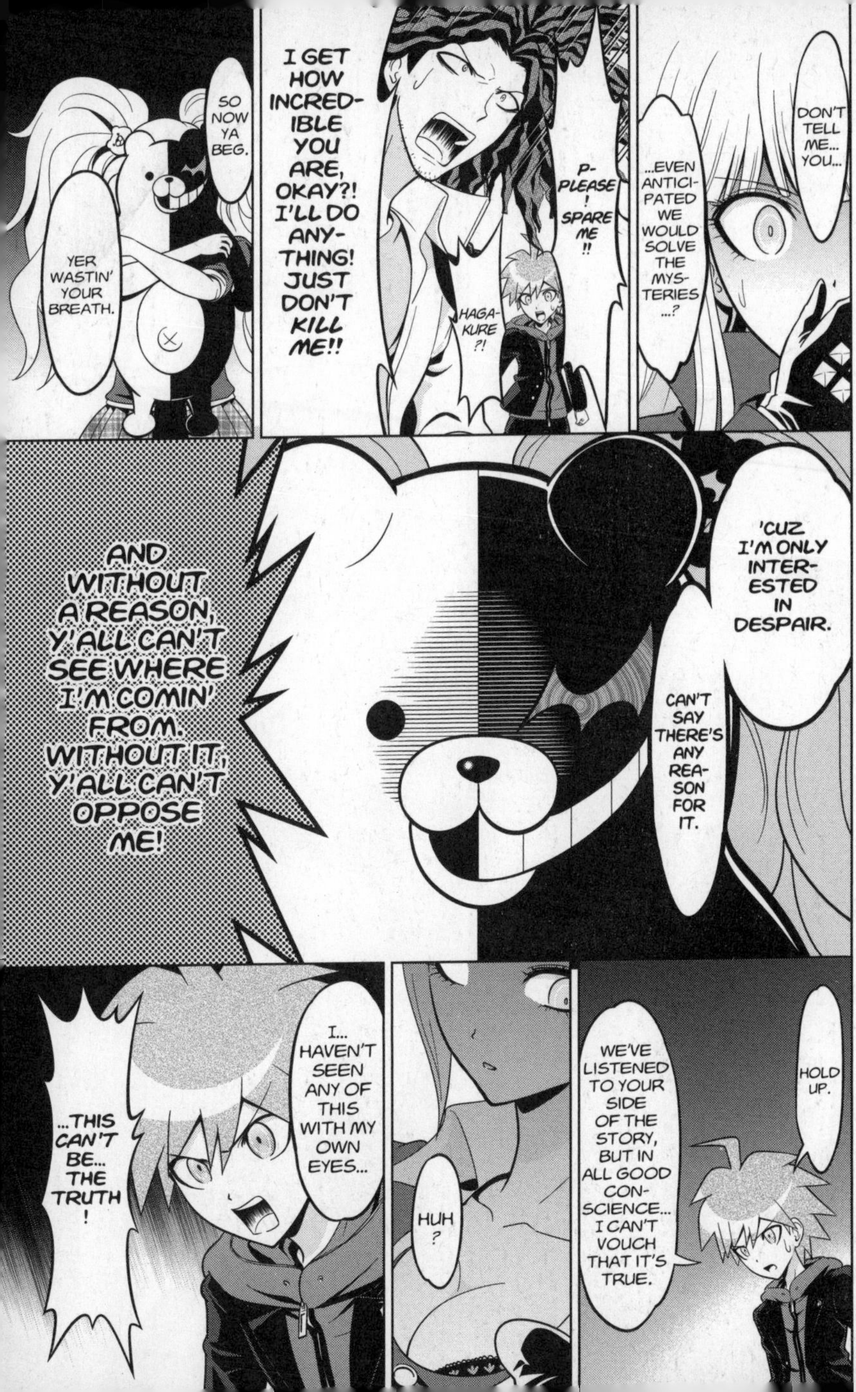
DON'T TELL ME... YOU...
...EVEN ANTICIPATED WE WOULD SOLVE THE MYSTERIES...?
I GET HOW INCREDIBLE YOU ARE, OKAY?! I'LL DO ANYTHING! JUST DON'T KILL ME!!
P-PLEASE! SPARE ME!!
HAGAKURE?!
SO NOW YA BEG.
YER WASTIN' YOUR BREATH.
'CUZ I'M ONLY INTERESTED IN DESPAIR.
CAN'T SAY THERE'S ANY REASON FOR IT.
AND WITHOUT A REASON, Y'ALL CAN'T SEE WHERE I'M COMIN' FROM. WITHOUT IT, Y'ALL CAN'T OPPOSE ME!
HOLD UP.
WE'VE LISTENED TO YOUR SIDE OF THE STORY, BUT IN ALL GOOD CONSCIENCE... I CAN'T VOUCH THAT IT'S TRUE.
HUH?
I... HAVEN'T SEEN ANY OF THIS WITH MY OWN EYES...
...THIS CAN'T BE... THE TRUTH!

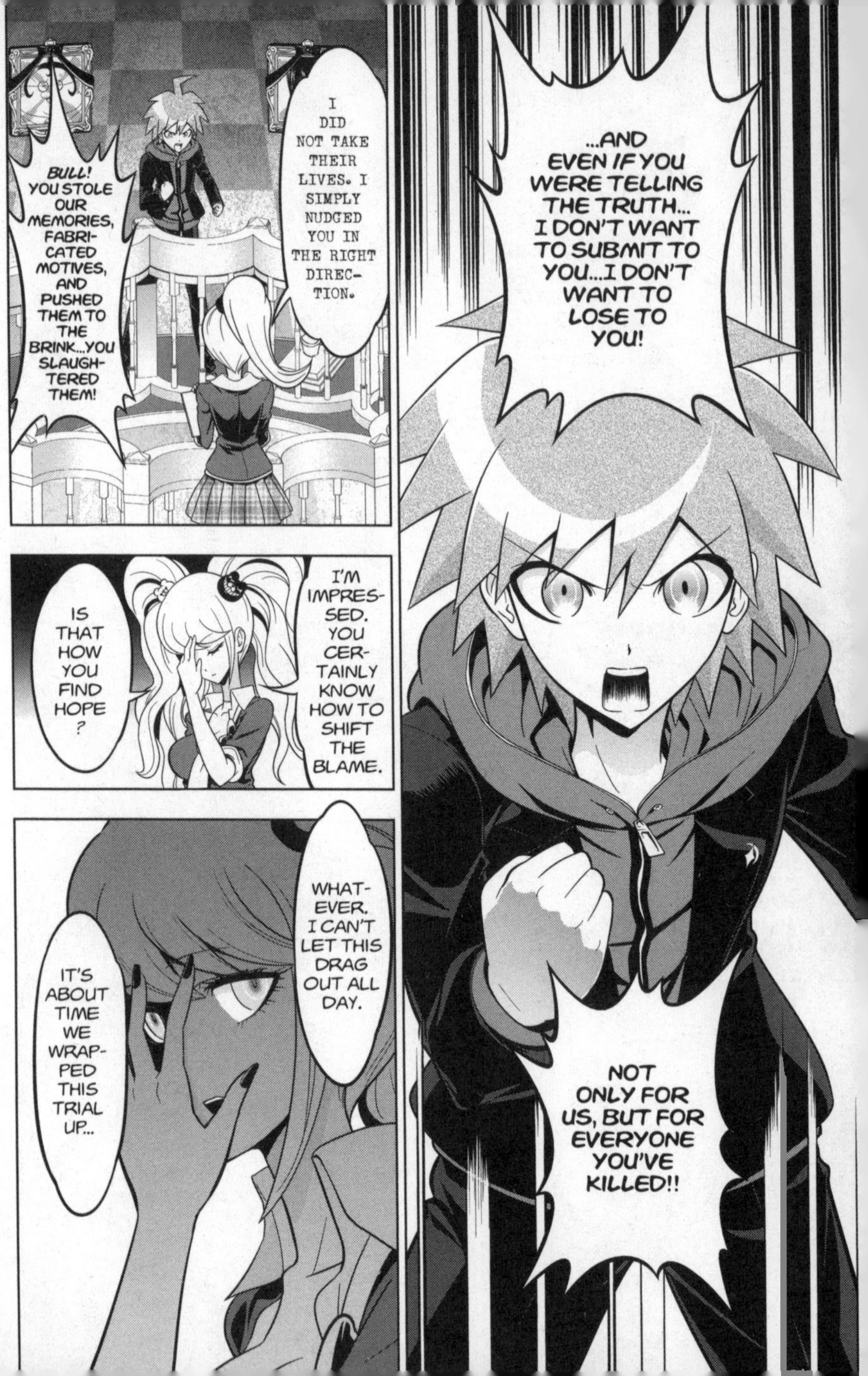
...AND EVEN *IF* YOU WERE TELLING THE TRUTH... I DON'T WANT TO SUBMIT TO YOU...I DON'T WANT TO LOSE TO YOU!
NOT ONLY FOR US, BUT FOR EVERYONE YOU'VE KILLED!!
I DID NOT TAKE THEIR LIVES. I SIMPLY NUDGED YOU IN THE RIGHT DIRECTION.
BULL! YOU STOLE OUR MEMORIES, FABRICATED MOTIVES, AND PUSHED THEM TO THE BRINK...YOU SLAUGHTERED THEM!
I'M IMPRESSED. YOU CERTAINLY KNOW HOW TO SHIFT THE BLAME.
IS THAT HOW YOU FIND HOPE?
WHATEVER. I CAN'T LET THIS DRAG OUT ALL DAY.
IT'S ABOUT TIME WE WRAPPED THIS TRIAL UP...

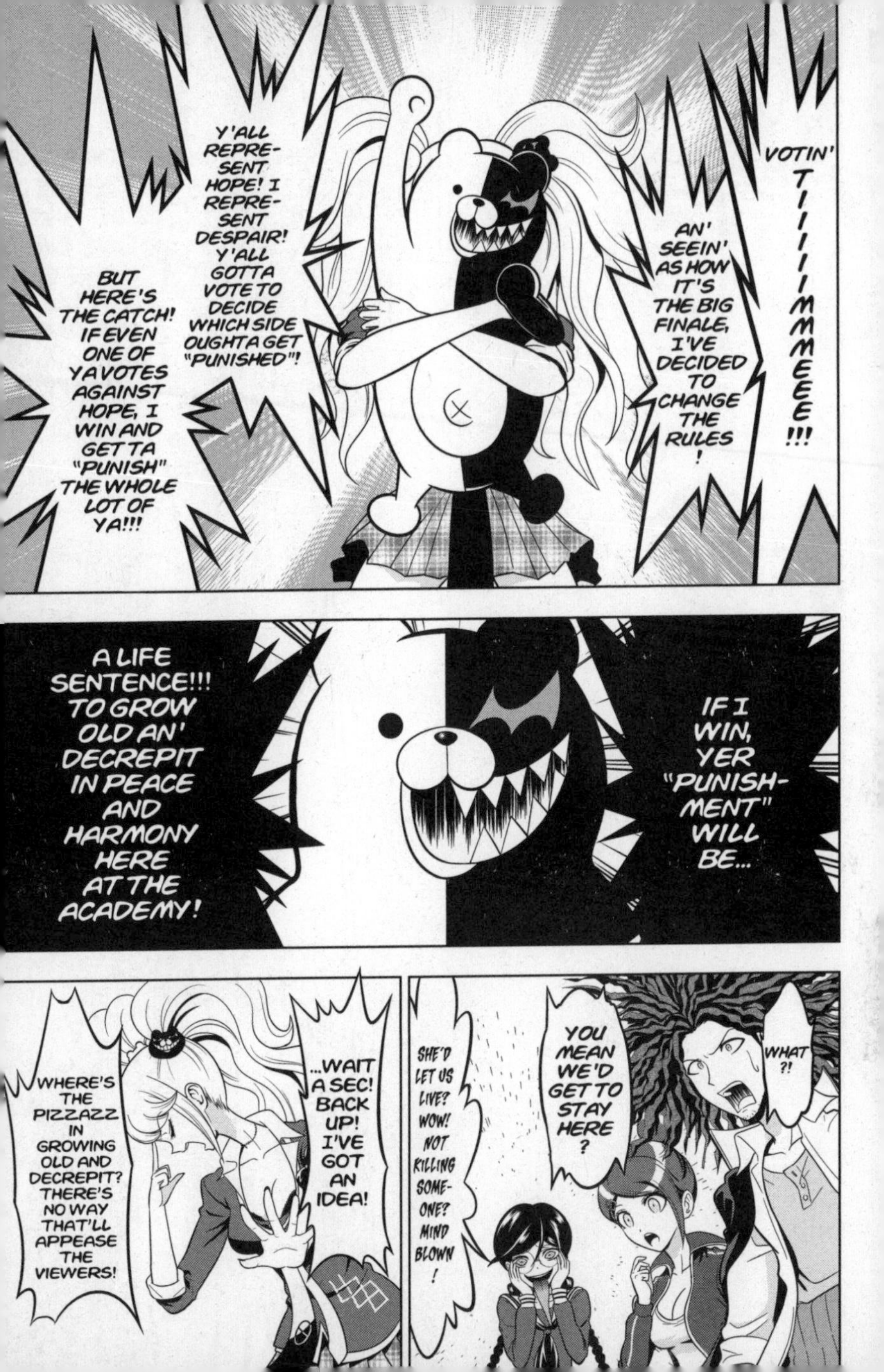
VOTIN' TIIIIIIIMMMEEE!!!
AN' SEEIN' AS HOW IT'S THE BIG FINALE, I'VE DECIDED TO CHANGE THE RULES!
Y'ALL REPRESENT HOPE! I REPRESENT DESPAIR! Y'ALL GOTTA VOTE TO DECIDE WHICH SIDE OUGHTA GET "PUNISHED"!
BUT HERE'S THE CATCH! IF EVEN ONE OF YA VOTES AGAINST HOPE, I WIN AND GET TA "PUNISH" THE WHOLE LOT OF YA!!!
IF I WIN, YER "PUNISHMENT" WILL BE...
A LIFE SENTENCE!!! TO GROW OLD AN' DECREPIT IN PEACE AND HARMONY HERE AT THE ACADEMY!
WHAT?!
YOU MEAN WE'D GET TO STAY HERE?
SHE'D LET US LIVE? WOW! NOT KILLING SOMEONE? MIND BLOWN!
...WAIT A SEC! BACK UP! I'VE GOT AN IDEA!
WHERE'S THE PIZZAZZ IN GROWING OLD AND DECREPIT? THERE'S NO WAY THAT'LL APPEASE THE VIEWERS!

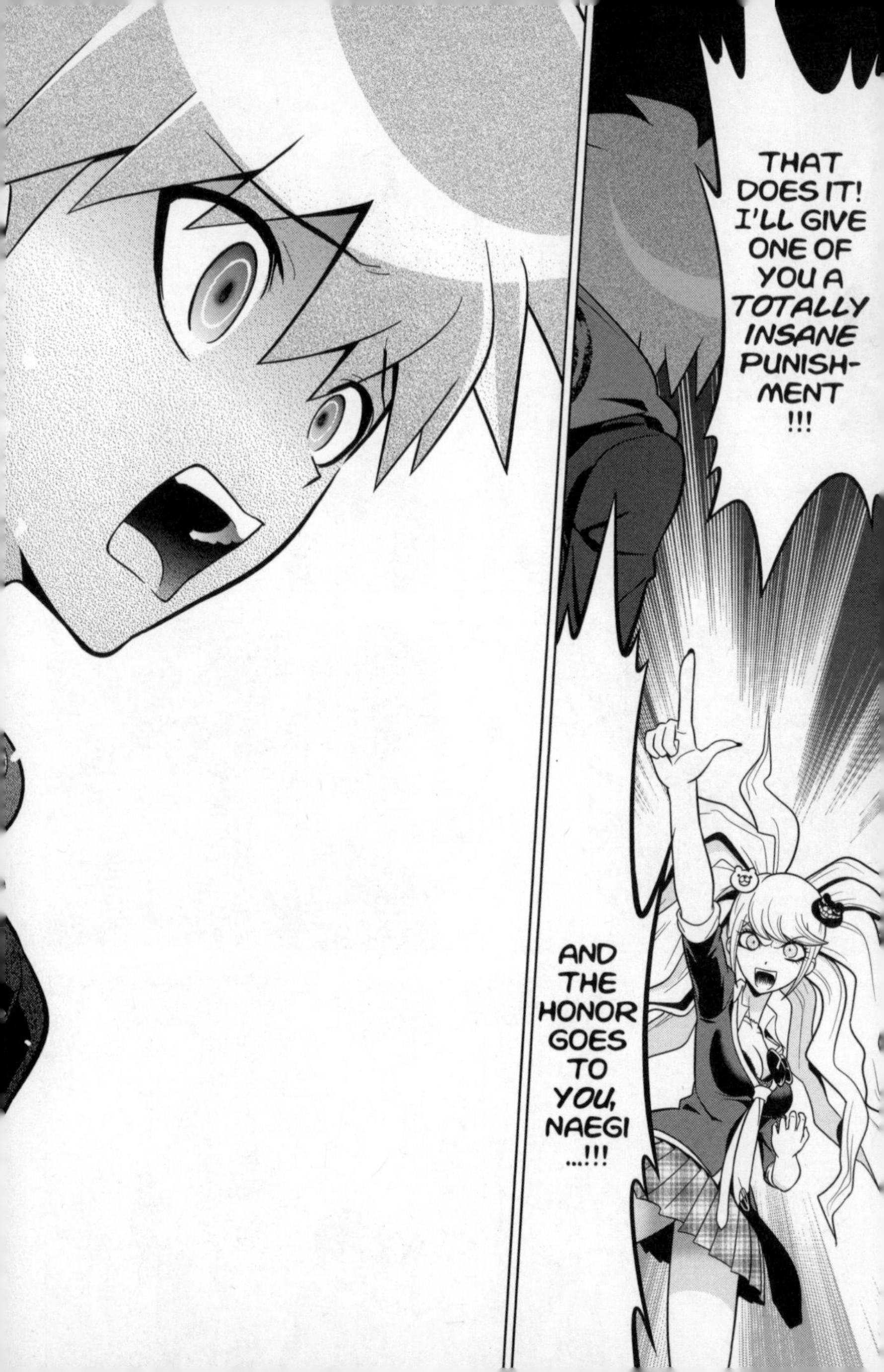
THAT DOES IT! I'LL GIVE ONE OF YOU A TOTALLY INSANE PUNISHMENT!!!
AND THE HONOR GOES TO YOU, NAEGI...!!!

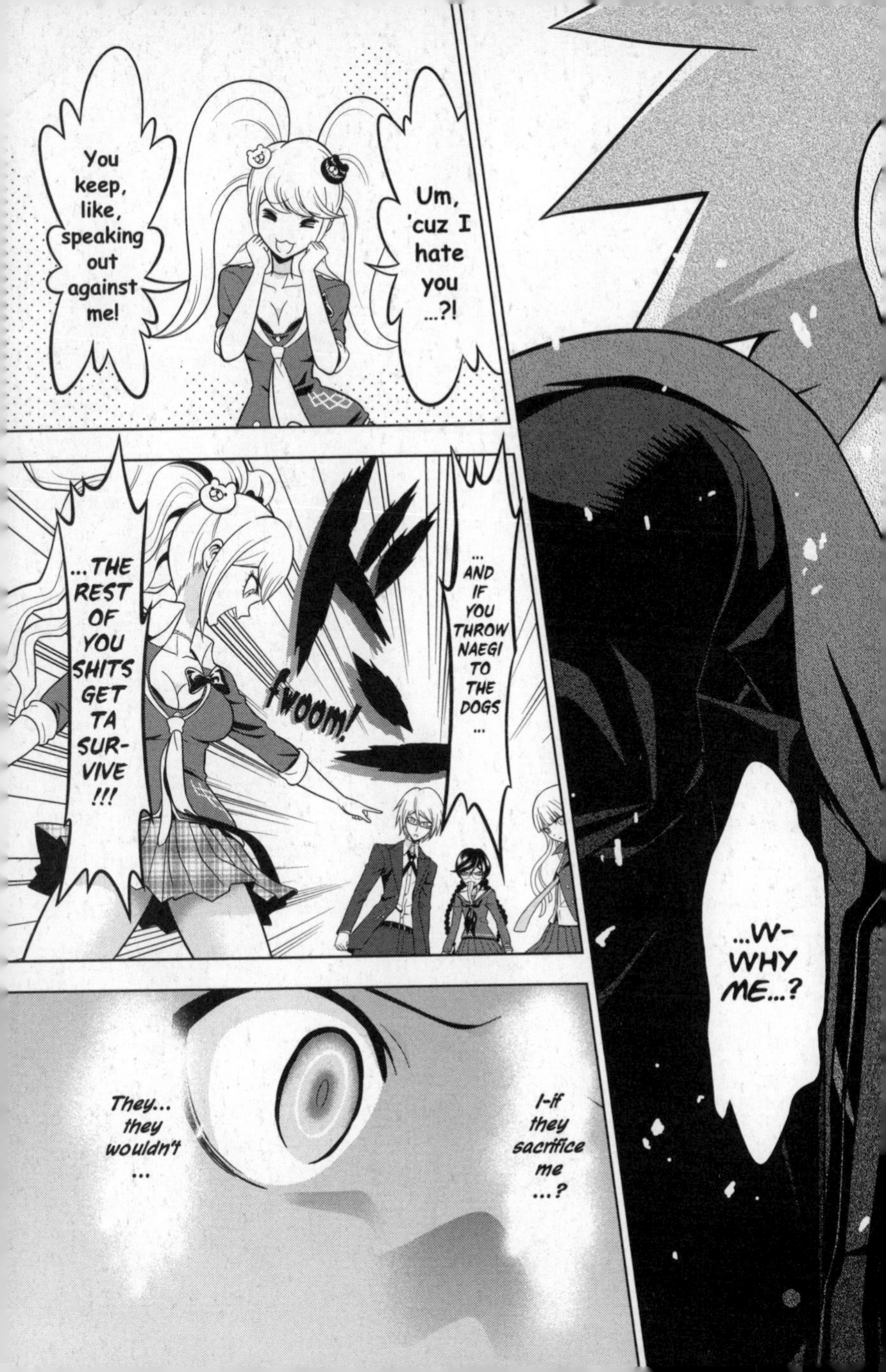
...W-WHY ME...?
Um, 'cuz I hate you ...?!
You keep, like, speaking out against me!
...AND IF YOU THROW NAEGI TO THE DOGS ...
fwoom!
...THE REST OF YOU SHITS GET TA SUR-VIVE!!!
I-if they sacrifice me ...?
They... they wouldn't ...

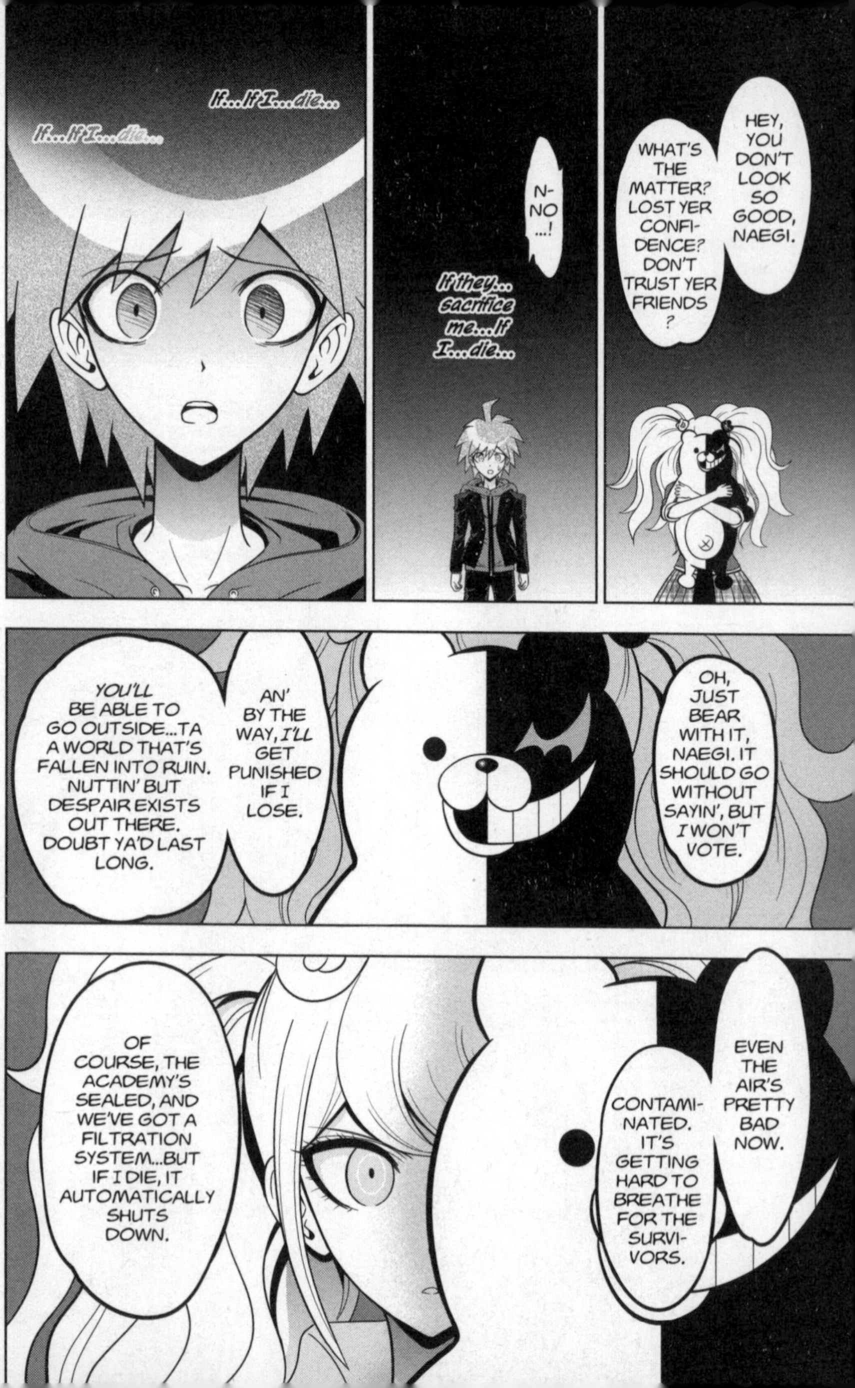
HEY, YOU DON'T LOOK SO GOOD, NAEGI.
WHAT'S THE MATTER? LOST YER CONFIDENCE? DON'T TRUST YER FRIENDS?
N-NO...!
If they... sacrifice me...If I...die...
If...If I...die...
If...If I...die...
OH, JUST BEAR WITH IT, NAEGI. IT SHOULD GO WITHOUT SAYIN', BUT I WON'T VOTE.
AN' BY THE WAY, I'LL GET PUNISHED IF I LOSE.
YOU'LL BE ABLE TO GO OUTSIDE...TA A WORLD THAT'S FALLEN INTO RUIN. NUTTIN' BUT DESPAIR EXISTS OUT THERE. DOUBT YA'D LAST LONG.
EVEN THE AIR'S PRETTY BAD NOW.
CONTAMINATED. IT'S GETTING HARD TO BREATHE FOR THE SURVIVORS.
OF COURSE, THE ACADEMY'S SEALED, AND WE'VE GOT A FILTRATION SYSTEM...BUT IF I DIE, IT AUTOMATICALLY SHUTS DOWN.

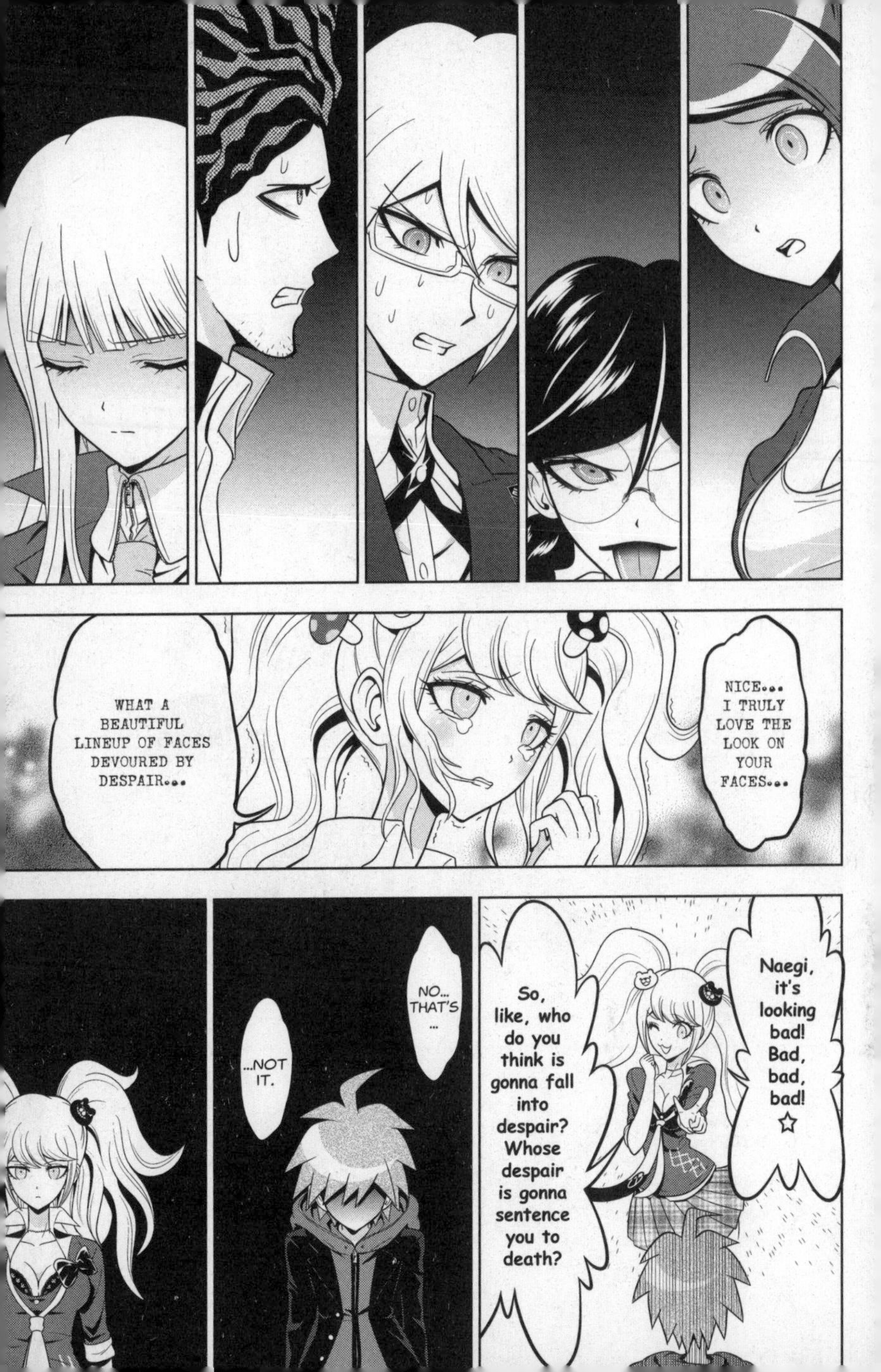
NICE... I TRULY LOVE THE LOOK ON YOUR FACES...
WHAT A BEAUTIFUL LINEUP OF FACES DEVOURED BY DESPAIR...
Naegi, it's looking bad! Bad, bad, bad! ☆
So, like, who do you think is gonna fall into despair? Whose despair is gonna sentence you to death?
NO... THAT'S ...
...NOT IT.

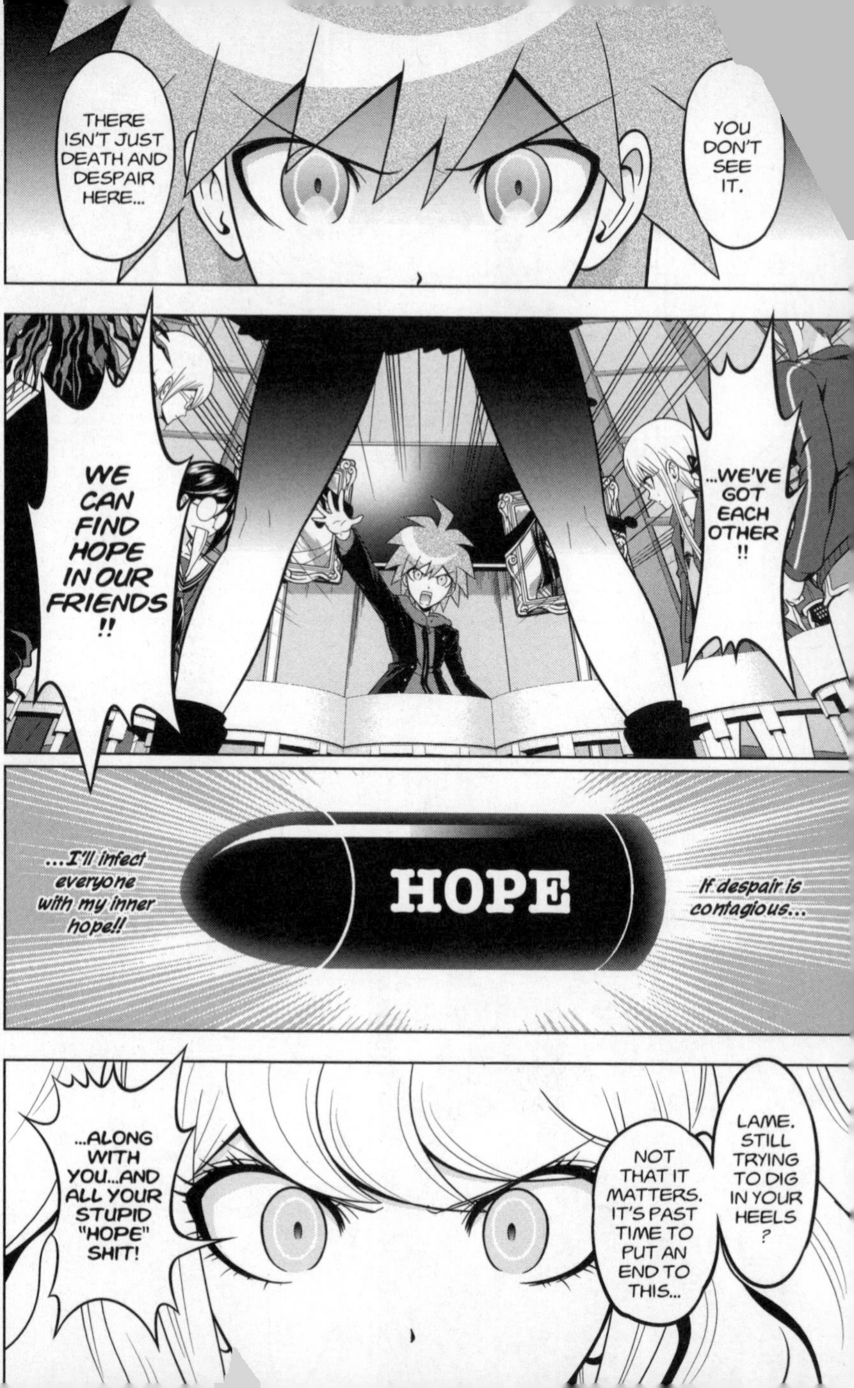

YOU DON'T SEE IT.
THERE ISN'T JUST DEATH AND DESPAIR HERE...
...WE'VE GOT EACH OTHER!!
WE CAN FIND HOPE IN OUR FRIENDS!!
If despair is contagious...
HOPE
...I'll infect everyone with my inner hope!!
LAME. STILL TRYING TO DIG IN YOUR HEELS?
NOT THAT IT MATTERS. IT'S PAST TIME TO PUT AN END TO THIS...
...ALONG WITH YOU...AND ALL YOUR STUPID "HOPE" SHIT!

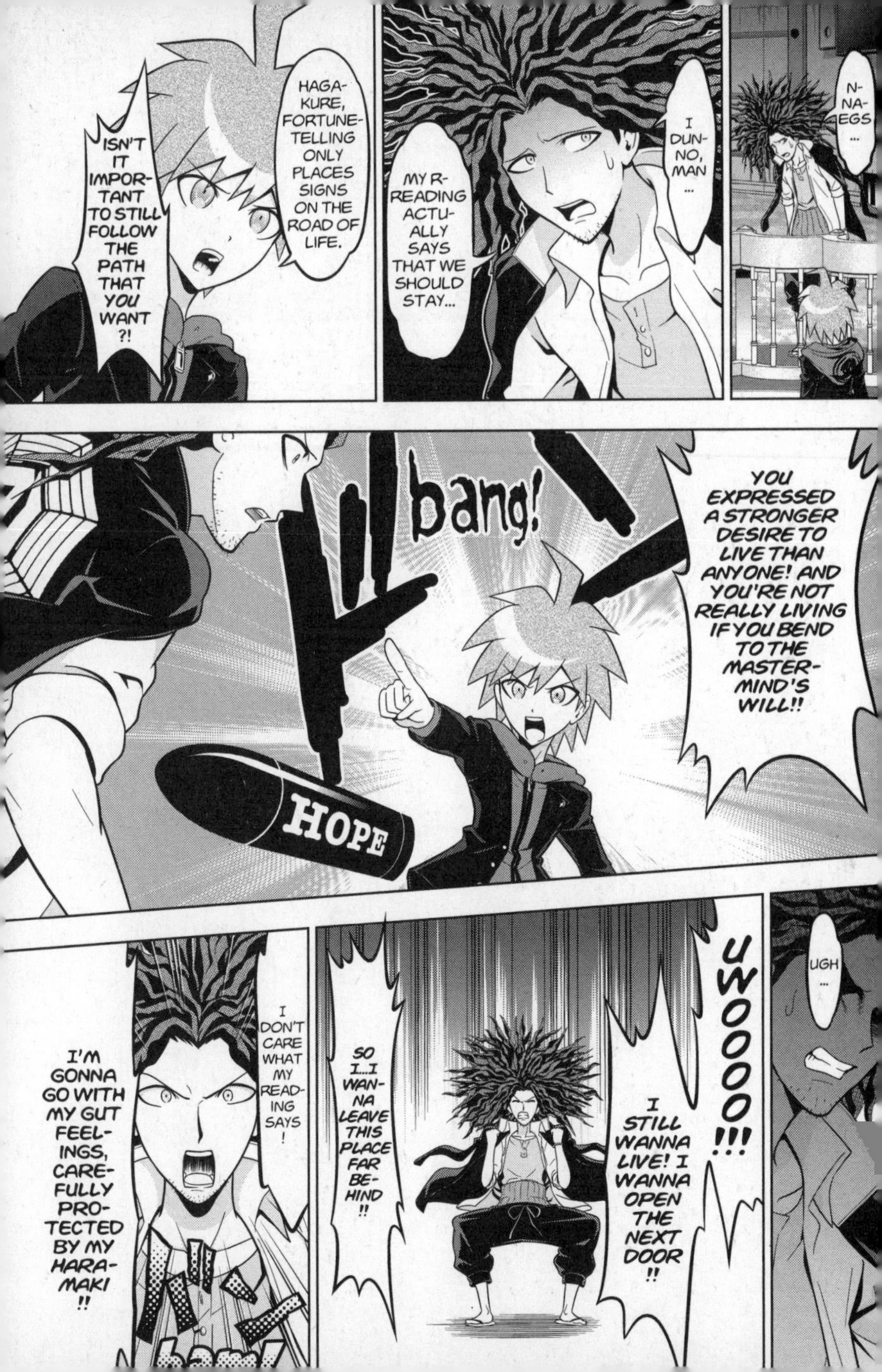
N-NAEGS...
I DUNNO, MAN...
MY R-READING ACTUALLY SAYS THAT WE SHOULD STAY...
HAGAKURE, FORTUNE-TELLING ONLY PLACES SIGNS ON THE ROAD OF LIFE.
ISN'T IT IMPORTANT TO STILL FOLLOW THE PATH THAT YOU WANT?!
YOU EXPRESSED A STRONGER DESIRE TO LIVE THAN ANYONE! AND YOU'RE NOT REALLY LIVING IF YOU BEND TO THE MASTERMIND'S WILL!!
bang!
HOPE
UGH...
UWOOOOO!!!
I STILL WANNA LIVE! I WANNA OPEN THE NEXT DOOR!!
SO I...I WANNA LEAVE THIS PLACE FAR BEHIND!!
I DON'T CARE WHAT MY READING SAYS!
I'M GONNA GO WITH MY GUT FEELINGS, CAREFULLY PROTECTED BY MY HARAMAKI!!

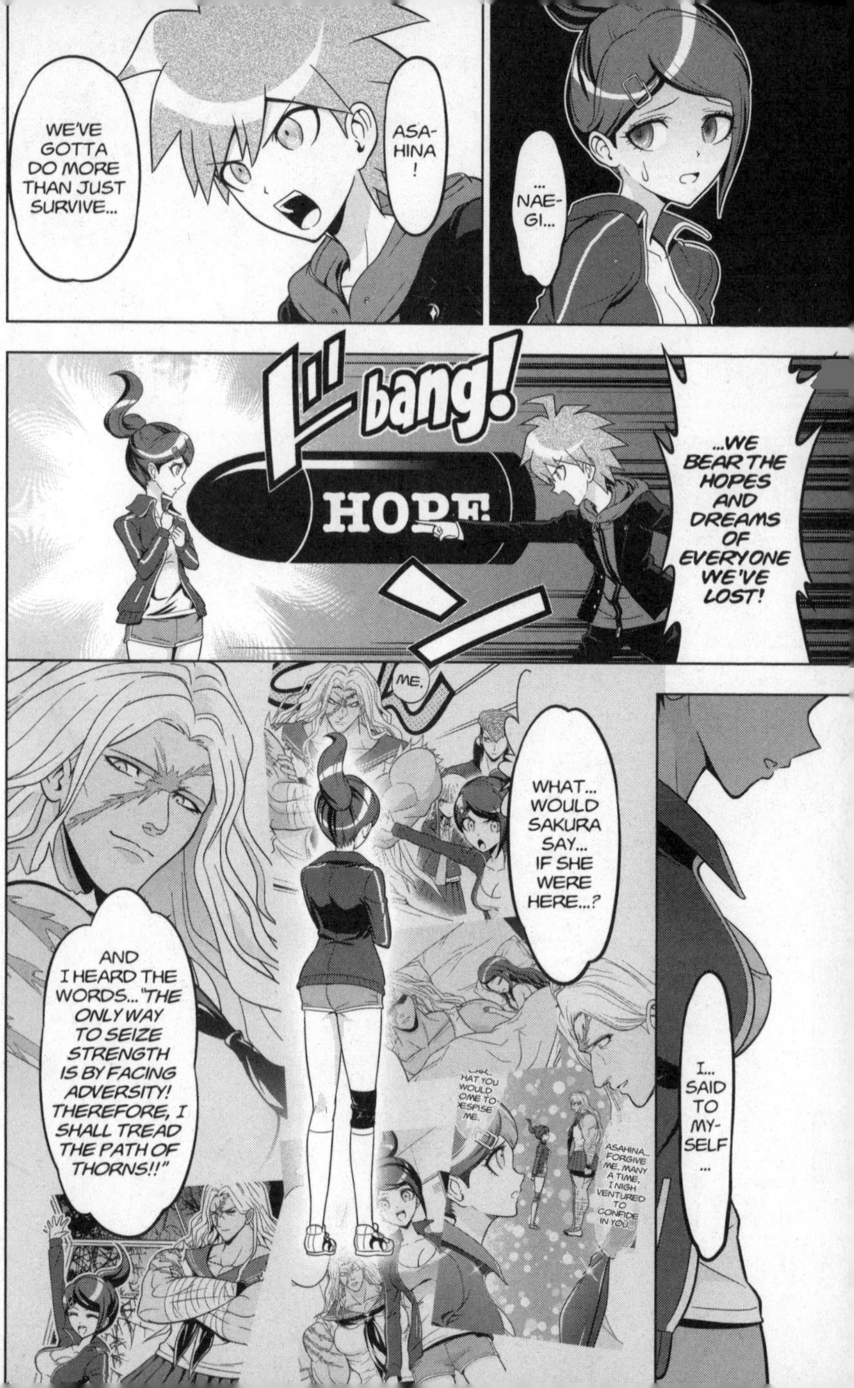
... NAE-GI...
ASA-HINA!
WE'VE GOTTA DO MORE THAN JUST SURVIVE...
...WE BEAR THE HOPES AND DREAMS OF EVERYONE WE'VE LOST!
bang!
HOPE
I... SAID TO MY-SELF...
WHAT... WOULD SAKURA SAY... IF SHE WERE HERE...?
ME.
ASAHINA... FORGIVE ME. MANY A TIME, I NIGH VENTURED TO CONFIDE IN YOU...
AND I HEARD THE WORDS... "THE ONLY WAY TO SEIZE STRENGTH IS BY FACING ADVERSITY! THEREFORE, I SHALL TREAD THE PATH OF THORNS!!"

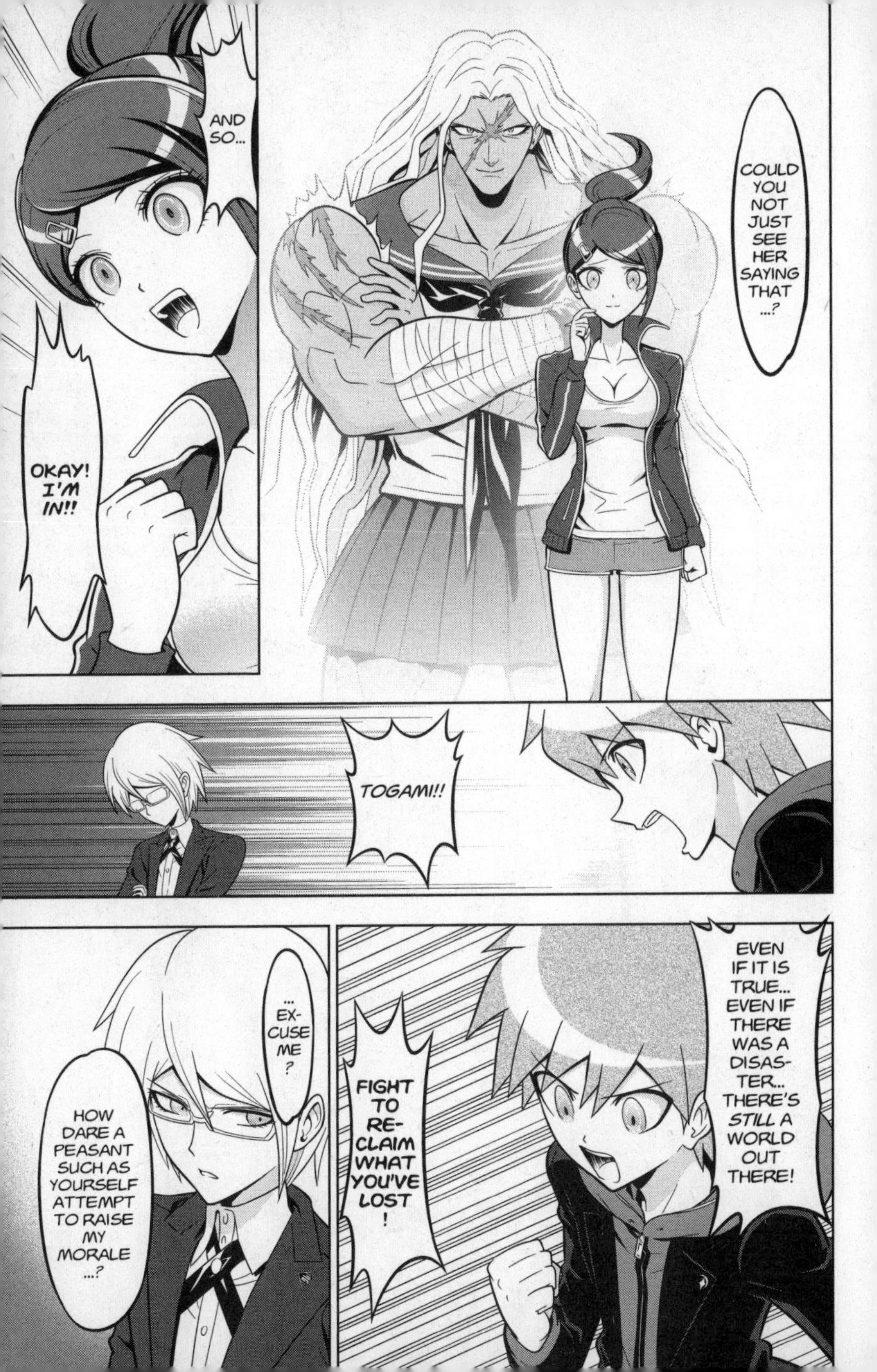
COULD YOU NOT JUST SEE HER SAYING THAT...?
AND SO...
OKAY! I'M IN!!
TOGAMI!!
EVEN IF IT IS TRUE... EVEN IF THERE WAS A DISASTER... THERE'S *STILL* A WORLD OUT THERE!
FIGHT TO RECLAIM WHAT YOU'VE LOST!
...EXCUSE ME?
HOW DARE A PEASANT SUCH AS YOURSELF ATTEMPT TO RAISE MY MORALE...?

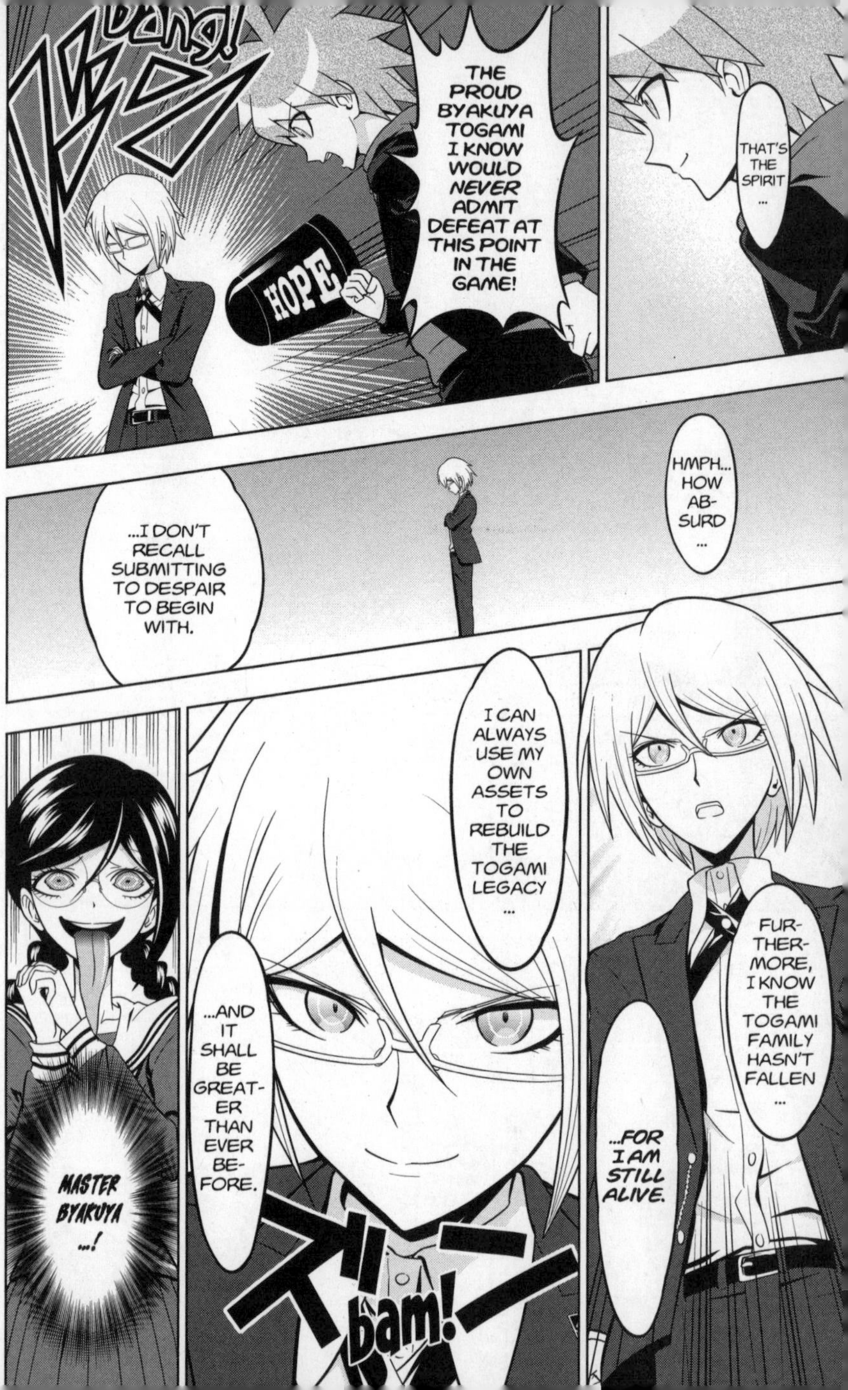
THAT'S THE SPIRIT ...
bang!
THE PROUD BYAKUYA TOGAMI I KNOW WOULD NEVER ADMIT DEFEAT AT THIS POINT IN THE GAME!
HOPE
HMPH... HOW AB-SURD ...
...I DON'T RECALL SUBMITTING TO DESPAIR TO BEGIN WITH.
FUR-THER-MORE, I KNOW THE TOGAMI FAMILY HASN'T FALLEN ...
...FOR I AM STILL ALIVE.
I CAN ALWAYS USE MY OWN ASSETS TO REBUILD THE TOGAMI LEGACY ...
...AND IT SHALL BE GREAT-ER THAN EVER BE-FORE.
bam!
MASTER BYAKUYA ...!

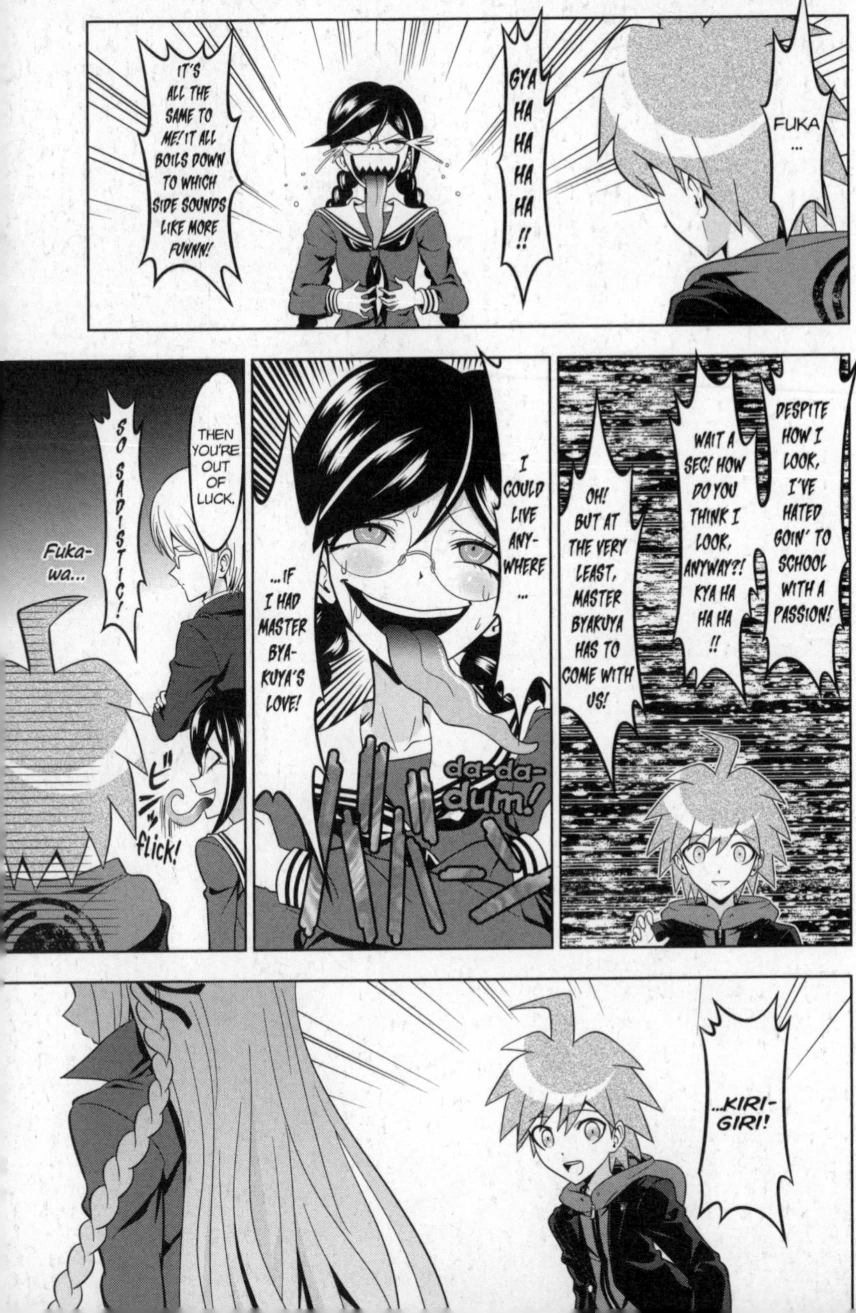
FUKA ...
GYA HA HA HA HA !!
IT'S ALL THE SAME TO ME! IT ALL BOILS DOWN TO WHICH SIDE SOUNDS LIKE MORE FUNNN!
DESPITE HOW I LOOK, I'VE HATED GOIN' TO SCHOOL WITH A PASSION!
WAIT A SEC! HOW DO YOU THINK I LOOK, ANYWAY?! KYA HA HA HA !!
OH! BUT AT THE VERY LEAST, MASTER BYAKUYA HAS TO COME WITH US!
I COULD LIVE ANY-WHERE ...
...IF I HAD MASTER BYA-KUYA'S LOVE!
da-da-dum!
SO SADISTIC!
THEN YOU'RE OUT OF LUCK.
Fuka-wa...
flick!
...KIRI-GIRI!

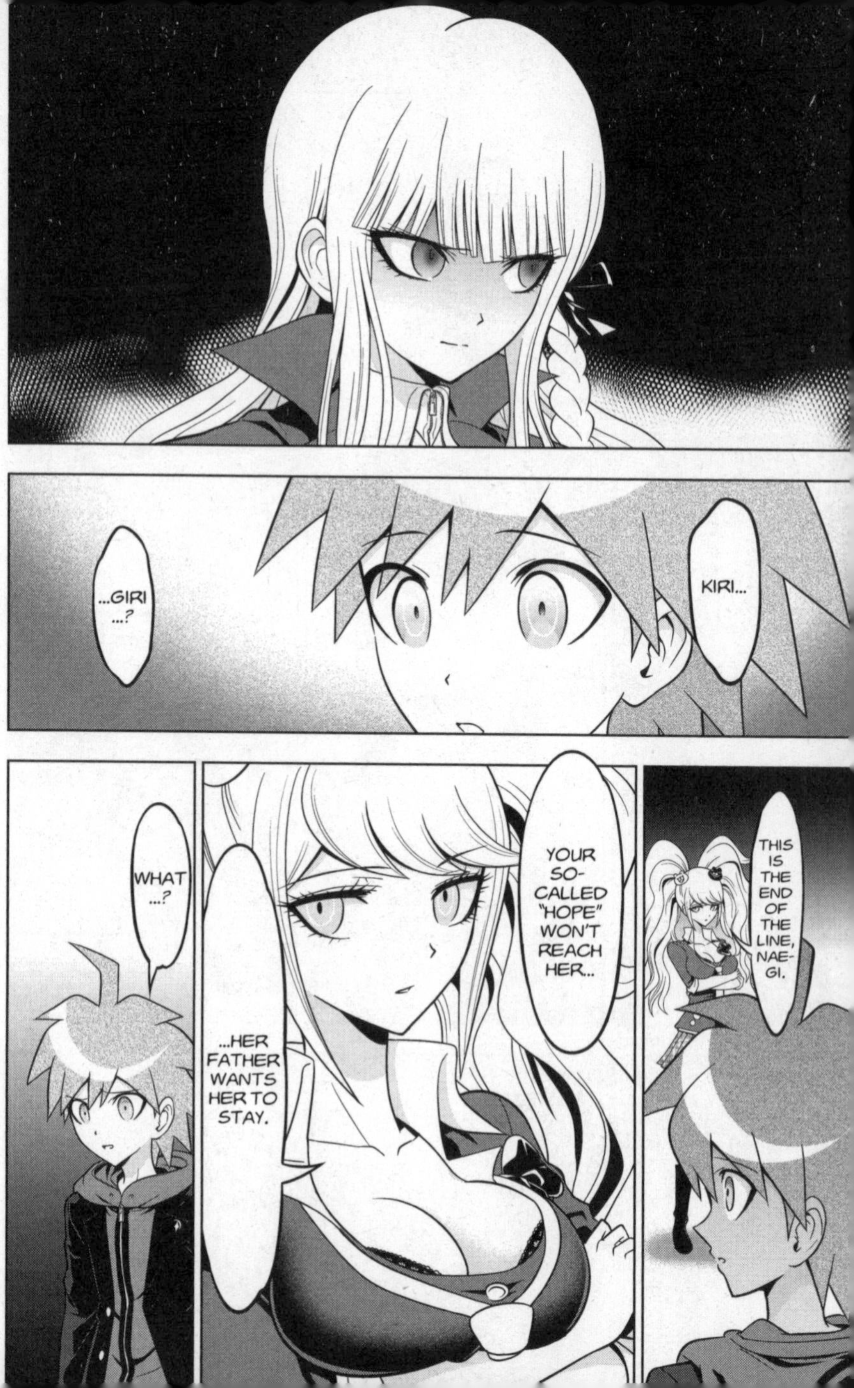
KIRI...
...GIRI ...?
THIS IS THE END OF THE LINE, NAEGI.
YOUR SO-CALLED "HOPE" WON'T REACH HER...
...HER FATHER WANTS HER TO STAY.
WHAT ...?

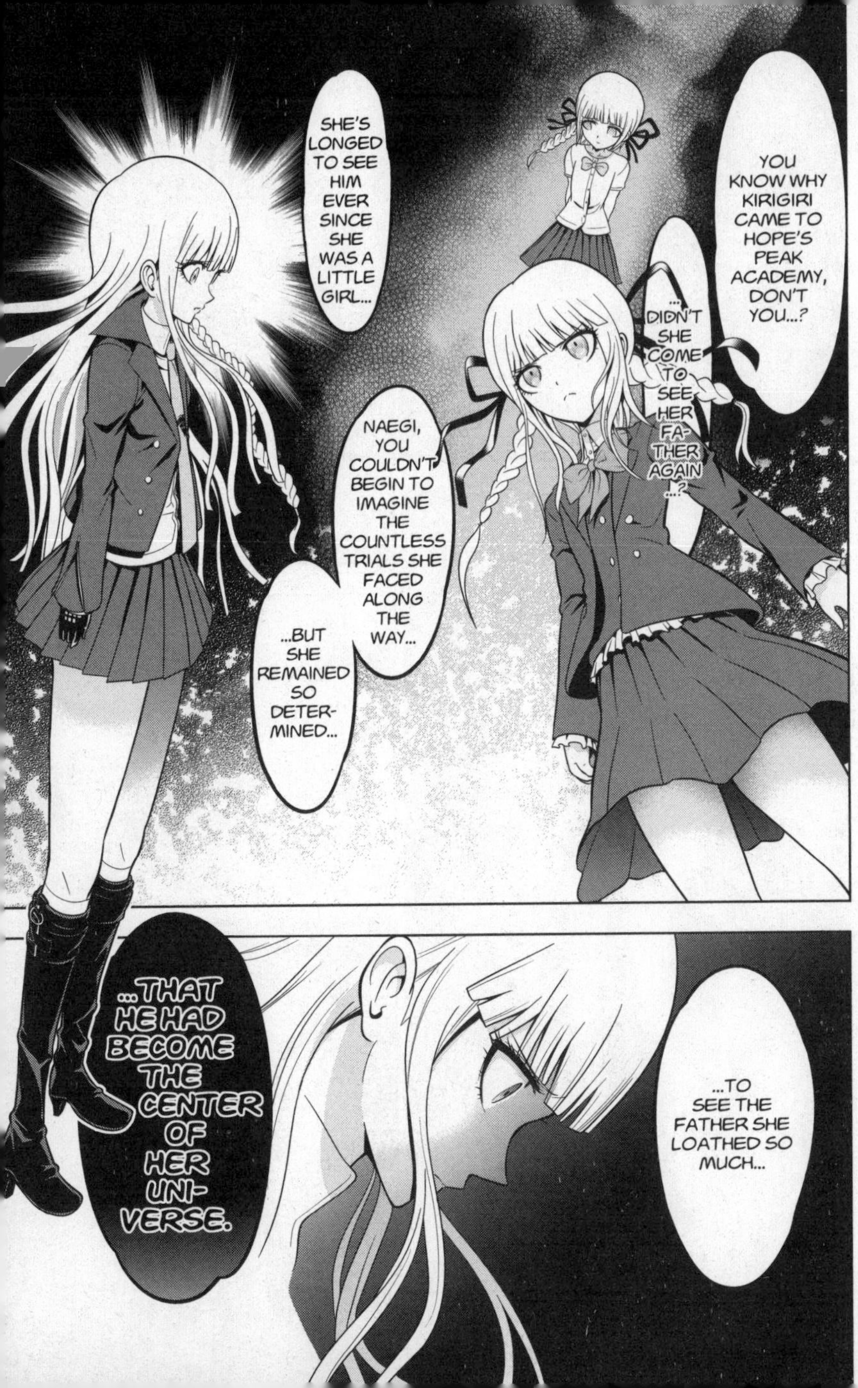
YOU KNOW WHY KIRIGIRI CAME TO HOPE'S PEAK ACADEMY, DON'T YOU...?
...DIDN'T SHE COME TO SEE HER FA-THER AGAIN...?
SHE'S LONGED TO SEE HIM EVER SINCE SHE WAS A LITTLE GIRL...
NAEGI, YOU COULDN'T BEGIN TO IMAGINE THE COUNTLESS TRIALS SHE FACED ALONG THE WAY...
...BUT SHE REMAINED SO DETER-MINED...
...TO SEE THE FATHER SHE LOATHED SO MUCH...
...THAT HE HAD BECOME THE CENTER OF HER UNI-VERSE.

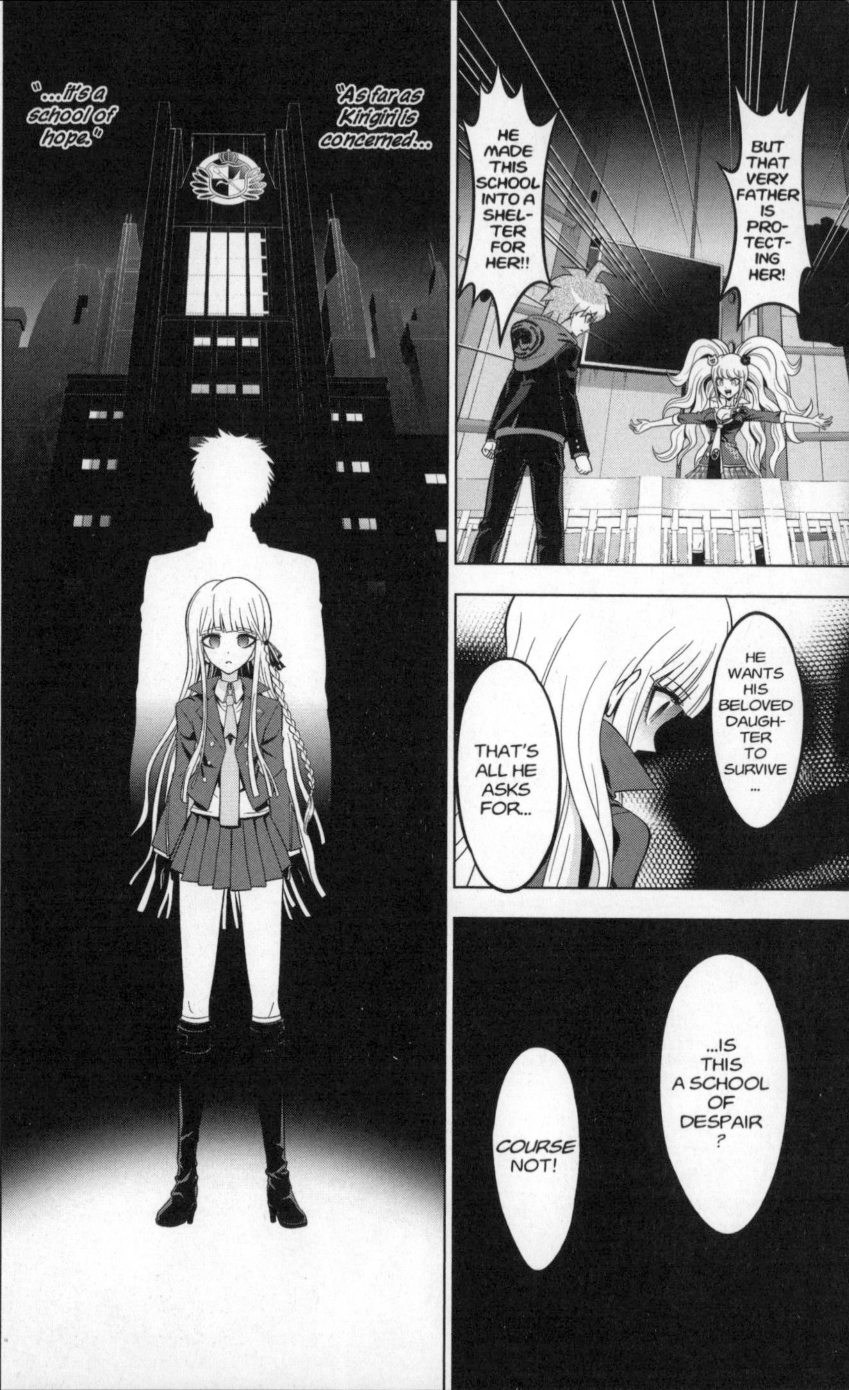
BUT THAT VERY FATHER IS PROTECTING HER!
HE MADE THIS SCHOOL INTO A SHELTER FOR HER!!
HE WANTS HIS BELOVED DAUGHTER TO SURVIVE ...
THAT'S ALL HE ASKS FOR...
...IS THIS A SCHOOL OF DESPAIR?
COURSE NOT!
"As far as Kirigiri is concerned...
"...it's a school of hope."

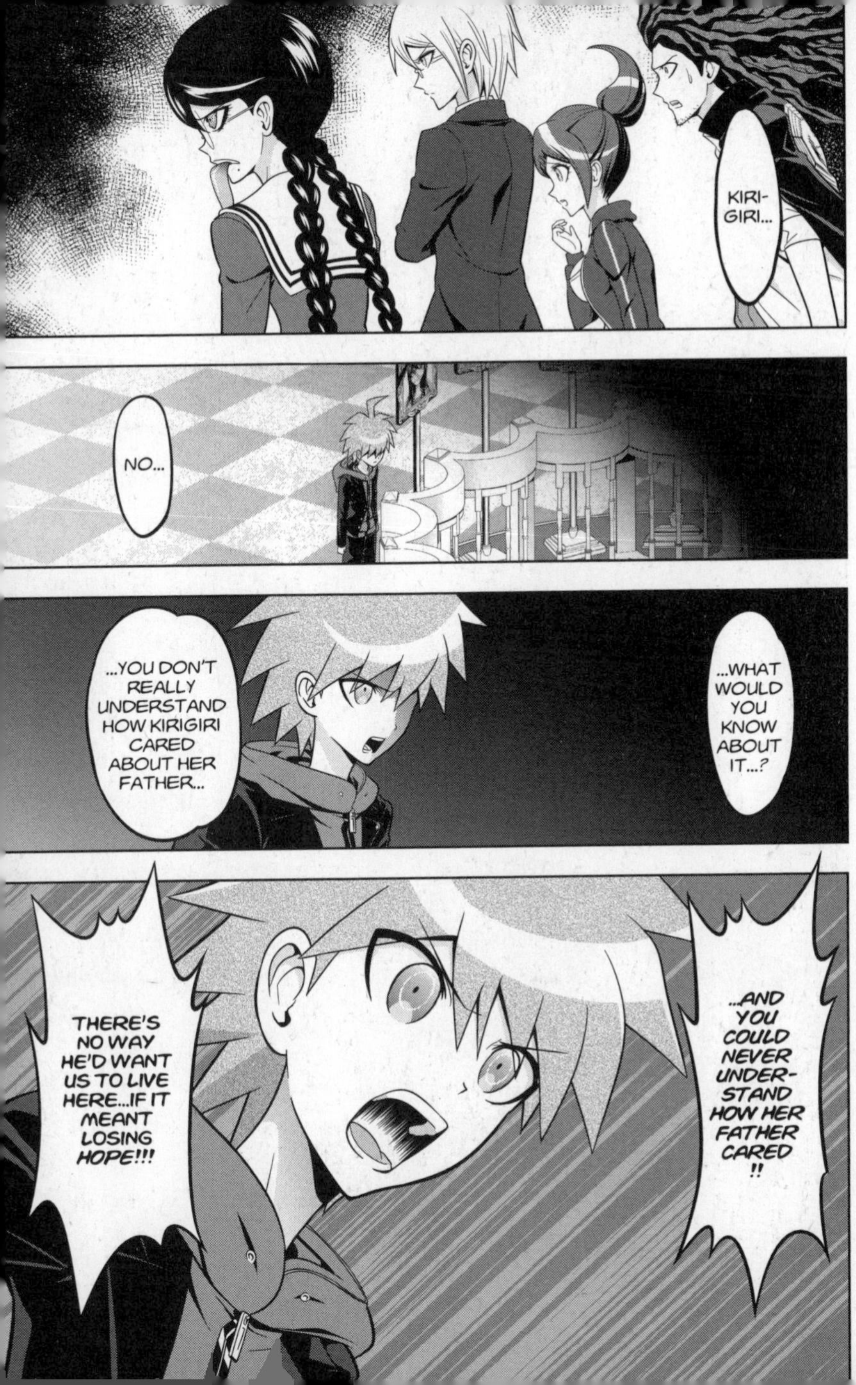
KIRI-GIRI...
NO...
...WHAT WOULD YOU KNOW ABOUT IT...?
...YOU DON'T REALLY UNDERSTAND HOW KIRIGIRI CARED ABOUT HER FATHER...
...AND YOU COULD NEVER UNDER-STAND HOW HER FATHER CARED!!
THERE'S NO WAY HE'D WANT US TO LIVE HERE...IF IT MEANT LOSING HOPE!!!

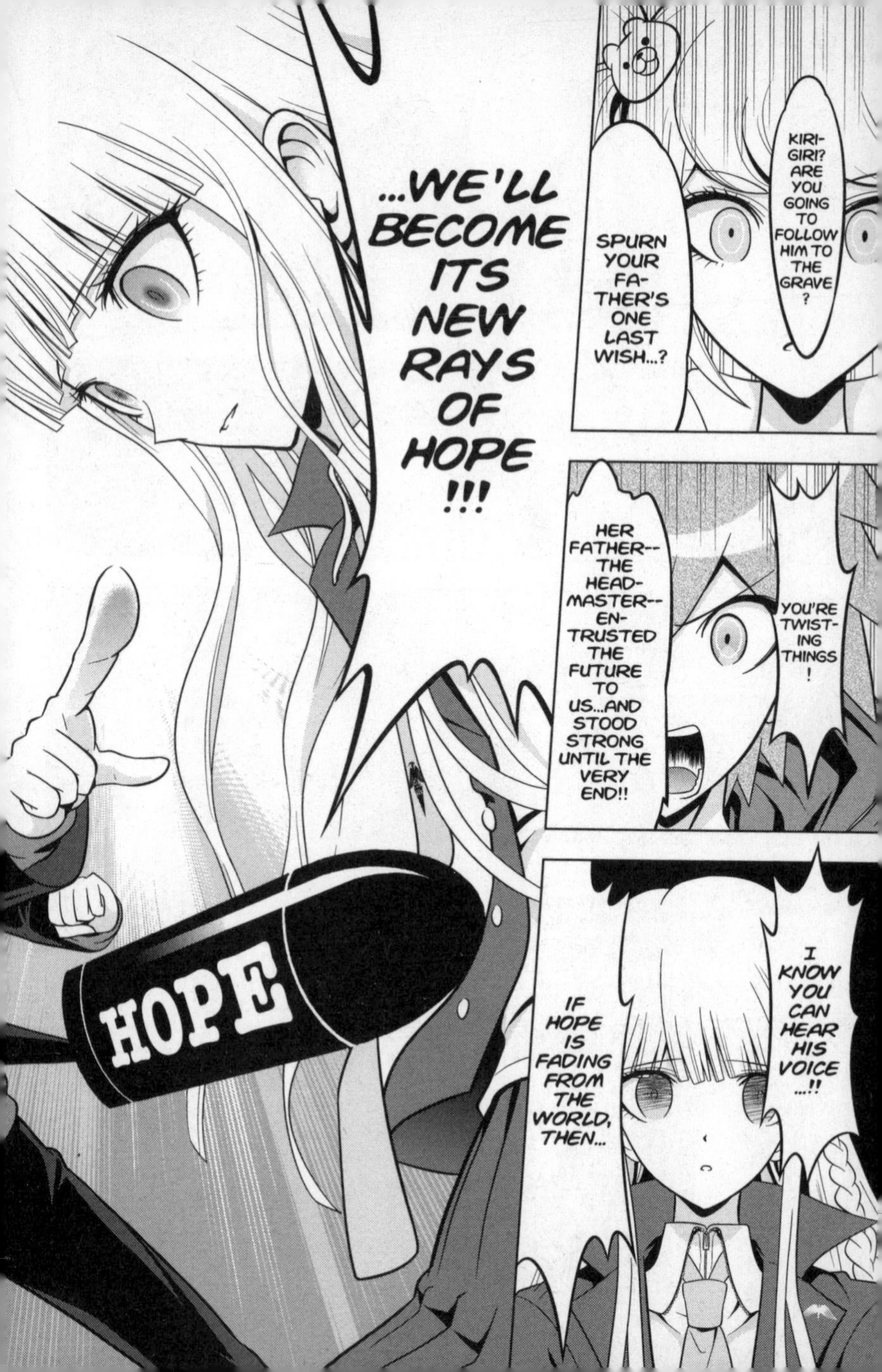
KIRI-GIRI? ARE YOU GOING TO FOLLOW HIM TO THE GRAVE?
SPURN YOUR FA-THER'S ONE LAST WISH...?
YOU'RE TWIST-ING THINGS!
HER FATHER--THE HEAD-MASTER--EN-TRUSTED THE FUTURE TO US...AND STOOD STRONG UNTIL THE VERY END!!
I KNOW YOU CAN HEAR HIS VOICE...!!
IF HOPE IS FADING FROM THE WORLD, THEN...
...WE'LL BECOME ITS NEW RAYS OF HOPE!!!
HOPE

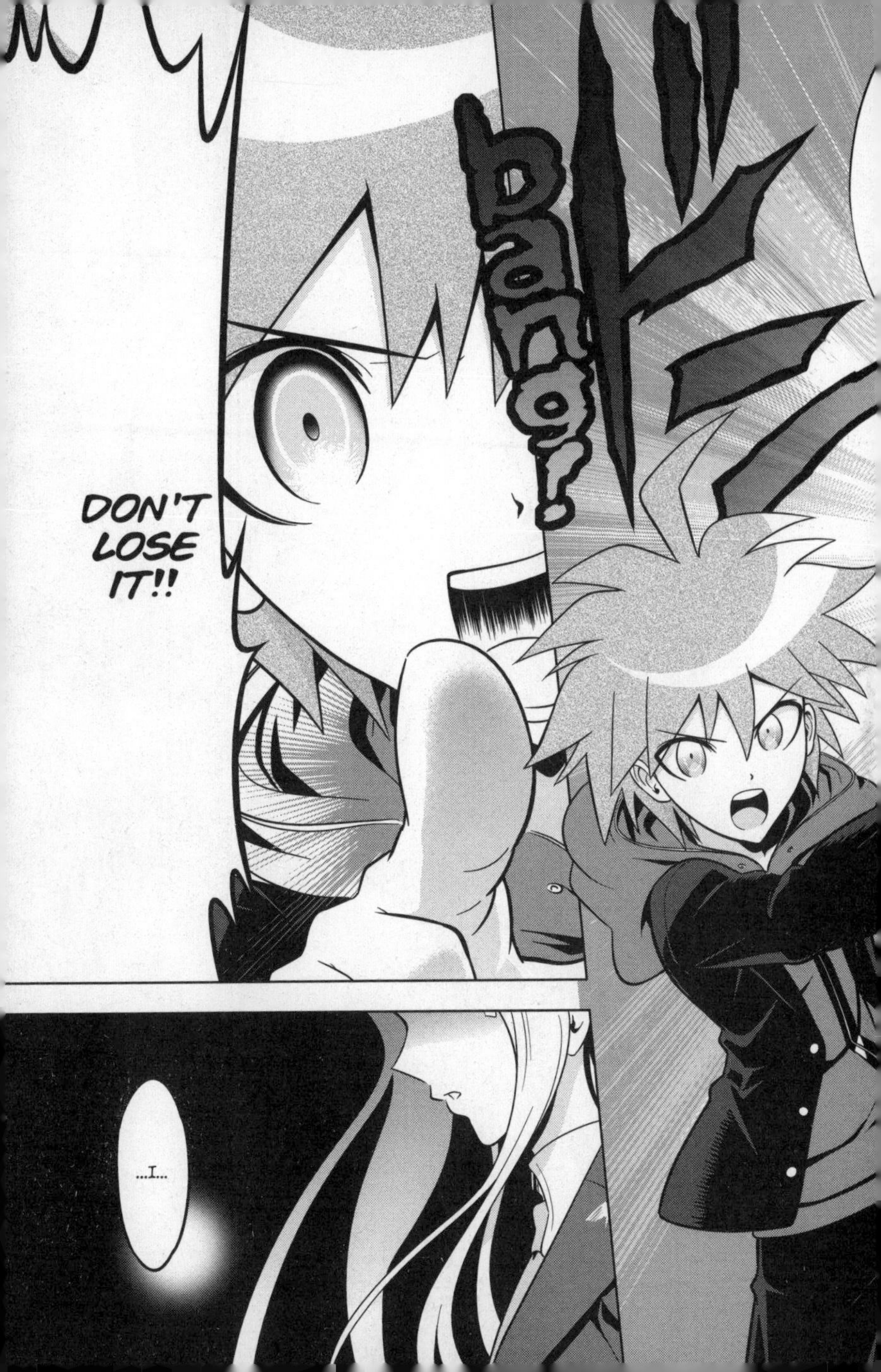
bang!
DON'T LOSE IT!!
...I...

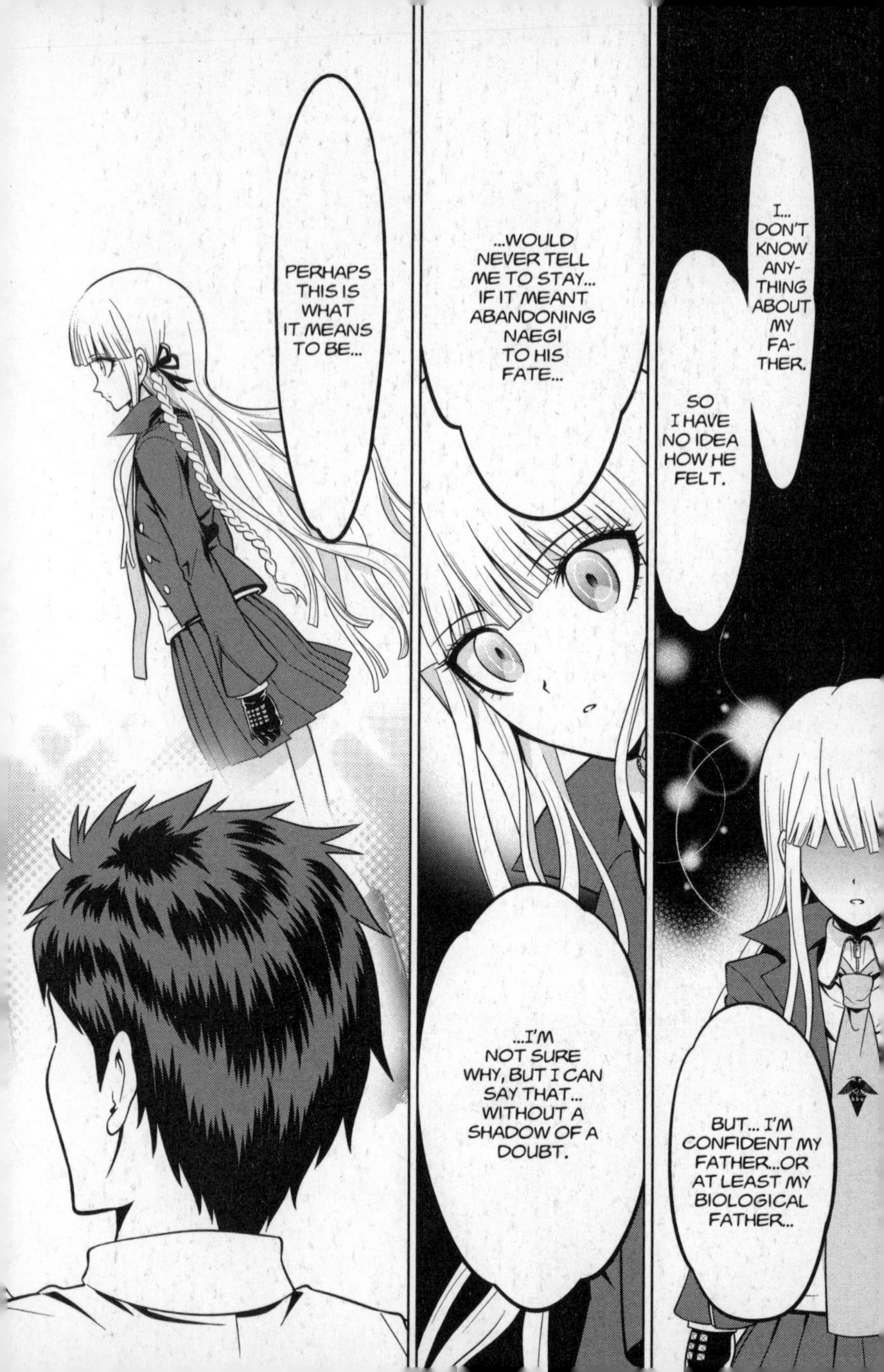
I... DON'T KNOW ANY-THING ABOUT MY FA-THER.
SO I HAVE NO IDEA HOW HE FELT.
BUT... I'M CONFIDENT MY FATHER...OR AT LEAST MY BIOLOGICAL FATHER...
...WOULD NEVER TELL ME TO STAY... IF IT MEANT ABANDONING NAEGI TO HIS FATE...
...I'M NOT SURE WHY, BUT I CAN SAY THAT... WITHOUT A SHADOW OF A DOUBT.
PERHAPS THIS IS WHAT IT MEANS TO BE...

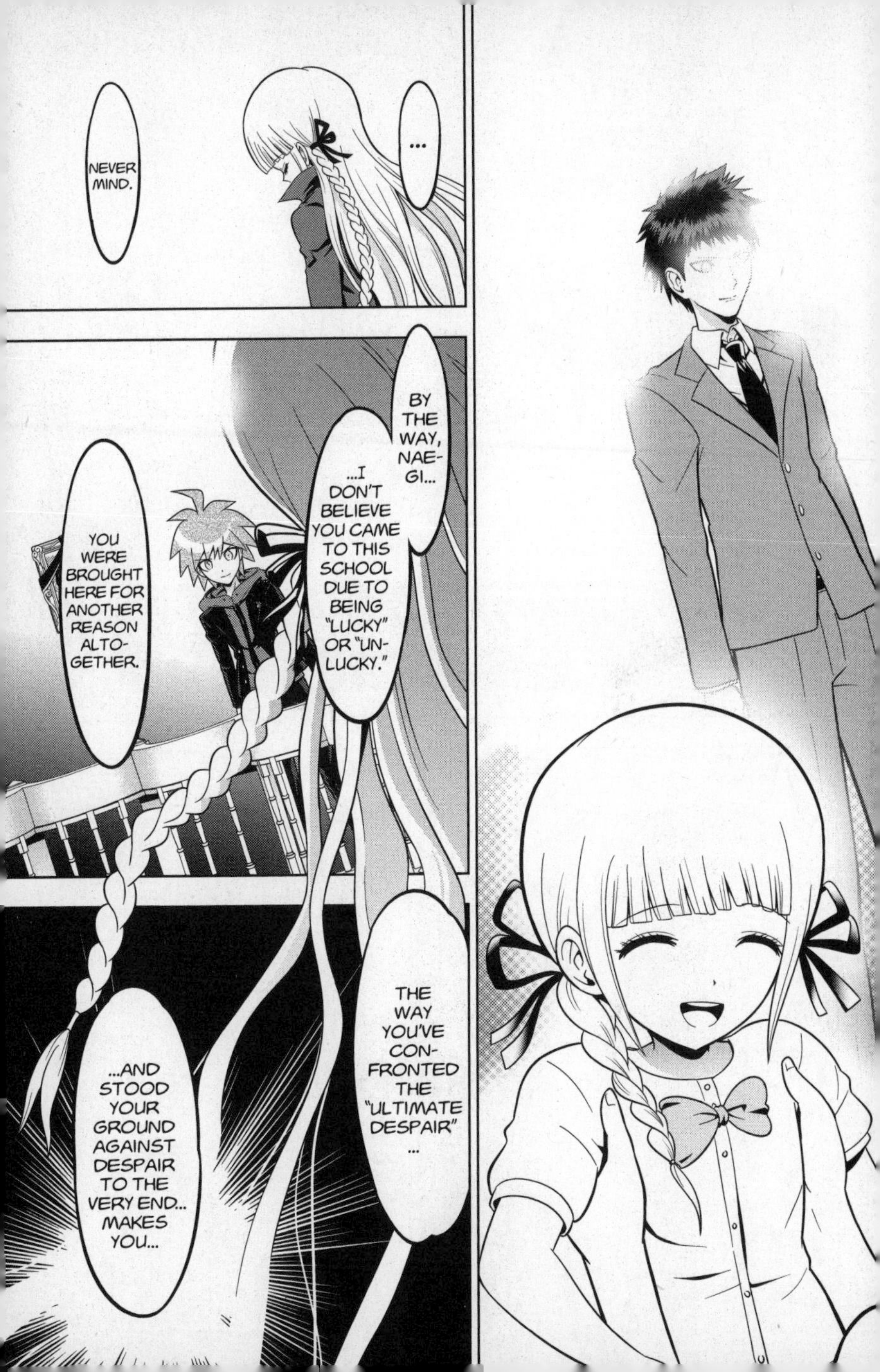
...
NEVER MIND.
BY THE WAY, NAE-GI...
...I DON'T BELIEVE YOU CAME TO THIS SCHOOL DUE TO BEING "LUCKY" OR "UN-LUCKY."
YOU WERE BROUGHT HERE FOR ANOTHER REASON ALTO-GETHER.
THE WAY YOU'VE CON-FRONTED THE "ULTIMATE DESPAIR" ...
...AND STOOD YOUR GROUND AGAINST DESPAIR TO THE VERY END... MAKES YOU...

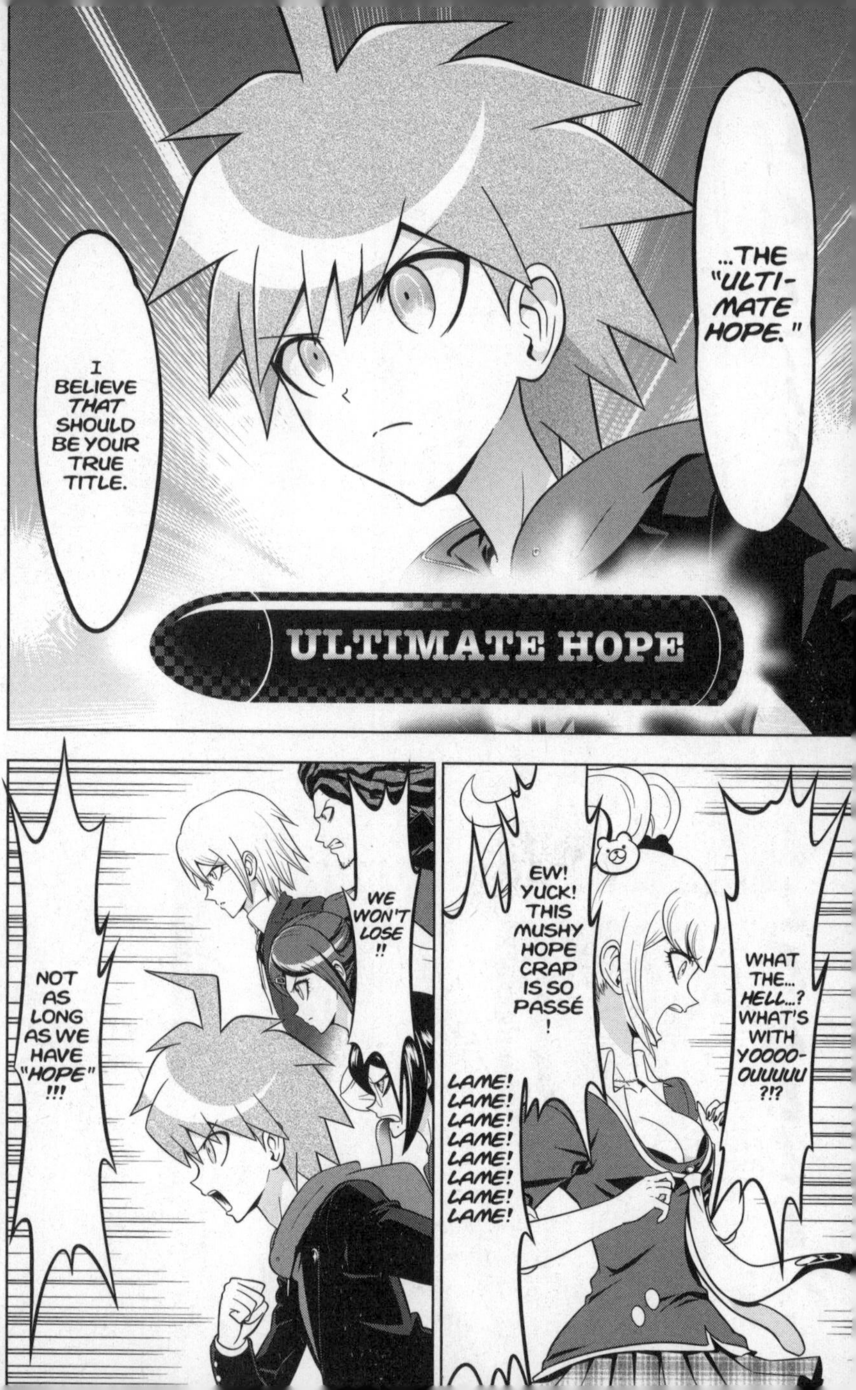
...THE "ULTIMATE HOPE."
I BELIEVE THAT SHOULD BE YOUR TRUE TITLE.
ULTIMATE HOPE
WHAT THE... HELL...? WHAT'S WITH YOOOO-OUUUUU?!?
EW! YUCK! THIS MUSHY HOPE CRAP IS SO PASSÉ!
LAME! LAME! LAME! LAME! LAME! LAME! LAME! LAME!
WE WON'T LOSE!!
NOT AS LONG AS WE HAVE "HOPE"!!!

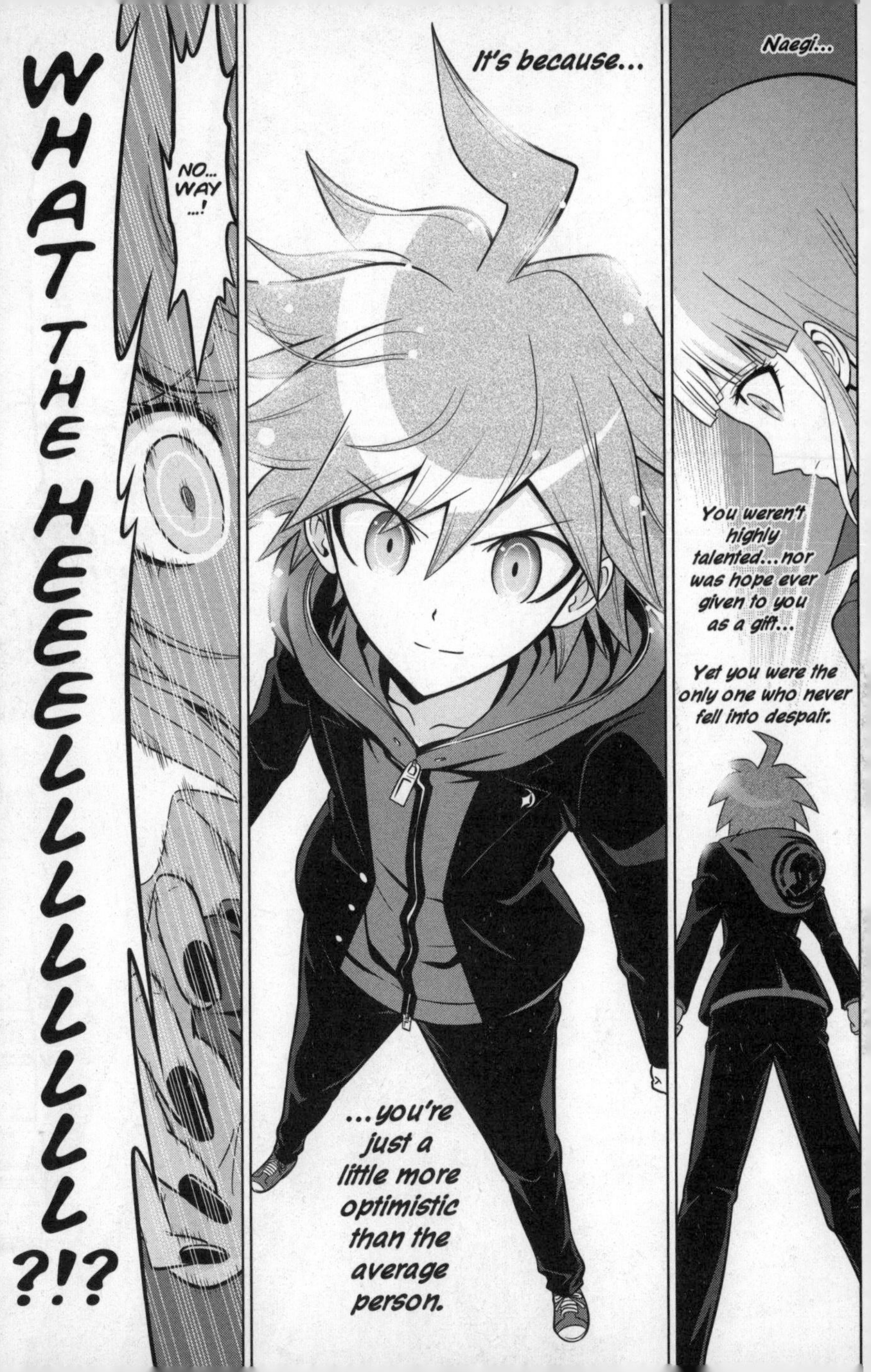
Naegi...
You weren't highly talented...nor was hope ever given to you as a gift...
Yet you were the only one who never fell into despair.
It's because...
...you're just a little more optimistic than the average person.
NO... WAY ...!
WHAT THE HEEELLLLLLL ?!?

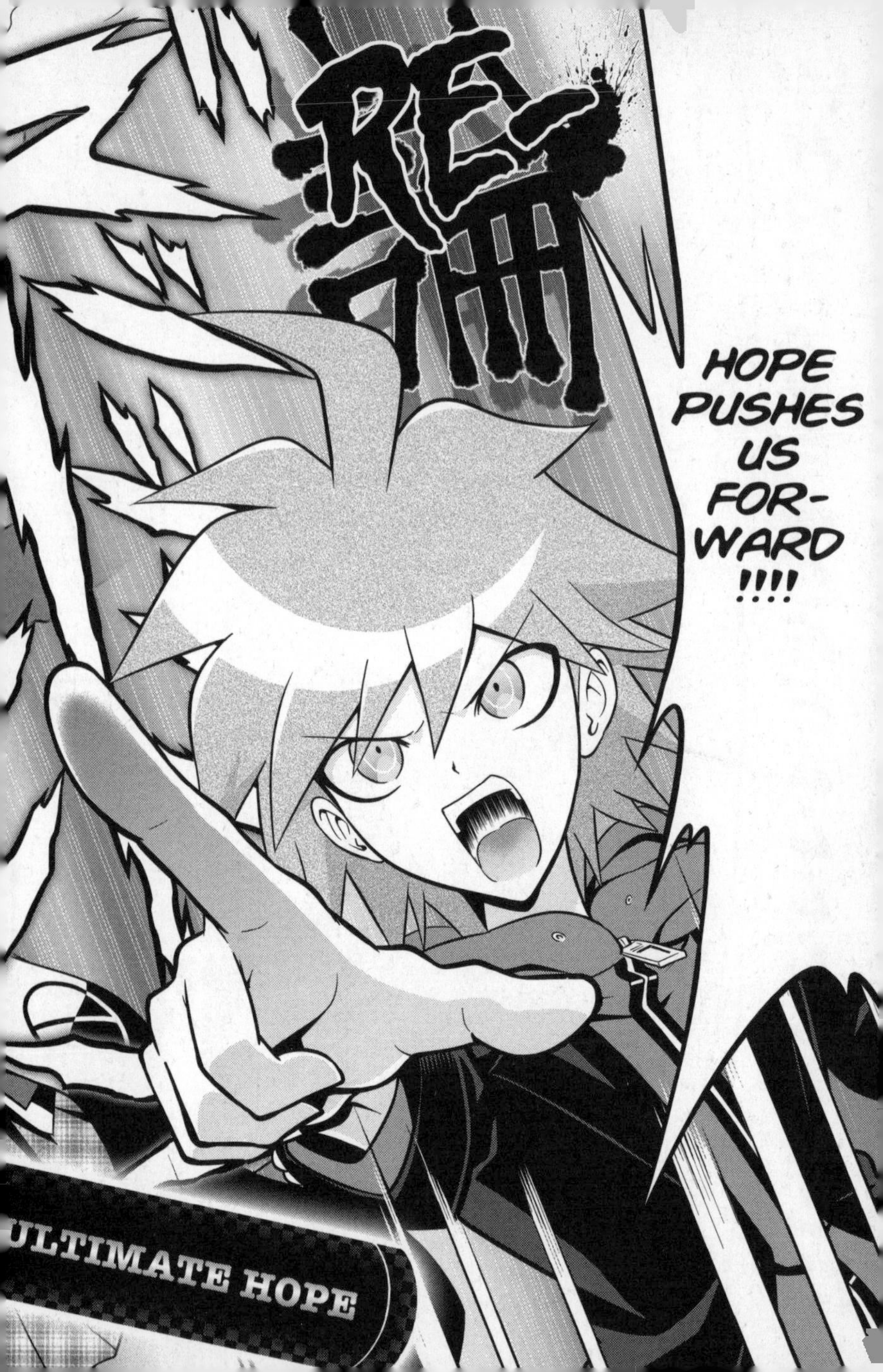

HOPE PUSHES US FOR-WARD!!!!
ULTIMATE HOPE

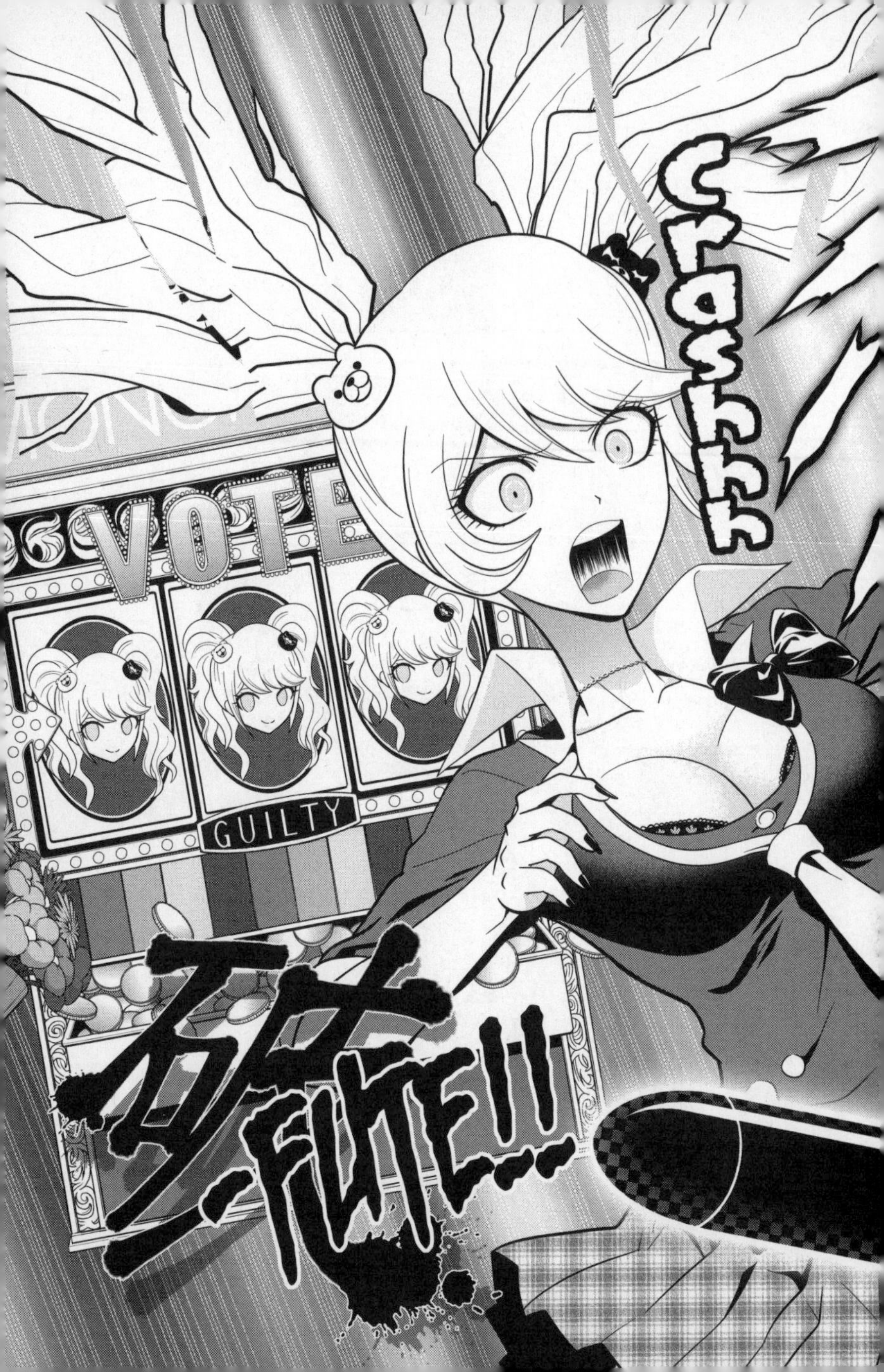
crashhh
VOTE
GUILTY

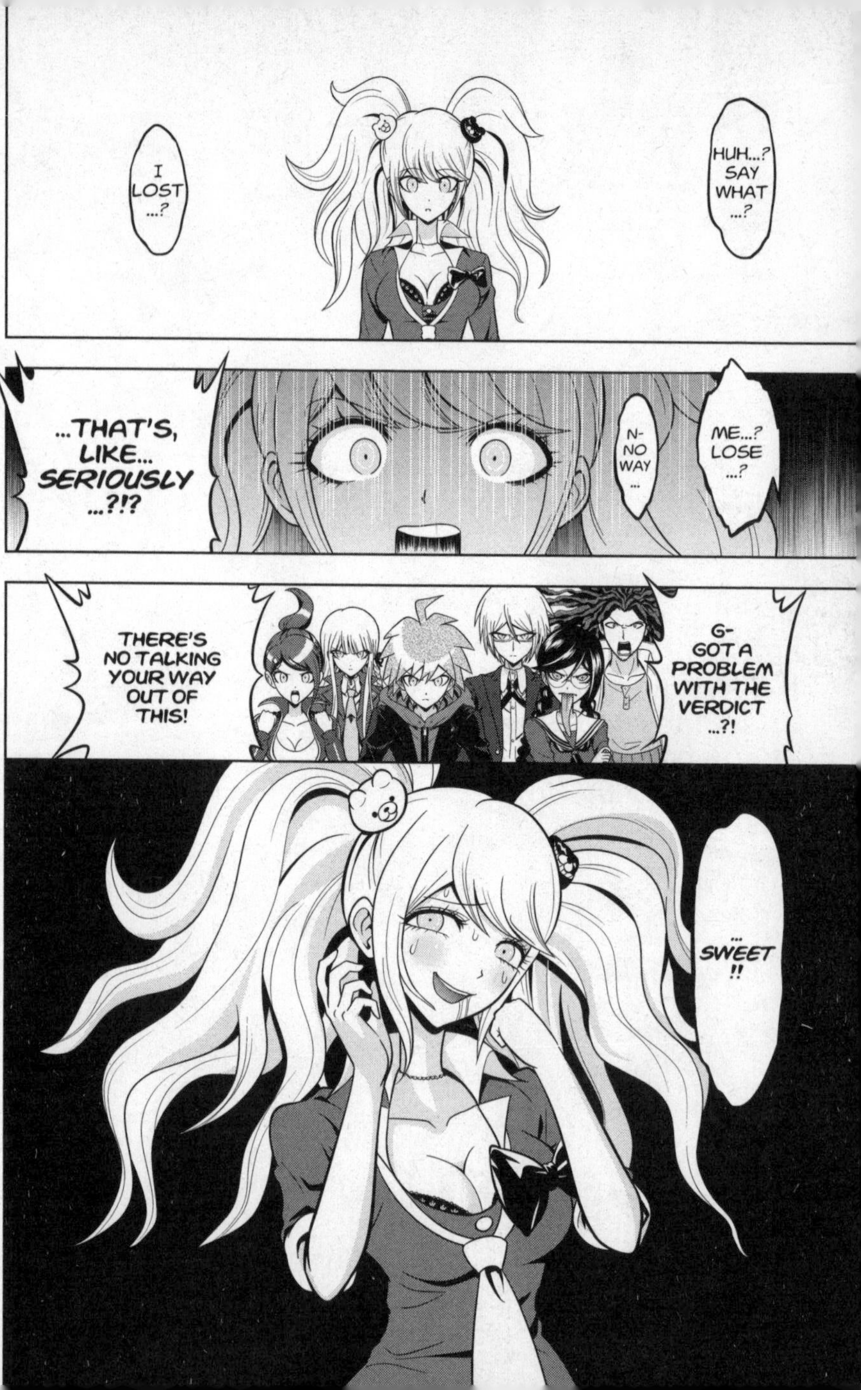
HUH...? SAY WHAT ...?
I LOST ...?
ME...? LOSE ...?
N- NO WAY ...
...THAT'S, LIKE... SERIOUSLY ...?!?
G- GOT A PROBLEM WITH THE VERDICT ...?!
THERE'S NO TALKING YOUR WAY OUT OF THIS!
... SWEET !!

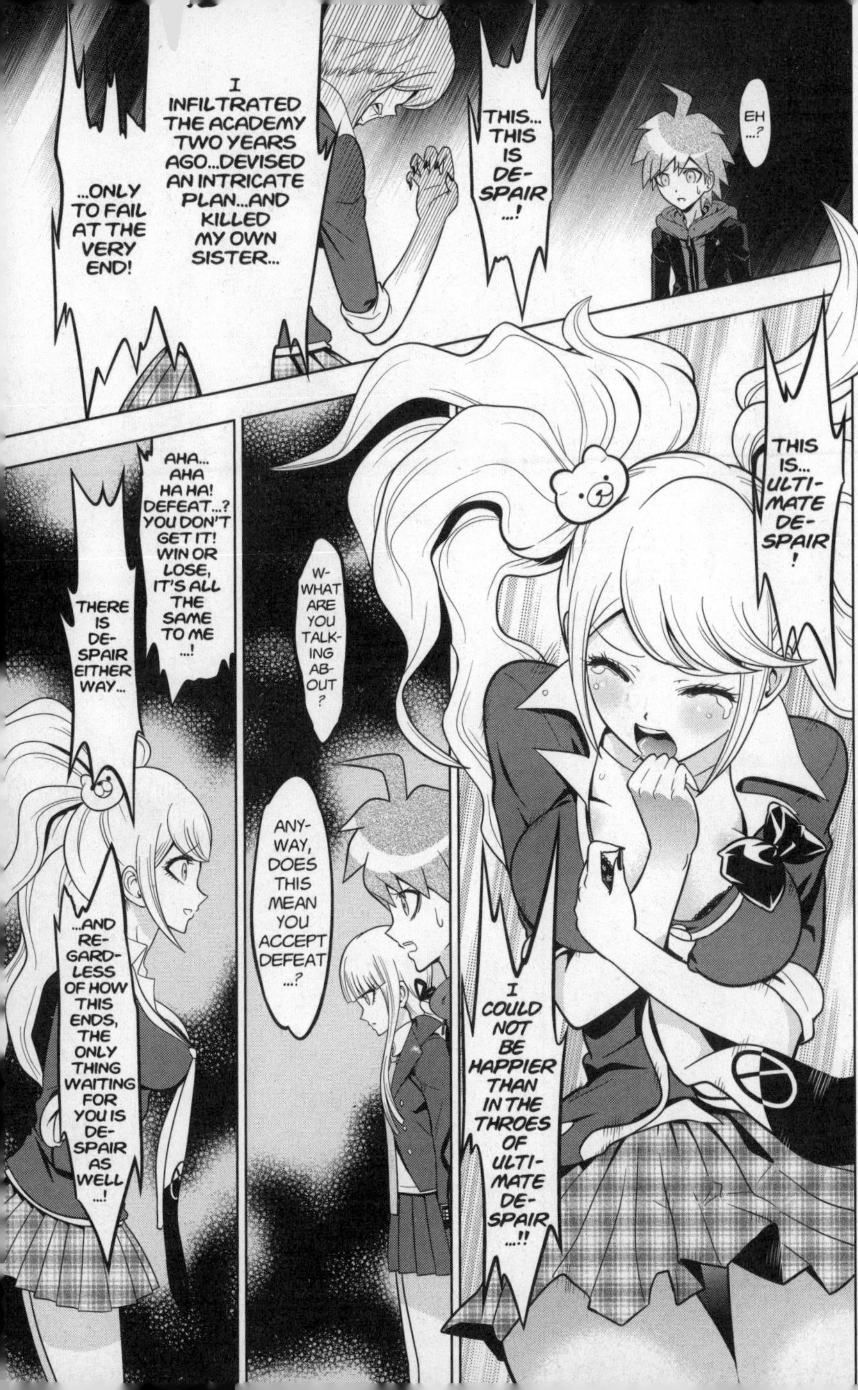
EH ...?
THIS... THIS IS DESPAIR ...!
I INFILTRATED THE ACADEMY TWO YEARS AGO...DEVISED AN INTRICATE PLAN...AND KILLED MY OWN SISTER...
...ONLY TO FAIL AT THE VERY END!
THIS IS... ULTIMATE DESPAIR!
I COULD NOT BE HAPPIER THAN IN THE THROES OF ULTIMATE DESPAIR ...!!
W-WHAT ARE YOU TALKING ABOUT?
ANYWAY, DOES THIS MEAN YOU ACCEPT DEFEAT ...?
AHA... AHA HA HA! DEFEAT...? YOU DON'T GET IT! WIN OR LOSE, IT'S ALL THE SAME TO ME ...!
THERE IS DESPAIR EITHER WAY...
...AND REGARDLESS OF HOW THIS ENDS, THE ONLY THING WAITING FOR YOU IS DESPAIR AS WELL ...!

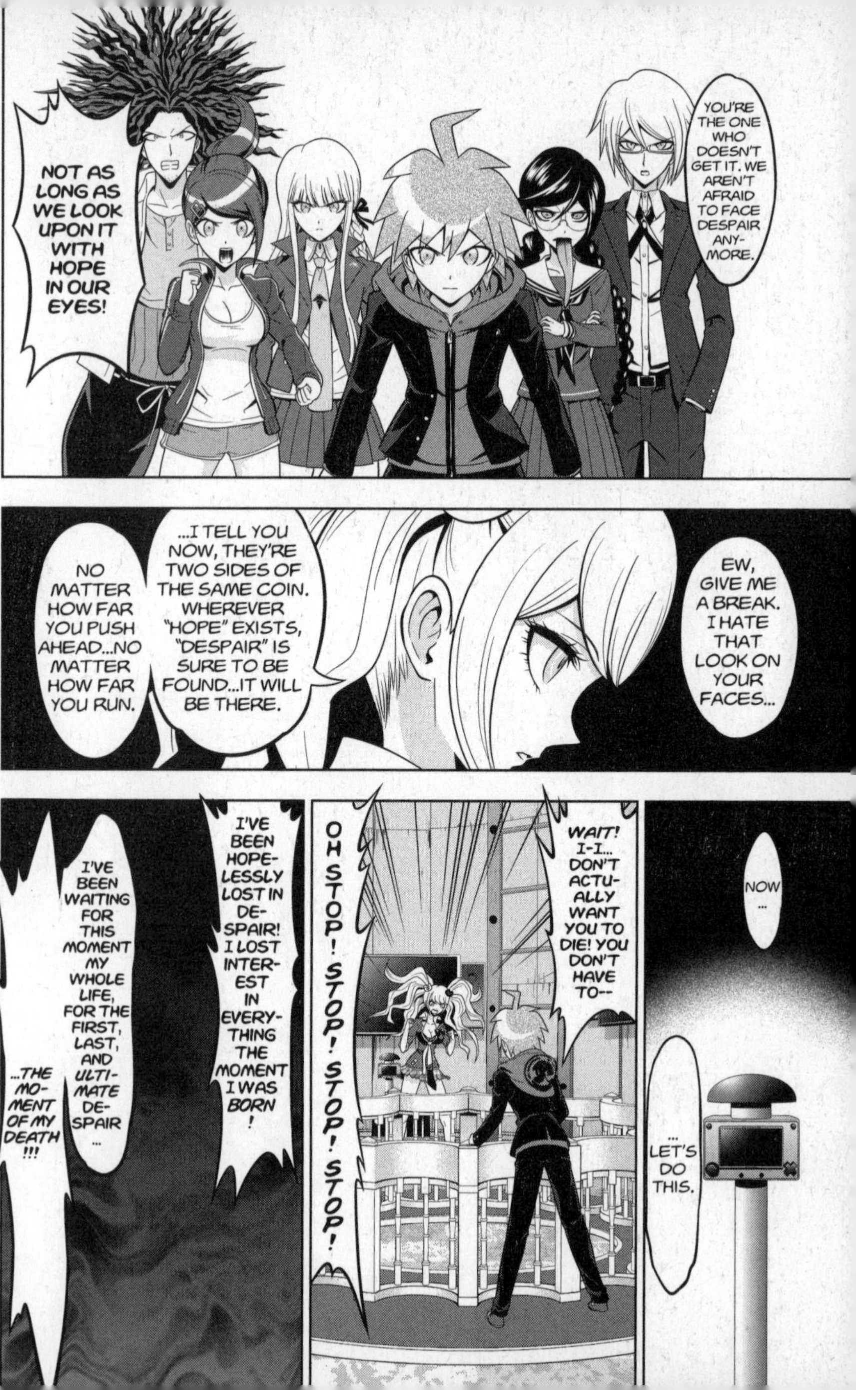
YOU'RE THE ONE WHO DOESN'T GET IT. WE AREN'T AFRAID TO FACE DESPAIR ANY-MORE.
NOT AS LONG AS WE LOOK UPON IT WITH HOPE IN OUR EYES!
EW, GIVE ME A BREAK. I HATE THAT LOOK ON YOUR FACES...
...I TELL YOU NOW, THEY'RE TWO SIDES OF THE SAME COIN. WHEREVER "HOPE" EXISTS, "DESPAIR" IS SURE TO BE FOUND...IT WILL BE THERE.
NO MATTER HOW FAR YOU PUSH AHEAD...NO MATTER HOW FAR YOU RUN.
NOW...
...LET'S DO THIS.
WAIT! I-I... DON'T ACTU-ALLY WANT YOU TO DIE! YOU DON'T HAVE TO--
OH STOP! STOP! STOP! STOP!
I'VE BEEN HOPE-LESSLY LOST IN DE-SPAIR! I LOST INTER-EST IN EVERY-THING THE MOMENT I WAS BORN!
I'VE BEEN WAITING FOR THIS MOMENT MY WHOLE LIFE, FOR THE FIRST, LAST, AND ULTI-MATE DE-SPAIR...
...THE MO-MENT OF MY DEATH!!!

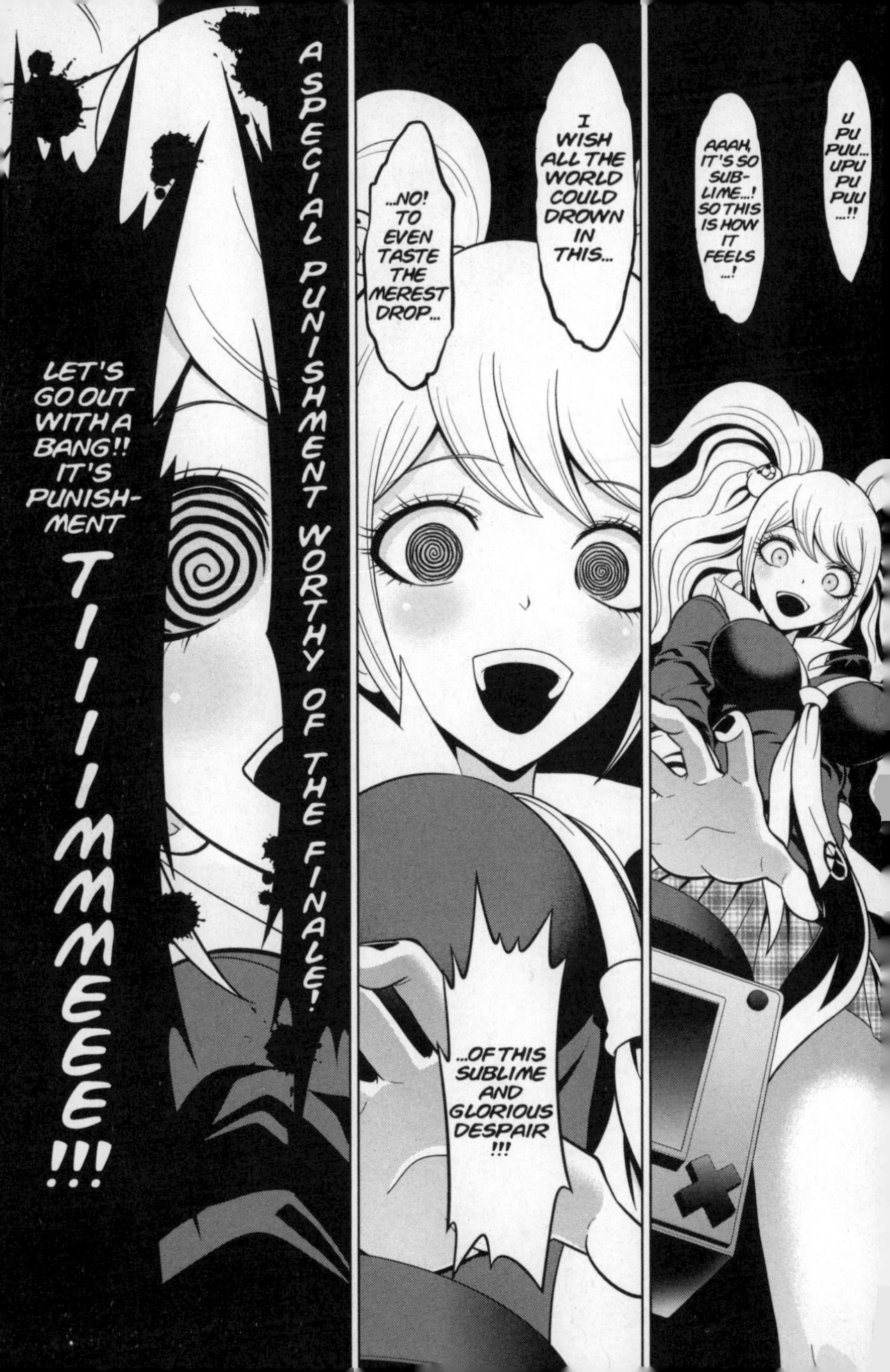
U PU PUU... UPU PU PUU ...!!
AAAH, IT'S SO SUB-LIME...! SO THIS IS HOW IT FEELS ...!
I WISH ALL THE WORLD COULD DROWN IN THIS...
...NO! TO EVEN TASTE THE MEREST DROP...
...OF THIS SUBLIME AND GLORIOUS DESPAIR !!!
A SPECIAL PUNISHMENT WORTHY OF THE FINALE!
LET'S GO OUT WITH A BANG!! IT'S PUNISH-MENT TIIIIMMMEEE!!!

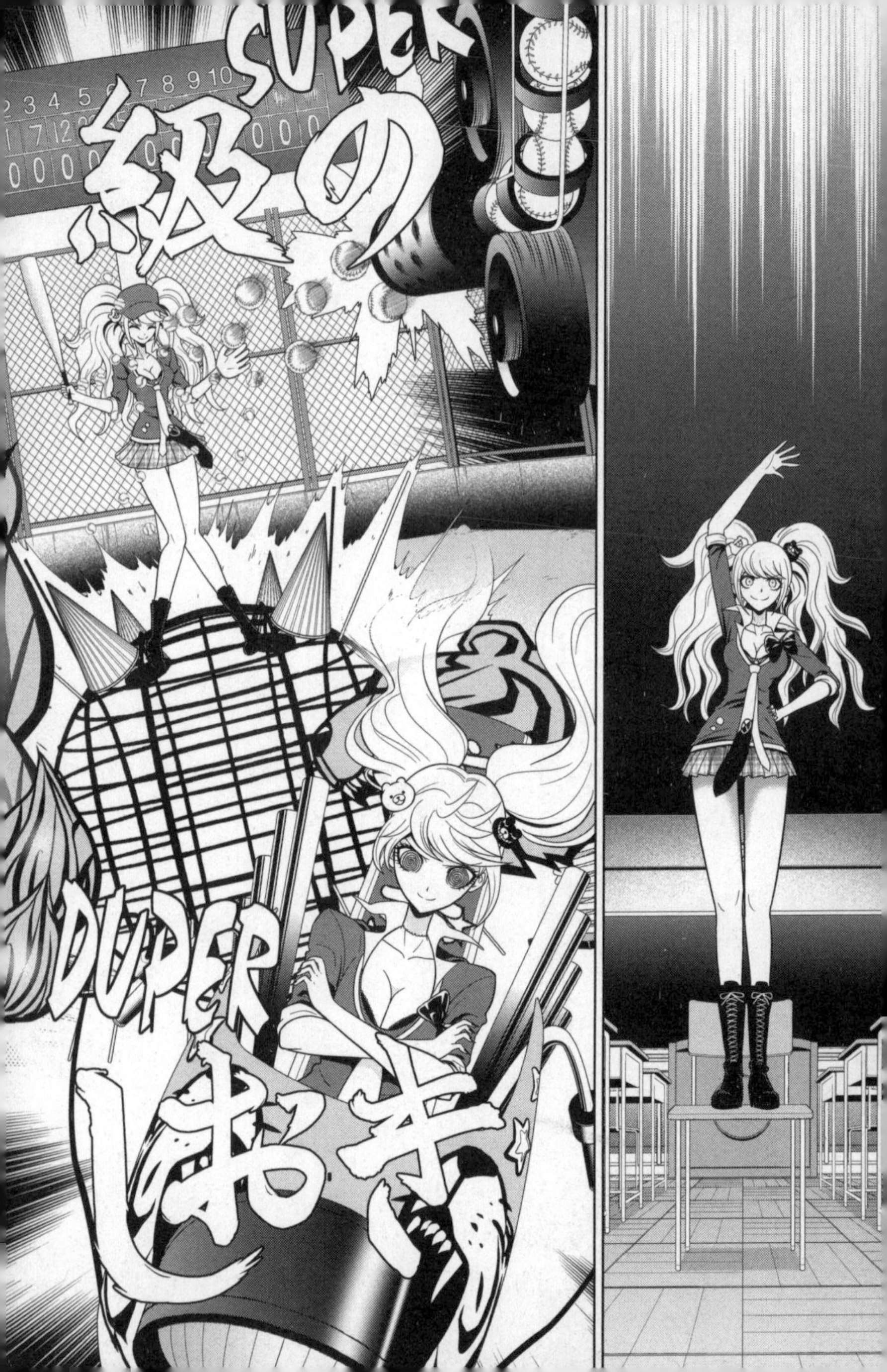
SUPER
級の
DUPER

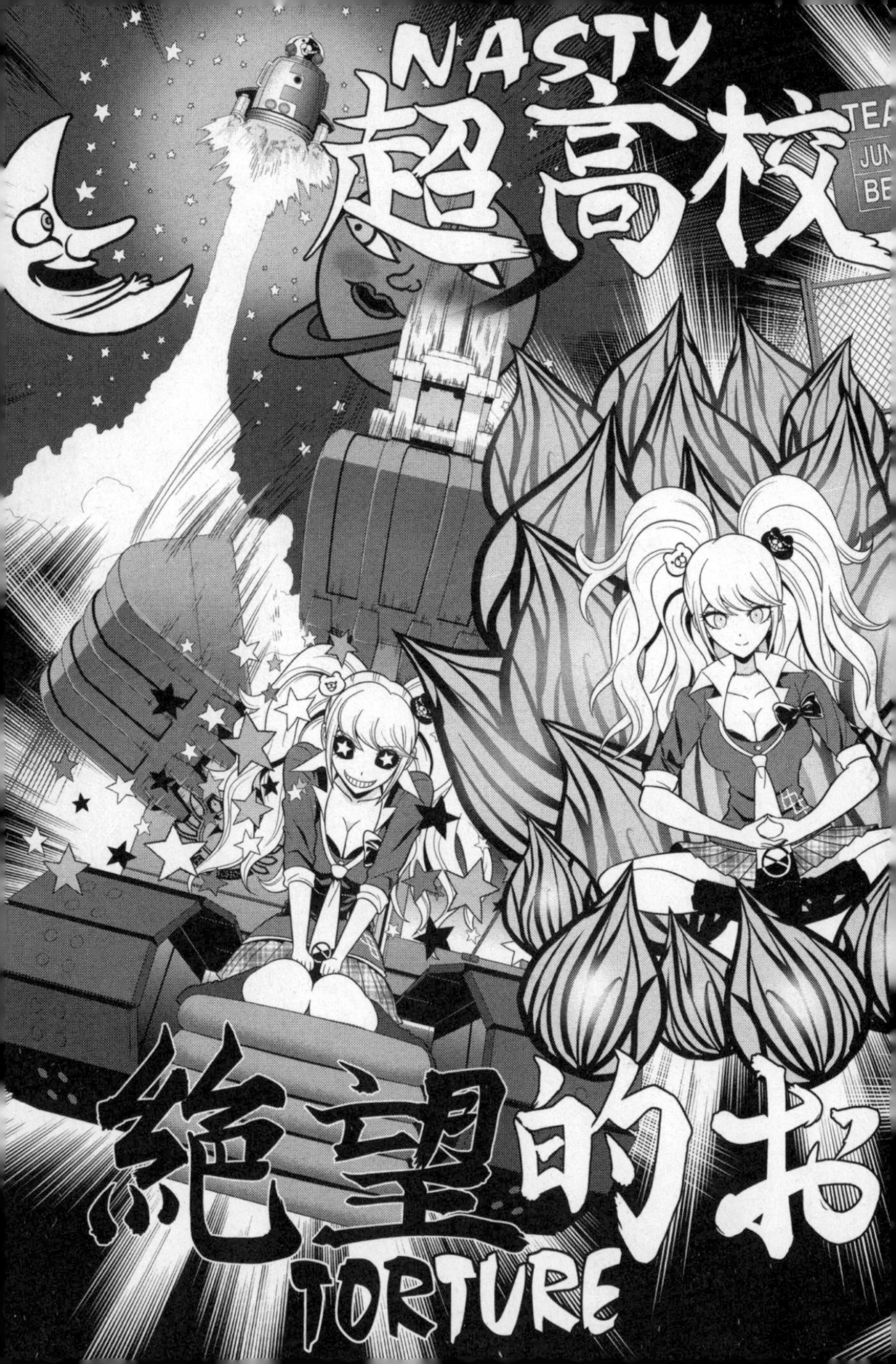
NASTY
超高校
絶望的お
TORTURE

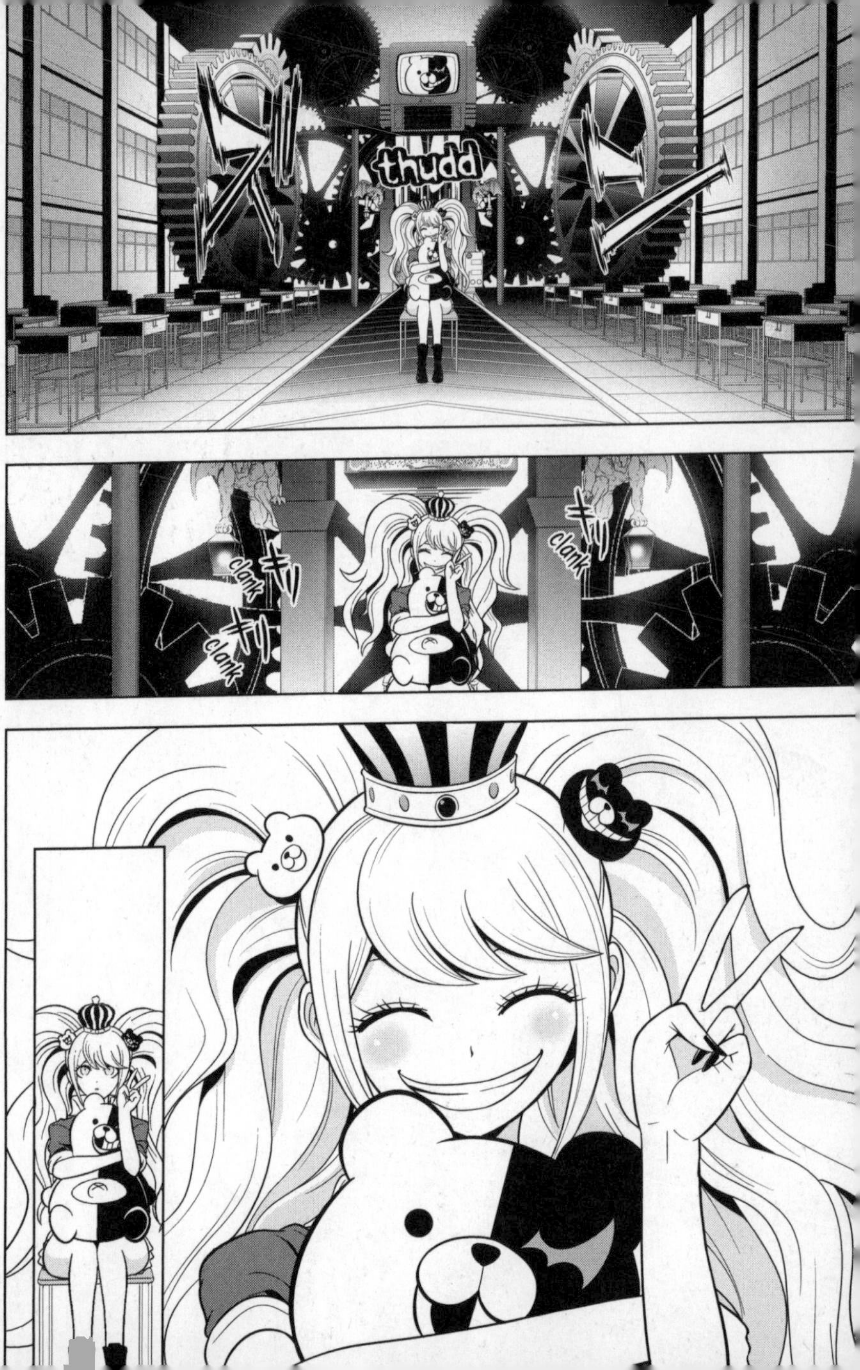
thudd
clank
clank
clank

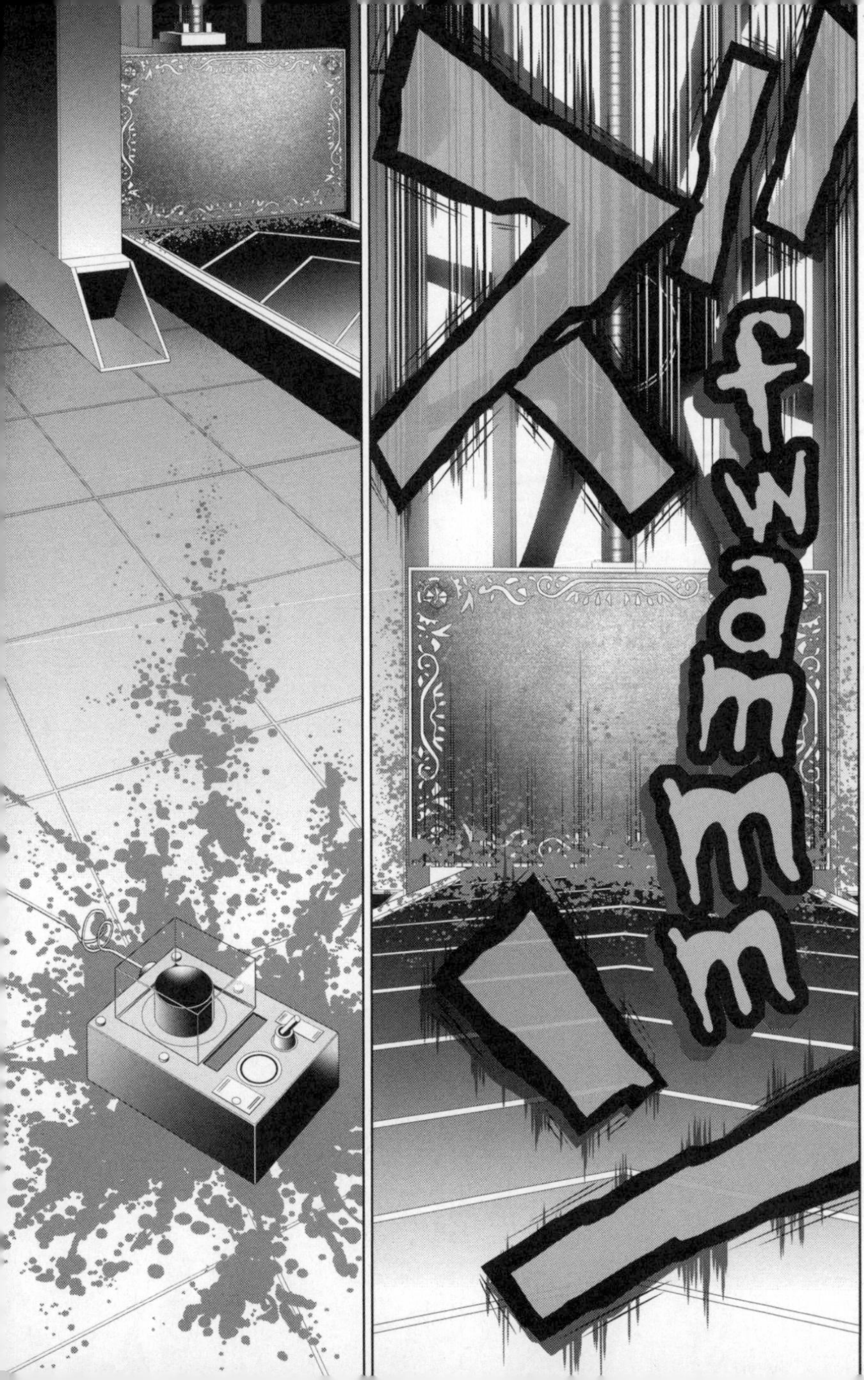
fwammm

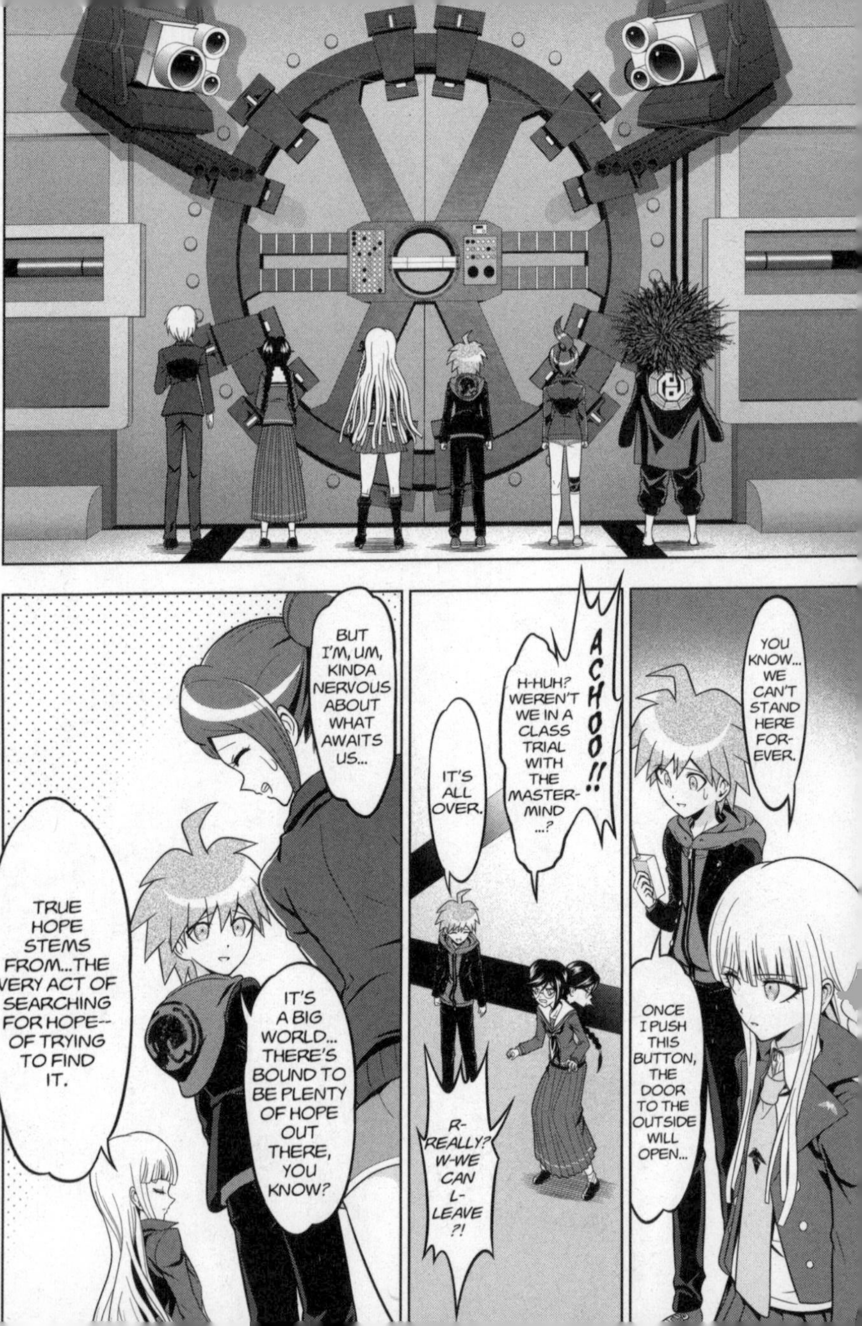
YOU KNOW... WE CAN'T STAND HERE FOR-EVER.
ONCE I PUSH THIS BUTTON, THE DOOR TO THE OUTSIDE WILL OPEN...
ACHOO!!
H-HUH? WEREN'T WE IN A CLASS TRIAL WITH THE MASTER-MIND ...?
IT'S ALL OVER.
R-REALLY? W-WE CAN L-LEAVE ?!
BUT I'M, UM, KINDA NERVOUS ABOUT WHAT AWAITS US...
IT'S A BIG WORLD... THERE'S BOUND TO BE PLENTY OF HOPE OUT THERE, YOU KNOW?
TRUE HOPE STEMS FROM...THE VERY ACT OF SEARCHING FOR HOPE-- OF TRYING TO FIND IT.

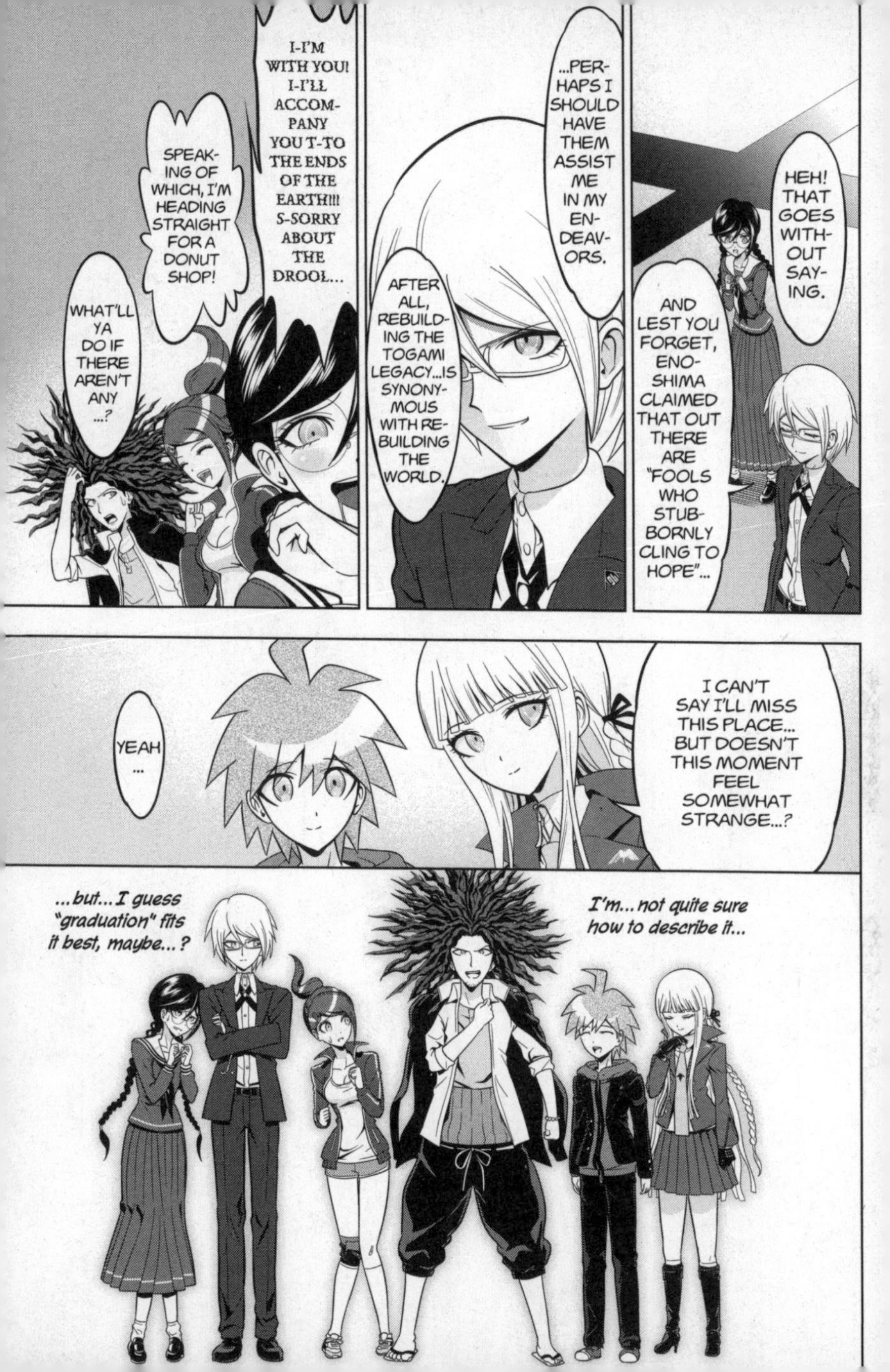
HEH! THAT GOES WITH-OUT SAY-ING.
AND LEST YOU FORGET, ENO-SHIMA CLAIMED THAT OUT THERE ARE "FOOLS WHO STUB-BORNLY CLING TO HOPE"...
...PER-HAPS I SHOULD HAVE THEM ASSIST ME IN MY EN-DEAV-ORS.
AFTER ALL, REBUILD-ING THE TOGAMI LEGACY...IS SYNONY-MOUS WITH RE-BUILDING THE WORLD.
I-I'M WITH YOU! I-I'LL ACCOM-PANY YOU T-TO THE ENDS OF THE EARTH!!! S-SORRY ABOUT THE DROOL...
SPEAK-ING OF WHICH, I'M HEADING STRAIGHT FOR A DONUT SHOP!
WHAT'LL YA DO IF THERE AREN'T ANY ...?
I CAN'T SAY I'LL MISS THIS PLACE... BUT DOESN'T THIS MOMENT FEEL SOMEWHAT STRANGE...?
YEAH ...
I'm... not quite sure how to describe it...
...but... I guess "graduation" fits it best, maybe...?

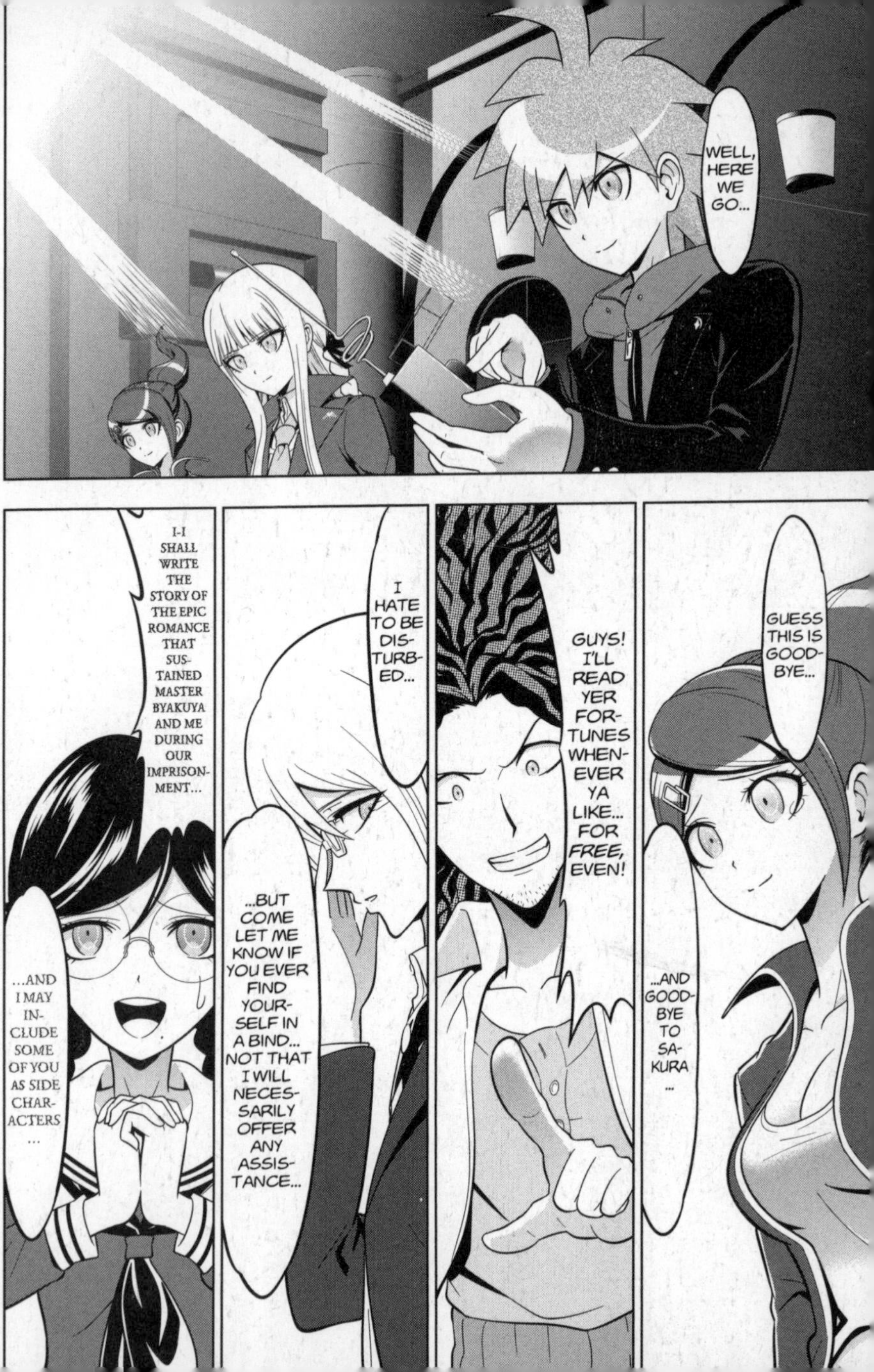
WELL, HERE WE GO...
GUESS THIS IS GOOD-BYE...
...AND GOOD-BYE TO SAKURA...
GUYS! I'LL READ YER FORTUNES WHENEVER YA LIKE... FOR FREE, EVEN!
I HATE TO BE DISTURBED...
...BUT COME LET ME KNOW IF YOU EVER FIND YOURSELF IN A BIND... NOT THAT I WILL NECESSARILY OFFER ANY ASSISTANCE...
I-I SHALL WRITE THE STORY OF THE EPIC ROMANCE THAT SUSTAINED MASTER BYAKUYA AND ME DURING OUR IMPRISONMENT...
...AND I MAY INCLUDE SOME OF YOU AS SIDE CHARACTERS...

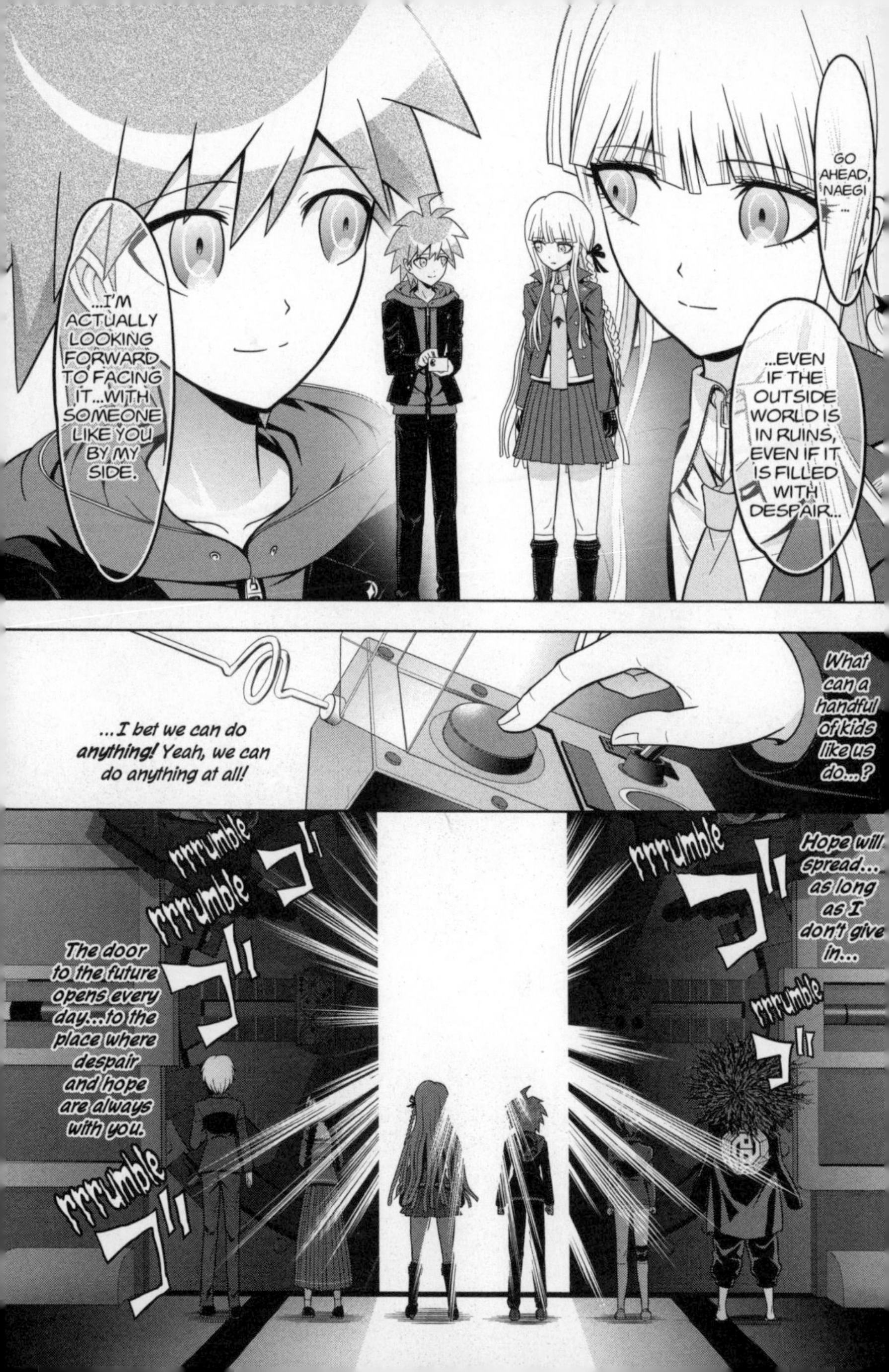
GO AHEAD, NAEGI...
...EVEN IF THE OUTSIDE WORLD IS IN RUINS, EVEN IF IT IS FILLED WITH DESPAIR...
...I'M ACTUALLY LOOKING FORWARD TO FACING IT...WITH SOMEONE LIKE YOU BY MY SIDE.
What can a handful of kids like us do...?
...I bet we can do anything! Yeah, we can do anything at all!
Hope will spread... as long as I don't give in...
rrrumble
rrrumble
rrrumble
rrrumble
The door to the future opens every day...to the place where despair and hope are always with you.
rrrumble

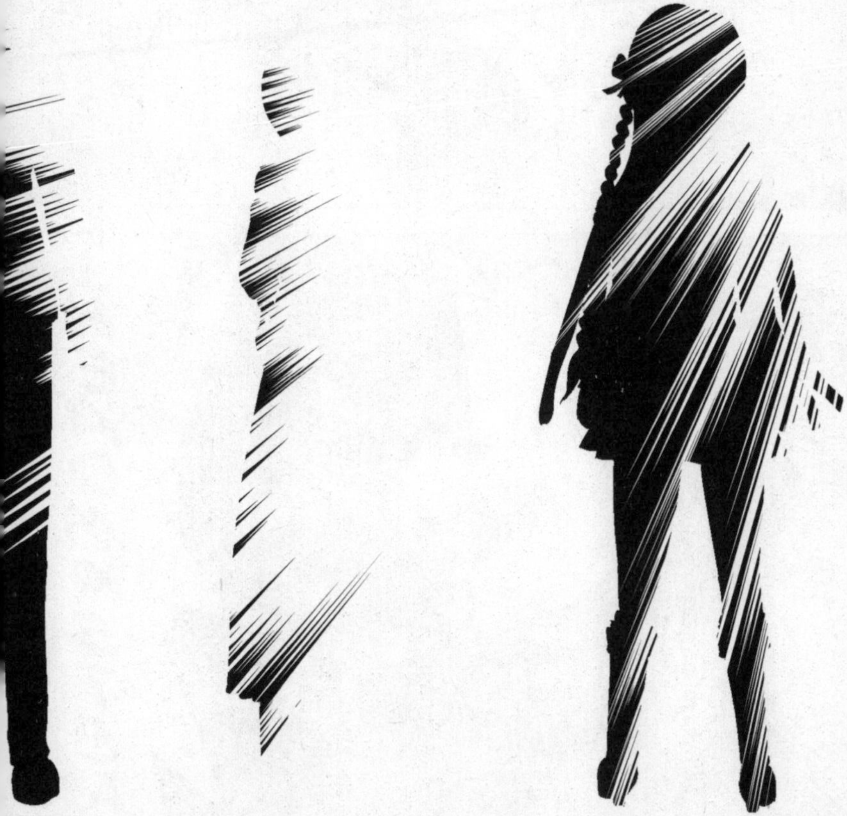

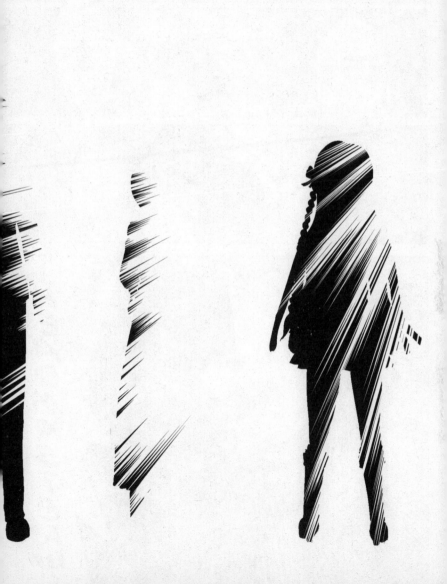

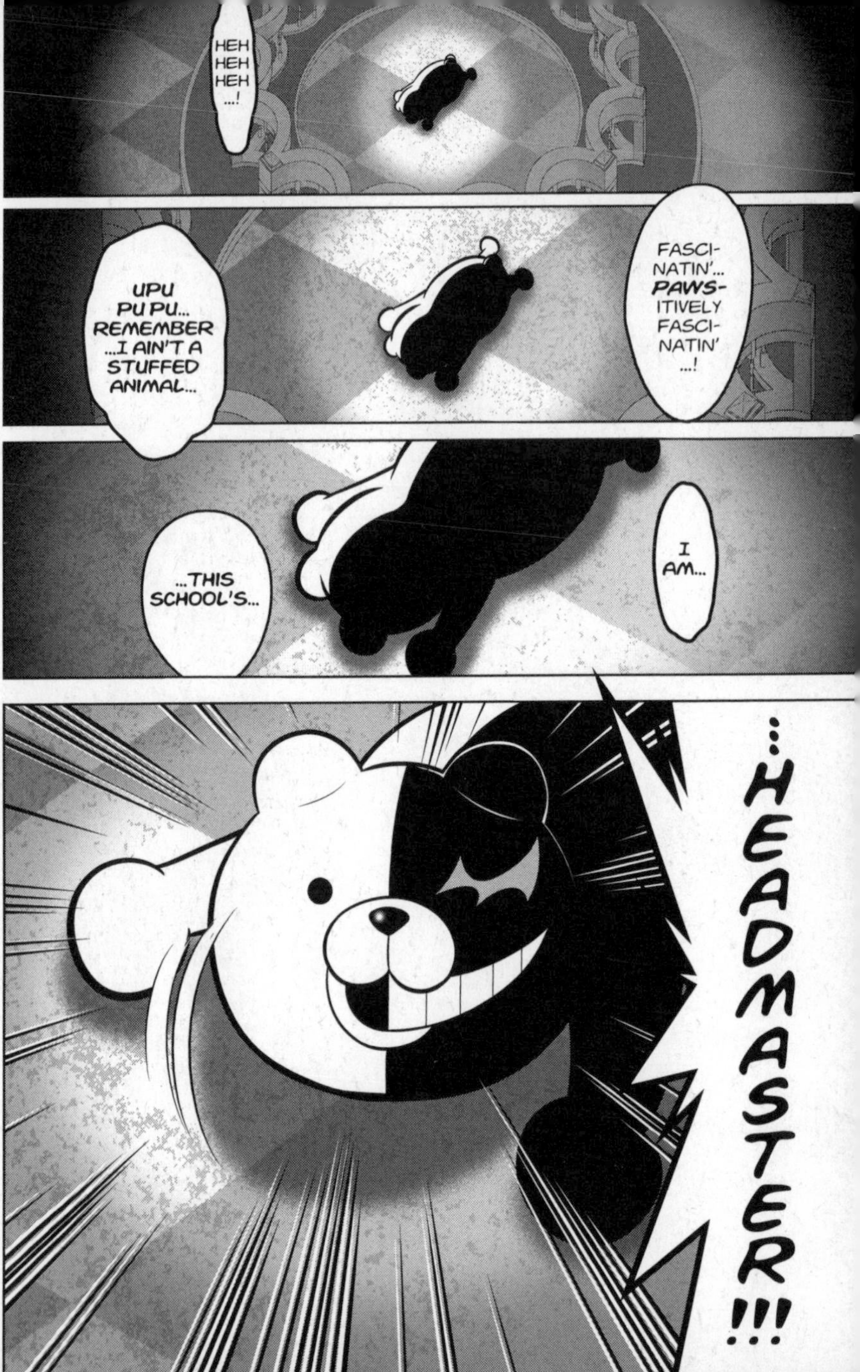
HEH HEH HEH ...!
FASCI-NATIN'... PAWS-ITIVELY FASCI-NATIN' ...!
UPU PU PU... REMEMBER ...I AIN'T A STUFFED ANIMAL...
I AM...
...THIS SCHOOL'S...
...HEADMASTER!!!

END

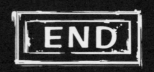

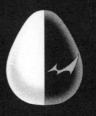

president and publisher
MIKE RICHARDSON

designer
SARAH TERRY

ultimate digital art technician
CHRISTINA McKENZIE

English-language version produced by Dark Horse Comics

DANGANRONPA: THE ANIMATION VOLUME 4

Published by
Dark Horse Manga
A division of Dark Horse Comics LLC
10956 SE Main Street I Milwaukie, OR 97222

LCCN: 2016003683
DarkHorse.com

To find a comics shop in your area, visit comicshoplocator.com

First edition: March 2017
ISBN 978-1-50670-136-3

8 9 10

Printed in the United States of America

DESPAIR MAIL

c/o Dark Horse Comics | 10956 SE Main St. | Milwaukie, OR 97222 | danganronpa@darkhorse.com

Welcome back to DESPAIR MAIL, the place for Ultimate Danganronpa Fans!
If you'd like to share your thoughts or comments on Danganronpa . . . pictures
of your Danganronpa cosplay . . . or your Danganronpa fan art—this is the place
for you! Send it to the address or email at the top of the page and remember to use
high resolution (300 dpi or better) for your photos or images, so they'll look good in print!

This is the final volume of this Danganronpa series, and so this is the last Despair Mail . . . for now,
anyway. However, we're working on publishing more translated Danganronpa manga in the future
(including manga based on the other games in the series, as some of you have requested), and if we
do, we'd love to include your fan contributions in those books as well!

I want to apologize to our Ultimate Digital Art Technician, Christina McKenzie, and our designer (surely
also Ultimate—but perhaps she declines to say so in case she gets assigned to Hope's Peak Academy
^_^) for waiting until the last minute to get Despair Mail ready . . . it's just that I wanted to include as
many of your contributions in volume 4 as possible.

As you probably know, we have to get each volume of the manga together some months before it
appears in your bookstore, so it's possible we may still get pictures or letters from you after the cutoff
date for volume 4. If so, please know that we do appreciate them, and, as mentioned above, we hope
to include them in another Danganronpa book sometime!

David Kusuma sent us this picture of his Danganronpa collection . . . thus far! I'm pleased to see this
manga series is represented in the bottom right . . . but looking at all these books in Japanese, I feel extra
motivated to get some more published in English here!

Emily Raine writes in to say, "I've loved Danganronpa for about a year now and now I'm going to be cosplaying Chiaki Nanami for Anime USA [an anime con in Washington, DC, if you didn't know—ed.]. When I saw volume 1 at Barnes and Noble, I got really excited because Danganronpa is part of my life now. I'm playing both 1 and 2 as well as watching both the Despair and Future Arcs (which I'm having my dad watch with me) . . . I just want to show my love for Danganronpa!" It's great that you're watching with your dad. Actually, someone at Dark Horse had a check-up recently and, mentioning that we were publishing the manga, found out that his doctor was into Danganronpa!

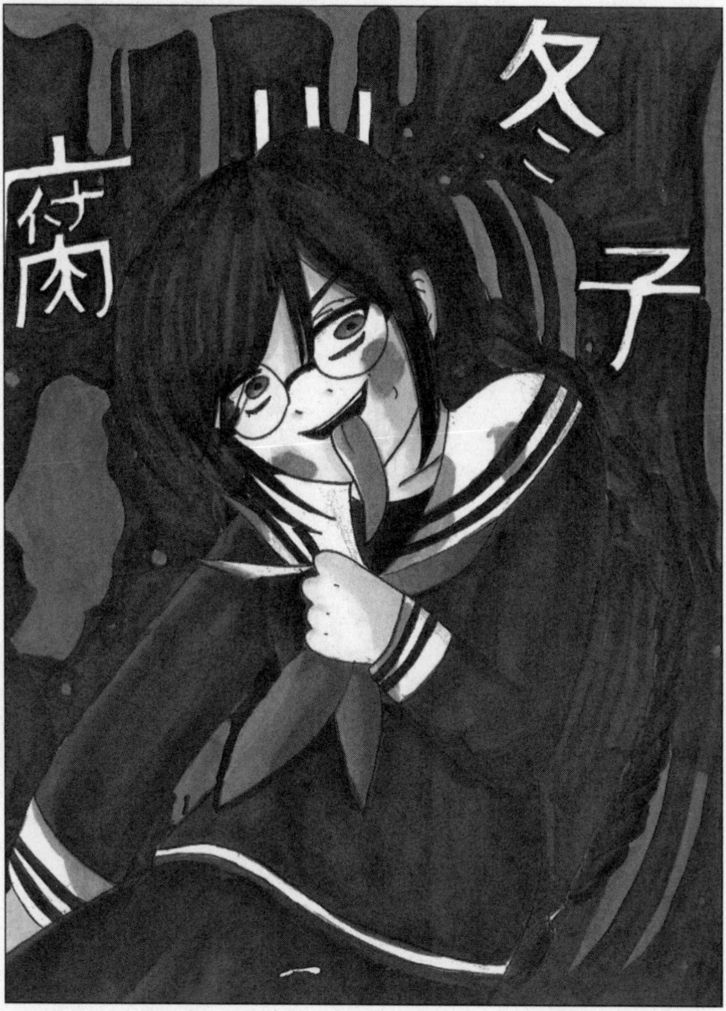
腐川冬子

Charlotte Zahn sent in this great rendition of everyone's favorite psycho, Toko Fukawa (or wait, I guess Fukawa's the "normal" personality . . . ?). ^_^

Sarah Haddad, whose sketches were also featured in volume 3's Despair Mail, sent this in too, saying, "Hey there, I drew another picture from Danganronpa and thought I would send it to you to see if it can make it into anything! :) Thank you!" Just in time, Sarah!

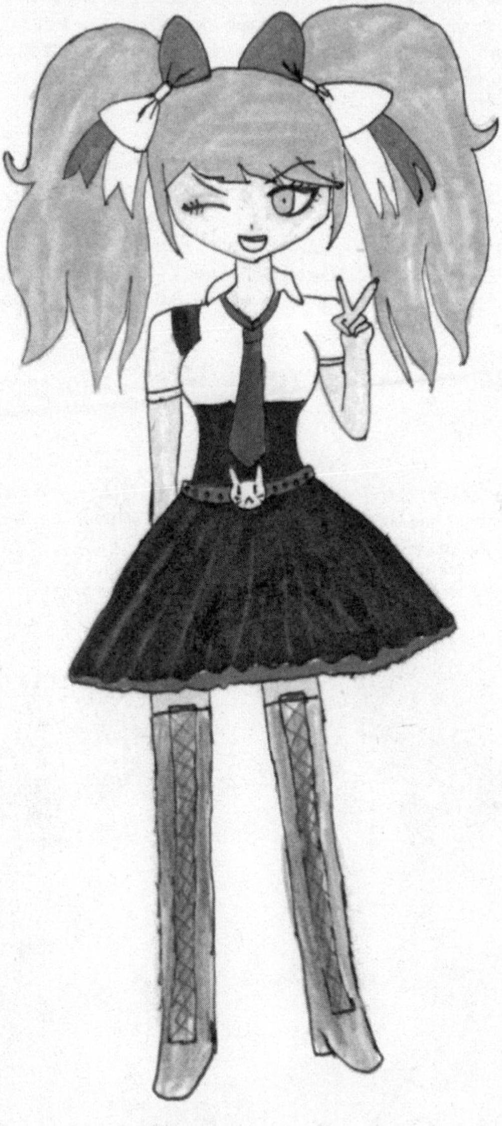

Well, as we all know, Junko Enoshima returns in the final volume . . . so we have to thank Megan Alesha Shorroc[k] for being so kind as to submit this fan art of her. Thank you, Megan!

lmedin A. sent in this letter to Despair Mail: "I just wanted to say I LOVE *Danganronpa*. My first encounter with it was vhen I watched YouTuber CinnamonToastKen play *Danganronpa: Trigger Happy Havoc*. Me being me, I saw the thumbnail ınd did not want to watch because it looked dumb (I judge stuff by their covers). HOW WRONG I WAS. The video acciden-ally played because of YouTube autoplay. I was too lazy to change the video. After that I was ADDICTED.

was sad when the game was over but the second game (*Danganronpa 2: Goodbye Despair*) was out, apparently. ;innamonToastKen said he was gonna play it and I was ECSTATIC (my favorite character was [and is] Chiaki). Sadly this neans I know when someone dies, why someone dies, and, well . . . who dies.

have noticed some differences between the manga and the game. Especially how they found out Chihiro Fujisaki is a lude. When I bought the manga I told my friend I would let them read it (I had told them about *Danganronpa* before, but *)anganronpa* isn't really the easiest thing to just explain through Facebook Messenger). They said they promised them-elves to not get addicted . . . but they failed.

m gonna buy every volume and if there's gonna be a manga for *Danganronpa 2* (or even 3) you can bet my wallet I'm ıonna buy that.

With a BEARful of love, Almedin A."

hanks for writing in, Almedin! In my day I worked on the same principle to discover new things, except back then, ıstead of YouTube autoplay, I was too lazy to change the TV channel on the remote control. But, as you know, ıziness can sometimes pay off big!

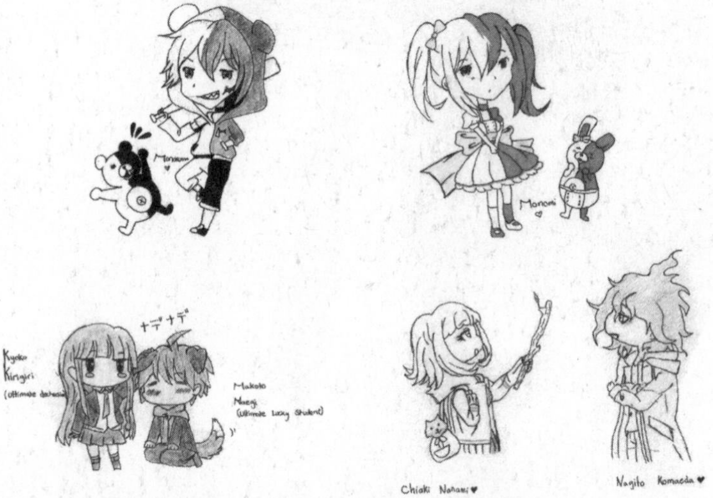
Monomi
Kyoko
Kirigiri
Makoto
Naegi
(Ultimate Lucky Student)
Chiaki Nanami♥
Nagito Komaeda♥

lindessa sent in these four drawings and said: "I'm so happy that you've translated the manga! Thank you and ıless your amazing souls. I'm a huge** Danganronpa **fan I love the games, anime, and now the manga 'cause now can finally read it!"

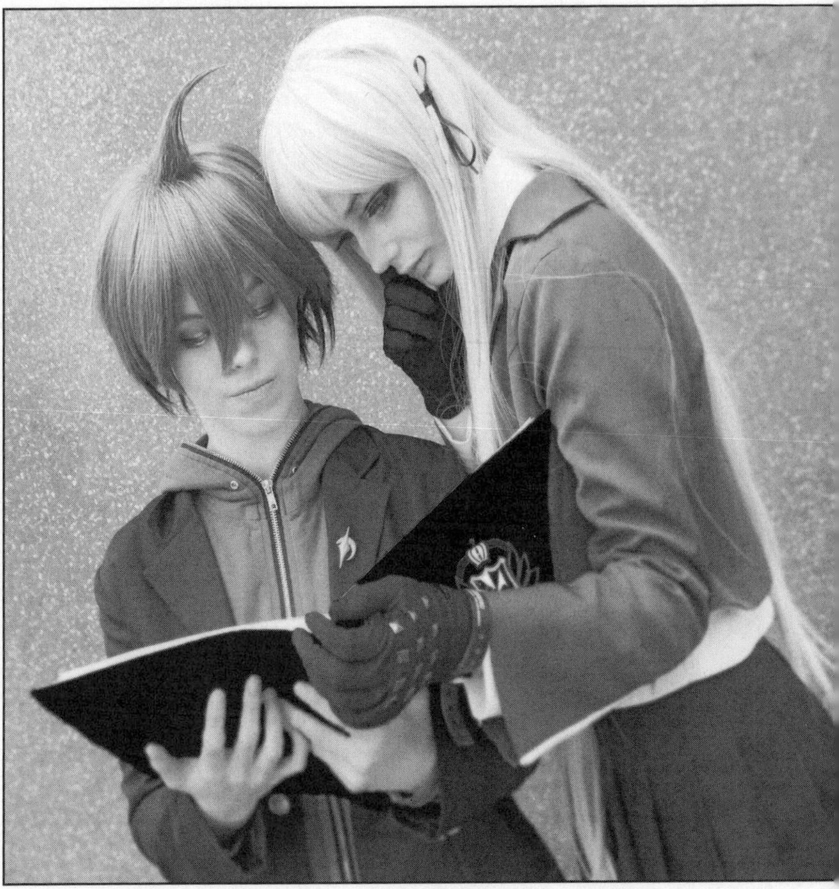

And finally, what could be more appropriate to end on than this shot of Naegi and Kirigiri looking for clues, wit Makoto Naegi portrayed by Kanon-No-Hana, and Kyoko Kirigiri portrayed by Emishima? Thank you both for thi great depiction!

Once again, thanks so much to everyone for your submissions, and your support of the Danganronpa *manga. A said above, we hope to do more* Danganronpa *books in the future, and if so, we'll hope to see you there! If yo ever feel like you're trapped inside someone's evil and corrupt game that's trying to set you all against each othe remember how to fight back: make friends instead . . . and don't give up on the truth.*

—CG

U PU PU PUU!!!

HEADMASTER MONOKUMA here, punks! This is a MANGA, so THAT means it's black and white with a li'l bit of color . . . just like ME! And it ALSO means it reads the other way, so why don't you PAWS a moment and turn this book around. If you knew that already, just BEAR with my little explanation. HAW HAW! Funny, ain't I? I kill me! But disobey the school rules—and I kill YOU!

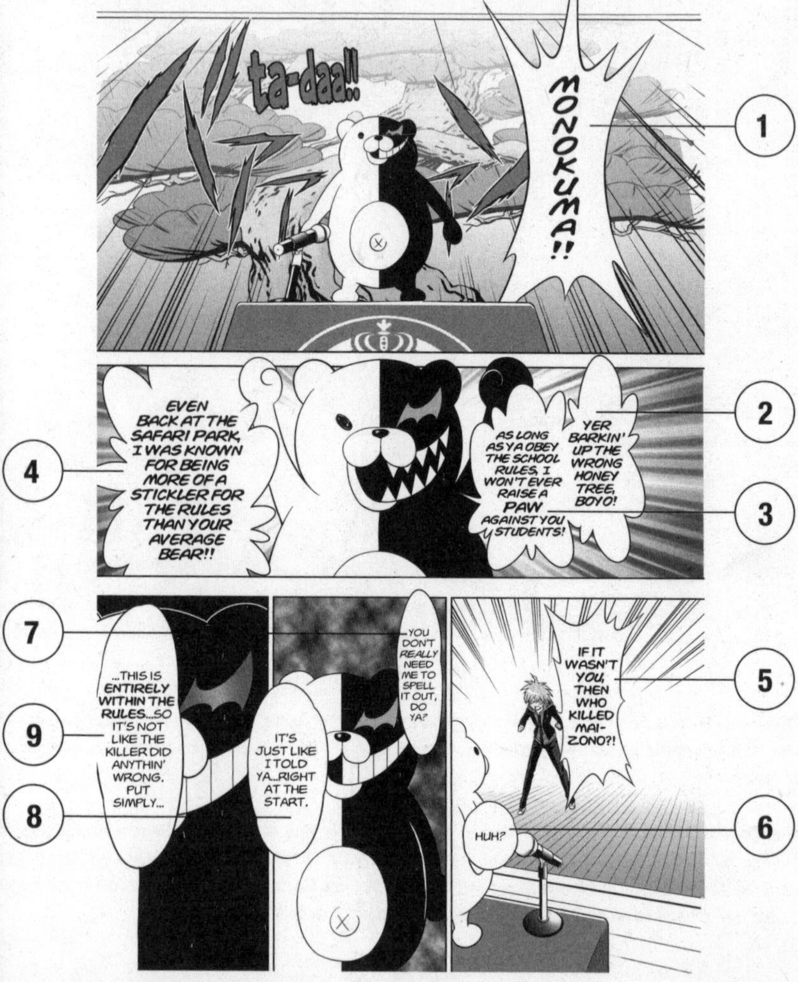
MONOKUMA!!
ta-daa!!
1
YER BARKIN' UP THE WRONG HONEY TREE, BOYO!
2
AS LONG AS YA OBEY THE SCHOOL RULES, I WON'T EVER RAISE A PAW AGAINST YOU STUDENTS!
3
EVEN BACK AT THE SAFARI PARK, I WAS KNOWN FOR BEING MORE OF A STICKLER FOR THE RULES THAN YOUR AVERAGE BEAR!!
4
IF IT WASN'T YOU, THEN WHO KILLED MAI-ZONO?!
5
HUH?
6
YOU DON'T REALLY NEED ME TO SPELL IT OUT, DO YA?
7
IT'S JUST LIKE I TOLD YA...RIGHT AT THE START.
8
...THIS IS ENTIRELY WITHIN THE RULES...SO IT'S NOT LIKE THE KILLER DID ANYTHIN' WRONG. PUT SIMPLY...
9